the office

the office

The Untold Story of the Greatest Sitcom of the 2000s

ANDY GREENE

DUTTON

DUTTON
An imprint of Penguin Random House LLC
penguinrandomhouse.com

LIBRARY OF CONGRESS CATALOGING-IN-PUBLICATION DATA

Names: Greene, Andy, author.
Title: The office : the untold story of the greatest sitcom of the 2000s / Andy Greene.
Description: New York : Dutton, an imprint of Penguin Random House LLC, [2020] |
Includes bibliographical references and index.
Identifiers: LCCN 2019037591 | ISBN 9781524744977 (Hardback) | ISBN 9781524744991 (eBook)
Subjects: LCSH: Office (Television program : U.S.)
Classification: LCC PN1992.77.O34 G74 2020 | DDC 791.45/72—dc23
LC record available at https://lccn.loc.gov/2019037591

Printed in the United States of America
1 3 5 7 9 10 8 6 4 2

BOOK DESIGN BY LAURA K. CORLESS

To my father, who taught me there's always a way

contents

author's note

This book was assembled from a number of sources, primarily from nearly ninety new interviews I conducted with members of the cast, writers, directors, producers, and crew along with various Hollywood executives, TV critics, and even the good folks at the Greater Scranton Chamber of Commerce. Since not everyone was available to speak, I also used archival material, including interviews I did with cast and crew over the past decade as part of my job as a staff writer at *Rolling Stone*, some DVD commentary, and other published interviews about the show and the people who starred in and created it. Brackets are sometimes used for clarity or to change the tense of a statement, and a full list of sources by chapter is in the back.

cast of characters

ACTORS

Devon Abner *(Devon White, Seasons 1, 2, and 9)*
Leslie David Baker *(Stanley Hudson, Seasons 1–9)*
Brian Baumgartner *(Kevin Malone, Seasons 1–9)*
Creed Bratton *(Creed Bratton, Seasons 1–9)*
Andy Buckley *(David Wallace, Seasons 2–6, 8, and 9)*
Steve Carell *(Michael Scott, Seasons 1–7 and 9)*
Clark Duke *(Clark Green, Season 9)*
Idris Elba *(Charles Miner, Season 5)*
Will Ferrell *(Deangelo Vickers, Season 7)*
Jenna Fischer *(Pam Beesly Halpert, Seasons 1–9)*
Kate Flannery *(Meredith Palmer, Seasons 1–9)*
Beth Grant *(Melvina, Seasons 4 and 9)*
Melora Hardin *(Jan Levinson, Seasons 1–5, 7, and 9)*
Ed Helms *(Andy Bernard, Seasons 3–9)*
Hidetoshi Imura *(Hidetoshi Hasagawa, Seasons 3–9)*
Rashida Jones *(Karen Filippelli, Seasons 3–5 and 7)*
Mindy Kaling *(Kelly Kapoor/Writer, Seasons 1–9)*
Ellie Kemper *(Erin Hannon, Seasons 5–9)*
Angela Kinsey *(Angela Martin, Seasons 1–9)*
John Krasinski *(Jim Halpert, Seasons 1–9)*
Paul Lieberstein *(Toby Flenderson/Writer, Seasons 1–9)*
B. J. Novak *(Ryan Howard/Writer, Seasons 1–9)*
Oscar Nunez *(Oscar Martinez, Seasons 1–9)*
Mark Proksch *(Nate Nickerson, Seasons 7–9)*
Craig Robinson *(Darryl Philbin, Seasons 1–9)*

Karly Rothenberg *(Madge Madsen, Seasons 1–8)*
Amy Ryan *(Holly Flax, Seasons 4, 5, and 7)*
Robert Shafer *(Bob Vance, Seasons 2–7 and 9)*
Phyllis Smith *(Phyllis Lapin Vance, Seasons 1–9)*
James Spader *(Robert California, Seasons 7 and 8)*
Calvin Tenner *(Lester/Calvin/Glenn, Seasons 2–9)*
Rainn Wilson *(Dwight Schrute, Seasons 1–9)*
Christopher T. Wood *(Chili's Manager, Season 2)*
Zach Woods *(Gabe Lewis, Seasons 6–9)*

WRITERS

Jen Celotta *(Seasons 2–6)*
Danny Chun *(Seasons 6–8)*
Lee Eisenberg *(Seasons 2–6)*
Owen Ellickson *(Seasons 8 and 9)*
Anthony Farrell *(Seasons 4 and 5)*
Brent Forrester *(Seasons 3–9)*
Amelie Gillette *(Seasons 7 and 8)*
Warren Lieberstein *(Seasons 5–9)*
Peter Ocko *(Season 7)*
Michael Schur *(Seasons 1–5)*
Aaron Shure *(Seasons 5–8)*
Justin Spitzer *(Seasons 3–9)*
Gene Stupnitsky *(Seasons 2–6)*
Halsted Sullivan *(Seasons 5–9)*
Caroline Williams *(Season 3)*
Larry Wilmore *(Seasons 2 and 3)*

DIRECTORS

J. J. Abrams
Jeff Blitz
Paul Feig
Tucker Gates
Bryan Gordon

Ken Kwapis
Ken Whittingham

PRODUCERS

Steve Burgess
Randy Cordray
Greg Daniels
Ben Silverman
Teri Weinberg

PRODUCTION STAFF

Shelley Adajian *(Standby Painter)*
Carey Bennett *(Costume Designer)*
Kelly Cantley *(First Assistant Director)*
Roxxi Dott *(Hairstylist)*
Randall Einhorn *(Director/Cinematographer)*
Briton W. Erwin *(Post-production Supervisor)*
Kim Ferry *(Hairstylist)*
Michael Gallenberg *(Production Designer)*
Sergio Giacoman *(Caterer)*
Richard Gonzales *(Second Assistant Director)*
Lisa Hans-Wolf *(Makeup Artist)*
Donald Lee Harris *(Production Designer)*
Dean Holland *(Editor)*
Allison Jones *(Casting Director)*
Jason Kessler *(Script Coordinator)*
Rusty Mahmood *(First Assistant Director)*
Ben Patrick *(Sound Mixer)*
Alysia Raycraft *(Costume Designer)*
David Rogers *(Editor)*
Henry Saine *(Graphic Designer)*
Claire Scanlon *(Editor)*
Peter Smokler *(Cinematographer)*
Matt Sohn *(Cinematographer/Camera Operator)*

Kasia Trojak *(Second Assistant Director)*
Mary Wall *(Assistant to Greg Daniels)*
Brian Wittle *(Boom Operator/Sound Mixer)*

NBC/GE/FOX EXECUTIVES

Bob Greenblatt *(Chairman of NBC Entertainment)*
Jeff Immelt *(GE CEO)*
Kevin Reilly *(NBC Entertainment Division President)*
Stacey Snider *(20th Century Fox Chairman/CEO)*
Jeff Zucker *(CEO of NBCUniversal)*

TV CRITICS/WEBSITE OPERATORS

Myles McNutt *(AV Club)*
Nathan Rabin *(AV Club)*
Alan Sepinwall *(Newark* Star-Ledger*/HitFix/Uproxx)*
Rob Sheffield (Rolling Stone*)*
Jennie Tan *(OfficeTally.com Webmaster)*

THE GREATER SCRANTON CHAMBER OF COMMERCE

Robert Durkin *(President and Chief Executive Officer)*
Mari Potis *(Director of Membership and Events)*

WRITER OF THE SONG "THAT ONE NIGHT"

Todd Fancey *(New Pornographers Guitarist)*

THE UK *OFFICE*

Ash Atalla *(Producer)*
Ricky Gervais *(David Brent/Cocreator)*
Anil Gupta *(Executive Producer)*
Andy Hollis *(Cinematographer)*
Ewen MacIntosh *(Big Keith)*
Stephen Merchant *(Cocreator)*
Jon Plowman *(Executive Producer)*

introduction

AN AMERICAN WORKPLACE

Throughout the nine-season run of *The Office*, the Dunder Mifflin warehouse set was the filming location for everything from a brutal all-staff roast of regional manager Michael Scott to the casino party where paper salesman Jim Halpert finally gathered up the courage to tell his longtime crush, receptionist Pam Beesly, that he was hopelessly in love with her. But near the end of the seventh season, in the spring of 2011, it was used for a far more somber occasion: the real-life goodbye party for Steve Carell.

The cast had spent the entire day fighting off real tears while Carell filmed his final few scenes as Michael Scott, and now they were finally able to let them out as he gave a private farewell address standing next to an enormous white cake shaped like his already-iconic World's Best Boss mug, a framed Dunder Mifflin hockey jersey, and four rectangular pizzas from his favorite Italian spot, Barone's. Someone had even had the foresight to place a box of tissues on a red table just a couple feet away from Carell's microphone, knowing tears were likely to come.

Nearly everyone who worked on the show—including John Krasinski, Jenna Fischer, Ed Helms, Mindy Kaling, and Rainn Wilson (still wearing the mustard-yellow shirt favored by his quasi-Amish beet farmer character, Dwight Schrute)—was crammed in front of a makeshift stage, and Carell addressed each department individually as he tried to keep the mood light after a rough day of shooting. "To construction," he said. "Thank you for making it strong, durable, and able to withstand a strong pounding." And then, with just minimal guidance from Carell, everyone gleefully yelled out Michael Scott's (slightly problematic by today's standards) catchphrase in unison: "That's what she said!"

He went around the entire room ("To set dressing and art, thank you for your constant tweaking and making something small look so big. . . . That's what she said! To production, thank you for keeping so many balls in the air. . . . That's what she said!") before he put down his prepared remarks, removed his reading glasses, and took a truly goofy moment and made it gut-wrenchingly sincere, just like many of the greatest episodes of *The Office*.

"I didn't prepare really anything else to say," he said. "This is overwhelming, obviously. It's been a fantastic seven years for me. I was talking to [my wife] Nancy about it a few days ago as this was all hitting me and she said something that I thought really nailed it. And that was, 'Well, your professional identity is wrapped up in this show,' which I knew. And then she said so simply, 'And they're your friends.' That's really it. You're my friends."

On that last word, *friends,* Carell choked up so badly he could barely get it out and he had to run offstage toward his wife as cries of "We love you, Steve" filled the cavernous space. "I remember somebody wanted to do an 'O Captain! My Captain!' speech," says Kate Flannery, who played boozy supplier-relations representative Meredith Palmer. "John Krasinski talked us out of it. I think it would have been too uncomfortable because Steve was just too emotional. We did put together a scrapbook for him with some old pictures. Steve actually gave us all Rolex watches that he had engraved. I wear it to this day because it reminds me that everything that happened did actually happen. I know it sounds crazy because things are so fleeting in the TV business, but we were family. We really were."

When that family had first come together to shoot the *Office* pilot seven years earlier, Carell was the most famous face in the group only because everyone else was a complete unknown, many still working day jobs to pay the bills. Carell had just wrapped up a long stint as a *Daily Show* correspondent, but his recent shift into the world of sitcoms with supporting roles on Julia Louis-Dreyfus's *Watching Ellie* and Tom Papa's *Come to Papa* had been catastrophic. Both shows were canceled within weeks of NBC's putting them on the air, leaving barely a dent in the public consciousness.

When *The Office* premiered on March 24, 2005, it seemed like it was destined to suffer a similar fate after airing a pilot that was practically a shot-for-shot remake of the original UK *Office*—a groundbreaking BBC show helmed by Ricky Gervais and Stephen Merchant—and was dismissed as a pale, pointless retread by critics. What saved it was Carell, who throughout the second season transformed Michael Scott from an unrepentant asshole to a genuinely lovable doofus acting out due to crushing loneliness and a desperate need for love.

The show would limp ahead for two seasons after Carell's farewell party, but even at the time most of the cast and crew knew that an *Office* without Michael Scott was a very dicey proposition. The main cast swelled to a ridiculous high of nineteen people in the final season, only underscoring the fact that, in the words of one writer, Michael Scott was a "load-bearing character" that the show simply couldn't function without, no matter how many bodies they crammed into the Dunder Mifflin bullpen.

But time has dimmed the bitter aftertaste of those last two years and restored *The Office* to its rightful place as one of the greatest sitcoms of all time, right up there with *I Love Lucy, Seinfeld, Cheers,* and *The Simpsons.* (Unlike those shows, however, *The Office* is a "single camera" show and presents the action through the eyes of a documentary film crew.) Bars across the country pack in hordes of college-age fans during weekly *Office* trivia battles, Comedy Central and Nick at Nite air the reruns nearly every night to enormous ratings, and Comcast recently shelled out $500 million to obtain the streaming rights from Netflix in 2021 so *The Office* can become the centerpiece of their new streaming service. (Netflix doesn't release numbers publicly, but according to multiple sources *The Office* is consistently their most popular offering, eclipsing even *Friends* reruns and their original hit shows like *Stranger Things, Black Mirror,* and *Orange Is the New Black.*)

The show started at a time when audiences had little reason to expect anything even remotely watchable from the four major networks beyond occasional brilliant flukes like *Arrested Development* or *Freaks and Geeks*. And after years of pathetic attempts to clone *Friends*, they'd resorted to soulless, paint-by-numbers sitcoms like *According to Jim*, *My Wife and Kids*, and *George Lopez*, complete with sappy music cues, wisecracking kids, and laugh tracks that went off after every lame zinger of a joke. Out of this scene somehow came a faux-documentary show about the sad, often desperate lives of the employees at a struggling paper company.

Amelie Gillette (Writer, Seasons 7 and 8): Nothing on TV was like *The Office* back then. The comedy was small and it was dry. The people looked like real people, which was a rare thing, especially for a sitcom. It proved that you could do something romantic without being dramatic and that you can do something that feels real, that feels grounded, even though there is this artifice of it being a documentary that tricks you into thinking it's real.

Jen Celotta (Writer, Seasons 2–6): What made *The Office* relatable, I think, was the fact that people were bored at their jobs. They felt like, "Oh, I can relate to this. I can relate to this feeling of having to sit at the desk next to someone who, outside of work, I wouldn't necessarily be friends with."

Lee Eisenberg (Writer, Seasons 2–6): We really liked cringe comedy and the show can be the cringiest of cringe comedy, but there was also a love story that was so compelling. You hadn't really seen anything like that before where the comedy was so great and then in the background was this story that you're just completely drawn to. You really gave a shit about all the characters.

Gene Stupnitsky (Writer, Seasons 2–6): In some ways it reminded me of a show like *Friends* where you laugh and you care. It's so hard to pull that off. To make you feel something is the hardest thing.

Ken Kwapis (Director): *The Office* had the idea that the comedy was behavioral. The stories weren't joke driven. The comedy focused on human behavior. And I think one of the secret weapons of the show is that not only is the humor dry, but the show is literally dry. There's no music.

J. J. Abrams (Director): I think what Ricky [Gervais] and Stephen [Merchant] created was a completely relatable, universal idea in the same way that [other British imports] *Sanford and Son* and *All in the Family* did as well. There are certain ideas—whether it's about being the underdog, living with a bigot, or being in an office setting with people that you're forced to make your family—that work anywhere. Obviously the David Brent character and Michael Scott were both a very relatable idea, the sort of inadvertently, unbearably offensive coworker. The nugget of the idea was so perfect and so rich that it could probably work in most any culture.

Clark Duke (Clark Green, Season 9): *The Office* replicated a thing that I love about Robert Altman movies in that it wasn't afraid of boredom and silence. Those things can be powerful tools if you use them correctly. And people love watching shows about rich people, but you rarely saw something about middle-class people in the middle of the country. It also wasn't about somebody that had an overarching goal. So many shows are about somebody trying to better themselves or they have some big goal they're trying to achieve, and that's not what most of life is for most people, and *The Office* is not about that. It was just about day-to-day life.

Oscar Nunez (Oscar Martinez, Seasons 1–9): The great, great, great sitcoms of yore all had a simple premise. It's character driven. *Taxi*'s just a fucking taxi place. *Cheers* is just a bar. That's all it is. And we were just an office.

Larry Wilmore (Writer, Seasons 2 and 3): *The Office* introduced a different rhythm to network TV. It showed you don't have to have these same rhythms. A lot of sitcoms were built around farce. It was always like, "Somebody doesn't know this. Ooohhh." *The Office* was just observational humor and comedy. It was very simple. Jim just looking at the camera is a joke as opposed to a structured joke punch line.

Jenna Fischer (Pam Beesly Halpert, Seasons 1–9): We had the benefit of some trailblazers before us who were starting to steer the ship in a different direction comedically, like *The Larry Sanders Show, Arrested Development,* and *Freaks and Geeks*. There was this turn and it was all sort of happening around the same time, so I feel like there has to be some credit given to those shows as well because together there was this kind of new movement that happened.

Melora Hardin (Jan Levinson, Seasons 1–5, 7, and 9): I absolutely feel like this show couldn't have been on the air at any other time in history. Back then, actors like me, and really the whole business, was turning their nose up to reality TV. We were like, "Uh, this is just awful," because all of us know there's nothing about reality TV that is real. It's completely made up. But I also feel like that reality TV paved the way for this show because this show walks that line where it's documentary-like even though it's actually completely made up. We got to play characters, but we get to play characters in a fictitious world that's trying to be real and seem real. I think without reality TV, America wouldn't have known what to make of *The Office*. They just would have been like, "What?" They would have never been able to wrap their brain around it.

Jason Kessler (Script Supervisor): Reality TV is what conditioned people for *The Office*. You had all these big splashy shows like *The Bachelor* and *Survivor* where people are used to seeing action where you cut to a talking head describing the interior emotions of what was going on in that moment. So once the language of that became familiar with audiences, it was a stroke of brilliance to bring that into scripted comedy. That allowed *The Office* to do those smaller jokes where you get to notice something on camera that's not exactly pointed to with a big, flashing light, but it's a little joke in the background, just like when you're watching a reality show and you kind of notice somebody doing something in the background and you're like, "Oh, that's interesting." You're able to catalog that more once you're familiar with the language of that style.

Paul Feig (Director): People had seen reality shows and all that, but they weren't consuming comedy that way. I always credit YouTube for changing the way we look at things because so many people were having a lot of fun looking at real videos shot by real people, which were loose, and they weren't jokey. If you look at just how comedy and TV, and movies, were before that, it was very joke driven. It's setup, punch line, characters being a little bit broad and over-the-top and everyone was wisecracky and very Neil Simon–y, for lack of a better term. But then YouTube was real life captured and you have *The Office*, where the humor is all behavioral. It's about how people are reacting to each other. For a lot of people in the public, and especially for younger people, there's a strong aversion to jokes and the old style of comedy. People get very frustrated by jokes now.

Larry Wilmore: Some of the most interesting moments, to me, are the quiet moments. Seeing Michael through the glass in his office and seeing him lonely in there is very poignant sometimes. You're seeing Pam torn at her desk, just torn with feelings over her boyfriend when there's this guy in the office she has a crush on. You're seeing Stanley just exhausted by Michael and he doesn't even have a line, but he's just exhausted. That would always make me laugh.

Alan Sepinwall (TV Critic, Newark *Star-Ledger*/HitFix/Uproxx/*Rolling Stone*): It's an unusual structure in that Jim and Pam are the traditional protagonists in terms of narrative structure. They're the ones you're rooting for, they're the ones who are progressing. They're mostly not the ones generating the comedy though. Pam is almost entirely a straight woman. Jim is sort of wry and making fun of Dwight and Michael and looking over at us, but the comedy is being generated by Michael and by Dwight. It's almost like a Marx Brothers movie where you've got the young ingénue and her love interest. They're part of what passes for plot in a Marx Brothers movie. And then Groucho and Harpo and Chico are actually the ones you're coming to see.

Paul Feig: Before *The Office*, all comedy had to be super clever, super written, or it had to be really crazy and broad. What *The Office* did was they were just normal people, but they're really quirky, and they're stuck in a situation just like you and the weird people you work with. You're the normal person. You are Jim Halpert. You are Pam Beesly, the normal one of the office, and you're going, "Look at all these fucking lunatics that I work with." That resonates huge with an audience because they're in on the joke, because the world around them is a joke. They are not surrounded by a world of jokes.

Nathan Rabin (TV Critic, AV Club): The British version and the American version have this incredible element of pathos. So many TV shows are aspirational. They're attractive people who live in really cool apartments and they have exciting lives and sexy jobs. And here's one where even the most successful people and the most likable people have a depressing fucking job and live in a depressing community.

Rob Sheffield (TV Critic, *Rolling Stone*): I think of Michael Scott as the archetypal TV figure of that decade based on the idea that the guy in charge is this total idiot, just like George W. Bush. You can't picture Michael Scott as a lower-level employee in the office. There's no way that actually doing a job is something that he could do, just as there's no way George W. Bush could've held any office besides president. That became the comic prototype of that era, not just in TV but in movies like *Anchorman* or *Talladega Nights: The Legend of Ricky Bobby*. The tagline for Will Farrell in *Talladega Nights* was "A man who could only count to number one," and that's kind of the archetypal position that George W. Bush and Michael Scott occupied.

Aaron Shure (Writer, Seasons 5–8): My personal theory about why *The Office* was so successful then is because Bush was president and it was sort of the zeitgeist of, "What does it mean when the people in charge are incompetent?" And I sort of saw the central foible of Michael Scott was that there was a switch in his head and if he had flipped it most of his stories would go away. And the switch in his head was set on, "Your employees can and should be your friends." And if someone flipped that switch he wouldn't have as many problems, he wouldn't have as many stories. I think part of why *The Office* is so popular today is there's a different type of meditation on incompetence, who's in charge and why.

Clark Duke: I'm not even sure you could make the show now because it was just so unrelentingly real at times. I feel like a lot of the stuff that came in its wake, even like *Parks and Rec*, was tonally so much brighter. But I like the darkness of *The Office*. That's what made it so great to me.

Oscar Nunez: We knew we hit the lottery when we got that show. We'll never be on a sitcom like this again. We can never top it.

Creed Bratton (Creed Bratton, Seasons 1–9): I don't know what season it was, but we were sitting around on the set one day and Steve looked around at everybody and said, "We'll never, ever have it this good again." He's not one to be making these generalized overview statements to everybody, waxing pedantic, but he did that time. It registered and I thought to myself, "He's probably right," and he was right. We'll never, ever be on a TV show like that again. It's just impossible.

chapter 1

THE ORIGINAL *OFFICE*

("I became fascinated with embarrassment.")

Long before Ricky Gervais and Stephen Merchant met and created The Office, *they worked at actual offices around London. Gervais—who spent much of the eighties trying in vain to become a George Michael–like pop star—took a job as the assistant events manager at the University of London in 1989. Merchant, meanwhile, bounced all over the city, taking menial gigs that made him desperate to find a line of work that could utilize his comedic talents. Years later, their experiences would prove to be invaluable when creating the show.*

Ricky Gervais (David Brent/Series Cocreator): I was happy with my life back then. I walked to work and I had a good time when I got there. I was with my mates and we drank in the bar after work. But they say that drama is real life with the boring parts taken out and I was obsessed with the boring bits at the office. I was obsessed with the minutiae of an excruciating social faux pas, and someone making a joke that isn't good and falls flat, and then the aftermath. I became fascinated with embarrassment.

Stephen Merchant (Series Cocreator): One of my early jobs was working for a mail-order company in the complaints department. I would go down to the warehouse and I'd always have to interact with the people down there. I became interested in the divide between the blue-collar and white-collar worlds. I felt like I somehow could talk to the warehouse guys because we had similar backgrounds, but I'm sure they didn't really see me that way. I also worked at a charity for a while where I had to stuff envelopes. I just remember using humor and pranks to get through the day.

In 1997, Gervais landed a new job at the startup radio station XFM.

Ricky Gervais: My job there was to write material for the DJs, but because I'm so lazy I ended up going in there and doing the bits myself. I'd pop in and do funny little things. Someone from Channel 4 was listening and they gave me a new show called *The 11 O'Clock Show*, which was like *Saturday Night Live* without restrictions. It was a spoof of a news show. I had a character that was supposed to be a straight news reporter, but I'd always start editorializing and saying crazy stuff. It gave me a bit of a profile.

Stephen Merchant: I had an urge to get into radio, which was something I had done while at school. One day I read in a music magazine about a new station that was launching in London called XFM, which had just won a radio license. I sent my CV and a cover letter in the hope there'd be some work. And I got called up for a meeting with Ricky to work as his assistant. I've joked over the years that my CV was probably the first one on his pile. I think Ricky would generally agree that he liked to take the path of least resistance. When we met he said to me, "I don't really know what I'm doing. I've sort of sweet-talked my way into this job. You have some radio experience. If you scratch my back, I'll scratch yours." After I started, we would goof around a lot in the office and developed a good rapport.

Around this time, Gervais began playing around with the idea of an oddball office-manager character named David Brent.

Stephen Merchant: My memory of it was that he had a handful of observations about the types of people that he'd encountered at offices over the years. One was the sort of guy who liked to joke, but then would quickly turn real serious. So there's a sort of gag about joking with the receptionist, "Oh, I'm having a barbecue this weekend. I've got to cut down on my burgers since I'm watching my weight." And the secretary would sort of say, "Yeah." And he'd say, "Well, what do you mean by that? Are you saying I'm fat?" Then there was him giving a job interview and slightly lecherously using it as an opportunity to leer at this young interviewee.

Ricky Gervais: I saw David Brent as a Frankenstein of all the men I'd met growing up and then worked for. When I was seventeen I went along for a job interview at one of those recruitment places to get a job during the school holidays. It was me and another guy. And this guy went to us, "I don't give shitty jobs. If two guys come to me . . ." And he phoned up his mate and he went, "Hey, it's me, yeah. I got two guys for you. Yeah, they're perfect. Yeah, of course they're eighteen." I remember thinking, "Hold on, we're meant to trust him because he's lying to a friend? That's an odd way to ingratiate yourself to two strangers." That bit made it into the character.

Gervais and Merchant lost their jobs at XFM in August 1998 when the radio station was bought out by Capital Radio.

Stephen Merchant: In 1998, I took the training course at the BBC and drew a lot of inspiration from it because even though it was the BBC, it doesn't mean it's a world of glamour and showbiz. It's still people squabbling over chairs and staplers. Anyway, the course required me to make a little documentary. Other people made documentaries about the local barbershop or a local service station. And I said to Ricky, "Why don't we do something using these character observations we've made at offices over the years?"

Ricky Gervais: When Stephen suggested that, I was watching a lot of docuseries where these ordinary people would be followed by cameras and they'd get their fifteen minutes of fame. There was one called *Driving School*, which just followed a woman who couldn't pass her test. There was one called *Hotel* set in Liverpool. It was just people at work.

Ash Atalla (Producer): The program makers somehow found these eccentric characters in everyday situations and followed them and wove the equivalent of a narrative complete with multiple A, B, and C story lines and cliffhangers. It was a genre that didn't exist up until that point.

Stephen Merchant: We were quite entertained by one [*Troubleshooter*] where a guy called John Harvey-Jones went around trying to fix problems with struggling companies. He met a bunch of small, family-run firms where there'd be lots of squabbling or just incompetence. We ate through a lot of those when we began putting together *The Office*. They gave us lots of ideas.

Ricky Gervais: You were hooked in because they found funny characters that I think people sort of think, "Oh, that could be me." There's something aspirational about, "Oh, he's famous now, and he worked in a factory, well I could do that."

Stephen Merchant: When we started working on ideas for our show we literally sat around and just talked about the offices we worked in and the kinds of people that we'd worked with. And quite quickly, we felt like there was a crossover of types that both Ricky and I had worked with. There was the person who didn't really want to be there and was just getting through the day, which was probably both of us in different ways. And then there was the sort of people who wanted to make sure everyone was doing everything by the book. They normally had a little bit of authority but no real power. I had a boss at the BBC for a while in one of the jobs I did there who tried to be the fun guy, which kind of undermined his own authority.

They filmed a short demo called Seedy Boss *where an early, crude version of David Brent tries to impress a potential hire by lying to his supervisor on the phone right in front of him, essentially a re-creation of Gervais's teenage experience.*

Stephen Merchant: We were pleased with it straight off the bat, but I think it was a slightly slower gestation in thinking, "Oh, maybe we can make this into a show." I just remember people sort of started to see it and there was some interest in it. It very quickly took on a life of its own. I had to take it back to the BBC and I managed to get in to see some of the executives there and show them the tape and they were very impressed by it.

Ash Atalla: *Seedy Boss* was passed around in comedy circles. There was a bit of a buzz growing around it. And a few producers and directors started circling. And then we set up a meeting with Jon Plowman at the BBC to see about turning it into a series.

Jon Plowman (Executive Producer): What I remember most about my initial meeting with Ricky and Stephen is their chutzpah. Most people come into a situation like they were in with a degree of humility. I looked at them and I could see that they'd already won a Golden Globe in their heads. There was such confidence. One of them said, "I've got a great show," and the other one said, "I'm gonna star in it."

Stephen Merchant: He asked why should we direct it, and I remember in all seriousness saying, "We might be the next Orson Welles." And he said, "You might not be." And I said, "You don't know, we might be." Now I realize how absurd that sounds. At the time, it wasn't that I thought we were geniuses. I think we just thought, "No one knows. Maybe we're really good?" It was bizarre. I don't know if it was a kind of complete arrogance. I think it was a naïveté probably about, "Well, how hard can this be? We did this thing and this is pretty good."

Anil Gupta (Executive Producer): Jane Root was in charge of BBC Two at the time. We played her the demo tape after meeting with Jon Plowman and then explained to her it was a mockumentary about an office. I remember her turning to the guy to her left, a guy named Liam Keelan, who was the scheduler, and there was a pause when the tape finished. She turned to him and said, "Is that funny?" He said, "Yeah." She said, "All right." That was them commissioning the pilot.

Ricky Gervais: I think we got it approved because no one really cared. It was low risk. They were going to put us on Monday nights in the summer. It didn't cost anything and we didn't get paid much.

The show is presented from the point of view of an unseen documentary crew chronicling the mundane lives of workers at an everyday office for a company called Wernham Hogg, which sells paper. The office is managed by David Brent, a failed musician who uses cringe-including humor as a desperate means to impress and befriend his employees. His lead salesman is Tim Canterbury, who dreams of finding a more fulfilling line of work but stays around because he's desperately in love with Dawn Tinsley, a receptionist who is engaged to a selfish, insensitive warehouse worker. Dawn and Tim kill time by playing jokes on Gareth, an oddball salesman completely obsessed with the military. At almost no point does any actual work get done.

Ash Atalla: Doing a pilot was a big leap from a demo tape. David Brent had to become a much more well-rounded character, not so much obsessed with women but obsessed with the low-level corporate world. Alongside him, we had to create other well-defined office types. We had all worked in offices and we talked about the archetypes. One we came up with was the everyman, the guy that should have moved to London but stayed in his hometown. That became Tim, played by Martin Freeman. Then we knew that a lot of offices have a mum, someone that makes everything tick. That can be a receptionist or an office manager. That became Dawn. Then there's the guy obsessed with the military. That became Mackenzie Crook as Gareth.

Ricky Gervais: Gareth was based on a kid I went to school with who was in the TA [the Territorial Army, the UK equivalent of the National Guard]. He was a real macho man, but when Mackenzie Crook came in for the audition it was even funnier because he's a guy that looks like a baby bird talking about how he's able to kill a man. Suddenly it became twice as funny.

Ash Atalla: We wanted to cast people who were as naturalistic as Ricky. And that's where you need a bit of luck, the sort of alchemy that comes together on every great show. Ricky had seen Martin Freeman at a sketch show. You could see very quickly that he was a very naturalistic, classy actor. Lucy Davis walked in the door and I did my first audition with her and I was absolutely bowled away by her heart and naturalism, down to the smallest detail of her performance. I mean, you just couldn't see the acting.

They set the show in Slough, England, a sleepy town about twenty-five minutes west of Central London.

Stephen Merchant: It's just the perfect sort of anonymous town. We used to talk about how if you live in Slough you didn't quite make it to London. You're so close to the bright lights, but you're just not quite close enough.

Ash Atalla: Slough is Nothingville. When you said Slough, nothing particularly [came] to mind. It was an archetypal working-class British town, the likes of which you find all up and down this country.

Stephen Merchant: We were originally going to set it at a paper and dye company, but then we researched it and found out that they didn't really exist. But there were paper companies, obviously. That became interesting to us. It's something everyone uses, but you never really think about the manufacture or the sale of it. It's just something everyone has. There's also something just about the blankness of it, and the anonymity of paper and the idea that in the case of Dawn, it's something she could draw on that could be really creative and fulfilling. But at the moment, it's just sort of blank. At one point, I went down to a paper company and sort of wandered around the office and spoke to them and took notes about the sort of mechanics of how it worked.

They shot the first season over just a couple of months in early 2001.

Anil Gupta: We found an old production office and shot there. Everything was very cheap. We didn't really use lighting. We also didn't have to sit around and wait for the actors to show up. Everybody turned up at the beginning and they stayed the whole time. We didn't even have a call sheet.

Stephen Merchant: I remember, on the first day, trying to reassure everyone that even though we were kind of inexperienced, that they were in safe hands. And I remember saying something like, "Yeah, we know all the terms. You know, *cut, action, roll over.*" And the first AD went, "It's *turn over.*" And I said, "*Turn over.* Right." So we had no idea what we were doing, really. We just knew what we wanted to see on the screen.

Andy Hollis (Cinematographer): Stephen always wanted the interviews to look as shitty as possible. He wanted their skin to look really green, like the camera hadn't been set up right.

Stephen Merchant: We had this idea that the tapes of the show had been sat on the shelves of the BBC for a long time, and no one had ever aired it and then they'd found it one day and stuck it on to fill up a time slot. So we had the idea that the color had faded like in an old photograph.

Ricky Gervais: We reveled in the slowness of the show because it was funny. It's not choreography. It's supposed to be real life and in real life people talk over each other and fluff their words. There's that juxtaposition between how you see yourself and how other people see you. That was a big one for me. It was all about that blind spot. That's why it was a fake documentary. I honestly wanted people to think it was real.

Stephen Merchant: There were things that struck us when we sort of realized, "Oh, if you shoot a scene through a window, you put the window between you and the action and then that gives it all that distance. And so therefore, you could believe that they have forgotten they were being filmed at that moment." We called them spying shots. And then we started to get this vocabulary of what was a spy shot and what was in the room and so we started to build up this kind of grammar that became a sort of shorthand as time went on.

Jon Plowman: Normally the ratio of film to cut film is twelve to one. That means you shoot twelve minutes to get one minute. They were doing thirty to one.

Stephen Merchant: I remember in the first week of filming the producers came to us and they were like, "Okay, you shot three times more footage than anyone's ever shot." We didn't know, so we were just covering everything, from every angle, every possible iteration. And they said, "You have to shoot less 'cause we just can't keep up with this amount of tape." It was quite a steep learning curve about technique. There were stacks and stacks of tapes just getting sent off to the editing suite.

This led to a tedious work environment where Gervais was always trying to break the tension.

Stephen Merchant: Ricky used to work hard to make the other actors laugh, particularly Martin. I'm not quite sure why. I think it was probably partly just to keep levity on the set. And I think also probably just that Ricky likes to keep his mind stimulated and keep himself energized. And I think that's a fun way to do it.

Ewen MacIntosh (Big Keith): When the camera wasn't on Ricky, he would do anything to make us laugh. He'd draw a picture of genitalia and point to it just as you were trying to concentrate. He'd do anything to make us crack up. They had a lot of trouble getting scenes finished.

Stephen Merchant: There was one where Ricky gives Tim an appraisal that just took forever, in part because Ricky kept trying to make Martin laugh. And I used to get kind of frustrated because I was worried about the clock and running out of time. And I would shout at him, "Come on, Rick, for God's sake."

Ewen MacIntosh: After about thirty takes people would be like, "Come on, we have other stuff to do. People want to go home." But I think Ricky needed an environment like that. He needed to blow off steam. He and Stephen were directing it all day and then going to a hotel room and putting a rough cut together every night. They needed to blow off steam just to stay sane.

Andy Hollis: A normal shooting day would be eight A.M. to seven P.M. At one point, we were shooting the same week as the World Cup. If there was a big match on, we'd set up one of those big tellys and watch it during the shooting day, which would be unheard of on a normal show.

Fine-tuning the characters to make them seem grounded and realistic was a constant focus for Merchant and Gervais.

Ricky Gervais: We always tried to do little things so David didn't seem too narcissistic, too nasty and too seedy. We made him a bit of a twit. We made him desperate. And as soon as people realized that he was trying to be famous, and he was trying to do the right thing, and he was basically decent but had been sold a dodgy bill of goods, and they could feel his discomfort, they didn't hate him. When David Brent looks at the camera, he's looking at you. And you feel it, you feel his pain. It's like you want to look away because you can't help him. And I never thought he was a bad person. I thought his biggest crime was that he confused popularity with respect.

Stephen Merchant: In British TV there's that long tradition of [the] fairly unlikable protagonist, whether it's Basil Fawlty [from *Fawlty Towers*] or [Steve Coogan's character] Alan Partridge.

Ricky Gervais: In the end, it's not even about working in an office. It's about being thrown together with random people for eight hours a day and all the tensions that come with that. Those themes are universal. Everyone has a boss they don't like or they think they know better. People always worry they're wasting their lives. Boy meets girl, sitting next to an idiot, all these things are universal.

And while David Brent's antics generated the most laughs, it was Tim's desperate, unrequited crush on Dawn that drew in many viewers. In a climactic scene, he pulls her into a conference room, tears off the mic, and confesses his feelings even though the audience can't hear a word. He then slowly walks back to his desk, puts on his mic, and simply says, "She said no, by the way." They didn't actually get together until the final moments of a Christmas reunion special that wrapped up the entire show.

Stephen Merchant: I was always a big fan of *Friends* and I always loved the will they/won't they thing with Ross and Rachel. And I was also a fan of *Northern Exposure,* which had a really great will they/won't they story at the core of that. I was also aware, having watched those other shows, of the dangers when you bring the characters together. There's a sort of air that's let out. There's a tension that goes. That's sometimes hard to come back from. Certainly it was tricky on *Friends,* and so I think we were aware that basically when they got together it was probably the end of the road. So we never intended to get them together until we decided to complete things.

Ricky Gervais: When it's done, it's done. It's Alfred Hitchcock's philosophy that the bomb must never go off.

The show debuted on July 9, 2001, to minimal ratings and mixed reviews.

Stephen Merchant: I was on a train a few days after the pilot had aired, and there were two women opposite of me talking to each other. One of them said, "Did you see that documentary the other night about an office?

It was hilarious." And the woman next to her said, "Oh, I don't think that's a documentary. I think that's a comedy." And the other woman who just said she was loving it said, "Oh. Well, it wasn't very funny then." The speed with which she turned was extraordinary. I took a real delight in that, in thinking that we'd fooled her.

Ash Atalla: Traditionally, you didn't really want it to be out in the summer, because it's a little bit of a dead time and it's silly season and people are on vacation and nobody's really focusing. The flip side of that is that you're not up against big launches because everyone launches in winter and autumn.

Jon Plowman: But then people began coming back from their summer holiday and a weird thing started happening where ratings for episodes five and six actually began going up, which rarely happens. They then did a very unusual thing for the BBC where they repeated the whole series just three months later. Then it became a hit.

The first season was a scant six episodes and Merchant and Gervais decided to pull the plug after a second, six-episode season and a two-part Christmas special.

Stephen Merchant: It's laughable really, looking back. But by the end of the second series, I really think we felt we'd run out of steam. I think we were worried we were gonna start to repeat ourselves. That we had sort of made so many of the observations we wanted to make, and we'd explored it. And again, through naïveté I think, we probably thought, "Yeah, let's wrap it up and move on to something else."

Jon Plowman: It was a big hit show. We would have done a third series in a heartbeat, but Ricky wanted to do that Christmas special and then move on.

Stephen Merchant: As you get older and more experienced you realize, "Oh, actually, there was probably more to explore." We probably would have perhaps kept it going, but at the time it just felt like we'd sort of said everything, really. We didn't want it to get tired and stale and feel like it was just, "How is David going to embarrass himself this week?" It just felt like the right decision.

Ash Atalla: There probably could have been a third, fourth, or fifth season. At the time, it didn't feel like there was any sort of *Office* fatigue. But does the show end perfectly? I think it does. Absolutely. It feels complete.

Stephen Merchant: We wanted Tim and Dawn to get together, and that was always the long-term intention. And so I guess we worked backward from that on those Christmas specials. And we wanted David to sort of have a little bit of an epiphany. We wanted to feel like he'd moved on a couple of stages in his maturity. Tried to get some self-awareness. That seemed like a sweet victory.

Ricky Gervais: I think I might have got the idea to just do twelve episodes from *Fawlty Towers*. Add that to my laziness. I've got the attention span of a toddler and I want to do the next thing while I'm doing this thing. The only thing that gives me an adrenaline rush is the idea. I wish I could just have the idea, watch it on telly, and not actually have to do anything.

chapter 2

COMING TO AMERICA

("The Americans will ruin it.")

Midway through the run of the series, Gervais got a call on his cell phone from a number he didn't recognize.

Ricky Gervais: The voice said, "Hi, Ricky, it's Ben Silverman." I didn't know who that was.

Ben Silverman (Executive Producer): I was an agent for William Morris in the late nineties living in London. I watched as the Europeans, particularly the Brits, were doing more and more creative things, including in reality television. They were doing docusoaps and amazing game shows. They were reinventing TV. One day I was back in London staying at a friend's house while on a business trip. I was flipping through the channels and I came across *The Office* on the BBC Two. For the first couple of minutes I was like, "Are they doing a reality show or making fun of a reality show?" Then I just started to laugh. I thought it was absolutely brilliant. I saw Ricky Gervais's name in the credits and I got his cell phone number through a mutual friend.

Ricky Gervais: He said, "I work for a company, I make remakes for America." Oh yeah, you and everyone else. And you know, obviously at that time, there hadn't been a successful remake since the seventies. But he said, "I'm in England, where are you?" I went, "I'm on Wardour Street," and he went, "I'll come and meet you." I went, "All right." So, he got a cab and we met in Starbucks on Wardour Street [in Soho].

Ben Silverman: I looked at him and I said, "I want to remake this. I know how to do this. I see a vision for how this could work in America and what we'd need to change. I'd love to do this with you." We talked for two and a half hours.

Ricky Gervais: I looked at it like, "Well this is exciting and it's no skin off my nose," which I thought it wasn't. I thought it was just me giving them permission to do a remake.

Ben Silverman: From there, we met with his agent and they contacted the BBC, who also owned the rights, and began a long process to negotiate for it.

Ash Atalla: We all sort of felt that we should distance ourselves from that American version because we didn't know what it was going to be like. And there were a lot of people here saying, "You sold out. It's going to be shit. The Americans will ruin it."

Ricky Gervais: Their first stab at it was saying I could play the Brent character. And I said, "What's the point of that? I've done mine. This should be made by Americans, for Americans." I said, "*The Office* worked because I knew what it was like to work in an office in England at the turn of the century, that's why it worked."

Stephen Merchant: I'd always been something of a kind of historian of TV and comedy. And I was always very aware that not many shows had successfully transferred across the Atlantic. And my observation was that one of the problems seemed to be that the original creators had tried to do it themselves, and that they'd perhaps come stuck 'cause they just tried to replicate what they'd done in England. The ones that did succeed—like *All in the Family* and *Sanford and Son*—had the original writers involved, but they'd obviously had great showrunners in the US and that's why they sort of blossomed. I thought it seemed important that we didn't do it ourselves.

Ben Silverman: I met with a ton of different potential writers and directors, including the directors and writers who had partnered with Larry David on *Curb Your Enthusiasm* early on. Then I also met with Greg Daniels, who I had always wanted to work with because I loved his work both on *King of the Hill* and *The Simpsons*. I knew he was a Harvard-educated intellectual as well as a great writer.

Greg Daniels (Creator of American Series/Executive Producer): I got a tape of it from my agent and thought it was a really cool, brilliant show. I didn't really think it would ever be on American television, but I thought it would be a cool meeting to take just to meet those guys. It turned out they were big fans of American television, particularly *The Simpsons* and an episode I had written of *The Simpsons*. . . . It was "Homer Badman," from the sixth season, ten years ago, when Homer tries to remove a gummy bear from a babysitter's bottom. He gets caught in a whole sexual-harassment kind of story, so they liked that. I think maybe that was an *Office*-y kind of moment. We kind of hit it off based on that.

Watching The Office *in America at this point required either tracking down the DVDs or catching it on BBC America when they began airing episodes in 2003.*

Ben Silverman: We talked and talked and talked about it, but he was really nervous that the underlying material was too beloved. I said to him, "When people are buying books to remake, they're not looking for the shittiest book. They're looking for the best bestseller they can buy." I said, "I have gone after underlying material that was unwatchable and was able to turn it into a good show, but I think this puts us in a head-start position."

Ricky Gervais: I wanted to go with Greg Daniels because he went on about the Tim and Dawn love story more than anyone else we met. We thought that was important. He understood the heart of *The Office*.

Stephen Merchant: Of all the many people we met, he just seemed the one that was most in tune with the show and with the sort of humanity of the show and the romance. We spent a lot of time in London with him just talking about why we'd made certain choices and what the corollaries would be between Slough and America. There were little differences we didn't realize at the time, like the tradition of the pub quiz. That is a big thing in England, but less so in the States. There was also the Territorial Army, which Gareth is a member of, and talking about what would be the equivalent in the US. It was him just trying to understand the psychology of the characters so he could build the American equivalent, really.

Ben Silverman: I told Greg that we had to keep it without a laugh track, which every single broadcast television show, no matter how inventive it was, had. I also wanted to keep it single camera even though every single broadcast television show was multicamera. [*To be fair,* Arrested Development, Malcolm in the Middle, *and a small handful of other shows were also single camera and didn't use laugh tracks.*] And a lot of these people can't be famous that we cast. It will break the environment that we're creating if we have movie stars appearing in the show. Greg and I agreed on all of this. And I said, "But the hard part's going to be getting the network to agree to it." He laughed and knew that.

As all this was going down, the four major networks were struggling to adjust to a new world in which they had to compete with cable and the Internet for viewers. HBO—which had spent twenty years relying on six-month-old hit movies and soft-core pornography for ratings—was suddenly the home to groundbreaking shows like The Sopranos, Curb Your Enthusiasm, *and* The Wire. *Meanwhile, NBC, ABC, CBS, and Fox were churning out lifeless sitcoms like* Two and a Half Men, *along with moronic reality shows like* My Big Fat Obnoxious Fiance *and an endless slew of procedural dramas like* CSI: Miami *and* NCIS. *When a truly original show like* Freaks and Geeks *somehow made it past the network gatekeepers and onto the air, it was canceled within months. A decade after* Friends, Frasier, *and* Seinfeld *had reinvigorated the sitcom, nothing had come along to replace them.*

Alan Sepinwall: *Friends* was a great show that was the worst thing that happened to TV sitcoms, because it convinced everyone that all you needed was a bunch of really good-looking people in front of the camera. The market became flooded with multicam shows about sexy young people in the city.

Rob Sheffield: It was almost like the Mad Libs. Take the name of a slightly faded nineties indie film starlet and put her in a city, and the city was always New York, and give her this wacky black female friend and the wacky gay friend. If it's Julie Delpy it comes out one way, if it's Heather Graham it comes out another way, but that was the template of the time.

Jeff Zucker (CEO of NBCUniversal): The format had become a little stale. There had been very few new successes outside of what Chuck Lorre was doing for Warner Bros. and CBS.

Rob Sheffield: Somebody at a network was saying, "Damn it, I refuse to believe America has fallen out of love with Jim Belushi. Let's take the chick from *Melrose Place* [Courtney Thorne-Smith] and marry her to Jim Belushi and then have that sitcom [*According to Jim*] that runs for-fucking-ever." That template had completely run out of any sort of inspiration. Workplace sitcoms of the time just didn't have much of a workplace feel. They never felt like real offices because everybody was a character. It was always, "There's an office and there's six people and one-sixth of them are Andy Dick or David Spade or some combination thereof." They had not evolved at all past *The Mary Tyler Moore Show.*

Nathan Rabin: My wife is seven and a half years younger than me so other than *Seinfeld,* basically, if something has a laugh track, it is incredibly annoying to her. I think there was this whole generation that came to see that as not just artificial and irritating and annoying, but as somehow invalid. I feel like there were people who were trying to find something that was less obnoxious.

Kevin Reilly (NBC Entertainment Division President): We were coming off twenty years of sitcoms' being at the center of network television. By that point, there was a lot of entitlement in the creative ranks. The real groundbreakers of the past had been street fighters and scrappers. They had really unique points of view about things and they were fearless. But now you had a generation of writers who had grown up on staff making millions of dollars a year, without ever really having to stick their chin out and kinda take a chance with anything. It created a negative feedback loop where the writers were in a system where they were making a lot of money, the networks were asking for sort of a version of the same old thing, and I think too many writers were willing to do the same old thing to keep the gravy train going. When they did step out and failed, their reaction was, "I'm not making that mistake again." Ultimately, they were not getting rewarded for being very creative or breaking the mold.

Alan Sepinwall: A lot of people were being promoted above their experience level and ability. I watched a lot of shows that were run by people who had no business running shows, just because they had worked on *Friends* or *Frasier* or *Seinfeld*.

And so when Ben Silverman tried shopping around a single-camera, laugh-track-free show about a struggling small-town paper company, he faced a lot of resistance.

Ben Silverman: HBO was like, "We don't do formats." CBS was like, "There's no way we would do a comedy like this. Maybe we're down to do a workplace comedy, but no way do we want to do this comedy as you're envisioning it." I went to Fox and was like, "This is a Fox comedy. It's in the tradition of *Married . . . with Children* and *The Simpsons*." And Gail Berman there was just like, "Ugh." She just had no vision and was terrible. I really thought Fox would be the one since they do this kind of stuff, but sometimes you get the wrong management at the wrong time. But FX was into it. Nick Grad worked there and was a friend of mine. He was really into smart TV and he was way into it. His boss at the time was Kevin Reilly.

Kevin Reilly: Nick handed me a tape of the British series and I freaked out. I said, "This thing is brilliant." I was already negotiating at that point to go to NBC, which was not really ultimately the best career choice. But I said to Ben, "I think this would be good for NBC." At that point, I was looking at NBC coming off of the *Friends* and *Frasier* era. There were a lot of derivative sitcoms chasing versions of *Friends*. I felt like, "Man, we need something fresh in the comedy space." The workplace comedy was a foundational sitcom idea, but it had really gotten stale. Nothing seemed to be working in the space. And I just looked at this and said, "This is the freshest reinvention."

Ben Silverman: Everyone else passed, didn't want to hear it, or only wanted to do a workplace comedy with significant changes. I thought it could be an NBC show because of NBC's tradition of upscale comedies. They were the coastal network. They were the intellectual network. They were the home of the shows on broadcast I watched growing up. They were the *Hill Street Blues, St. Elsewhere, Cheers, Seinfeld, Cosby* network. So I felt like it was in their tradition, and then I also thought *Saturday Night Live* was actually of the tradition that we were going to go for with *The Office* as well.

NBC was in a minor state of panic because Friends *and* Frasier *were kicking off their final seasons and* ER *was running on fumes.*

Jeffrey Immelt (GE CEO): Our heads were spinning around NBC at that time. GE had acquired Universal in 2004. We were about to have a pretty stinky year in 2005 because our big feature movie was *King Kong* and it was crap. [It cost over $500 million to make and barely grossed over $200 million worldwide.] And we had a massive erosion in our ratings at NBC. Two thousand four was the second year of *The Apprentice,* which I don't care what anybody says, nobody ever thought that it would be a hit. It was almost our lead show going into 2004. We were trolling around the bottom.

Their big plan for the 2004–05 season was to launch Joey, *a* Friends *spin-off starring Matt LeBlanc. It came straight out of the* Frasier *playbook where a popular character was taken from a hit show that had just wrapped up a long run and moved to the other side of the country. Unlike* Frasier, *it was a disaster that cost NBC a lot of money and audience goodwill.*

Jeff Immelt: That tested higher than any show we've ever tested, and it just sunk like a log.

Jeff Zucker: At the end of the day, *Joey* just wasn't fully developed enough and wasn't funny enough. These multicamera situation comedies have to be funny and it just didn't hit.

Kevin Reilly: I was given *Joey* coming in the door. It sounds very self-serving to say now, but I always thought it was a bad idea.

Jeff Zucker: We needed to rebuild our comedy lineup. The holes in it were substantial. We had had some success with a single-camera comedy, *Scrubs,* in a way that ABC or CBS had not. And so we were certainly more comfortable with the idea of a single-camera comedy than they were. We had seen the prototype from the UK of what *The Office* could be and that gave us the confidence that it was a shot worth taking.

The news that NBC was working on a remake of The Office *hit the Hollywood trade publications just as the network began airing* Coupling, *another remake of a British sitcom produced by Ben Silverman and Teri Weinberg. It was so horrendous that the network pulled it after just six episodes even though they'd paid for ten. The fiasco created a toxic buzz around* The Office.

Teri Weinberg (Co-Executive Producer): *Coupling* was a provocative look at friendship and sex. It was really *Friends,* I guess, on a sexy steroid. I think the blessing and the curse was people weren't ready for a new *Friends.*

Alan Sepinwall: The NBC version of *Coupling* was just remakes of the original BBC episodes, only shorter because there was less running time. It was just god-awful. There was no life to it. It was just repeating ideas that somebody else had.

Rob Sheffield: I remember just assuming the American *Office* was going to suck. There was certainly no reason not to think it was. It was based on a UK sitcom and we'd seen so many track records of failure in that department. Of course, we'd seen lots of successes. Like most Americans who grew up in the 1970s, I loved *Sanford and Son,* I loved *Three's Company,* and I had no idea, I'd never heard of [their UK counterparts] *Steptoe and Son* or *Man About the House.* Whatever they'd lost in translation, they more than gained. But by the 2000s it seemed like *The Office* was a classic case of networks taking a really cool, innovative, and unduplicatable show and just trying to do an American knockoff. It seemed like the UK *Office* was just impossible to duplicate because it was so driven by the personality of Ricky Gervais, and because he and Stephen Merchant had such a tight grip on the creative control, it didn't seem like a template you could give to somebody else and see what they'd do with it.

Larry Wilmore: *The Office* is so well regarded now that people have forgotten the original feel people had about it. Before it aired, so many people were negative about it. "Oh my God, they're going to ruin it." This is because of *Coupling.* I kept hearing, "This is going to be terrible." I'd tell people what I was working on and they'd go, "Oh my God!" Then they'd try and be nice and be like, "Oh, okay!" But it was so condescending. They felt sorry for me. I wanted to say, "Guys, it's going to be great! Believe me! It's really going to be great." Nobody believed me.

chapter 3

CASTING

("She just looked like a person who'd work at a paper company for twenty-five years.")

Once they had a green light from NBC, Greg Daniels and Ben Silverman had the difficult task of assembling a cast that could live up to the UK originals and somehow stand on their own. Allison Jones—a veteran casting director responsible for everything from Freaks and Geeks *to* Arrested Development, Veep *and* Curb Your Enthusiasm*—was their first pick to lead the process.*

Greg Daniels: I was very interested in working with her after *Freaks and Geeks* because I thought that was the best-cast TV show I'd seen in years.

John Krasinski (Jim Halpert, Seasons 1–9): Allison Jones could be the most talented woman in show business.

Allison Jones (Casting Director): I met Greg Daniels in a little bungalow on the Universal lot. He mentioned *Freaks and Geeks,* wanting real people and just similar vibes as the British cast. We just sort of assumed we'd be crucified doing an American version of *The Office* so we just wanted to do the best we could. I had a lot of people in my head already. At our first casting session we had half the people, I think, who eventually got cast.

Greg Daniels: The combination of [Jones] and the British show brought in everybody you can imagine. I had such a joyful time reading people. For three or four months we saw just every cool, alternative comedian, comedy actor, and improv person you can think of.

Ken Kwapis: What made this casting process unique was that we never brought the actors to the network to audition in front of executives. That's the key difference. The usual way broadcast network shows are cast is that you narrow it down to a handful of candidates, and you basically parade them in front of the executives and have them read scenes. Sometimes in a small room full of executives who are sometimes watching, sometimes checking their devices.

Allison Jones: Reading in front of network executives is torture for everybody, including the poor actors. This is the first time we ever did it like this. We said to the executives, "Because of the nature of the show, reading live in the room is not gonna show you anything."

Ken Kwapis: That wouldn't have worked with these characters and the kind of comedy that Greg had written because a lot of it is behavioral. It's not jokey. A lot of it is small things that are observed and that wouldn't play. You're not playing to the rafters. And so all credit to Greg, he convinced the network that the proper way to cast these parts was to put people on tape in improvised sessions in the location itself. Sometimes we worked with the scenes from the pilot, but sometimes we set up improv sessions. But they were done on location in the place we were going to shoot, in a somewhat dressed bullpen.

These descriptions of the cast went out to agents all over town:

Story Line: "The Office—An American Workplace" is based on the BBC show "The Office." The American show is aiming to capture the humor and poignancy of the original. It is a single-camera mock-documentary that portrays in a realistic style some ordinary American office workers trapped in a confined space with their immature, inappropriate, bizarre, or deluded coworkers and one horribly over-confident supervisor. . . .

Michael Scott, 34–44: Michael Scott is the manager of the office and the boastful, unreliable narrator of the documentary. He is a legend in his own mind, who thinks he is a comic genius, fountain of business wisdom, and his employees' cool friend. He believes in his version of reality with the sincere enthusiasm of a nine-year-old child thinking he can do karate. However, the documentary reveals the truth: he is a buffoon, a pathetic mid-level bureaucrat overdue for a midlife crisis, whom decent people pity as a "sad little man" when his inappropriate behavior hasn't appalled them into silence. Horribly overconfident, he is a trainwreck of bad leadership characteristics, only redeemed by his childish enthusiasm. Despite continual proofs that he's an ass, he clings shamelessly to his deluded self-image like a shipwreck survivor clinging to a scrap of wood.

We need: an actor who can play a juicy comic character. Someone with an expressive face to get a laugh or a smug look: Someone with the heart of a nine-year-old, but who plays between 34 and 44. Someone whose face and physique do not command natural respect (i.e. not buff and handsome). Boyish, not rugged. Capable of high-spirited, sunny energy as well as small, specific acting. Perhaps someone used to creating a character and improving as that character.

Dwight Schrute, Late 20s–30ish: Dwight is the team leader and Michael's sidekick. He actually admires Scott, although it is unclear if this is due to Scott's personality or Dwight's officious inclination to look up to whoever is above him in the hierarchy. Dwight is obsessed with survival, personal security tactics, and other grandiose nerd action fantasies, probably because he got his ass kicked a lot as a kid. A volunteer policeman on the weekend, he takes any excuse to go on a power trip in the office. Yet his survival training appears to be more Gilligan's Island than Green Berets. Although aggressively horny, he has no idea how to behave with women. His unpleasant personal habits and annoying personality suggest an unsocialized loner, a sort of Caliban or Gollum. If stuck in an elevator, he would probably start drinking his own urine after ten minutes. His lack of social skills render him the butt of office jokes and thus bearable. If Scott is redeemed by having the heart of a nine-year-old, then Dwight can perhaps be pitied for his interior teenage geek.

We need: someone who can look a little grotesque or at least be believable as a geek. Someone who has no desire to be likable or please an audience, except through total identification with his character. Someone who can seem reasonable to himself while saying insane things, who understands the comedy of playing it straight.

Jim Nelson [*This was later changed to Jim Halpert*], 30ish: Jim is the sales rep in the office, who has to share a workspace with Dwight. He is an ordinary, decent person with good taste leading a life of quiet desperation. He likes people, is a good listener and wants to be a psychologist. His clever sarcasm and takes to camera are a little defense against the vulgarity that surrounds him, although they make Pam the receptionist laugh. You wish he would be more assertive in love and work. After playing with Pam, his chief enjoyment in the office is using his superior social and emotional skills to prank Dwight, although you sense that when he indulges his immature impulses he is letting the environment defeat him.

We need: Someone likable, around 30, who can get laughs by raising an eyebrow or doing a take to camera. He needs to be pleasant-looking enough for you to root for him to get the girl, without being a hunk in any way. Although hidden by his ordinariness and bad haircut, Jim is the romantic lead.

Pam Beesley, 26–29: Pam is the receptionist and Jim's friend. Pam is decent, reasonable and friendly. She has the manner of a nice kindergarten teacher or future mom. She is an ordinary woman with a sense of humor. She allows her loutish boss and fiance to push her around some, but can exhibit flashes of working class toughness in protecting her friends. She's not cynical or a smartass, although her way of disagreeing is gentle sarcasm. She's not arrogant or glamorous or overtly sexy, but she is cute compared to the other office workers, and she loves to play with Jim, who understands her better than Roy, her fiance. Jim and Pam would probably not have met without being thrown together in the office, but they have become true friends, and their flirting is more serious than they acknowledge.

We need: Pam needs to be soft and kind and vulnerable. Pretty too, but definitely not a head turner—more of a likable, accessible pretty. A working-world girl-next-door type, who can deliver sarcasm with a light touch, yet a touch of a tragic waif. Pam is the other romantic lead.

ADDITIONAL CHARACTERS:

Ryan: *The twenty-something college-boy temp.*

Jan Levenson-Gould: *The attractive, no-nonsense boss above Michael Scott.*

Todd Packer: *The crude traveling salesman.*

Stanley: *The lifer at the office, a worn-out cart-horse.*

Kristen: *An irritatingly bland stupid nice girl with no depth. [This character was ultimately eliminated.]*

Big Keith: *A stolid accountant with no affect but an odd mind. [This character ultimately became Kevin.]*

Roy: *A masculine, working-class hunk.*

Two or three employees to sit in the back and work, but who we might develop. They should not be better looking than Jim or Pam, feel like they are in the world of the show as actors and have a sense of humor. At least one should be African American.

Bennett: *A male employee who appears to be the statistical average in everything. Very real—should feel like somebody's brother that wandered onto the set. [This seems like an early, very crude version of Oscar or perhaps Devon.]*

Phyllis: *A female employee with experience as a straight woman in burlesque. [They clearly already had Phyllis Smith in mind when they wrote this description because she had a background in burlesque.]*

Anton: *A dwarf or midget. [Before they eliminated this character from the pilot, they discussed having Peter Dinklage come in to read for it.]*

Auditions began on November 6, 2003. The very first person on the sign-in sheet was Rainn Wilson, who came in to read for both Dwight Schrute and Michael Scott. The thirty-seven-year-old had been knocking around Hollywood for six years at that point, taking small parts in Almost Famous, Galaxy Quest, *and* Monk. *Earlier that year, he had begun a thirteen-episode arc on* Six Feet Under *that finally got him some industry attention.*

Rainn Wilson (Dwight Schrute, Seasons 1–9): I was excited beyond words as I loved the project so much. I sat in the waiting room, clutching my pages, literally more eager for this audition than any of the hundreds I had been on in the past. . . . I gave the world's lamest audition for Michael Scott. I simply did a very bad Ricky Gervais imitation with a lot of tugging on my tie and eye rolling. In the back of my mind, I knew the best was yet to come.

Allison Jones: He came back the same day and read for Dwight. He just was so good and just had brilliant comedy timing. He was hilarious and completely believable as the most annoying guy you've ever sat next to in an office. He was skilled beyond belief comedy-wise, but it still wasn't 100 percent, though. We wanted to look at other people.

Rainn Wilson: I heard they were auditioning every living and breathing comedy actor in the Western Hemisphere.

Seth Rogen, Judah Friedlander, Patton Oswalt, Matt Besser, Matt Price, and Jarrett Grode also tried out for the role, and Rainn wouldn't get a callback for well over a month. That same afternoon, Jenna Fischer read for the part of receptionist Pam Beesly. She was up against Mary Lynn Rajskub, Anne Dudek, and Kathryn Hahn. Fischer was married to future Guardians of the Galaxy *writer/director James Gunn but had struggled to get her own career going since arriving in Los Angeles five years earlier. At one point, she was working as an actual receptionist.*

Jenna Fischer: I had known Allison Jones before, so when I got my first call to audition I spoke with her and she said her notes were to really downplay my looks, like don't at all try to be pretty, no makeup. And I said, "Really?" That's because usually casting directors say, "Okay, be really hot. Be hotter and sexier than you need to be." But she said, "Be as plain as possible and dare to bore me." I said, "Really? Bore you?" She said, "Don't try to be funny. Please, please don't come in here and do a bunch of shtick and try and be funny."

Allison Jones: Jenna always seemed like the right type for it. We tested a few people that were good, but she always seemed on the money. She's also hometown pretty. It's trite, but I would just say that Jenna has that sort of the girl-next-door thing, and also not that exciting, if you know what I mean. She's not threatening in any way.

Rainn Wilson: The other actresses were kind of nervous and flustered in the waiting room, but Jenna just sat there, reading *Wired*, a John Belushi biography. I remember asking her about the book and her offhandedly saying something about how it was a book Pam would probably be reading.

Ken Kwapis: I have a very specific memory of my first meeting with Jenna, because I remember she was sitting with some of the other actors who were there to audition for Pam. And the other actors were chatty and gossiping, talking to each other. And Jenna was very quiet, and as I recall, sitting a little bit off to the side. And she seemed so shy that I wondered for a moment whether she was actually mistakenly there thinking she was interviewing to get a receptionist job. And watching her audition, it was hard to imagine that someone was acting.

Jenna Fischer: My take on the character of Pam was that she didn't have any media training, so she wouldn't know how to give a good interview. Also, she didn't care about this interview, because this was some weird project her weird boss was forcing her to do. The first question that they asked was, "Do you like working as a receptionist?" I took a long pause and said, "No." And that was it. I didn't speak any more than that. I wanted to stay true to the "dare to bore me" direction that Allison had given. They waited for me to say more, and I just didn't. I sat there. They sat there. The silence went on for what seemed like an eternity. And then, they started laughing. I committed to the same tactic. I gave yes and no answers. I felt like the comedy would come in watching me think about what I wasn't going to say, instead of the words that I said. It felt great. Greg and I clicked, and he clearly liked my take on Pam.

Greg Daniels: After her first audition I was like, "How did you do that? Are you a real receptionist?"

Allison Jones: Mary Lynn Rajskub also came in that first day for Pam and she was also fantastic. There were so many good readings, just slightly different interpretations of the same thing. So it wasn't easy to decide.

A casting memo shows that Paul Rudd, Steve Zahn, Aasif Mandvi, Robert Smigel, Michael Showalter, Zak Orth, Josh Radnor, Ron Livingston, and Colin Hanks were all considered very early on for the part of Jim. John Krasinski, who wound up getting it, had far less experience than anyone else who landed a lead role in The Office. *He had finished attending college at Brown only two years earlier and was eking out a living in New York as a waiter while taking roles in commercials and off-Broadway plays.*

John Krasinski: I definitely had fun being a waiter. I can't say for sure that I was a good waiter. I think that I made people have a good time. I probably couldn't tell you what was on any of the plates I was serving, so probably not great for the house. But being a waiter, I think I was a lot like any other actor in New York. I had credits because I'd work lunches during the week, and then on a Wednesday would be lucky enough be in a movie like *Kinsey*, go shoot for a day and come back.

Allison Jones: Steven O'Neill, who did the New York casting, gets the credit for bringing in John. At first he was gonna bring him in for Dwight. But then John said, "I'd rather read for Jim." And that was fine of course, so he read for Jim. He sort of combed his hair a little bit like Martin Freeman from the British version. So it was a little bit like he was trying a little too hard.

John Krasinski: There were like seven actors auditioning and six of them went in separately and then, for some reason, it stopped with me. The casting director said, "We're going to take a five-minute break for lunch. Is that okay?" I said, "Yeah," but in my head I was thinking, "No, just do one more." And then through the front door came a guy with a salad who sat across from me on the couch and he said, "Are you nervous?" And I said, "Not so much for the audition, but I'm really nervous for the people who are making this show because so often these translations are just such garbage and I really hope they don't screw it up because so many people are waiting to kill this show." And Greg Daniels said, "I'll try my best. I'm Greg Daniels. This is my show."

A horrified Krasinski called his agent and told him what happened. He urged him to go into the room and still give it his best shot.

John Krasinski: I went into the room and everyone was laughing at me because I was such a moron. Everyone was like, "Is this the jackass that told you the show was going to be ruined? Go for it, kid." Weirdly, because everyone was already laughing, the room was really warm and ready to go.

Ben Silverman: He felt like our Jim like immediately. He was so likable and thoughtful and he was handsome, but not too handsome. He didn't look like a young Brad Pitt or anything like that. He looked like you could put him in a tuxedo and he'd be handsome, but that wasn't what was driving his look. He also had this slightly muted, humble intelligence. His performance was kind of layered and that's what you needed from Jim, because you needed to think, "Why the fuck is this guy there? Why isn't he going to break out of it? Why wasn't he just nailing Pam the first week?" We needed somebody who had this kind of working-class struggle within him, and was smarter than those around him but wasn't an operator or political animal.

Greg Daniels: It's a hard role to cast. Very infrequently, I think, do you find an actor who is very, very good at comedy and extremely sincere and vulnerable, and capable of being like a masculine leading man. And I really felt that when all the different people came through, it was very clear John was the best.

Ken Kwapis: Greg wanted to populate Dunder Mifflin with people who the audience wouldn't recognize from other shows to reinforce the idea that we were making a documentary about a real place. He wanted to create the illusion that we were in fact documenting life at a paper company in Pennsylvania.

That was taken to an extreme when Phyllis Smith, Allison Jones's casting assistant, was brought on to play meek, matronly paper saleswoman Phyllis Lapin.

Ken Kwapis: Her job during the casting process was to sit beside the video camera and read the off-camera lines to whoever was auditioning. I would be sitting next to her watching the actors. And what occurred to me, after several auditions one day, is that I was much more interested in looking at Phyllis than I was at the actors who were auditioning. There was something about Phyllis's whole vibe I found just very appealing. And I said to Greg Daniels, "This woman really feels like she should be working in a paper company." And Greg said, "Let's ask her to be in the background of the pilot."

Allison Jones: I remember this a little differently. We had two days of testing. I was reading and Phyllis was filming. Ken came up to me and said, "Ask Phyllis to read to see if she can do it, because she'd be great in the background." And I was like, "Yeah, she would. Look at her, she's Phyllis." So she started reading with the actors and it was clear that she could do it.

Phyllis Smith (Phyllis Lapin Vance, Seasons 1–9): I was being auditioned for the show and didn't know it.

Allison Jones: So then Ken asked her to play a part in the pilot. And we were thrilled 'cause she was gonna make a day rate of a SAG, which was, I think, at the time $700, and that was like, "Holy cow, that's amazing!" She had been in casting for twenty years. She had a Midwestern and completely regular feel in kind of a pure way. She was also a different generation than most TV sitcoms that were casting at the time. She just looked like a person who'd work at a paper company for twenty-five years.

Phyllis Smith: I didn't believe it was real until I got a call from wardrobe saying they needed my measurements.

Stand-up comic Craig Robinson came in to read for the part of warehouse foreman Darryl Philbin after Greg Daniels watched a funny music video that he created with fellow comedian Jerry Minor.

Craig Robinson (Darryl Philbin, Seasons 1–9): When I went into the audition, Greg Daniels said to me, "I saw your video. It doesn't get much funnier than that." I said, "Thank you." But now the pressure was on. I had to outdo my video. I had to read one of those talking-head paragraphs. I love deadpan comedy like Leslie Nielsen and Peter Sellers and Harvey Korman. So I went in and I knew to do it deadpan and they took to me.

Ben Silverman: The longest part of our process was finding Michael Scott. We were circling Bob Odenkirk. He was available and was a great comedic actor. He had an incredible reputation among the comedy world, and he hadn't yet become famous. He wasn't well-known. We also had really liked David Koechner, who ended up being on the show in a great role [as Michael Scott's obnoxious friend Todd Packer].

An early memo reveals that Christopher Guest, John C. Reilly, Eugene Levy, Cedric the Entertainer, Rick Moranis, Dan Aykroyd, Matthew Broderick, Owen Wilson, Jason Lee, Steve Buscemi, Stanley Tucci, Jon Favreau, William H. Macy, Gary Cole, Hank Azaria, Robert Townsend, Jeff Garlin, Stephen Colbert, Dave Foley, Mark McKinney, Richard Kind, Kevin Nealon, Horatio Sanz, Thomas Lennon, Dan Castellaneta, David Arquette, and Paul F. Tompkins were all considered for the role, though many of these names never got past the discussion phase.

Allison Jones: Louis CK also came in to read for Michael Scott. I was so bummed we couldn't get him 'cause he was great, but he had a deal at CBS at the time. Ben Falcone and Jason Segel tested for Michael too.

Oscar Nunez: I remember Andy Richter and Damon Jones being up for it.

Ben Silverman: We wanted somebody with the kind of generic Americana appeal that most TV stars of the time had. Tim Allen, Seinfeld, all of these people were not the most extraordinary looking. They were Americana, and that I think was something we knew we needed in our lead as well.

Allison Jones: They made an offer to Paul Giamatti, and that was the days when movie stars did not do TV. So he said no. Then we tried Philip Seymour Hoffman and he said no as well. Back then, actors like that did not touch TV. It was seen as the bottom of the barrel, let me tell you.

Ben Silverman: I didn't watch *The Daily Show*, but I was aware of Steve Carell because I had just seen him in *Bruce Almighty*. Stacey Snyder, who was the chair of Fox movies until very recently, was the chairperson of Universal Pictures. She knew I was making *The Office* and was very excited I was doing it and was a big supporter of mine and friend of mine. She said to me, "I'm telling you, Carell is the guy. We're going to do another movie with him that stars him. You should grab him."

Stacey Snider (20th Century Fox Chairman/CEO): It was easy to recommend Carell because he was just in *Bruce Almighty* and his character had that same unctuous personality as Michael Scott. Remember Ted Baxter [from *The Mary Tyler Moore Show*], who everybody just rolled their eyes at? He couldn't read the room and he couldn't read how people responded to him. That is what Carell conveyed in his very small part in *Bruce Almighty*. When we were previewing *Bruce Almighty*, Carell just killed it and would steal the scenes from Jim Carrey when they were together.

Kevin Reilly: Stacey sent me footage from *Bruce Almighty* and said, "You should see this. He might be the guy." I then pushed for Steve all summer.

Stacey Snider: When I get enthusiastic about something like Steve Carell or a brand-new mascara, whatever it is, I push. I am that person that says, "No, you have to watch this," or "You have to love it." There's certain things that I get to a point where if you don't like it as much as I like something, I'm not sure we can be friends.

Kate Flannery (Meredith Palmer, Seasons 1–9): Steve had done so many failed pilots at that point. Because my boyfriend had photographed most of a lot of them, he said he used to have a joke that if they saw Steve on a pilot, they'd go, "Oh, there goes the show."

Ben Silverman: The problem with Carell was he was on another show [*Come to Papa*] as like the fourth lead on NBC. We had heard that show would be canceled, but the network wouldn't let us—even though it was on their air—get with Carell until they confirmed that it was canceled.

Kevin Reilly: Bob Odenkirk really wanted the part. He was excellent and had a good take on the character.

Allison Jones: But Bob has an edge to him. His take on Michael was just as funny as Steve's, but it was darker.

Ben Silverman: We just weren't sure Bob was soft or likable enough. He was a little tougher and meaner.

Jeff Zucker: I only vaguely remember this, but *Come to Papa* wasn't taking off and it wasn't a terribly difficult decision to let it go so they could bring in Steve.

Steve Carell (Michael Scott, Seasons 1–7 and 9): The auditions were very different than any other show I'd ever auditioned for. They were more of a workshop. Generally when you get to the point of a network audition there will be a bunch of people from the network weighing in on how it's going. This was very unlike that. It was just Ken Kwapis and the other actors and a camera, and they shot the audition like a documentary. That was my first taste test of what it would be like. But I met Greg and we talked briefly before I auditioned, probably a week or so before, but I'd never seen the show. I'd only heard how great it was and I kept myself away. I didn't watch it for the sole purpose that I'd heard it was so great and Ricky was so fantastic that I would have an inclination to copy him if I watched that, essentially I would try to emulate him, and I wanted to go in with as clean a slate as I could.

Allison Jones: How often do you have two solid people like Steve Carell and Bob Odenkirk testing for the same role? But Steve wasn't really very threatening and he was just sort of a jerk and a douche as opposed to an asshole. There wasn't really much edge to him at all, so that I think worked. Everyone thought that would translate better to an American audience. It was a relief when we were able to decide to go with Steve Carell after much angst. The worst thing I've ever had to do ever is tell Bob Odenkirk's agent that he didn't get *The Office*. Luckily, Bob did fine afterward. But at the time, believe me, it was a bummer to make that call. And I do suspect the show would have worked with Bob Odenkirk.

Before any of the other roles were finalized, groups of actors were called onto an

Office set in Los Angeles to see how they'd interact with each other. The finalists for Dwight were Matt Price, Rainn Wilson, Robert Baker, T. J. Thyne, Hugh Davidson, Ben Falcone, and Mathew Maher. The finalists for Jim were John Krasinski, Michael Weston, Thom Sharp, and Lance Krall. The finalists for Pam were Jenna Fischer, Ever Carradine, Erica Phillips, Kirsten Gronfield, and Maggie Lacey.

Allison Jones: We had ten or twelve VHS tapes filled with the different combinations of actors doing the roles together. It was a difficult choice for everybody to make for some of those roles, until they started reading with each other.

Jenna Fischer: They filmed us doing scenes on camera for two days, mixing and matching us. It was basically a fully produced screen test, something I'd never done before. . . . Over the course of two days, I was asked to read with John Krasinski a lot, which I thought was a good sign since he was definitely the best Jim.

They shot an improv scene where they gently flirted near a copy machine. They had an immediate rapport.

John Krasinski: The moment I sat down with her I thought, "This girl is going to get it." When we were walking out I was like, "You are going to get it. I know it."

Jenna Fischer: It was exactly as sweet and cute and supportive as anything Jim would say to Pam. I smiled really big and said, "I'm so glad you said that because you're my favorite Jim and I don't think anyone could do it except for you." It gave me a big confidence boost to know we were rooting for each other.

John Krasinski: The first question I asked when I got the part was, "Did Jenna get the part?" She said, "That's the first question I asked too." So it was this weird thing going already, this chemistry that had already started, which was pretty awesome.

The role of office temp Ryan Howard went to B. J. Novak, a recent Harvard graduate just beginning to make a name for himself through stand-up comedy and appearances on the MTV prank show Punk'd.

B. J. Novak (Ryan Howard/Writer, Seasons 1–9): Greg Daniels saw me do stand-up.

Greg Daniels: He started off with this joke where he said, "I just graduated from college, but I didn't learn much. I had a double major. Psychology and reverse psychology." I immediately knew I wanted to do something with him.

B. J. Novak: He called me in for a meeting with him; he thought I would be good for this small role that he was considering putting in, of the temp. He also knew that I had been a writer, and was interested in trying out writer/performers for the show, and was willing to read some of my writing samples. We talked for over an hour—it was the most exciting meeting I had ever had—about the British *Office* and his theories of comedy, and he drew me these Venn diagrams explaining his theory of television comedy, and it was so intellectually stimulating and inspiring; it was all I wanted to do. So I was discovered first, I guess, as an actor, by about fifteen minutes. And I had other things I could have done—I'd just been on *Punk'd* as an actor—and all I wanted to do was this show that everyone thought was such a terrible idea to remake.

Novak went to high school in Boston with John Krasinski and even wrote a high school play he starred in.

B. J. Novak: Total coincidence. I mean, whenever I really stop and think about it, it's just so crazy I stop thinking. We were friends for, I don't even know how long. And our first collaboration was actually eerily similar to this: Our senior year in high school. It was called *The Senior Show.* It was an original comedy show with a couple of musical numbers—mostly a parody of the school, its teachers, etc. John played an English teacher we liked, Mr. Todd, who dressed himself as a ghost and visited four "types" of students on the last night of eighth grade and gave them missions to accomplish in high school. I played Mr. Yasi, an eighth-grade teacher with a cheerful Boston accent who taught the American presidents class that John and I both took; I also played a student with a propensity for creatively dumb questions.

Ben Silverman: B. J. went to Harvard and John went to Brown, so they also had this Ivy League connection. There was a big Boston posse that we connected to, but B. J. was hired as a writer at first, and then we gave him an acting role. Same with Paul Lieberstein [who played HR rep Toby Flenderson] and the same with Mindy Kaling. They were all hired as writers who could then become characters on the show. They were thoroughbreds and great smart people, mostly in their twenties. We were hiring them because we thought they could write for the younger characters.

Smaller roles were given to Oscar Nunez (Oscar Martinez), Leslie David Baker (Stanley Hudson), Angela Kinsey (Angela Martin), and Brian Baumgartner (Kevin Malone).

Allison Jones: They all came in for the pilot for the small background parts, and who knew they would grow into the regular parts? We didn't know.

Brian Baumgartner (Kevin Malone, Seasons 1–9): I had seen every episode of the British series and had been doing theater. I had just moved to Los Angeles about three months before *The Office* started. I actually came in to read for the role of Stanley. I knew if I was going to get cast on the show it was going to be as the Kevin character, so I went in and read the role of Stanley like how I saw Kevin and was lucky enough that they saw something in that too.

Allison Jones: He was just a good face and a good vibe and a little bit like the Keith character [played by Ewen MacIntosh] that they had in the English series. He was just kind of a big teddy-bear doofus. And I'd just seen Oscar a month before on *Reno 911!* and couldn't believe how funny he was.

Oscar Nunez: I was still catering and I was still babysitting when I got the audition. Prior to that, things trickled in for me, like an episode of *24* and *Reno 911!*. I improvised a couple of scenes at my audition. They were like, "How do you feel about working at a paper company?" I said something like, "Oh, I know what you're thinking. We use paper and paper comes from trees, but I gave a tree. My friend from Israel, you know, there's a charity and you can donate a tree and I've given several trees, so I feel okay about this." They thought that was funny.

Leslie David Baker (Stanley Hudson, Seasons 1–9): I went in to meet Allison Jones and I had on my little suit and tie because [my character is] working in an office. I went in, read the part, and she said, "Great, I want you to go back to the callback. It's in two days. But don't go in dressed as nicely as you're dressed. You want to look kind of rumpled and kind of crinkly-wrinkled, like you've been actually working." I ended up going to the callback. I had another audition scheduled that day, drove to the office and they had like fifty people there. I looked around and said, "I've got time to leave and go to my other audition." I got in my car, drove to Culver City and then to Hollywood, went to the audition, left the audition, and school was out and every old person in Los Angeles decided they wanted to come out and drive that day. So there's old people driving slow, children darting in the street, locusts falling from the heavens, whatever could slow me down, trains stopping in the middle of the track, anything that could happen happened. So I got back to the callback and I was sweaty and wrinkled and irritable and grouchy.

Allison Jones: I guarantee you that helped his audition, because he was funny and he was cantankerous and that was the character. It is really fortuitous when that happens.

Most people who came to the auditions were strangers to Greg Daniels, but Angela Kinsey was married to his brother-in-law, future Office *writer Warren Lieberstein.*

Allison Jones: Greg didn't want anybody to know that, so we had a plan that we weren't really gonna say that. And I sort of secretly pushed her for the part, knowing she was right for it, but we didn't want to say that because that always looks like it's nepotism. But, again, she was perfect for it. We had a plan that I was going to say, "I think Angela is great," and that I was gonna push her, not Greg. Now, Greg would never remember this and Angela doesn't know this, but when I did that, Greg opened up his mouth and contradicted my excitement for her! He objected to her! I think he was trying to use reverse psychology or something. But I was like, "Fuck, you just fucked up our whole plan, Greg!" He objected with some ridiculous logic I can't recall, but still she got the part. So whatever his logic was, I was pissed at him because I had a plan that he wasn't going to open his mouth and he did.

Kinsey was indeed perfect for the part even though her character is as sour and miserable as she is sunny and cheerful.

Angela Kinsey (Angela Martin, Seasons 1–9): When I first came to town I temped, so I had a lot of time working in offices, and there are these people out there who kind of approach life, or definitely approach their job, with this sort of disgruntled kind of filter. That's how I saw Angela Martin. And within that world of always being put out, she could also have moments of happiness, sadness, love, but they were all like seen with a glaze of, just, disgruntle. [*Laughs*]

The vast majority of the cast had spent years trying to get their careers going and were more than a little skeptical this weird British import would get picked up to series, let alone become a hit.

Oscar Nunez: I figured we'd probably shoot the pilot and that'll be it. But then Greg Daniels said, "There's not going to be a laugh track. We're going to let the scenes go really long and awkward." I thought that was amazing and I thought to myself, "Okay, we have a chance."

chapter 4

SETTING THE STAGE

("It looked like they were shipping aluminum out of there.")

To create the Dunder Mifflin set, the producers rented a tiny, nondescript studio at 3322 La Cienega Place in Culver City, California.

Larry Wilmore: It was a very bizarre place to work. It looked like they were shipping aluminum out of there. It just didn't seem like showbiz.

Jason Kessler: A lot of small studios have offices for production staff to work in. And instead of using those for working, they actually dressed that as a set and that became the *Office* set.

Donald Lee Harris (Production Designer): They hired me to build the set. When I first walked in, it was pretty much just a big, giant, empty room. There were no cubicles or anything like that. There was nothing. No offices, none at all. I felt that the space could work if we divided it up and created some of the office cubicles around the bullpen. We built the offices out of that aluminum sash that you use for storefronts. I designed and built all of those around the bullpen.

Ken Kwapis: Greg and I spent a lot of time discussing the layout of Dunder Mifflin, and in particular how the desk arrangement would reinforce certain relationships in the series. Dwight and Jim, for example, not facing each other exactly, but being at a slight angle to each other. The idea that Pam is always facing Jim, but Jim is turned slightly away from Pam, so that it takes . . . this sounds very small, but it's important . . . he has to make a choice to turn to look at her. In the early episodes, this enabled me to frame a lot of interesting shots where we're looking past Jim toward Pam, and she is gazing at him. And he's either unaware that she's looking at him or pretending to be unaware she's looking at him.

Donald Lee Harris: I wanted Jenna's desk to be curved so that she wasn't just facing one direction. She could swivel her chair to any direction in the room and also have a vision of the whole space, and not just be locked into a standard square desk where you're just looking one way.

Ken Kwapis: There were a number of things that I wanted to do in the bullpen that are not realistic. For instance, most bullpens have cubicles where people are separated by walls. And it was important obviously that people be able to see each other. The accountants have a glass partition between them, but everyone else works in an open bullpen. It's more like a classic newspaper bullpen, like *The Washington Post* in *All the President's Men.*

Donald Lee Harris: Two small stages were attached to it, one of which we actually converted to the warehouse. We went to some warehouses in Los Angeles to see how they were set up, how they stacked materials and they used the chain link to separate different areas. It's very helpful for somebody like me, who may not have much experience in the paper business.

Randall Einhorn (Director/Cinematographer): The first set we filmed on was J. J. Abrams's office back when he was doing *Felicity.*

Matt Sohn (Cinematographer/Camera Operator): A number of seasons later, J. J. came in to direct an episode. On his first day on set, he was walking around and he was like, "This is so weird. . . ."

J. J. Abrams: I was struck by this uncanny feeling like I had been there before, and I couldn't figure out what the hell it was. And I hadn't ever noticed it on the series watching it, but I couldn't shake this feeling like something very weird was going on. And then it struck me that the room that was Michael's office had been Matt Reeves's office when we worked on *Felicity* and then I was doing *Alias*, and that the conference room was my office. It was a complete, unexpected mind bender.

Carey Bennett (Costume Designer): I'd never worked in an office before, luckily, so I actually researched and found this paper company in Glendale called Economy Office Supply that was about the same size as what we were trying to create. I invited myself over there and I just couldn't believe it. It was just so juicy, full of amazing details, even inspirational quotes that had been printed off of a computer and then taped to the wall, but in a big, long string of papers. And all the characters were there for me. This one woman had these great long dresses and these really comfy shoes and was just as sweet as can be. She became Meredith. There was a guy that always had on these T-shirts with wolves on them and gamer stuff on his desk. That became Dwight. I took a million pictures of this place and I presented this little photo presentation that I had from this office to Greg and everyone. They were just like, "What is this place? How did you get these pictures? Where did you find this?" So, we all went back over there. We took video cameras and videotaped this whole place. I think we even ended up using all of their supplies and stuff for the set. It's what fueled me the entire time I worked on the show.

Henry Saine (Graphic Designer): Everything always had to look very boring, which meant I had to unlearn everything I knew about design. I designed all the signs and everything with Microsoft Paint instead of normal tools like Photoshop and Illustrator. If I had to make a birthday banner I'd think, "They're going to just use an old Helvetica font and put a bunch of exclamation points at the end." When I created the Dunder Mifflin logo, I worked really hard on eight of them and at the last minute I made a ninth where the words weren't even lined up right. That's the one they picked.

They decided to set the show in Scranton, Pennsylvania. Much like Slough from the UK series, it's a working-class town relatively close to a huge city.

Carey Bennett: At an early meeting about the show, we had a map out and we were all like, "Where should we place our show?" Daniels literally hovered over the map and was like, "Well, we need to be close to a big city, but it needs to have been maybe a city that had, at one point, had some industry, but now it was sort of on the downswing." He just circled his finger around the map and found Scranton. And that was that.

Greg Daniels: I was reading John O'Hara stories at the time. He's a great writer and sets a lot of his stuff [in Scranton]. Paper Magic is a company that does children's valentines and it says "Made in Scranton" on the back of Scooby-Doo valentines that I had gotten around the same time for my kids. I think it was still maybe floating around when John Krasinski came there before the pilot with some buddies and shot the footage that's in our opening title sequence. He interviewed different Scranton paper personalities at Penn Paper and Paper Magic, and the behavior of him going around with a camera crew, asking the managers of these paper companies to show him around, it mimicked exactly what we were going for. We were like, "Thumbs up. That works."

Carey Bennett: I also worked on *Scrubs* and one of the PAs was from Scranton. I hired him to take pictures for me when he went back home of every single person he could see. He came back with a thousand photos of everybody from police officers to kids on the street to people working in stores. I needed every walk of life and he came back with a whole disk full of pictures.

Mari Potis (Greater Scranton Chamber of Commerce, Director of Membership and Events): I got a call from Phil Shea, their property master, and he told me they were doing a pilot for a TV show about a fictional paper company that would be set in Scranton but shot in Van Nuys, California. He wanted to use a Scranton Chamber of Commerce sign for the walls and then asked if I would help with some other items for the set. Then for the next nine years, I became the person that got them authentic Scranton props for the background. Greg Daniels wanted everything as authentic as they could [get] to Scranton. Eventually, we sent them truckloads of items submitted from local businesses that lined up to donate them at Steamtown mall, hoping to get free advertising on TV. It was that yellow Froggy 101 radio station sticker [from Dwight's desk], pizza boxes, newspapers . . . whatever they needed.

Donald Lee Harris: We did the whole first season there in that warehouse and upstairs, which is also very difficult to work in. There was no elevator or anything, so everything had to be hauled up the stairs.

Randall Einhorn: Ken Kwapis was really responsible for everything in the office actually working. You turn on the faucet, you wanted that to work. That doesn't happen in normal television production. If you need the faucet to work, you need to get a special effects guy in who could hook it up with pressure and someplace to attach it. It was really smart to make it feel like a place where you could sell paper.

chapter 5

THE PILOT

("That seems kind of dangerous.")

In a decision that most everyone involved lived to regret, they shot a pilot for The Office *in 2004 that was essentially a re-creation of the UK* Office *pilot. Ken Kwapis was hired to direct.*

Ben Silverman: Our first move was to emulate the British show and be a little slavish to it.

John Krasinski: The pilot was pretty much word-for-word the British show, which I know we weren't all super excited about, but we could understand why we had to do it to see how it stacked up against the other show.

Paul Feig: I had heard that Ricky's deal with them was that they had to shoot the exact pilot from the British *Office* to the script. I was kind of like, "Ooh, that seems kind of dangerous."

Ricky Gervais: I thought it was odd they just redid our pilot. I don't know why they did that. I thought there was no point to it. It got better when they went on their own.

Larry Wilmore: It's a great pilot, but it's very difficult because that script was specifically written by Ricky and Stephen for Ricky's voice. I thought Greg still did a good job but had kind of an eerie feeling watching it, almost like there were ghosts doing it.

Greg Daniels: The pilot was shot a lot like the original UK *Office*, which I felt was necessary to test NBC and see if they really had the stomach for a show of this nature, since the dominant show of the time was *Will and Grace*, which has a completely different sensibility.

It was also an opportunity for the cast to learn their characters and adjust to the mockumentary format.

Creed Bratton: Greg Daniels sat everybody down the first day and said, "We're going to shoot this without a laugh track. We're going to have long silent pauses, very uncomfortable pauses. I don't know if people are going to like it or not, but we're going to give it a shot. We're going to assume that there'll be some intelligent people that will find this amusing."

Melora Hardin: At one point, my cell phone rang just before we were going to rehearse a scene. I was like, "Oh, so sorry!" and I clicked it to silent. Ken said, "Oh, no, no, no. Don't do that. Leave it on. I want someone to call you in the scene when we're rolling. I think that's great. Just leave your cell phone on." I was like, "Really?" He's like, "Yeah, yeah. If they do call, answer it." Most people would be like, "Turn your fucking phone off." That was super fun. I knew immediately when he said that, I was like, "Oh, I'm gonna love this guy."

Peter Smokler was brought on as the director of photography. He only worked on the pilot, but he played a crucial role in setting the look for the rest of the show.

Ken Kwapis: He was also the DP on *This Is Spinal Tap*, so he had his mockumentary bona fides by the time he came to *The Office*. He was really helpful in setting the style.

Peter Smokler: The DP for most sitcoms sits on a dolly and has an audience behind him. But I was a documentary cameraman and that's how I filmed *Spinal Tap, The Larry Sanders Show,* and eventually *The Office*. Greg Daniels had really only worked on animation up until that point, so he really leaned on Ken to make it come alive.

Carey Bennett: When we finally got everybody on set I realized that three different people had white shirts on, would never happen in a real show. As a costume designer, you're trained to make it look like a painting, basically. You are doling out your colors in a specific way. And I was kind of in a panic since we were getting ready to shoot. I said, "Oh my God, Ken! Three people are wearing white shirts!" He stopped me and he goes, "You know, I think because this bothers you, it's correct."

John Krasinski: At the beginning of the day before we started, Ken did about forty-five minutes to an hour of just letting us work, not only to get us in the mood of just being in one place for a very long period of time, but also to capture moments for cutaways, which helped tremendously. There were a lot of moments where I didn't even know he was shooting.

Ken Kwapis: Everyone was on the call sheet all day, even if you didn't have a scene during the pilot. Everyone got their own desk and they personalized it. Every day of the pilot started off with us shooting general views. I wanted to see the Dunder Mifflin staff at work. People who didn't have dialogue, Phyllis Smith, for example, would be on a fake phone having an imaginary sales call.

Jenna Fischer: The Wite-Out moment of mine [from the opening credits] was just picked up during one of the morning sessions where I just made it my business to white some things out some day. . . . Angela would pass me little sticky notes over the wall during the day. They'd say things like, "I'm having a cat party for my cat Sprinkles. Would you like to come this weekend?"

Ken Kwapis: Finally after a half hour or so of just shooting people at work, we would segue into a scene.

Steve Carell: Ken Kwapis set a great tone right from the beginning. He essentially cleared the set of everyone but himself as the documentarian, the cameraman, and the sound man. It was just us. So he created this environment of these people in an office and this documentary crew. I think that really helped the tone and the mood. I think we all felt that we were sitting in this office and we were being followed around by a camera crew. You kind of got lost in that.

John Krasinski: Ken would be very hesitant to talk to you [out of character] in the talking-head [interviews] when we were alone with the camera. For like ten minutes he was asking me, "So, did you go to college in Scranton?" I was like, "Oh, we're *actually* acting now."

Rainn Wilson: Ken would never say *action* because he didn't want it to seem like a set, so he'd go, "Ooookay. Let's go ahead."

Jenna Fischer: One time Ken called cut and Leslie [David Baker] continued to make fake phone calls for about ten minutes. It was like he had to finish it up. He hadn't finished the sale and he wanted to finish it.

Steve Carell: Jenna made me laugh a lot when filming the pilot. Whenever I came at her with something completely inappropriate, her face would register a combination of disgust and horror and anger, and yet she wouldn't be doing very much, but her face would register five or six things at the same time without doing anything.

B. J. Novak's character of Ryan Howard serves as the audience surrogate in the pilot as Michael Scott shows him around the office and introduces him to the entire Dunder Mifflin crew. The episode establishes Jim's unrequited love for Pam, who is engaged to warehouse worker Roy Anderson, played by David Denman. It also establishes Jim's rivalry with Dwight and the fact that Dunder

Mifflin is facing financial hardships that may require letting an employee go. Near the end, Michael mock-fires Pam as she sobs uncontrollably. It's an exact mirror image of a scene from the UK show, but it comes off as far less playful.

Ken Kwapis: Michael Scott humiliates Pam in front of Ryan. I think that felt more like the Ricky Gervais version. I remember Ricky once distinguishing between the character he created and the character Steve created by saying that his character was a jerk, but Michael Scott was a boob. We used that as an important way to classify things. We'd say, "Is that something a jerk would do or is that something a boob would do?" The firing was a thing a jerk would do.

Paul Feig: When I watched the pilot I was kind of like, "I don't know, man, this is kind of hitting all the stuff that I was concerned about," which is the brilliant Steve Carell really trying to imitate Ricky Gervais's role. When they had the scene where he fake-fires Pam and she starts to cry, I'm going, "Oh man, I think American audiences are going to flee from this."

B. J. Novak: Jenna probably had to cry, like, fifty times that day. This was a lot of people's favorite scene and a lot of people's least-favorite scene.

Steve Carell: My favorite shot in the episode is the pan-over and B. J. is shaking his head. If you look closely, you'll notice that [we] have little, if any, makeup on and very little attempt is made to make us look good.

Alan Sepinwall: I watched the pilot and I really didn't like it. I had known Greg a long time by that point and he said, "Alan, what do you think?" I said, "Greg, I don't know. The moment when Michael fires Pam, I really kind of hated him." And Greg took a step back and said, "Well, that's not good!"

Many of the critics agreed with Sepinwall's assessment.

The *New York Daily News:* "Compared to the BBC version, in which every portrayal of the four key character types is utterly perfect, NBC's version is so diluted there's little left but muddy water."

The Washington Post: "Reality check: Carell, who was so brilliant on Comedy Central's *The Daily Show*, overdoes it at times and certainly is no match for the wonderful Ricky Gervais, his counterpart in the British version."

Entertainment Weekly: "The curious pilot is so faithful to the BBC version, it's almost Van Santian. [*This is a reference to Gus Van Sant's critically panned shot-for-shot remake of* Psycho *in 1998.*] For aficionados, it won't work: You can't help but see Gervais' roly-poly ghost in every scene."

The Kansas City Star: "The first mistake NBC made was giving the Brent role to Steve Carell. He was a riot on 'The Daily Show' but is ill-suited for this part. Up until now I've taken Carell in small doses, like the white-collar worker he played in a series of 30-second shipping commercials. One gets the sense that was how he got hired for 'The Office.' Here, Carell crawls under your skin faster than Nancy Grace, which is saying something."

The ***Los Angeles Times:*** "Lost in translation is the sadness behind the characters on the BBC series, the utterly dreary lives outside the office from which the comedy inside the office emanates. Yes, these poor blokes are being derided, but at the same time the show elicits your compassion for them. . . . There's a menace to Carell's character that I didn't want to feel, a sociopathic, beady-eyed quality that's too cartoon, and that gives the show a colder edge. This 'Office' will have to rely less on him as a guiding voice than 'The Office' relied on Gervais."

USA Today: "The insurmountable problem for this version may prove to be Carell himself. He's an amusing sketch comic, but he comes across as an actor doing a bit, not a person running an office. Worse, he makes the character too one-dimensionally unsympathetic. He captures Michael's delusions of grandeur but misses the poignancy in his mad dash for popularity. But then that's what happens with copies. Inevitably, something great gets lost."

Ricky Gervais: I remember they tested it and Greg Daniels sent me a disappointed e-mail saying, "It scored very low." I wrote back, "Congratulations! The [UK] *Office* tied with women's bowling for the lowest test score ever and we didn't change a thing." And I said to him, "That's a good sign. Anything to do with innovation suffers on the test score because people go, 'That's not what I expected.' They mark it down because it's not like the sitcom they thought it was going to be. You can't let that stop you."

KEY EPISODE 1

"Diversity Day"

About six months after the pilot was shot, NBC picked up The Office *for five additional episodes. For the first one of the new batch, they moved away from the UK series and created something all their own with "Diversity Day." It revolves around two mandatory diversity meetings in the conference room that go horribly wrong. The idea was hatched when Ben Silverman, Greg Daniels, and his manager Howard Klein traveled to England to meet up with Ricky Gervais and Stephen Merchant before they formally began working on the series.*

Greg Daniels: One of the things we talked about was that a big issue in American offices would be race. Huge. Bigger than class . . . That's why we hit it dead-on.

Michael Schur (Writer, Seasons 1–5): It was completely and utterly different from any of the British *Office* episodes that had aired, which I think was really important. The tone was still the same, which was that the boss is doing something humiliating, but there wasn't a direct equivalent at all in the British series. So, I remember thinking, "Boy, that's a really smart move to show people, we're not just taking the scripts from the British show and re-creating them."

Larry Wilmore: B. J. Novak wrote the episode, but *The Office* was one of those shows where it didn't matter who thought of the idea, someone else could write the episode. That's how Greg did it. Everyone would chip in and write. It was very much a communal writing process as well as an individual writing process. This episode definitely was in my wheelhouse of the type of stuff I was pitching at the time. We knew we wanted to push the envelope in terms of the content.

It begins with an outside diversity expert named Mr. Brown (played by Larry Wilmore) coming into the office to conduct a seminar after Michael insulted many in the office by delivering an infamous Chris Rock comedy routine from Bring the Pain, *which contains numerous uses of the word* nigga.

Larry Wilmore: I didn't want to take a part on the show that could have gone to an actor that really needed the work, but they asked me to read it at the table read since we didn't have it cast yet. At the table read, I just killed. I really got a lot of laughs. But I kept saying, "We really should get an actor." I don't know how many people they auditioned, maybe one or two, but I feel like they were sneakily trying to get me to do it. I'm glad they did because it turned out to be one of the funnest things that I ever did.

Kate Flannery: It was so hard not to laugh because Steve was so real and so funny and Larry was coming in being so earnest.

Larry Wilmore: Steve Carell had me crying laughing. I had to keep a straight face during that scene. He was just really saying that bit over and over, "And the niggas . . . and the niggas . . ." He just said it over and over and I was crying with laughter. I don't think you could get away with that these days.

Ken Kwapis: In the original script, Michael Scott's diversity training seminar was held all over the office, all over the bullpen. I just had a gut feeling that if everyone was stuck in that conference room it would be funnier. I think that had an important impact on the episode, and it also had an impact on the series in general. It is hardly an original thought, but look at the stateroom scene in [the Marx Brothers movie] *A Night at the Opera*. People crammed into a small space is funnier than people having plenty of elbow room. Everyone is stuck in there for this poorly conceived seminar and just that by itself, I thought, was going to help the comedy. And moreover, the conference room became an important space for storytelling.

Larry Wilmore: That conference room scene has everything in it and it sets everything up for the rest of the series.

Greg Daniels: I had an expression that I used in the writers' room to describe a scene where the situation was charged, several characters had different opinions, and there was an excuse for them to all sit around and fire off great lines one at a time. I called it a killing field, like it was just nonstop joke joke joke. They were usually scenes like a diversity training seminar in the conference room.

During Michael's follow-up meeting, he required everyone to wear a notecard on their head that said things like "Asian," "Jewish," or "Black."

Greg Daniels: The game of them putting cards on their foreheads happened to Tom Huang, our writers' assistant at the time, who's an independent filmmaker now. That's something that he had suggested that had happened to him in a job. That was a great thing to be able to use. Something real.

Angela Kinsey: Mine was Jamaica. Jenna was Jewish. I'm sitting next to her and I look at her and Steve Carell was, as Michael Scott, giving his speech about diversity, and I just lost it laughing. I just bust out laughing. He was sitting right in front of us, he had turned his chair backward and was leaning forward to us, and I had the hardest time keeping a straight face. I thought, "This is really cool. This feels like lightning in a bottle. This chemistry. This group of people. I think we have something here."

Greg Daniels: We had some wonderful cards we didn't use, like "Szechuan" was one of my favorite cards that Michael had written down.

Steve Carell: Looking at people with cards on their heads all day, that was almost impossible to get through the day without laughing every time you looked at someone. It was just the most ridiculous visual.

Larry Wilmore: The camera keeps landing on uncomfortable faces, which of course Gervais did in the original as well. But we found our way to do that with our type of story.

Steve Carell: When the dailies for this show were being filtered about NBC, this Chris Rock routine [with multiple uses of the word *nigga*] was being played on most computers at NBC.

Greg Daniels: I woke up in a cold sweat that this was going to get out before the show with the un-bleeped version. I ran to the editing room and bleeped it on the master.

The episode marked the first appearance of writer Paul Lieberstein as HR rep Toby Flenderson.

Michael Schur: I remember Paul Lieberstein's extreme reluctance to act in that episode even though he only had one line: "Are we all going to have to sit Indian style?" And Michael Scott, who is on this mission to prove that he's culturally sensitive, immediately kicks Toby out of the meeting.

B. J. Novak: Paul has such a fun natural demeanor that we kept saying, "Paul should be in the show! Paul should be in the show!" And I believe I'm the one who said he should be named Toby.

Michael Schur: Kevin Reilly, the president of NBC, saw the dailies and said, "Who is that redheaded guy? Get him in the show more."

Jim spends much of the episode trying to close a big-money deal with a client, which Dwight winds up stealing for himself. But near the end, Pam falls asleep on his shoulder in the conference room, giving them a rare moment of semi-intimacy. "Not a bad day," Jim tells the unseen camera crew.

Ken Kwapis: That more than makes up for everything else that went wrong in Jim's day. It took a lot of takes because Greg and the writers had so many thoughts about this small moment. I think we must've done it a dozen times. It wasn't so much Jenna leaning her head as it was how John reacted. We did it over and over and over again. Between takes we'd have these big discussions about what the meaning of that reaction was. It's the simplest little thing, and yet it was discussed with such eagerness by everyone. I think everyone sort of related to that moment in their own way. I remember B. J., Paul, Greg, and I all standing around discussing this quiet little moment. How surprised should Jim be? How happy or how obviously happy should he seem? It's a moment that you can actually play in a lot of different ways. And we did. And as you know from many series, sometimes romances proceed at a glacial pace. But what was wonderful about this is it sort of made a big leap forward in the form of a tiny moment.

Larry Wilmore: Moments like that are more powerful than other things I've seen where there are big, fiery speeches because it reminds you of real life. I'll never forget how John was frozen there a little, but then decided it was a delightful treat and he was going to enjoy it. It was such a nice little moment that played at the right speed. John is conveying that, "This isn't completely what I want, but you know what? I'm happy and that's okay. It's okay to be happy right now. At the end of the day, I'm selling paper. This is bonus land right here."

Oscar Nunez: As we're shooting this episode I was thinking, "This is really, really funny." I remember talking to Brian outside the building and I was like, "Brian, I can see us in three or four years getting an Emmy for writing or acting for this show." I knew there was nothing else like it on American television.

Larry Wilmore: It was one of those breakthrough moments. I feel it is where we really put a stamp on what that American show should be, the way that we wanted to do it.

Paul Feig: "Diversity Day" was the episode where I was like, "This show is genius." But, at the same time, I kept thinking, "I don't know if they're going to keep it on, because it's really mean." But that's why it's funny.

Ken Kwapis: But for a while there were pundits who said, "Oh, the show took a while to get its bearings and find itself." And when you hear things like that you just kind of bite your tongue and move on. But inside I was saying, "Are you kidding? Watch 'Diversity Day.' Episode number two!"

chapter 6

SEASON ONE

("It felt like we were making a student film.")

"Diversity Day" was a breakthrough episode, but then they had just four more episodes to prove themselves before NBC decided on whether or not to give the show another season. The cast and crew showed up at the crack of dawn each morning at the Culver City lot, determined to prove all the doubters wrong and get a renewal order.

Jen Celotta: There were no trailers for the actors that first season so they would basically walk onto the set and be there all day. They had to sit in the background for other people's scenes since there was nowhere else to go. They were just sort of trying to create that feel of being at work and being a little bit bored. You just couldn't get up and go to your trailer and do something.

Larry Wilmore: It felt like we were making a student film in some ways.

Randall Einhorn: We would do these morning things that first season, like in the pilot, where it was just general views so we could watch people be people. I would watch Stanley at the copy machine or Phyllis scratching herself or whatever. I spent forty-five minutes in the morning watching them in character.

Kate Flannery: The first season they told us that we needed to bring our own paperwork since they wanted us to be busy. They really wanted us to really figure out how to be in an office without speaking. I brought my tax paperwork and I brought this really thick Ruth Gordon autobiography that I was hiding. And our computers didn't work back then, so I didn't even have the luxury of playing solitaire.

Matt Sohn: There was a theory that it was getting everybody into the mind-set of *The Office*, and it gave us a ton of B-roll and footage to use in different places during the show, whether it was paper coming out of the copiers, or just the wide boring shots of the office's people doing the mundane work.

Randall Einhorn: I remember there was one point that Greg actually joked about, and I'm not *entirely* so sure he was joking, but he said that we should start *actually* selling paper. I thought that was really funny, man. We should sell some paper. Why not? It would help with the catering budget. Let's sell a few reams of paper, sure. I thought that was ingenious.

Jason Kessler: The first season really felt like it was an experiment. We only got five episodes, which is such a tiny, tiny order, so it was clear that NBC wasn't putting all of its chips on *The Office*. I absolutely loved it, and getting to read the scripts every week was such a treat for me as an aspiring writer. But I don't know if I believed that a network audience as a whole would get it. It's just a very specific, dry brand of humor.

Ken Whittingham (Director): We were still trying to figure out how the show worked. At one point, Greg and I were talking and I said, "Man, it might be kinda cool if we shoot through the blinds and see that Steve is actually playing with a truck even though he said he was really busy." I believe that was the first time we did the spy shot and that became a signature thing for the show.

Ben Silverman: We opened out of *The Apprentice,* which was, like, interesting, but a little tough because the ratings expectation was so high. That was their number one show. There was this sense they'd work well together because they were both set in workplaces, but they were so different. Our first rating was huge and then we moved away from *The Apprentice* and our ratings weren't as good and they were like judging us.

The actors were making only modest amounts of money and had no idea if the show was going to last beyond these six episodes.

Ken Whittingham: When we first started filming "Health Care" [the third episode] I was also working on *Scrubs.* John Krasinski pulled me aside one day and goes, "Ken, man, do you think you could get me on *Scrubs*? That would just be wonderful. I would just love that!"

Kate Flannery: I kept my restaurant job actually through the first season. I was a waitress at Kate Mantilini in Beverly Hills. Sometimes Greg Daniels would come in to talk to me. I'd be holding a tray of food and he'd be like, "I've got to talk to you about saying the word *vagina* [in 'Health Care']. We're going back and forth with the network on that, but I really want you to keep it."

Jason Kessler: My job that season was to drive around town and drop people's scripts off at their houses. I very specifically remember going to John's apartment in West Hollywood and he was playing video games with a friend. He invited me in to play. Normally, I would drop a script off at the door or I'd knock on the door and hand it to him, and someone would say, "Oh, thank you very much," and just go in their house. John's the only person who ever invited me in.

Episodes two through six ("Health Care," "The Alliance," "Basketball," and "Hot Girl") weren't as strong as "Diversity Day," but they fleshed out the world and showed the potential of the characters.

Ben Silverman: Those first episodes took a while to find their own soul.

B. J. Novak: I remember the leap that we made when we did the batch of episodes two through six. The pilot was very strong and it got us on the air, but after that the staff got together and we started breaking the rest of the stories. Having seen Steve Carell and Jenna and John and Rainn and having caught glimpses of these other people, it was easier to write the little nuances and quirks of the characters.

Ken Whittingham: I remember talking to Rainn about making his character his own. He didn't want to be anything like Gareth. When we shot "Health Care" [where Dwight is put in charge of picking a new health care plan] he wanted a little more intense and a little more OCD and very self-righteous. Gareth was just a little more laid-back and just a little unaware.

Ken Kwapis: We knew that people held the original show in high regard, and so we knew that among other things, we couldn't go too far away from the original show in terms of it being behavioral and observational and a mock documentary. We weren't going to suddenly turn it into a joke fest.

Ken Whittingham: In "Health Care," Michael has promised the staff a big surprise at the end of the day. They're all just waiting outside of his office. It was written that we would take this long uncomfortable beat since he didn't have anything and he knew he didn't have anything. It was just a super, super-long beat where everybody just sort of slowly just kind of walked out of the room and left him there. One of my biggest concerns was like, "Wow, is this a long time for this uncomfortable silence? How does this fit into this twenty-one-minute or twenty-two-minute show?" My first cut was ten minutes over.

Greg Daniels: The editor's cut on ["Basketball"] was forty-four minutes long.

Steve Carell: It was a little bit more difficult for us being broadcast on NBC and aired in the US because the UK version had twenty-nine minutes and we twenty minutes and thirty seconds. In order to let the show kind of breathe and let those awkward moments play out, it's a little bit tougher to do that in twenty minutes.

Greg Daniels: You have to leave a lot of good stuff on the floor.

Crucially, they always made sure to keep in the pauses and awkward silences, even if it meant cutting other great jokes. The scene in "Health Care" where Michael pauses after promising to deliver a big surprise lasts an excruciating one minute and thirty-five seconds.

Paul Feig: Watching those first six, as hilarious as they were, it was like, "Wow, I don't know if this is going to survive." But we were hoping it would, because we saw how funny it was.

John Krasinski: I remember every week being told that this would be our last episode, and unfortunately we weren't going to keep going. I remember saying, "Is there any way I could get a DVD of this to show my mom, because this is definitely the best thing I've ever done." And I was happy with that, and I actually still have that DVD. So for us, it was just like we were in the best regional theater group in the world. We just thought no one was necessarily paying attention, but we were having a blast.

Oscar Nunez: At the end of the first season, Kate Flannery and I quit our jobs around the same time. I'm like, "I'm going to quit. Are you quitting?" She's like, "Yeah, I'm going to quit. Fuck it. Let's quit." The manager at her restaurant said, "You'll be back." She hasn't been back.

chapter 7

THE FIGHT FOR SURVIVAL

("Things literally got insane.")

The pilot premiered strong with 11.2 million viewers, but ratings dropped nearly in half to 6 million just five days later when "Diversity Day" aired. By the end of the season, they were down to 4.8 million. Ominously, each episode did worse than the previous one. A second season seemed like an extreme long shot.

Jeff Zucker: It wasn't even close to being successful that first season.

Jason Kessler: We didn't think it was going to get another season. In fact, the entire production staff went to work on another pilot called *Early Bird* with [*Office* co-executive producer] Kent Zbornak. I took a job as the writers' assistant on the Borat movie. We all thought *The Office* was over.

Larry Wilmore: The person that saved us was Kevin Reilly, who was running NBC at the time. He was in the show's corner.

Teri Weinberg: If not for Kevin Reilly, we would not have seen the light of day. And I still say it to Kevin over, and over, and over again, because he never wavered, he never stopped loving the show, he never stopped fighting for it.

Kevin Reilly: NBC used to have this screening process where you had all these executives from the head of the company to head of business affairs, the head of affiliates, the head of research, the head of cable, the head of syndication . . . Everybody weighed in with their opinions. And most of the room voted thumbs down for *The Office*, like a resounding thumbs down. But at the end of that couple of days we had one room that screened it that was full of the assistants and the interns and the new young executives that we call associates. It was a room of about forty young kids. And they said to me, "*The Office* is the only show you're making that we'd actually watch." They loved it. And I said, "There it is!" To me, right then, in that moment I said, "I'm falling on my sword for this, because these are the people that are getting really bored with sitcoms and that's who I want to watch this." But then I had to go through really an excruciating process of dealing with some very heavyweight executives who were really quite sure that this was a terrible, terrible decision. I don't want to name names.

Ben Silverman: Jeff Zucker wasn't into it.

Teri Weinberg: We broke the fourth wall, so it felt more like a reality show than it did any other kind of traditional comedy. So I think that maybe Jeff didn't quite have the understanding of it, or [it] just wasn't quite his taste.

Jeff Zucker: You have to remember I had the overall responsibility for the network, so none of these decisions were made in a vacuum. And so obviously it wouldn't have gotten on and wouldn't have continued if I didn't support it, right? So at the end of the day, obviously, I clearly supported it and had wanted it to come back. But listen, these weren't slam dunks and it certainly wasn't a no-brainer.

Alan Sepinwall: Jeff Zucker was not an entertainment guy, he was a news guy. He was brought in because he had made the *Today* show absurdly profitable, and he never really seemed interested in or knew what to do about the entertainment side of things. He was really just not interested in running the entertainment division of a major broadcast network.

Zucker may have been head of NBC, but he was still outranked by the corporate brass at GE.

Jeff Immelt: I always say that things are only funny because they're true. I started my career in sales offices, so I had seen these people before, and I knew that this show would resonate vis-à-vis people who have worked in offices and who have jerks for a boss. And my daughter was in her twenties and it was one of the only shows she would watch on NBC. I also just found it to be really, really, really funny. I would watch thirty minutes of *Friends* and not laugh once, but I would watch thirty minutes of *The Office* and be like completely engaged. So I liked it from the start and I was extremely supportive of adding it. I was kind of urging Jeff [Zucker], saying, "Look, we should add it, because, look, we suck so badly, what harm can it do?" But he was very unsure about it. He thought it was too quirky and just too narrow for a broadcast network to put on.

Jeff Zucker: Kevin Reilly was a very big proponent of it, as were others, but at the end of the day, I made the decision to go forward with it.

Jeff Immelt: I love Jeff and we had a great working relationship. But once or twice I would say, "Hey, look, let's just do it my way." I was smart enough to know what I didn't know, and to a certain extent those jobs are so public and they are under scrutiny every day that I didn't feel comfortable doing too much. But in the case of both *The Office* and *30 Rock*, which he was also skeptical about, I definitely put my thumb on the scale.

Ben Silverman: I was on a plane with my best friend at the time, David Benioff, who created *Game of Thrones*. We were going from the premiere of *Troy* in Cannes to Tokyo, picking up Brad Pitt along the way in Amsterdam. I can describe Brad's sleep to you. It was like an animal growling and moving. It was like something I had never witnessed before. Anyway, Eric

Bana was there too. We were in the lap of luxury. We land in Siberia to refuel, where we're met by these Russian soldiers. I look down on my phone and see that I have, like, nine missed calls. They picked up *The Office* for a second season. [The Japanese premiere of *Troy* took place on May 17, 2004, ten months before *The Office* pilot aired. It seems like he's confusing at least part of this story with the initial series order.]

Kevin Reilly: We ordered a big whopping six episodes.

Ben Silverman: It wasn't the thirteen originally budgeted, and they would only do it for like 50 percent of what it's going to cost. I had to get everyone to reduce their fees and figure out a way to make the budget work. Literally, I'm doing this from a Siberian tarmac, speaking to Ricky and Stephen, who agree to defer and reduce their fees on the first six episodes, doing it with Greg Daniels and his manager [Howard Klein], who was also a producer on the show. Then I have to call the line producer [Kent Zbornak] and explain to him how we can shoot practical, we don't need to build sets. Then we can use Randall Einhorn as a cameraman and to direct so we don't need to budget as many cameras. I basically was teaching them how to do a reality-style production and cut the budget down by 50 percent. By the time I landed in Tokyo, I was doing all the follow-up and negotiating.

Ricky Gervais: We had to defer some wages to give it a chance, which everyone did.

On May 16, 2005, NBC announced that The Office *would come back for a second season, airing at nine thirty* P.M. *on Monday nights between* My Name Is Earl *and* Law & Order: SVU. *Kevin Reilly even filmed an* Office *parody video he presented at the Radio City Music Hall upfronts poking fun at NBC's difficult year. The response in the entertainment press was not kind. "Surprisingly, these guys—both Jeff Zucker and Mr. Reilly—love their* Office,*" wrote Virginia Heffernan of* The New York Times. *"They keep acting like it's a daring art project instead of a dark, low-rated reminder of how much it is not the real* Office. *They want us to give it a chance. And they even want to be able to joke self-deprecatingly about how they themselves are like the* Office *dud, just fatuous, small-time branch managers. That joke is a luxury. It's for winners. I think it's spooking people here."*

What nobody in the audience at the upfront realized was that a new movie called The 40-Year-Old Virgin *was three months away from hitting theaters and turning Steve Carell into a huge movie star. The Judd Apatow–directed film would gross $110 million on a $26 million budget and usher in a whole new era of R-rated comedies on the big screen. The timing couldn't have been better to help* The Office.

Ben Silverman: It was incredible. I called the head of marketing at Universal and said, "Would you please tag your *40-Year-Old Virgin* spots with *The Office*? I'll go ask NBC to put the money in." It was one of the first times ever a movie studio and sister network did ads with this star and brought up the show and the movie. There were *40-Year-Old Virgin* and *Office* radio spots airing during the summer.

Kate Flannery: I remember going to the premiere. We were working on an episode that day and I had a really intense moment after that movie in the parking lot. I thought, "Oh my God, this show could actually go. He has a power and a charisma that could be enough to make this job go." And I was right. Steve becoming a star was profound for *The Office.*

Jason Kessler: That movie was a turning point and this gigantic success that I don't think anybody could have predicted. At the time, R-rated comedies weren't killing it at the box office, but *40-Year-Old Virgin* was such a massive success that I think no matter what the show was, if Steve Carell was on a TV show, people were going to watch it.

It still wasn't enough to convince everyone at the network to pick up The Office *for a full second season.*

Kevin Reilly: Things literally got insane. It got to the point in the second season where I'd order more episodes, put it on the schedule, and then I'd meet with finance and I wouldn't see it in the budget. I'd say, "Where's *The Office*?" And they'd stare at me and say, "You gotta take it out." And I'd say, "No, I just left the meeting where it's in. When did this happen?" They'd say, "Well, an hour ago. You need to go back and talk to Jeff [Zucker]." This happened about five times. I kept being told it was in, but the money people would be told it was out. So it was really bonkers. Really, really bonkers.

Season two began on September 20, 2005, right after the debut episode of My Name Is Earl.

Kevin Reilly: The crazy thing is that *The Office* would never have made it if not for *My Name Is Earl,* which premiered at a six rating. Even at that point, that was inconceivable for comedies. It was the biggest comedy premiere the network had had in years. And *The Office* was behind it. So all of a sudden it had a little bit of a protection and it was getting sampled by that audience.

The cast did everything they could to build an audience.

Matt Sohn: A bunch of the cast members were on MySpace and they began communicating with fans while they were at their desks on the set in the background. That kind of helped kind of build some momentum for the show and build that fan base, because people could actually touch base with them. And a lot of the actors had so much time to spend online doing that in the background of shots that they were doing it a real lot.

Jennie Tan (OfficeTally.com Webmaster): One of my favorite early episodes was "The Fire," written by B. J. I wrote him on MySpace about a specific line in the show which I thought was hilarious where Michael [unironically] quoted Andre Agassi and said, "Image is everything." He wrote me back and said, "Thank you so much. I didn't know if it would work. It happened as kind of an off-the-cuff add-in at the last minute. But I'm glad you appreciate it." I started writing to B. J., Jenna, Angela, and Kate Flannery on MySpace and they'd write me back. That's how I got the idea to start OfficeTally.

Kim Ferry (Hairstylist): In addition to MySpace, they tried to book themselves on talk shows. They would call their agents and say, "We really want to try to get on David Letterman. We want to talk to Jay Leno. We want to get the word out. How can we do that?" My experience with actors, normally, is they don't ask for that, but they were very proactive, for sure. I think it saved our show.

One month after The Office *began its second season, the iTunes store began selling TV shows. It marked a sea change in the way consumers viewed television shows.*

Jeff Zucker: It took us some time to make a deal with iTunes, and that's a story for another day.

Jeff Immelt: Steve Jobs called me because Jeff [Zucker], appropriately so, was being a hard-ass on using content on iTunes. The only things he wanted was *30 Rock* and *The Office*. Jobs was like, "This guy Zucker is being such an asshole. You got to help me out here, because we need *The Office* in order to have compelling content." They didn't want to see *Law & Order*, they wanted to see *The Office* and *30 Rock*.

Ben Silverman: It was one of the first deals between Apple and a TV show. We felt that it was brand-aligned for the show. We got a lot of free marketing from them. The next wave of it was they had us in the storefronts. It was us and Bono. *The Office* and U2 were the two elements of the iTunes store, music and content, that drove the iTunes sale. They were smart to bet on series and not movies because there was more permanence and repeatability.

Kevin Reilly: We did some novel deals with iTunes allowing them to feature episodes, and we gave them some previews. Those deals had never been done before. At the time, when you went to an Apple Store, they had the iTunes posters on the wall, and there was *The Office*, prominently featured in the iTunes ads. And all of a sudden, kind of the newness of iTunes and people sampling on iTunes, and the extra publicity, helped the ratings go up.

Mary Wall (Assistant to Greg Daniels): People would be able to watch it on iTunes, and then they caught up and started watching it on TV. It gave us a huge uptick in the ratings.

Teri Weinberg: As a result of being exposed to this new digital world, people knew we were out there. We had so many episodes in the top ten that all of a sudden our numbers went up on the network. That was really a turning point for us. It gave this really juicy hidden demographic of young people that didn't fit into the eighteen-to-thirty-five or -forty-nine. They were fifteen, and sixteen, and seventeen. And so, those were the kids that were picking it up on iTunes and we became known to younger people. And then suddenly, we became critical darlings too.

Larry Wilmore: There was a blog at the time called Television Without Pity. That was Twitter from back then. *The Office* got a whole section on it and people were pouring out love and opinions for *The Office* and the fan base really started growing during the season.

Ken Whittingham: College kids jumped on it and started downloading and it really became popular amongst that demo. That gave NBC the courage to bring it back for a whole season.

Kevin Reilly: I remember around Thanksgiving, I woke up one morning and I saw that the *Office* rating had grown for the first time. And I hate to admit it, but I think I kind of welled up with tears. But I thought of it as my Christmas present because from that point forward, *The Office* started to incrementally grow from there until Christmas. It allowed us to order a full twenty-two-episode season. And I realized then that the whole fight was worth it.

Teri Weinberg: We just had built such a strong family during this time that we just said, "We're going to get up every day, and we're going to have fun, and we're going to be funny, and we're going to make people laugh, and we're just going to keep doing our jobs. And if we do them well, hopefully we'll be able to maintain longevity." That might be my personal optimistic view, but I feel like every day we all stepped on the set, that we just said, "Let's have fun and let's be creative and have fun." And we just kept doing it.

chapter 8

DWIGHT

("He would have made a good Nazi.")

It took the writers well into the second season to flesh out the Dunder Mifflin universe and give each character their own distinct personality, but they had the peculiarities of Dwight figured out from the very beginning. He is loosely based on Gareth Keenan from the UK Office*, and both characters do have an obsession with authority, a bitter rivalry with a charismatic paper salesman who sits one desk away, and a surprising ability to attract beautiful women despite being a nerd without any self-awareness or discernible sense of humor. But the* Office *writers took Dwight in a totally different direction by making him a beet farmer with an almost Amish existence who still somehow finds time to obsess over* Battlestar Galactica, Harry Potter, *and heavy metal music. It's a wild mass of contradictions that made him the most eclectic character on the show, and it's hard to imagine anyone but Rainn Wilson playing the part.*

Rainn Wilson: Someone described Dwight as being a fascist nerd, and I think that really sums him up pretty well. He's into hierarchy, power, and structures.

Rob Sheffield: Dwight was always so much more dimensional than Gareth. I love Gareth, but Dwight was such a disturbing character since he yearned for authority of his own and felt so trapped. I remember about ten years ago [Rainn] came into the *Rolling Stone* offices for a staff lunch and he had this really funny, breathtakingly candid thing to say about how easy it was to create that part. He said, "People going out for roles in sitcoms are comedians, they're not actors, so they don't know how to create a character. This was no problem at all for me. I knew I was going to be able to do this."

Rainn Wilson: It was very important to me that I have the least-flattering haircut possible to my head—which I designed specifically. . . . And also the fact that he still wears a beeper, which is about eight years after beepers have been completely discontinued, because he probably has some number that someone might still have. But all of these things put together, and then it kind of comes into your body. And I think your job as the actor is to let these impulses flow through you and not stifle them. He has this love of hierarchies and this love of power. Well, he's going to assert his power with his pelvis and maybe stand inappropriately close to someone. And it's kind of like an alpha-male type of thing.

Creed Bratton: Rainn Wilson is an absolute genius, one of the naturally funny people on the planet. His instincts are impeccable and he never censored himself.

Caroline Williams (Writer, Season 3): I feel like it's got to be based on someone Greg knew because Dwight came in very fully formed, though obviously Rainn brought a lot to the character. There was so much that was northeastern Pennsylvania in him with the obsession with muscle cars combined with farming and the obvious sort of Amish suggestion.

Danny Chun (Writer, Seasons 6–8): Dwight in a lot of ways is like an archetype of sort of [the] surly nerd or the annoying coworker. But then early in season-two stuff they added all these odd extra dimensions, which just gave him so much specificity, and that gave us so much to work with.

Rainn Wilson: He's a beet farmer and that makes total sense, 'cause you ever meet a farmer, they can't quite ever fit in, in society. They may try as hard as they want. They can play it cool, they can do whatever they want; they can't really fit into city life no matter how much they try. They're just more in tune with the dirt and the tides and the seasons and the wolves than, you know, human interaction.

Justin Spitzer (Writer, Seasons 3–9): It's interesting because he had these two very distinct parts of his character that kind of don't make sense together. I always preferred the part of him that was into hot-rod cars and playing heavy metal and rocking out as opposed to the fascist stuff. Then there's a part of him that's this weird quasi-Amish beet farmer. Again, they don't make sense together but sometimes that's what gives people dimension, these contrasting characteristics.

Nathan Rabin: Most times if you're playing a nerd you play it as somebody who's embarrassed by themselves. Somebody who knows that they're geeky, who knows that they're not attractive, who knows that it's awkward for people to spend time with him. With Rainn Wilson, I think what he did that was absolutely brilliant is he played it as a position of delusional strength. Also, he kind of had what Michael Scott had, which is this combination of being very arrogant but also being very unself-aware and being very unself-critical. He fucking went for it and he had a sex life and he had a girlfriend.

Jeff Blitz: Rainn somehow understood from the beginning that this is a character that doesn't exactly exist in the real world that some of the other people on the show exist [in], but he just had an amazing intuitive sense for how far he could take it. He also found a way to play it so that the emotional heart of it was true and the factual stuff didn't need to be true.

Larry Wilmore: Dwight loves rules. He can't get enough of rules. He's very dramatic in that way, even at his own expense. That's my favorite thing about him. He's arrogant in a way that just never works, which is really funny too. I have no idea how the character was even created. It just kind of happened organically. I feel like that is all Greg Daniels though. It all just happened to come out of his brain and we just happened to get on that train.

Owen Ellickson (Writer, Seasons 8 and 9): Mackenzie Crook did not do it the way Rainn did it, but I think the brilliance of Rainn was that Dwight and Gareth are fundamentally weak characters, but Rainn always played Dwight to absolute maximum strength, which then made his being stymied by the realities of the stories he was in even funnier. He really thought he was omnipotent. It felt like you were watching Stalin or something, then he would get upended every twenty seconds. There was just something brilliant about that.

Rainn Wilson: I think the greatest comedy comes from people taking themselves seriously. The circumstances can be absolutely absurd, but if the person is taking the stakes really seriously and taking themselves really seriously, it really is a great comedy mine to dig from.

Jason Kessler: There's a major difference between acting like you're weird and being weird. I think Rainn's weird in a great way and he was able to bring a specificity to that role that you can't fake. He's a very thoughtful actor and really cared about the dynamics of Dwight in a way that some actors maybe wouldn't have. One of Dwight's major characteristics is loyalty. That could be very cartoonish, and that could be very real, and I think the sense of reality that Rainn brought to the role is making that loyalty feel like he wanted it in the same way that Michael wants to be friends with everyone. I think Dwight just wants a friend, and he wants that friend to have power over him and to tell him what to do and be proud of him when he does those things. He found that in Michael.

Randall Einhorn: Michael needed Dwight because Dwight was the only person who took him seriously. They needed each other and were codependent in a really wonderful way.

Owen Ellickson: There was real magic in the Michael/Dwight pairing. Michael was so unsure about everything he believed that that just really put Dwight in such stark relief as a guy who was in complete control of his own bad life.

B. J. Novak: There are so many beliefs in Dwight's head it's a wonder he can ever think about anything else. There's religion, there's tradition, there's every science fiction thing he's ever seen, probably everything he's read, every old wives' tale—every belief is somewhere on a ridge in Dwight Schrute's brain.

Owen Ellickson: Rainn made him so remarkably self-assured that you believed every new corner of Dwight's personality just because Dwight so palpably believed them.

Halsted Sullivan (Writer, Seasons 5–9): Greg always described Dwight as the law-and-order character and that's pretty much how I saw him. He was someone who knew if he followed the rules, things would work out. But then that's why Jim had such a fun time pranking him, because Dwight was a predictable character. He knew that Dwight would act and react in a certain way 'cause he was a rule follower. And he definitely was the self-imposed office cop and the self-imposed disciplinarian, often to his own detriment, because he became so predictable.

Danny Chun: A lot of the character is in Rainn. I love Rainn. He's a wonderful human and very sort of soulful, but he's also kind of intimidating. He kind of cultivates a little bit of a grumpy persona, but deep down he's just a wonderful, sweet guy. And he's also just incredible, he can memorize a huge talking head in like a minute and spit it back to you. He was so adept and it was a real treat to write for him because he was funny, he brought stuff to it but he was also very appreciative and gracious toward the writers. I always felt like it was a joy to work with him.

Mark Proksch (Nate Nickerson, Seasons 7–9): Rainn's an interesting guy and he's eccentric in the best ways possible. He came into the show with a definite point of view of what this character should be. And you'll either get cast as that or they'll pass on you as that, but it's not like he was going to change that character dramatically to fit what they wanted. That's a big thing if you're casting a show. If a person comes in that can do something really well and it's not quite what you had in mind, you should take them, because they're going to make the character their own, and it'll become a stronger character instead of just a watered-down goofy guy. I think Rainn did that and that's why that character was always so strong and never faltering at all . . . because Rainn honed in on what he wanted for that character to be and then never really relented. People may think it's a cartoony character, but it worked in that show so well.

Caroline Williams: Dwight embodies a kind of masculine insecurity that compensates with a sort of ridiculousness and doesn't realize how that's not actually swagger, it's just tragic. He always struck me as sort of the most insecure because of his need to overcompensate. And I think someone who is insecure innately seeks a leader to bring them purpose. There [were] always jokes about how Dwight would've been like the perfect henchman for a truly evil despot because it's not about ideology. It's his own psychology. That came up a lot. I remember a lot of the writing staff was Jewish, and they found a lot of humor in these sort of ideas. And I was always like, "Oh, God. That is horrible. How dare we talk about this?" Terrible things, but it was very funny.

Gene Stupnitsky: I remember early on trying to write a Dwight talking head where he was talking about his grandfather fighting in World War II and you realize at the end he was a Nazi. I remember Michael [Schur] fighting me on that. He was like, "He can't be that! He can't be that!" I was like, "No, we can make this work! He has a Nazi heritage." We were very unsure of it, but we did it and it just became part of his canon. That's who he was and it was accepted. His grandfather was a Nazi.

Lee Eisenberg: You can't go back on that.

Rainn Wilson: He would have made a good Nazi.

Rob Sheffield: My favorite Dwight episode ever is the one where he gives a speech ["Dwight's Speech"] and Jim doesn't tell him it's a speech he took from Mussolini, and Dwight delivering that speech is so intense. And honestly, it tells you more than you want to know about Mussolini as well and where Mussolini's psychology must have come from. But Dwight loves that incredibly stupid and disturbing fascist speech and he is so happy in that moment; it might be the happiest he ever is in all the years that we spend with him. It's always a disturbing episode for me.

Gene Stupnitsky: There are many sides to Dwight. He would have been a great Nazi, but there's also Dwight the ladies' man, which is so unexpected.

Lee Eisenberg: What's unexpected about Dwight sometimes comes from Rainn. Rainn is musical. He plays guitar, so Dwight plays guitar even though you don't especially think Dwight would like music.

Gene Stupnitsky: The character is round. It would be easy to have every Dwight line be like, "I am a disciplinarian. I am humorless." But Dwight has a sense of humor. It's just different from our sense of humor. Dwight probably watches YouTube clips of people getting punched in the nuts and he thinks it's great. Everyone has an interior life on the show and I think that's what's great. No one is just their one joke.

chapter 9

SEASON TWO

("It's a love story disguised as a workplace comedy.")

Dwight needed just a few adjustments when the second season began, but Michael Scott was a very different story. The writers knew he came off as intensely unlikable in the first season, and their primary goal when they started off the second one was to find a way to fix that.

Jason Kessler: On day one Greg Daniels came in and said, "Michael's got to have heart." That changed the entire show.

Lee Eisenberg: Greg created a manifesto, like the Unabomber, about how to make Michael less of a dick. The change was he went from being an asshole to being pathetic.

Jeff Zucker: When you're watching a show on television, you wanna have somebody who you are rooting for. And even if they are not the perfect character, you wanna be able to spend time with them, and so there was a conscious decision to soften the character of Michael Scott a little bit.

Larry Wilmore: Steve has a very sweet quality and that hard edge, I think, just didn't play right. He can do it because he's talented, but I think it was working against him ultimately. If you look at Gervais in the original, any time he got a comeuppance it was due, because he was a horrible human being. He was so bad. He just made you laugh because he needed attention so desperately and he'd go to any depths to get it, whereas Carell's character, it wasn't that he needed attention, he needed love. And that was a big distinction. When the character needs love you can play that a little differently than when the character just needs attention.

Alan Sepinwall: David Brent was driven by a desire to be famous. Michael Scott was driven by a desire to be loved. And that is a very big difference. You couldn't have done a hundred episodes with David Brent. That would be unbearable. By the end of twelve episodes, it was kind of unbearable. They had to soften Michael Scott to make him work.

Kevin Reilly: What we were really looking for was the method to his madness. We wanted this to sustain for years at twenty-two episodes a year. To do that, we had to find more dimension to his character.

Jen Celotta: I love to understand the why of human behavior. You can see somebody that's acting in a way that seems frustrating or unlikable, but once you understand the why, then your perspective can be flipped. With Michael, it was understanding that he wanted to be friends with everybody that he worked with and the understanding that, to him, this was his family and he had their best interest at heart. You had to understand that he was insecure.

Kate Flannery: They learned how to write for him from watching *The 40-Year-Old Virgin.*

Paul Feig: I remember everybody in charge of *The Office* going, "How do we do this? How do we take what everybody loves about Steve in that movie and make it work for us on the show?"

Jen Celotta: I had seen *40-Year-Old Virgin* when I'd gotten the job. I saw his ability to play such a layered role. I was like, "Oh God, he's can play such depth. He can play such pathos. He is capable of doing anything we throw at him."

Larry Wilmore: He shot *40-Year-Old Virgin* after he shot the first season. He lost a lot of weight for that movie, so physically he looked a little different.

Mindy Kaling (Kelly Kapoor/Writer, Seasons 1–9): Steve came in at the beginning of the season having lost weight and was the handsomest we'd ever seen him.

Larry Wilmore: He had his hair slicked back like a used-car salesman that first season.

Kim Ferry: He had a Gordon Gekko look. [His hair] flipped down and it was really tight. He was trying to be slick and cool, but to me that made him not seem as likable in a way. It was just too extreme. When I met Steve the first thing I said to him was, "I just don't like your hair the way it was. It's not flattering. I don't really want to offend anyone, but I think we should definitely do something to change it." And he said, "Absolutely, I want the same thing." So we talked about it and we tried out a couple styles. I just tried to soften up a little bit and just make it a little more flattering. He just needed some height and some volume and we got it.

Larry Wilmore: Even a hair choice was a way to soften him up.

Alan Sepinwall: He's easier to look at, which is a really superficial thing, but it made a difference.

Michael's newfound vulnerability was first seen very briefly in "The Dundies," but it became more pronounced two episodes later in "Office Olympics."

Paul Feig: I remember going to the very first table read of the second season because they read four scripts in a row, and I was going to be directing one of them. "Office Olympics" was going to be my first one. They'd been reading the "Dundies" script, but they still hadn't quite softened up Michael yet. They made him less aggressively mean, just less of a total asshole, but the dynamic was still kind of floating. When I did the "Office Olympics" we stumbled into this thing that really worked. The whole episode was kind of a vulnerable episode for Michael because he's freaking out that he's going to buy this condo. He has a panic attack, and he accidentally pulls the burner off of the stove. He goes out on the patio, he can't breathe. That was humanizing for him.

The script didn't call for anything else to show Michael's human side, but Steve Carell found a little moment in the end to really emphasize the big change to his character.

Paul Feig: We shot the scene at the very end where they give him the yogurt lid at the awards presentation as a medal. They're basically making fun of him. It was supposed to be just kind of like he's taking it seriously, and he thinks it's great, and everybody else is laughing behind his back. But Steve made this decision that as they're playing the national anthem [he would] tear up. His eyes got red and started watering. Suddenly it was like, "Oh my God, this poor guy." He was so vulnerable and you see how desperate for anything good to happen to him and any kind of approval or validation. I remember I was like, "Oh my God. This is great! Let's do it again, really go with it!" Then Greg was really excited and was like, "That's it, that's it!" That was the turning point. I was like, "Oh, we can actually make Michael a nut, and overbearing, and ridiculous, and all these things, but we can find moments where he's vulnerable and human." As Greg and all the writers started to analyze, it was like, "Okay, let's give him a victory every once in a while." I remember Greg saying, "We can have it where he actually is smart a couple of times."

Ben Patrick (Sound Mixer): The show hit a different speed after that moment in "Office Olympics." It was the precise moment where I knew we had something special. When he got emotional, it wasn't just a comedy.

Your investment in not just his character, but everybody who reacted to him, just changed.

Jason Kessler: Michael was the enemy season one. The entire office was banding against him as this terrible boss. As soon as we came in season two to start breaking the season, that note from Greg saying "Michael's gotta have heart" changed it so much. It became "Michael wants us to be a family." And that's the core of the show. I mean, *The Office* is a workplace comedy that is secretly a family show.

Larry Wilmore: *The Office,* at its essence, isn't a workplace show. That's just what it looks like. *The Office* is a romantic comedy. That's how it was set up. It's really a love story. It's a story of unrequited love. That's true from Michael's point of view too since he requires love. So it really is a love story at its core. It's just that a lot of people don't know how to give it or how to take it. So it's not really a workplace comedy. It's a love story disguised as a workplace comedy. That's what is at its root. That's what we really, really went after in that second season. That story line of Jim and Pam is about that, and I don't think it was ever done better than it was that season. Even some of just the cutaways of Jim where you saw the unrequited, forbidden love just breaks your heart.

Paul Feig: They were always going to be kind of the Sam and Diane [from *Cheers*] of *The Office,* obviously, because that's what it was on the British *Office.* That camaraderie was there, and it was really strong between John and Jenna.

Jen Celotta: I wrote the episode with the jinx ["Drug Testing"] when they're out of Cokes and then they couldn't talk to each other for the day. It was a delight to work with them and see how much they could convey with just these little looks to each other.

Creed Bratton: I could get emotional just watching John and Jenna just filming a scene because of that unrequited-love feeling they were conveying. It felt romantic. I could be across the room, glance up, and see the look. It was all in the eyes. They had a real special rapport.

Gene Stupnitsky: The amount of time that we spent on Jim and Pam versus how much screen time these little moments actually had was insane. We would spend hours and hours debating these tiny things. The fans on the *Office* fan site OfficeTally [used] this phrase *squee*. Whenever Jim and Pam had a moment, like when they were playing jinx all day and one of them finally spoke or Pam putting her head on Jim's shoulder in "Diversity Day," those are all squee moments.

Lee Eisenberg: We would actually unironically talk about squee moments in the episodes. We'd be like, "We haven't had a squee moment in a long time. We need something. We need a squee."

John Krasinski: I remember that one episode where we were on the booze cruise. When I saw the episode they had allowed that incredibly long pause when Jim wanted to say that he loved Pam and he couldn't. I thought from then on I had full and total trust in anything [the writers] wanted to do.

Jason Kessler: If you look at season one, it really feels like Roy is going to be a main character. I think the writers realized that the Jim and Pam connection was so strong, even stronger, I think, than in the Dawn/Tim relationship in the British *Office*. I think that that kind of forced the Roy relationship to take a backseat. But I definitely remember each moment being obsessed over, and talking a lot about the Jim-and-Pam of it all.

Gene Stupnitsky: At the beginning, it was like a Victorian-era love story where Jim sees Pam's ankle, and that's enough to sustain him for, you know, like half a season.

Jen Celotta: I remember overall an enormous amount of discussion about how quickly to progress them. We wanted to have obstacles in their way that felt real. There was something very beautiful about them pining for each other. Even when you didn't focus on it in a given episode, it was always there in the background.

Kate Flannery: John always had this sort of star quality to him. Jenna is a slightly unexpected heroine. She's not the Jennifer Aniston. Her beauty is more subtle. There was such a sense of balance there.

Randall Einhorn: They had a very, very natural rapport and they just felt at ease together. They just felt safe with each other, which is paramount when you're putting yourself out there like they were. There's nothing worse than two actors that don't get along trying to have a romantic scene. I've been in those situations and it's just painful. It doesn't look real. It doesn't feel real. It was great that they felt so natural together because it came across really natural. You rooted for them. You wanted them to be together because of that. It felt like it should be great together.

During "Booze Cruise," Jim foolishly tells Michael that he had a crush on Pam. Michael, of course, immediately tells the entire office. To limit the fallout, Jim tells Pam that he had a crush on her "years ago" in "The Secret" two episodes later.

Lee Eisenberg: The scene between Jim and Pam in the kitchen is one of my favorite scenes that we've ever written, where he's like, "I used to have a crush on you but now I don't." Then Michael reveals the secret to everyone in the office. He's so excited that Jim confided in him and he's like, "I will hold on to that secret for as long as I can." It felt so real and in character.

The other romance that began in season two was between Michael and Jan, even though they were destined for a far worse fate.

Melora Hardin: I remember a conversation around the time of the pilot where Greg Daniels and me and Steve Carell were having lunch together.

I think Steve and I both said something like, "God, Jan and Michael are just so funny together." I don't remember which one of us made the point, but one of us said that there was a spark between them because they were both angry at each other and angry at the world. There was something really a little bit hot about them. We were talking about how, "God, if this show gets picked up, wouldn't it just be crazy if Jan and Michael hooked up sometime?" I remember Greg Daniels saying that for him it was tricky. He used to say to me, "You're this beautiful, strong woman who's his boss. Why would you ever be attracted to him? We got to find a way to make that work. We need to find a way to make the audience buy that choice."

They pulled it off by having a recently divorced Jan witness Michael land a huge sale with a representative for the county (played by Tim Meadows) during the course of a long, boozy dinner meeting at Chili's. They make out in the parking lot at the end and speed off together into the night. It was the first time that Jan seemed a little unhinged.

Melora Hardin: Tim Meadows and Steve just kept cracking me up. I could not hold it together that day. They were just so frickin' funny. We all knew that we were heading toward hooking them up. There was something so wrong and right about it that it was very appealing to me as an actor. I just love when things are a little bit off.

Many of the smaller characters were slowly fleshed out as fully formed characters in the second season, including Darryl Philbin.

Ben Silverman: Darryl is the smartest guy in the building, but he's running the warehouse and Michael Scott's running the office.

Michael would often come down to the warehouse to learn about black culture from Darryl.

Craig Robinson: Michael idolized Darryl in so many ways. Darryl treats Mike with kid gloves. He knows he doesn't mean harm, but it's like, "Yo, you go too far each and every time." He tries to keep the kid gloves on him, but at the same time, he has to exercise patience.

Midway through the season, Dunder Mifflin CEO David Wallace makes his first appearance. He was portrayed by Andy Buckley, who had largely given up on acting by the time he got the role and was working as a financial adviser for Merrill Lynch.

Andy Buckley (David Wallace, Seasons 2–6, 8, and 9): I knew Allison [Jones] for years and one day I ran into her in our neighborhood farmers' market. She said to me, "What are you doing these days, Buckley?" I said, "Well, I'm a stockbroker. I'm an adviser at Merrill Lynch and I'm married. We have a son." She said, "If something comes up would you ever want to do something?" And I said, "Yeah, sure. If it was just a smaller thing or I didn't have to leave town. I can't leave town." And I gave her my card.

Months later, he found himself auditioning for the role of David Wallace against Charles Esten.

Andy Buckley: I was like, "Oh man, they're gonna hire this guy." Luckily they hired him for the other part [of Stamford branch CEO Josh Porter]. Allison called the next day and said, "All right, they hired you, Buckley. They're gonna give you glasses and they're gonna gray your hair a little bit just so you seem a little older and perhaps more mature."

And that was it. Buckley became yet another perfect comic foil for Steve Carell. Just weeks before Buckley's debut episode aired, Carell beat out Larry David, Charlie Sheen, Jason Lee, and Zach Braff for the Best Performance by an Actor in a Television Series award at the Golden Globes. Nobody saw it coming. "I really did not expect this," he said after Pamela Anderson handed him the statue. "Thanks to Ricky Gervais and Stephen Merchant for creating such a groundbreaking piece of television and to Greg Daniels for his talent, courage, and sheer audacity. . . . Thanks to my parents for not making me go to law school and finally, to the light of my life, my wife, Nancy."

Melora Hardin: They didn't have a big enough table for all of us to go, so most of us were upstairs. We were in the same building, but upstairs on the terrace or something. It was all decorated and fancy, and they had big TVs and I just remember just screaming and being so excited when we won.

Kate Flannery: When Steve won that Golden Globe, we all went crazy. We were working that day and nobody there knew who we were and nobody thought he was going to win. It was just amazing. We couldn't even be in the room that night. We were only in the viewing party, but everyone went crazy.

Oscar Nunez: We were on the roof because only Steve and Greg Daniels and Nancy were downstairs. When he won we lost our shit, jumping everywhere until we formed a dog pile. People were like, "Oh yeah, that's the *Office* people!" It was really cool.

Melora Hardin: It wasn't very long before Steven came up and we got to all celebrate him and give him big hugs. It was very, very exciting. I still was in a haze. I was just so excited for him.

It was the clearest sign they'd had yet that the show was going to go the distance.

Jason Kessler: Everything really clicked in season two.

Matt Sohn: The show was truly becoming its own and breaking away from the English version.

Creed Bratton: In the second season, I remember driving out to Saticoy Street on Woodman and right before we make a left to go to the stages there was Steve's picture up on a billboard for *40-Year-Old Virgin*. It was like, "Wow! This is really weird." Everything just coordinated and synchronized for him amazingly, like a comet.

KEY EPISODE 2

"The Dundies"

"The Dundies" wasn't the first episode filmed for season two, but it came out so strong they used it as the premiere, meaning it was the first time anyone saw the show after its light reboot.

B. J. Novak: Very important episode, I think, maybe the most important in the show in terms of turning season one into season two, which I think is a very, very big difference. The colors are brighter. Steve is calmer and more likable. The show is less dark and more optimistic and more celebratory.

Jenna Fischer: We also introduce all of the characters in this office. Everyone gets a little moment.

Much of the action takes place at a Chili's where Michael is handing out awards to the staff.

B. J. Novak: We didn't want to invent a fake, similar-sounding restaurant, like "Pepper's" or "T.G.I. Wednesday's." Since this is supposed to be a realistic show, about realistic offices, we thought setting [it in] a place like Chili's would be refreshing.

Jason Kessler: That was the first episode where we went out of the office set and went on location. It's really interesting to see the characters outside of the office environment, and how they interact with each other.

Randall Einhorn: That place was pretty ghetto. It was the Black Angus Steakhouse, before we went into it. The carpet, it just smelled like cooked cow. It was pretty rough.

Kate Flannery: It was a failed Black Angus so it was kind of shitty.

B. J. Novak: We got permission from Chili's and spent weeks, with their help, reconstructing, with painstaking detail, a Chili's restaurant in the empty abandoned building.

Jason Kessler: It was dressed to look like a Chili's, and we had Chili's executives on set making sure that everything fit into the brand.

Michael Gallenberg (Production Designer): Chili's even gave us tables, chairs, and props from a store they were updating in the Bay Area.

Kate Flannery: I remember that Chili's suddenly got very involved with the episode and it almost drove Greg nuts.

Greg Daniels: We had only a verbal agreement with Chili's. At one point during the shooting of this they wanted to back out.

B. J. Novak: On the first day of shooting, it turned out that Chili's hadn't read the script, which involved, at a crucial moment, a drunk woman vomiting and a character responding by running through the Chili's yelling, "A woman has vomited!" Well, for some reason, a vomit-filled pit of inebriation was not how the Chili's people wanted their restaurant to be portrayed on television.

Greg Daniels: But we'd already shot two days and we all froze. We had to shut everything down.

Michael Gallenberg: As we waited for the lawyers to work out the deal with Chili's, the cast and writers were crashed out all over the place. I have a picture of Mindy sleeping under a table.

Greg Daniels: And Steve, who I have to credit because as a longtime improv teacher, his brain didn't freeze and he came up with a fix . . . having the manager come out and address the problem head-on [by saying that Pam had taken drinks from other customers]. That solved the problem with Chili's and we were able to move on.

Jenna Fischer: [In one scene] Jim and I are doing an interview for the camera and in the middle I was supposed to turn and puke all over the bar. I guess the corporate lawyers at Chili's didn't like this idea so they changed it to having me fall off a stool instead.

Randall Einhorn: Playing drunk is really hard. She was written as being hammered, but a happy hammered and a little bit behind-it drunk. You could see when people are drunk and you say something to them and they think about it for a little bit and then you see the penny drop. They're just so slow. You see the wheels turning. She did all that so beautifully, but infused with the spirit of the character.

Jenna Fischer: When I got the script for this episode, I was very nervous. I couldn't remember what it was like to be drunk and I didn't want to do a caricature of a drunk person. B. J. Novak suggested I go out and get drunk one night for research. I laughed him off at first, but then decided it was a pretty good idea. I took B. J. with me and made sure I didn't have to drive. It only took four drinks. After each drink, B. J. would check in with me, asking, "How do you feel now? What's different?" He made me describe, in detail, the various levels of drunkenness. . . . I totally drew on my experience of that night when we shot this episode. I realized that when you are drunk, you laugh at stupid things, talk closer to people, get touchy, and basically act like a more obnoxious and unbalanced version of yourself. You lose control a little. So, that's what I did with Pam.

Jennie Tan: It's an episode where everyone gets a chance to shine. Phyllis gets the "busiest beaver" award and Kelly gets "spiciest curry."

The most crucial scene comes when a group of unruly bar patrons pummels Michael with food and he gets incredibly dejected until the office cheers him on and restores his spirits. It was the first moment in the show where Michael truly seemed vulnerable.

Jenna Fischer: You can make fun of your family, but somebody else can't. The office really rallies for him.

Jason Kessler: When you're in your house, the older brother picks on the little brother constantly. But when you go out in public and somebody picks on the little brother, the older brother's there to stand up.

It's also the first time that Pam and Jim kiss, even though it happens very briefly when Pam is incredibly drunk and not fully in control of her faculties.

John Krasinski: Everyone is always asking me about the kiss in the finale, but I thought this was the big kiss. We'd never made physical contact.

Greg Daniels: That was something my wife was really big on. [The writers] weren't really big on it. She kept saying, "You gotta put that in. It's good."

Mindy Kaling: I thought the kiss this early was a mistake.

The lore around this episode states that the Chili's employee who speaks to the camera and bans Pam from the chain for life is an actual Chili's manager. In reality, it was character actor Christopher T. Wood.

Christopher T. Wood (Chili's Manager, Season 2): I think at least some of the extras were Chili's employees, and the only reason I say that is because almost everyone assumed that I was actually a Chili's manager. On Twitter I've tried to debunk this any time it flashes up. People will put out, "Hey, fun fact, the guy in that episode was actually a Chili's manager." And I'm like, "No . . ." I've had people say, "No, you're a Chili's manager." I'm like, "I kind of promise you I'm not. I don't know how else to say this." But what can you do? I take it as a compliment toward my acting.

KEY EPISODE 3

"The Injury"

The premise of "The Injury" couldn't be simpler: Michael burns his foot one morning on a George Foreman grill and Dwight suffers a concussion when he races to his condo so quickly to help that he crashes his car into a pole. The rest of the episode is just everyone reacting to Michael's absurd claims that he's horribly injured and Dwight's obliviousness to his actual severe injury, which causes such a major personality shift that he actually starts acting friendly toward Pam. It was just the third episode written by Mindy Kaling.

Mindy Kaling: "The Injury" is probably the favorite episode that I've written. I think the original idea was that Michael had fallen asleep in the sun and had sunblock all over him except for his foot, and it started out as a sunburned foot. And actually the name of the episode was "My Grilled Foot" for the longest time until we thought that might be too weird for people to tune in and watch that. I was amazed that we based a whole episode that was basically about disability around Michael's crazy disability of having to eat bacon every morning when he wakes up.

Jen Celotta: Mindy Kaling is a genius and that episode was so well written. That speech about how he burned his foot was one of the funniest things I've ever read.

"I enjoy having breakfast in bed," Michael explains to the camera. "I like waking up to the smell of bacon, sue me. And since I don't have a butler, I have to do it myself. So, most nights before I go to bed, I will lay six strips of bacon out on my George Foreman grill. Then I go to sleep. When I wake up, I plug in the grill, I go back to sleep again. Then I wake up to the smell of crackling bacon. It is delicious, it's good for me. It's the perfect way to start the day. Today I got up, I stepped onto the grill and it clamped down on my foot . . . that's it. I don't see what's so hard to believe about that." A ridiculous monologue like this would be a hard sell for most actors, but Carell delivered it effortlessly.

Jenna Fischer: Steve Carell's bit at the top of the episode, where Michael explains how he burned his foot, is the greatest interview of the entire series. I think his performance is brilliant. Seriously, brilliant.

Jen Celotta: There's not a false note in that monologue because you believe that he's true in everything he does. He has his own set of rules and he plays by them. Even when he's doing ridiculous things, there's such integrity to him, and Steve protected his character and he knew his character.

Mindy Kaling: That's my favorite talking head he's ever done. "Sue me. I like to wake up every morning to the smell of bacon." Steve, I remember, when he read it, he's such a genius, because there's about seven crazy things, and he's just like, "And yes, every morning I have to have seven strips of bacon, and no, I don't like to go to my kitchen to do it. It has to be in my bedroom." And he just railed through it, and at the next meeting it was, "Give me something else." He's such a genius he could take something so crazy and make it something I love thinking about.

Randall Einhorn: That was outrageous and incredibly funny, just amazing. It is such a far-fetched idea that he cooks bacon in his bedroom while sleeping, but he appealed to everybody's love of the smell of bacon and made it very, very believable. It was a tremendous performance.

Dean Holland (Editor): As a viewer you were like, "Michael would one hundred percent do this." They did a great job at building stuff up like that and allowing themselves to take chances and go broad without it seeming broad. He treated that injury as if he was in a serious car accident and was like, "You all are not taking this as seriously as I am and this is a serious thing."

When Dwight crashes into a parking lot pole, he gets out of his car in a stupor and vomits all over the hood as everyone watches from an office window in horror.

Jen Celotta: The way you do vomit is you give an actor split pea soup and they spit it up. However, it was like six in the morning when we shot this. They put split pea soup in Rainn's mouth again and again and again for takes, and so I am certain that one of the takes he actually threw up a little bit. I think that was the one we used.

Bryan Gordon (Director): Mindy Kaling wrote the episode, so that's genius upon genius. And I think part of the appeal was that every actor likes to have an obstacle, and Michael and Dwight, their obstacles were they got injured. Michael's dealing with his foot and Dwight is dealing with getting injured and that gave them so much to work with.

Mindy Kaling: It is full-on loopy. It starts with Dwight throwing up, there's a *Flowers for Algernon* B story, Michael grills his foot. If it had just been weirdness for weirdness's sake, it wouldn't have really taken off. It was all about the framework—that's a Greg thing: It can't just be crazy—and the episode is really about injuries and people with disabilities. If you remember correctly, Michael decides that when people are mean to him, he's going to pull, "Oh, you're mean to people with disabilities." That's why it's so funny to me, because what happened to him is so stupid.

Bryan Gordon: What I love most about the episode is the reactions to Michael and Dwight that all the characters give, even when they aren't speaking. They go from, "I don't give a shit about this guy," to a little sympathy and then, "Is Dwight crazy? Is he out of his mind?" They get that all in there without speaking.

Mindy Kaling: It was a very broad episode. It's basically like *Flowers for Algernon*, but *Office*-style, with vomiting and monologues about grilling your foot. And the episode before, ["Booze Cruise,"] which Greg had written, was this very like romantic one, allowing there to be a minute where they don't say anything—the opposite in tone from mine. So it was nice that later in *Office* lore that became an episode that people remember fondly, because at the time, I remember no one was very happy with it.

KEY EPISODE 4

"Casino Night"

The second season ended with "Casino Night," which was both the most logistically complicated episode they'd shot up until that point and the most important in terms of advancing the Jim/Pam narrative. At twenty-eight minutes, it was also the first of many extended "supersized episodes" NBC let them air, a sign of faith in a show that was now pulling in about eight million viewers a night and retaining nearly all of the My Name Is Earl *audience. Greg Daniels and Steve Carell came up with the idea for an episode about a casino-themed party in the Dunder Mifflin warehouse on a flight from New York to Los Angeles after filming the Valentine's Day episode. When they got back, Daniels urged Carell to write it himself.*

Steve Carell: I said, "I don't know if I can give it my full attention, and I don't want to do a half-baked job of it." But he is a very persuasive gentleman, and I walked out of the meeting not only still writing the episode, but filled with all sorts of hope and excitement about the episode.

Greg Daniels: He came in with a great draft. And can I say, looking back on it, it was such a great move to have him write it, but also I feel like, as a staff, we were too close to it. It was good to have somebody write it who hadn't been sitting in the [writers'] room.

Steve Carell: I wasn't there for the rewrite sessions, I was off shooting. But the great part of it is that I didn't feel precious about the script. I felt like I had written what was a pretty decent half hour, but I knew it could be better, and I knew that all of the writers would make it better. They're all so smart and good and funny that I didn't feel weird about letting it go and letting it evolve.

Ken Kwapis: It was always a longer script, but I didn't really know what *supersized* meant. I don't think I'd ever heard that word applied to a TV episode.

Greg Daniels: It was our fans that got us the supersized thing. I mentioned in an article, and it ran in the *Chicago Tribune*, that we wanted to have a supersized episode.

Jennie Tan: So me and two other bloggers decided to put a petition together to supersize it. We got like a thousand signatures and a little publicity for it, and they supersized it. I wonder what impact we really had though.

Rainn Wilson: It was really clear in this episode that we could really use those extra six or seven minutes because moments can breathe and pauses can hang and it really helped the episode.

The longer running time gave them time to stretch out the plot, which featured Michael trying to balance two dates (Jan and Carol) at the party, Kevin demonstrating surprising skill as a poker player, and Jim finally telling Pam how he feels about her.

Ken Kwapis: It was a challenging episode because it had a lot of straightforward dramatic scenes in it. It was also so complicated to shoot. Besides "Booze Cruise," it was the first time I had to work with extras. We also had to turn the warehouse into a casino.

Michael Gallenberg: We pretty much dressed in different gambling stations in the warehouse with small drapery backings. We really didn't try to hide the warehouse, we really just embraced the space for what it was.

Jenna Fischer: Usually when we sit in the background of a scene we play on our computers and do a little work, but we actually played poker for two days.

Carey Bennett: Everybody needed to have these fancy outfits for that one, which was far outside of what I usually had to provide on that show. I had to think, "What do these people wear outside the office? How is it appropriately dowdy or sort of dated a little bit?"

Jenna Fischer: We spent so much time on [the clothing], like how much can each person be dressed up and why? Did they go home after work and get dressed? Did they bring it with them and change in the bathroom?

The entire episode builds to a climax where Jim tells Pam that he loves her in the parking lot after Roy drives away. She rejects him ("I can't. You have no idea what our friendship means to me . . .") and he walks away in tears. She then goes up to the darkened office to call her mother and he walks in and passionately kisses her right before the credits roll. Every single detail of the two scenes was obsessed over for weeks by the entire cast and crew, down to the blue dress that Pam wore.

Carey Bennett: Everything Pam wore always took such great consideration, and the night before we started shooting it I did not have a dress for her. We had all sorts of things we had tried, and nothing was really landing. I think it was literally seven P.M. the night before, which is unheard of. Normally something that was that important would have been decided on and altered and photographed, but we just didn't have it. I remember having a little breakdown about it. I sent two shoppers out right before stores closed and one of them came back with that blue dress. I think they got it at David's Bridal. We fit three or four things that next morning, but that one was just the one. She felt pretty in it, it fit great, we didn't even have to alter it.

Jenna Fischer: The idea was that it had to be something that Pam already had in her closet, so something she was either going to wear in a friend's wedding or wore in a friend's wedding.

Jason Kessler: On set, they had as few people as possible to make the Jim/Pam scenes feel as intimate as possible.

Jenna Fischer: We shot this episode over two different weeks, so we spent two weeks prepping for this scene alone. I met with Greg and Ken by myself and I met with John and we had a lot of discussions about how this scene would go down. I don't think we've ever prepared for a scene as much as we did this one because we wanted it to be perfect.

Ken Kwapis: The parking lot scene was tough to shoot from a stylistic point of view, because for the first time we decided as a director/producer/camera group that we couldn't be close to them. They wouldn't have had that exchange if they were aware that the cameras were on them. Our strategy was that the cameras sensed that something was going on. It's almost like being a wildlife photographer, you don't want to get too close. We had two cameras going and they were both quite a distance from John and Jenna. And at night on long lenses, there's always a danger you're gonna not keep something in focus, which, frankly, given the style of the show, was absolutely appropriate. But that was a case where we were spying on them. It required a real stealth approach.

Jenna Fischer: When we shot this, I was so excited that [John] was doing such a good job of acting that I just kept looking at him and thinking, "Oh my God, he's going to love this. He's going to flip out when he sees this, this is so good. . . ."

The kiss in the office was perhaps the most scrutinized scene in the history of the show.

Ken Kwapis: Greg and I discussed the idea that since the party's going on in the warehouse, that the bullpen lights would be mostly out. So there's just a few desk lamps. And the logic behind the scene is that we know, based on the parking lot scene, that Pam is distressed. And the camera operator, and the documentarian, me, we essentially follow her back up to the bullpen. So we bury ourselves in an adjoining room so we can see her as she makes a phone call to her mother. We don't know what she's about to do. But we just are interested in her because we know she's going through some emotional duress. What we're unprepared for is for Jim to enter. And so when Jim enters, the camera operator is sort of like, "Oh shit," and sort of stands up straight and quickly zooms to get a better image size. But the idea was in the little jittery movement, the camera operator signals to the viewer that we were not ready for this.

Randall Einhorn: That kiss is a perfect example of staying far enough away so that it could have felt like a real moment and giving the viewer a privileged moment that they would not normally see.

Jenna Fischer: We rehearsed the blocking but never rehearsed the kiss. Then, [Ken] sent us back to our trailers, with strict instructions that we were not to see each other until the scene began. We were separated for at least an hour while they set the camera up in a hidden location on set.

Ken Kwapis: We wanted to present it from a slightly oblique angle, so it doesn't feel like it's presented for the viewer. We wanted to catch it.

Randall Einhorn: Ken and I were the only ones in the room with them, but Ken was in the human resources area where Toby sits.

Ken Kwapis: John and Jenna had their own ideas about how to approach this scene. They were nervous about it. My job was actually to make it seem like we were just doing another scene. I didn't want to make them nervous. I didn't want to make a big deal out of it. I was like, "We're doing a scene. And then we're gonna do another scene. And then we're gonna do one after that." One of the things that they really wanted was to clear the whole set so they'd feel comfortable. They wanted the space to be their own.

Greg Daniels: Ken shot this like it was a nude scene in a movie. There was no one around. Paul [Lieberstein] and I were hiding in the kitchen. We didn't want to make our presence known.

Jenna Fischer: We literally cleared the set and I sat in my trailer and John was placed off camera down in that hallway. I was brought to set all by myself. The room was light like that and I sat in the place and the first time I saw John was when he walked in the room and kissed me.

Ken Kwapis: We knew that we wanted the camera at one angle. We didn't want to have coverage of this moment. When they kiss, the camera angle is slightly behind Jenna. You see John's face but not hers. You don't see her reaction. That seemed like that was really important. And I feel like in a way not seeing her face makes it more powerful. It allows the audience to kind of fill in the gap and it felt like a real event we were just lucky to capture.

Larry Wilmore: It felt very satisfying. It also felt like we didn't know what was going to happen next and we were fine with that since it might have been our finale. I remember having a feeling of "What's the next move in this? What do we do now?" Luckily, we didn't have to worry about it until we came back the following year. It did seem like the right tone to end the season.

chapter 10

THE RISE OF CREED

("I didn't know him from a hole in the wall.")

The second season is best remembered for the buildup to Jim and Pam's kiss and Michael Scott's personality shift, but another story was happening at the exact same time: Creed Bratton's gradual transformation from glorified extra to quirky fan favorite with impeccable comic timing. It came as a shock to nearly everyone since most people on the set didn't realize that quiet, gray-haired background actor could act. They certainly didn't know anything about his history as a founding member of the sixties folk-rock group the Grass Roots, best remembered for their top ten hits "Let's Live for Today" and "Midnight Confessions." Back in those days he toured with the likes of the Beach Boys and Buffalo Springfield, but he quit the band in 1969 and spent the next three decades doing whatever sort of work he could find in Hollywood, including the occasional bit role in a B movie and odd catering jobs. By the early 2000s, he was working as a stand-in on sitcoms and barely eking out a living.

Ken Kwapis: I directed the pilot of *The Bernie Mac Show* [in 2001]. And I remember one day while we were lighting a scene there were a few stand-ins. They're there to help out with the lighting. And two of them were talking to each other. One of them, who turned out to be Creed, was telling a story to the other stand-in about meeting Jimi Hendrix backstage at some concert in the 1960s and learning a guitar lick from him.

Creed Bratton: The Grass Roots did a show with Hendrix at Devonshire Downs in 1969.

Ken Kwapis: I was just walking by and overheard this conversation. I went, "What the hell?" I introduced myself to Creed and asked him to explain his story. He told me about being in the Grass Roots.

Creed Bratton: Ken had his assistant go out and get some Grass Roots records from Amoeba [Music] to sign because he's a big rock-'n'-roller.

Ken Kwapis: We became friends.

Creed Bratton: My fishing buddy Joe Moore was the first assistant director on *The Bernie Mac Show.* He mentioned to me one day that Ken Kwapis was working on the pilot of the American edition of *The Office.* By happenstance, Ken had given me his telephone number. If he hadn't done that, I never would have been able to get to him. I called him up and lobbied to get on that set.

Ken Kwapis: He was looking for more stand-in work. I said to him that the style of the show is supposed to resemble a documentary and that we're gonna have minimal lighting and no stand-ins. But I said, "But there's a couple of empty desks in the back of the set, in the back of the bullpen. If you don't mind, just come in and occupy one for the week or so that the pilot will be shot."

Greg Daniels: We needed people to sit in the desks in the background because the office had to have a certain number of people there, but we didn't have the budget necessarily for hiring actors to fill all these chairs.

Allison Jones: I didn't know him from a hole in the wall.

Creed was one of a handful of nonspeaking extras in the Office *pilot. When they shot the second episode months later, Kwapis was again the director and he made sure Creed still had a desk. The only other nonspeaking background actor was Devon Abner, whose main experience had been in the theater.*

Devon Abner (Devon White, Seasons 1, 2, and 9): Creed went out of his way to make me feel comfortable and to learn the ins and outs of what to do and what not to do. I remember when I first got there Ken said, "Tomorrow everybody come up with a little bit, and I'm going to go around the room and just film everybody doing a little thing that you like to do." I couldn't come up with anything interesting, but Creed came up with something funny involving a fishing pole. I thought to myself, "Wow, that's an extra step beyond what I could think of."

Creed Bratton: When we shot that second episode, "Diversity Day," I was in the bullpen with everyone else wearing a card on my forehead. I got to ad-lib and stuff with everybody, but not on camera because they couldn't give me lines yet. I wasn't part of the cast and they would have [had] to pay me for that more than just my day rate. The first AD didn't realize that and she had me interact with Phyllis where a camera could pick my up my voice. I was making up something crazy about sacrificing goats and she was laughing. Later someone said, "Wait a second. Creed was talking. We got his voice in the background of the scene." They ended up paying me just like a minimal fee for an actor. I just said, "Okay. This is a step. This is a step in the right direction."

Creed and Devon both stuck around for the rest of the first season and they were asked back when the show was picked up for a second one. When they returned, Creed was determined to show the producers that he was capable of more than just background work. With help from Joe Moore, he shot a video of himself in front of the venetian blinds at his apartment showing off an oddball character he'd created that was basically himself minus about fifty IQ points.

Creed Bratton: I brought it in and I handed it in to either Greg Daniels or Kent Zbornak, I can't remember.

Devon Abner: I thought, "Oh, man, he's going to get in trouble." That's because when you're in the background, you're never supposed to do stuff like that. But they loved it.

Right around that time, Larry Wilmore came up with a clever idea for a Halloween episode.

Larry Wilmore: I remember saying in the writers' room, "It would be funny if Michael had to fire somebody on Halloween while they were all in costume." I just thought that was a funny idea.

Greg Daniels: Michael had to fire somebody by the end of October and he had put it off and put it off and he had to do it at the Halloween party. He was very concerned with firing this person and still being friends with them. For the episode, we needed to have him pick somebody who hadn't really had a large profile but was in the room.

Jason Kessler: We knew we had to fire somebody and we had Creed and Devon and a choice just had to be made. I don't think we had any information about either guy, really. I think we knew that Creed had played in a band in the sixties, and Devon had been a theater actor, but I think that's about the extent of it.

Kelly Cantley (First Assistant Director): When they wrote that episode, honest to God, they had no idea if either one of those guys, Devon or Creed, could even talk.

Matt Sohn: Greg had talked to them and said, "Hey, look, one of you guys is going to get fired. The guy who's going to get fired will get a line and the other guy will still be around. So go talk amongst yourselves." I think maybe Greg didn't want to necessarily pick one and get rid of the other, so he let them discuss it. And ultimately Devon was like, "Well, I have a play that I'm doing in New York, so maybe it's better that I just get the line and leave."

Devon's memory of this is a little different.

Devon Abner: They pulled me aside and said, "We have some bad news. You're going to get fired in this one, but you can stay on as a stand-in." Creed and I were both utility stand-ins at this point. But it actually worked out perfectly because I was just about to give them my notice. I had gotten a part in a play in New York and was going to leave anyway.

Creed Bratton: A couple weeks after I gave them my tape, they dropped this script on my desk. It was Halloween. And it had a six-and-a-half-page scene with Steve Carell. It was like, "This is it, buddy. Show us what you got."

Paul Feig: I directed this one. I remember Greg coming up to me with the script and I read it and was like, "This is a huge role for Creed." So I said to Greg, "Can he act?" And Greg just kind of pushed his hands toward me like, "That's your job." I remember thinking, "Oh my God, this is a giant part for a stand-in."

Lee Eisenberg: I remember the table read for "Halloween." I don't even think I'd even spoken to Creed at that point, but he was so funny when he read it. I was like, "Oh my God, Creed is a genius."

In Creed's big scene, he is summoned into Michael's office dressed as Dracula. Michael is determined to fire him, but Creed manages to talk him into firing Devon instead.

Creed Bratton: That was the Rubicon. That was the big deal. I was quite aware into the deep marrow of my bones that this was the one where I had to deliver. I had a couple weeks to prepare and I learned those lines backward and forward. I knew this was a big deal. This was my shot. I even set a timer to turn on a recorder in the middle of the night so I would subliminally get the lines while I was sleeping that whole week.

When he showed up on the day of shooting, they told him the scene had been rewritten. He had to learn new lines on the spot.

Creed Bratton: They asked Steve if he was okay with the new lines and he was like, "Yeah, sure." Then they went, "Creed?" I gulped and was like, "Yeah . . . sure." I started sweating profusely. I was scared to death. Finally, I just took a deep, deep breath, put my hands out, and said to myself, "I have come this far. I know I can make people laugh. There's nothing for me to worry about. Just look at the lines, do it, have fun." I went in there, I breathed, and I just did it. I don't even remember what happened because it was going so fast. We were just flying.

Randall Einhorn: He killed it. I remember as soon as we started filming that scene we thought, "He's got it! This is going to be a great scene!" He killed it.

Paul Feig: All his weird, beautiful weird Creed energy just sort of came out and just kind of played into the scene. Steve was great too. Acting with Steve Carell is like playing with the greatest tennis coach in the whole world. Steve was playing with him and knew how to draw stuff out of him, and then Creed was surprising us with things he was doing. We were in Michael's office for like a half a day just shooting that scene over and over again. It was great.

Creed Bratton: The next day at craft service, [John] Krasinski and Rainn Wilson saw me when I was just coming in for the first part of the day. They both walk over and they give me a big hug and they whisper to me, "You knocked it out of the park, Creed." I had to walk off and cry a little bit by myself. Truly I never get unemotional thinking about it because it was life changing for me. I was a sixty-year-old guy getting a break like this. Thank God I was quirky enough that it worked.

Paul Feig: I just remember feeling bad knowing that Devon was going away. He was a really nice guy. It was like they were pitting each against the other and one had to convince the other to get fired. But I feel like they always knew that they were going to keep Creed. That's the genius of Greg Daniels. That's why he had writers on the staff be part of the cast. He just likes to take those kinds of chances. He knows he's got good people around him. He's good at picking people. When you allow the show to be loose, you can find the natural rhythms and talents of people.

Randall Einhorn: This could have happened to Devon if Devon had that chance.

Creed Bratton: I did feel bad about Devon.

Devon Abner: When people ask me about *The Office*, I always say how happy I am for all of those guys, but especially Creed. I've always been happy for him because he is such a great guy. He's just so talented and so funny.

As the season went on, the writers gave Creed a moment or two in most every episode. It didn't take long for this very eccentric character to become a fan favorite.

Greg Daniels: Creed didn't need to be as realistic as the other characters. It's kinda fun to have enough characters where there can be a guy who just has this mysterious four-toed backstory. The idea is that he's not just crazy. I think the idea is that there was enormous amounts of drug use at some point and what's left of his brain is very poorly connected.

Ken Kwapis: The writers began to draw upon Creed's real-life background as a 1960s rock-'n'-roller to start to shade his character a little bit. There's also a scene where he's giving Andy some romantic advice and he reminisced about dating Squeaky Fromme.

Greg Daniels: We'd grab anything from his life. He has a way of saying things with this intensity and certainty and it doesn't really matter whether the things are real or insane, he gives it the same commitment.

Ken Kwapis: When we did "Casino Night," we wanted to create this idea that Creed lived in the warehouse. I think that's partly why I think he's so excited to win that refrigerator. I think we shot a talking head with Creed where he basically talked about how he lived in the warehouse and subsisted on mainly nuts and raisins. It was cut for time.

Alysia Raycraft (Costume Designer): I remember one day I was talking to Greg at breakfast and he said to me, "You know what we say about Creed? He lives under his desk."

Creed Bratton: I thought there was a tunnel that he'd crawl under his desk when no one was looking around and he'd end up in the warehouse, where he had a bunch of boxes. He had a little place to live down there.

Ed Helms (Andy Bernard, Seasons 3–9): We liked to joke that Creed the actor and Creed the character are virtually one and the same, but the truth is the show actually takes Creed into some pretty hilariously dark places and I don't associate that much with Creed the person. That said, his sense of humor is dark and can be weird and close to Creed the character. But the character on *The Office* is kind of insidious and a little bit threatening, and there's nothing like that in the real Creed. But there is very much something off-kilter about both the real Creed and the character Creed.

Creed Bratton: I'd always have scenes, but there was never a Creed-centric episode until I was briefly the office manager [at the end of season seven]. In retrospect, it was the way to go because I might have just overdone my welcome. Creed is best in small bits. It leaves people wanting more of that character.

Creed didn't become a full-time cast member of the show until the fourth season.

Kelly Cantley: In season three the whole cast won a SAG Award. Creed was still just a day player and he didn't get a statue at the ceremony, so every member of the cast petitioned SAG to include one for Creed. A month or so after the award, another one came for Creed and the cast presented it to him on set.

Creed Bratton: I could cry now just thinking about that moment. You know, people come up to me on the street and go, "Creed, you're a national treasure." I'll go, "No, no, no, nope, nope. I'm a trinket perhaps, something you find in a curio shop." A national trinket? I can live with that, but I can't live with a national treasure.

chapter 11

MINDY

("I thought I had the scarlet letter on me.")

Creed wasn't the only Office *actor to join the cast through unorthodox means. Mindy Kaling—who played the gossipy customer service representative Kelly Kapoor—was first noticed by Greg Daniels when his wife, Susanne, took him to the hit off-Broadway play* Matt & Ben. *The low-budget, satirical production starred Mindy Kaling along with her real-life best friend Brenda Withers as bumbling versions of Ben Affleck and Matt Damon who stumble upon the screenplay for* Good Will Hunting *when it literally falls out of the sky. (Kaling and Withers wrote and directed the play together.) Daniels was extremely impressed by Kaling's sharp writing and her killer comedic timing, just as he was starting to hire writers for the first season of* The Office. *A meeting was set up at his office on the* King of the Hill *set after he read a spec script she wrote for* Arrested Development *that also blew him away.*

Mindy Kaling: Greg is the frequent perpetrator of crazy-long pauses in conversations. Like, minutes long. My meeting with him was about two and a half hours, but if you transcribed it, it would have had the content of a fifteen-minute conversation. . . . He likes to take people past the point where they can be putting on a show to impress him. Or, this is my interpretation. He might have just been zoning out and forgot I was there.

He zoned in enough to hire her as a staff writer for the first season just a week later. As an Indian-American, she was the only minority in the tiny writers' room. She was also the only woman, the least experienced writer, and very cognizant of the fact that NBC's diversity hiring program (which provided money to shows to hire women and minorities) was at least partially responsible for her being there.

Mindy Kaling: It used to really embarrass me because I thought I had the scarlet letter on me. *Diversity hire* inherently meant "less talented but fulfilling that quota."

In the early days of the first season, she felt extremely out of place.

Mindy Kaling: For some reason, I thought that Greg, B. J., and Mike [Schur] were all best friends because they had all gone to Harvard and been on *The Harvard Lampoon*. I'll never forget the day when Mike asked B. J. to go to a Red Sox–Dodgers game, while I stewed angrily on the other side of the room, feeling left out. "I'll get you, you cliquey sons of bitches," I thought.

It didn't take long for Kaling to prove her incredible talents (she wrote the season-one episode "Hot Girl," where Michael and Jim both pursue a traveling saleswoman played by Amy Adams), and in the second episode, "Diversity Day," Daniels decided to try her out in front of the camera.

Greg Daniels: I always thought that she would be a great writer-performer from the very beginning. I hired her as a writer just with like a little subclause in the deal that was a writer-performer deal.

Mindy Kaling: I didn't know this, actually, when I signed my contract, because I was a staff writer, but there was a performer clause in the contract. Greg snuck it in there.

Her big moment came at the end of "Diversity Day" in a conference room scene when Michael does an obnoxious, stereotypical Indian accent directly into her face and she slaps him hard.

Ken Kwapis: I believe that's her first network television appearance. I don't remember how many takes we did of her slapping Steve Carell, but there's a kind of awkward silence within the group. And Steve finally looked up and said, "Now she knows what it's like to be a minority." That wasn't a scripted line. I'll never forget that improv.

Oscar Nunez: When Michael Scott was like, "Mama-gamush ba-gush" [*it's actually, "Welcome to my convenience store. Would you like some googi, googi? I have some very delicious googi, googi, only ninety-nine cents plus tax. Try my googi, googi!"*], and she slaps him, Mindy just could not keep a straight face. So she would storm out and we would start laughing. When Mindy had to keep slapping Michael, she couldn't keep it together, then we would all laugh. We had to do that scene so many times.

This was a rough prototype of the Kelly character at this point, which is made clear by the decision to pin back her hair into a tight bun and dress her in highly unfashionable clothing.

Carey Bennett: I don't wanna say she was an afterthought, but she kind of came in at the last minute as just sort of a background character. We'd kind of imagined her playing her sort of more like a first-generation immigrant. We thought she had a deer-in-headlights vibe and wasn't very savvy.

Greg Daniels: She was kind of constructed just to be insulted.

Mindy Kaling: The way I dressed that first season, you would have maybe assumed that English was not my first language, and that I was sixty-three years old.

When the show came back for the second season, Kaling was not only writing many of the strongest episodes, but her character of Kelly had a complete transformation, both look-wise and attitude-wise.

Greg Daniels: Mindy was always chasing at the Kelly that we created, trying to get her to have better clothes and cooler hair and stuff like that. She pretty much single-handedly swerved that character away from the original conception.

Lee Eisenberg: Kelly season one and Kelly season two are two completely different characters.

Mindy Kaling: I think [Kelly came into her own] in "Valentine's Day," in season two, when she had hooked up with Ryan, and you get to see her. When Jim asked her, "Hey, how are you?" and she goes on for a page and a half of dialogue about what happened to her the day before, I really felt like I had an idea of what Kelly was about.

Her monologue to Jim in that episode set the tone for all future Kelly appearances: "Last night, Ryan and I totally, finally hooked up. It was awesome. And it was so funny 'cause we were at this bar with his friends and I was sitting next to him the whole night and he wasn't making a move, so in my head I was like, 'Ryan, what's taking you so long?' And then he kissed me. And I didn't know what to say. So I said, 'Ryan, what took you so long?' And I just said that to him, can you believe that? Oh my God, Jim, is that embarrassing? I'm embarrassed. . . . Oh, thank God, because I was nervous, Jim, you will not believe. So nervous, but now—now I have a boyfriend!"

This established not only Kelly's fast-talking Valley Girl vibe, but also her infatuation with Ryan. They'd have an on-again/off-again relationship throughout the entire run of the show that, unlike the Jim/Pam dynamic, was never mined for anything but laughs. In real life, however, Kaling and Novak grew very close after spending countless hours together in the writers' room and on the soundstage.

Mindy Kaling: We became friends when we were still super young, and also because we were working sometimes sixteen-hour days at *The Office*, and we did it for eight years. So it was like going to college twice together.

B. J. Novak: No one, including us, ever really knew, "Is this dating? Is this not dating?" We were never really dating, we were never really not dating. We didn't know. No one knew. All you'd know for sure was that you'd always find one of us next to the other, even if we weren't getting along.

Richard Gonzales (Second Assistant Director): I would always make sure everybody knew it was time to come back from lunch for touch-ups or whatever. One time I knocked on Mindy's door and B. J. answered. I was like, "Uh . . . we're back from lunch, guys. Let's get the touch-ups." And it was just weird. It was like, "Wait, what are you doing in there?" I guess they were a couple for a little while.

B. J. Novak: Sometimes viewers would ask, "Are Ryan and Kelly together right now, not together?" It's not even that I wouldn't know. I thought the question was missing the point. Write whatever you want. So, Kelly needed a boyfriend this week, so Ryan goes on a date. Ryan and Kelly are getting engaged. . . . I think it was sort of expressive of the relationship that we were in.

Around the time of the third season, Kaling auditioned for Saturday Night Live.

Mindy Kaling: They didn't offer me a part, but the audition went pretty well, and that night, they were like, "Do you want to come write for the show?" Greg used to write for *SNL*, and he had known that being on *SNL* was my great dream. He said, "Listen. If you get cast on the show, I'll let you break your contract and go do it, but if they ask you to write, I can't, because you have a job writing here, plus you're on the show. So I'm not going to let you leave the show so you can go be in New York." At that time, I missed New York so badly. I hated LA for a long time, and I wanted to leave it. I had these fantasies of going to *SNL* and falling in love with some writer on *SNL*, of getting married and living in New York. That was really heartbreaking to have to turn down.

But after just a few years, many of the other writers from the earliest days did leave and Kaling—once a frightened newcomer—was suddenly a grizzled vet, churning out brilliant episodes like "Branch Wars," "Frame Toby," and "Secret Santa" while somehow finding time to play Kelly Kapoor in nearly every episode. The other writers marveled at her ability to juggle it all.

Jen Celotta: Mindy was incredibly impressive. She would turn a script around so fast and it was always so good. I would sometimes hear that three days before a script was due she hadn't started it, and then she'd turn in this brilliant script. I was just like, "What the hell? I don't understand this." Maybe she just worked incredibly well under pressure, but she was able to turn around something so fast that was so good. "The Injury" is still one of my favorite episodes, along with "Dinner Party." When I first came into *The Office* and read her—I think it was "The Dundies"—I was intimidated, in a good way. It made me want to push and work hard to try to keep up.

chapter 12

SEASON THREE

("All of the Hondas and Toyotas turned into Mercedes and BMWs.")

The cast and crew of The Office *went into the third season riding an incredible high. They'd just won an Emmy for Outstanding Comedy Series, NBC had finally given them a full-season pickup of twenty-two episodes, much of the cast had gotten a raise, and all of the agonizing battles of the past were behind them.*

Jason Kessler: When we came back for the third season, you started seeing new cars in the parking lot.

Matt Sohn: All of the Hondas and Toyotas turned into Mercedes and BMWs.

Randall Einhorn: Craft services in season one and two was like sausage links, a bunch of deviled eggs, and some sandwiches. By season three, I'd be sitting there with a forty-pound camera on my shoulders and this guy would walk up to me and say, "Crab-stuffed mushroom?"

Kim Ferry: It was so exciting. You definitely felt like you had job security finally. It's not like "I'm gonna have to go on unemployment. I'm gonna have to start looking for work." "I'm gonna have a job for a whole year. This is great!" People started buying houses.

Kate Flannery: I met my boyfriend at the end of season two. He came to my Lampshades [sketch comedy] show and he asked me out after that. And so we actually dated between season two and three. So when I came back season three I was like, "Oh my God, I'm over forty. I'm a female in LA, I have a boyfriend and I got a show. This is nuts!" It was just this wonderful new reality.

Larry Wilmore: Season three felt more like a regular sitcom. That feeling of guerrilla filming and being a renegade and all that was long in the rearview.

Brent Forrester (Writer, Seasons 3–9): The pressure came off them significantly after that second season. I kind of felt like the troops had won their victory.

Ken Whittingham: Things started to feel a little different by season three because from time to time there might be a little pushback on certain things from the actors in ways they wouldn't before. They'd start saying to me, "Well, I don't know if my character would do that."

Jen Celotta: As we became more successful, and potentially had more money for things, every department wanted to do a better job. Lighting wanted the cooler lightings. Wardrobe wanted better clothes. Everybody wanted cooler, neater things. But that puts a wall up between you and the character when everybody's just starting to look a little bit too like perfectly put together. There were certain things that really helped people connect to the characters and I think, like, the blandness of the office, the grays, the lighting, everything really helped that.

Carey Bennett: Ricky Gervais came to set at this point. He said, "Hey! So how's it going for you?" And I'm like, "You know what? I'm just holding the line. I'm trying, but everybody wants to be fancy. They all want this fancy stuff. They want to be in fancier, cuter outfits. And I'm trying to hold the line." And he said, "Oh man, tell me about it. After the first season of the

UK show, everybody came back and their teeth were whitened and they had tans."

The season begins with "Gay Witch Hunt," where Michael learns that Oscar is gay and tells the entire office about it.

Oscar Nunez: Greg Daniels wrote that script and he was very concerned about it. He said, "Do you mind if we make your character gay?" And I said, "No, I don't care," and he said, "Oh, good, because we wrote this script." What would you have said if I was crazy and had said no? But it was a great, great script.

The episode climaxes in a conference room scene where Michael forcibly kisses Oscar to somehow prove that he's comfortable with homosexuality.

Oscar Nunez: We kept doing the scene over and over again and we kept hugging and we kept hugging. I guess Steve felt something was missing, and he was right. It was a nothing scene. Michael should have been more awkward or aggressive. And so maybe the fourth or fifth take, he's coming in for the hug, but he's not diverting his face. His face is coming toward me and I'm like, "He better go left or right because we're going to smash faces. Where is he going? Where is he going? Oh no. This is happening now. . . ." And we kissed. As they say, the rest is history.

Jen Celotta: That kiss was not scripted and it was one of the best moments in the series, I think. Steve leaned in to hug him and then he just went for the kiss. Thank God Oscar is a genius and he had improv training and he did not break, but we had to work to find a reaction where everyone wasn't breaking because this was not supposed to happen.

Brian Wittle (Boom Operator): I'm six feet away from them booming the scene and I remember thinking, "He's gonna kiss him! He's gonna kiss him!"

Randall Einhorn: It just kept going and going and nobody pulled out. Oscar wasn't going to pull out. Steve certainly didn't. We all knew that it was just genius.

Oscar Nunez: I remember thinking, "I hope they get this take because I don't want to do it over again." And I knew the reactions were awesome. There was laughter, which was totally normal. It was very funny.

Kate Flannery: That was improvised and it was nuts. I was like, "Don't anybody fuck this up. Don't anybody speak over this. Don't let anybody get in the way. Let it happen." It was so great, so wonderful.

Ken Kwapis: Once the kiss ends, Steve ad-libbed a line. Under his breath he goes, "See, I'm still here." That was not in the script. It's just this strange idea in some fairy tale that he was going to, what? Kiss Oscar and turn into a frog? I thought that was such a wonderfully perfect Michael Scott head-scratching observation. And it's very appropriate that it takes place in that conference room. It's almost like that room is like the crucible where all of the interpersonal dramas within the office come to a boil.

In that same episode, the world of The Office *grew with the introduction of the Stamford branch of Dunder Mifflin. This was a mirror of the second season of the UK* Office, *when the Slough branch of Wernham Hogg absorbed the Swindon branch. Jim transferred to Stamford after Pam rejected him at the end of season two.*

Caroline Williams: Opening that other office was a real left turn, something unexpected. There was nothing really like that on the British show, though by this point we'd really diverged from that. But the Stamford branch was also an opportunity really to do something completely different. Also, I think Stamford was brought up as somewhere that would be a little bit more sophisticated than Scranton. Suddenly the office feels smaller than it already was.

Ken Kwapis: I remember talking to Greg about wanting to make sure that on some level, Jim feels out of place in Stamford. That there's an adjustment required, a learning curve. It's not quite as homey as it was in Scranton. Clearly it's a branch that's very professional. It's totally different than Scranton. You wanted to really show that this is a place that actually functions like an actual office. We built the set in our warehouse.

Brent Forrester: Once that Stamford office was created, of course you get to cast a whole bunch of new people and hope to create some more lasting stars.

The first one they hired was Ed Helms. Like Steve Carell, he came from an improv background and first got widespread recognition as a correspondent on The Daily Show.

Teri Weinberg: We'd always been huge fans of Ed and it was just a time to open up our cast, to bring in someone who was crazy talented, that had something really fun to offer to the relationships on the show.

Justin Spitzer: Ed Helms was someone that I think Allison Jones had been suggesting for a while that the show use. We were all familiar with him from *The Daily Show.*

Allison Jones: I think it was probably Greg's idea. Greg probably said to me, "Do you think Ed Helms would be good in the show?" And I'm sure I said, "Absolutely, he'd be great."

Brian Wittle: I remember Ed being the new guy and watching him. We're all trying to figure out, "Is he gonna be around for a while?" He was really funny and really nice. Everyone knew him from *The Daily Show.* He just gelled right away. He had the right sense of humor and the right attitude. He was a perfect choice for an addition to the show. It was like in the early *Saturday Night Live* when they added Bill Murray in the second season and then he became this huge star, but he wasn't a member of the original cast.

Randal Einhorn: As soon as he came, we knew this guy was going to fit right in here.

Creed Bratton: I just think his arrival boosted everything up. It just gave it a jolt of energy, because he's a wild card. I mean that in the best possible way. He's like a live wire. I can't see anybody else pulling it off as well as he did.

Ed Helms: For my part, it was very daunting because I was already a big fan of the show. I was very anxious. I was very excited because I love the show, but I was very nervous because I didn't know how I'd fit into that kind of vibe. Very early on, I was opening up to John [Krasinski] about my anxiety. And he was like, "Dude, we're all here to support you. We're a basket and you can feel like you can nestle into it." It actually was such a nice sentiment and it was so genuine and it totally put me at ease.

Caroline Williams: My memory of creating the Andy Bernard character is that Michael Schur had a friend who would introduce himself by saying his name followed by his hometown. So it was like, "Joe Schmo, Chicago, Illinois." And this person was somebody that some of the other staff knew and it had a real comical resonance with them. And so it became, "Okay, this guy's going to be like Andy Bernard. He's going to be that guy." There was also a running joke in the staff about where people went to college. College was a big topic of conversation in the writers' room. There was something about Cornell that preexisted Andy Bernard, mostly coming from Michael Schur.

Justin Spitzer: I'm pretty sure Mike Schur was the one who came up with the idea that Andy went to Cornell and he's always bragging about having gone to Cornell. That probably had something to do with the fact that so many of the staff went to Harvard.

Gene Stupnitsky: I remember during lunch once we went back to our offices and I was reading that Cornell is the black sheep of the Ivy League.

Lee Eisenberg: People that went there are very insecure about that.

Gene Stupnitsky: I didn't know that, but I thought, "Hey, that is hilarious. Let's make Ed go to Cornell and he's really proud of it and insecure about it and shoves it down everyone's throat in Scranton."

Ken Kwapis: His energy at first was making up for the fact that Dwight wasn't sitting across from Jim once he moved to Stamford. Clearly, Andy was his own character, but there was a little sense that he was functioning, in a way, the way Dwight did as well.

Caroline Williams: Andy was also a counterpoint to Dwight because Dwight's rage was much more expressed and Andy's was sort of withheld. They're totally different. Andy, as the kind of Dwight of the other office, his mask was just so chipper. That's a reason to kind of love him.

Gene Stupnitsky: Ed can sing, so we had the character sing. And Ed played the banjo, so Andy played the banjo.

Ed Helms: Andy was just an amalgam of people that have annoyed me over the years. I tried to do a sort of armchair psychoanalysis of those people and then take that analysis and insert them into Andy. It's incredibly fun to play someone that you don't like. It exorcises your own demons in a way. It's cathartic. We all have things that we don't like about ourselves, little things. And I get to amplify those things and put them out there. It's fun and it has a cleansing effect.

Lee Eisenberg: Ed brought such bluster to the character. That sort of energy didn't exist before he came on. He's a cocky nerd, but so different from Dwight. He was also bragging about all the wrong things. We had a thing where he's like, "I worked at Wells Fargo." He worked at all the places that have gone down. He worked at Enron. You realize he's a fool.

Gene Stupnitsky: I remember that one time Mike [Schur] ordered tuna for lunch twice in a row and someone was like, "Tuna!" That went into the character.

Jason Kessler: I think Andy is very much like Michael in that he's always looking for a group to belong to. He's constantly looking for love, either romantic love or social love. I think that's why he was in an a cappella group. I think that's why he's in sales. And Ed brought so much sensitivity to the character that maybe you wouldn't get if it was just played as a preppy douchebag. There's a big difference between Andy Bernard and Bradley Whitford's character in *Revenge of the Nerds II*. They're both the polo shirt frat guy, but the sensitivity that Ed brings to Andy, and the sensitivity that's inherent in the character, pushes out the dickishness and gives you a real person that you can care for and want to see succeed, even when they are just over-the-top in terms of who they are as a person.

The separation of Jim from the rest of the office was disconcerting for the cast and crew.

B. J. Novak: It was tough to write for because it wasn't the energy of the whole gang together. It was smarty story-wise and we got to introduce some great people in Rashida and Ed and we're better for it, [but] it was hard not having Jim in the office.

Rainn Wilson: We never saw John. There [were] like eight episodes where John would just come in on the days where we weren't there . . . it was very interesting being in the office without John there.

Leslie David Baker: The whole dynamic changes.

Rainn Wilson: It really did, and it suffered because his energy playing off people and being the straight man in the office is so important.

Rashida Jones's character of Karen Filippelli was also introduced at the beginning of season three. She also worked at the Stamford branch and took an immediate liking to Jim.

Allison Jones: We auditioned a lot of people for that. Laura Benanti was up for it as I recall. I thought they were all too pretty, kind of, to be on it. But then everybody said, "No. All these women can be plain too." So it was like, "Okay, fine." But Rashida was the best.

Greg Daniels: When we were looking for Karen and I saw Rashida's name on the audition list, I [thought], "This is a friend of people who work here, so let's be nice, but it's just not going to be her." But the thing that's great about her is that she's very beautiful but doesn't seem aware of her beauty. She leads with her intelligence. And she felt like a good contrast to Pam. When she read scenes with Jenna [Fischer], that's when we said, "This is cool."

Brent Forrester: The writing staff was so enamored and proud of the cast that it was always a test to see if an incoming actor could remain. It was taken very, very seriously. Rashida did not just get a free pass at first. In fact, I think even after they shot a couple of episodes with her there was still this idea of, "We could recast her if she isn't up to par." It was taken really, really seriously. But she quite correctly survived and then rose to the level of the cast because she's just unforgettable.

Caroline Williams: A big part of bringing on Rashida Jones was bringing in someone for Pam to feel threatened by. And she was the opposite of Pam in every way.

Rashida Jones (Karen Filippelli, Seasons 3–5 and 7): The first day on set I was terrified. I kept saying to Ed Helms I felt like I had won some radio contest and they had thrown me into my favorite show. "How is this possible? What am I going to do?"

Ken Kwapis: What's nice about Rashida is just her energy. She completely fits within the world of the show, and yet her energy is very different than Jenna's. Right away, there was just a nice contrast in energy between the two women in Jim's life. This is a strange way to put it, but I feel like Pam always feels very Midwestern to me, and Rashida's character always feels like she comes from the coast. And as soon as we meet Rashida, we think, "Oh my gosh, this is gonna pull him further away from Pam."

Caroline Williams: The idea for Karen was definitely not to make her negative. We wanted the audience to love her so there was genuinely a sense of being torn between Pam and Karen. It would've been really easy to bring in somebody that was dumb or annoying or just really antagonistic or evil in some way that maybe Jim didn't know. But there would be no threat, and the audience wouldn't be torn. We wanted her to be genuinely likable, because the audience is going to hate anyone in her position because they loved Pam so much. The audience is going to be inclined to root against this person. And that was the challenge, to make people root for her so that there was real tension. And then, by the end of the season, it's like you almost feel bad for her when you see her eyes when Jim and Pam are being goofy together and she seems hurt. You're surprised in yourself that you're caring about the person who would come between them.

Gene Stupnitsky: We knew we had to do something with Jim and Pam in the third season, but we were always talking about shows like *Cheers* or *Moonlighting*. "How do you keep them apart?" One way is to physically keep them apart. The first way we did that was by creating the Stamford branch and introducing this Karen Filippelli character, who was basically an ideal fit for Jim to forget Pam. We thought it would give the audience a lot of angst, and it did.

Rashida Jones: I had anxiety before the show aired because I just didn't know how people were going to respond to me. I was afraid I was going to go out and people were going to launch eggs at my face and just not be psyched about me. I was a huge fan of the show before I was on it and I was rooting for Pam and Jim. It put me in a weird position, but because the writers are so good they made me likable. They did a really good job of making it confusing for viewers, too, I think. I knew that people were Pam/Jim loyalists and I never expected to be able to break that. The fact that anyone was rooting for me at all made me so happy.

Caroline Williams: At the end of Phyllis's wedding, Karen sings. And part of that was because Rashida Jones is a great singer, but it was also to kind of make her even more threatening. Not only is she ambitious and kind of excels at things that Pam doesn't, she's also good with stuff that Pam does, like kind of being a free spirit. So that kind of ups the stakes as well. It's like, "Oh, she's also fun."

After seven episodes where Jim lives in Stamford and begins dating Karen, the two offices merge when the Stamford branch closes and many of the employees there move to Scranton.

Kate Flannery: We weren't there all day, every day for a while during the Stamford period, which made me nervous. I was like, "Oh my God, is the whole story line going to go to Stamford?" Then when they merged, it was like, "Oh, my God, this is crazy." I thought it was so ballsy for them to create that other office so soon. I thought it was totally in the spirit of a documentary to explore an idea much bigger right away, sooner than later. So that was kind of fantastic.

Lee Eisenberg: I think that the Stamford story line is the type of thing where you try to mine as much as you can out of something without making it tired. I think if it was the entire season, people would miss the Scranton stories. You want the core of the office together. You want to see Michael and Jim together.

Brent Forrester: It was always the intention to bring Jim back to Scranton. I was really excited that they handed me the episode [to write] where Andy and Dwight would meet for the first time, "The Merger." Seeing the two offices finally come together was the thrill of it for me, comboing up characters that had never been comboed on the show yet. In particular Andy Bernard and Dwight. I was like, "Oh. That's going to be a great combo."

Caroline Williams: Greg had a very good plan for merging the offices together. He knew what he wanted to do. I always wanted Jim to come back and I always wanted it to be as quick as possible. For me, *The Office* was Jim and Pam, and I wanted them reunited. I don't remember if everyone else felt the same. Greg had his plan for just how much he could push the audience to the point where we wouldn't lose them. Obviously, the longer they were gone, the more tension would build, and that helped storytelling. But you also don't want to alienate the audience by having them check out because so many of our favorite people aren't together. So I remember wanting Jim back and being very concerned that it was going on too long. But then ultimately, watching the season, it was the perfect amount of time.

Ken Whittingham: I directed "The Merger." I remember Greg saying to me, "Where do you think the new people would sit?" It took about half an hour or so to kinda just figure it out and then I gave him kind of a new layout of the office. He was like, "Why?" So I kind of broke down the relationships, who would be actually looking at who, and how that would play, and where Jenna and John would be and how it would impact their relationship. I had a reason for why everyone sat everywhere.

Caroline Williams: The separation forced Jim and Pam's relationship back, which was good. I remember a lot of conversations with Greg about keeping them apart because all the audience wants is for them to be together and have a happy ending, and that is just the death of storytelling. So he was so good at protecting that tension but not giving in to what the audience wants. It's a fine line between making the audience happy but keeping the story going and keeping it exciting and interesting. If they had followed what the message boards were saying, Jim and Pam would've been together from the beginning. And then what? Where does it go from there? Because they were the heart of the show.

Jim and Karen are dating by the time they move to Scranton, and when Pam breaks up with Roy for good in episode seventeen ("Cocktails"), their situation from season two reverses and she becomes the lonely single pining after him.

Caroline Williams: It was a really tumultuous year for Pam because before she got to be the object of affection, and now she was the pursuer. I think it really unsettled her and it ultimately allowed her to find her voice.

In one of the season's more poignant moments, Pam enters her work into an art show. Roy comes and is barely able to mask his disinterest, while Michael doesn't arrive until the very end and is overjoyed when he realizes she's drawn a portrait of the Dunder Mifflin building. Nobody else from the office besides Oscar shows up, not even Jim. The rest of the episode ("Business School") is devoted to Michael delivering a disastrous speech at Ryan's business school and the office battling a loose bat.

Lee Eisenberg: That episode is kind of a perfect encapsulation of the themes of the show. Pam feels ignored by Roy. He doesn't get her. You have Michael and Ryan at the school, where we have Michael making an ass of himself, but at the end the characters come together. Michael's there to support Pam. He goes to see her art show but then he sees that she drew a picture of the building. To Pam, I think it was probably just something to draw, but to him, he's like, "You drew *our* building. There's my car right there. How much is it?" All these different agendas come together and it's so sweet.

Gene Stupnitsky: I actually got choked up when I first saw it. When he shows up at the art thing, it's so great.

Rainn Wilson: It's truly touching. I think that Michael is such a child and this is when his childlike enthusiasm works, because he's like, "Wow, you did that? It looks so real." And he's so touched by it in this open-hearted way and that affects Pam. It's where you see one of the great sides of Michael.

Lee Eisenberg: Something I didn't appreciate at the time is how well the show mixed melancholy and joy in the same space. It's hard to do, but when it works it's very special. I mean, in that same episode, there's a bat in the office and Dwight thinks Jim is a vampire.

Gene Stupnitsky: We put an amazing line in that one about Dwight shooting a werewolf, but by the time he got to it, it had turned into his neighbor's dog. What a dark joke.

The love triangle of Jim, Pam, and Karen wasn't the only romance in the office that season. Dwight and Angela were keeping their relationship on the down-low, while Jan was finally willing to debase herself by publicly dating Michael.

Lee Eisenberg: Melora was so funny as a straight woman who Michael basically ruins. He takes her down a bit.

John Krasinski: Melora was so good on our show. She was really our secret weapon, because I think it's hard to play the straight character in a show like that. She played the severe girlfriend so well and ended up being a great comedy duo with Steve. Steve found her very funny and I think that had she not been so hard-core, it wouldn't have been nearly as funny. Her character had so much ambition and so much power in her, which was the exact opposite of Steve. It was almost like an S & M relationship, like he loved being tortured by her or something.

Lee Eisenberg: When Melora first came on the show, she hadn't done a ton of comedy. I felt like she was a little bit anxious, because everyone had come from these improv backgrounds. The comedy was that she's straight, and then Michael . . . she's the opposite. And then the comedy started drifting more toward her, where she actually got jokes, rather than being the straight person and being the reaction shot. Her character started to develop. She really embraced it.

Rainn Wilson: I love how Jan went from the perfect type of corporate straight person in season one to become more and more and more warped as we found out more information about her.

Melora Hardin: I remember in season three when Greg Daniels came up to me and started talking about Abbott and Costello. He said, "Costello was the funny one, but they paid Abbott more. That's because it was much harder to find a good straight man to set up the jokes than it was to find the silly guy that was gonna be able to land the jokes and do the silly funny bits." I was like, "Really? That's so interesting." He's like, "I'm just letting you know that." I just thought that was really cute and sweet. He was basically saying that I was very valuable to the comedy of the show.

But Jan unraveled as the season went on and Michael eventually dumped her, though she won him back by getting breast implants.

Melora Hardin: We were at the upfronts one year, and we were on the sideline about to go on and we were watching another cast out there onstage. I remember turning to Greg and going, "You know what I think is interesting?" He's like, "What?" I said, "It's interesting that none of the women on our show seem to have fake boobs, and that when you look at all the other casts, there's like that woman, she's definitely got fake boobs. She's definitely got fake boobs, and she's got fake boobs." I'm pretty sure that that gave him the idea.

Carey Bennett: Those were her real boobs in there. And we created this whole crazy super bra. These are like ancient costumer secrets and I don't know if I can fully reveal them, but basically that bra could stand on its own. Her ladies were just sitting on top of it basically.

Melora Hardin: I called them my strap-on boobs.

Jenna Fischer: You start at the beginning thinking Jan is the one together person. Then look what happens to her. Nothing is what it seems on this show.

Throughout the entire season, Pam deals with one indignity after another until she has her epiphany after walking on the hot coals during "Beach Games" and finally tells Jim how she feels about him in front of everyone, including Karen. At the same time, a job opens up at Dunder Mifflin's corporate office in New York because Jan is about to be fired over her erratic behavior. Michael, Jim, and Karen all apply for it, setting up the season-three finale, "The Job."

David Rogers (Editor): When we saw the New York footage we were all like, "Wow, Jim and Karen look really good together. Why is he leaving Karen?" Paul Lieberstein said, "The heart wants. It's just love. He loves Pam."

Near the end, Jim seems to be on the verge of a job offer from David Wallace, but he sees a note that Pam left in his bag along with the yogurt-lid gold medal from "Office Olympics." You don't see him decline the job, but you do see him drive back to Scranton and walk into the conference room while Pam is being interviewed by the documentarian. He asks her if she's free for dinner that night. "Okay then," he says as Pam beams with shock and euphoria. "It's a date."

Melora Hardin: It's so sad and happy in a weird way. This is such a mixed moment to watch Jim on the precipice of being his biggest, best self and taking that step down to staying where he's safe and comfortable and finally, in a way, addressing this relationship that is so sweet and right.

Jenna Fischer: It's so cool. On the one hand, he's taking a huge risk personally, but he's still going to be held back professionally.

Ken Kwapis: This was a transcendent moment. It was hard for me to sit there without crying. I was crying.

Midway through the season, The Office *beat out* Desperate Housewives, Entourage, Ugly Betty, *and* Weeds *to win Outstanding Performance by an Ensemble in a Comedy Series at the Screen Actors Guild Awards.*

Melora Hardin: When we won the Emmy, Greg took that home. But with the SAG, we all got one. They're super, super, super heavy. They're bronze, and they've got a giant marble base. I carried that little sucker around all night, and I woke up the next morning, and my bicep was so sore that I could barely lift my arm from carrying that around all night long. That was what it took for me to believe that we were a hit. It was my sore bicep. I needed physical proof.

KEY EPISODE 5

"Beach Games"

In the penultimate episode of season three, Michael becomes so convinced that he's going to get promoted to the CFO position at Dunder Mifflin's corporate office in New York that he organizes a series of competitive games at Lake Scranton where the staff will compete for the regional manager position. It was directed by Harold Ramis and written by Greg Daniels and Jen Celotta.

Jen Celotta: As soon as Greg and I landed on the idea that Michael would choose a successor we thought, "How would he do that? Oh, he would absolutely have a *Survivor*-like competition that's just ridiculous."

Brian Baumgartner: This is a big moment not just for the season, but for the series. We're putting everything forward and having several people in the office now competing for this job and really solidifying that the CFO is kind of an important character.

Jen Celotta: Kent [Zbornak] came to us with a photo of a beautiful lake that looks just like Lake Scranton. We were saying, "Let's do it at a lake that looks just like Lake Scranton." And we saw it and it was so gorgeous. We were like, "We need to find a lake that's the lake equivalent of *The*

Office, like the bleakest lake we can find." So we went to an area called Hansen Dam.

The cast drove down there in a bus. Along the way, they sang songs like children on their way to summer camp.

Jen Celotta: That was so much fun. I think we had one scripted song. Then we said, "Just, guys, keep singing." Then we just started throwing out song titles.

Brian Baumgartner: I had no idea we were going to sing. They were in a little car and over a God mic Harold just suddenly said, "Kevin, sing something."

Ed Helms: We sang "Tiny Dancer" [as a nod to *Almost Famous*] and Rainn led the *Friends* theme song. I think I started *Flintstones* as a nod to the bus scene in *Planes, Trains and Automobiles*.

Jen Celotta: We were trying to think of the public-domain song titles at a certain point just to make sure we didn't go over our music budget. So we might have done [the nineteenth-century folk song] "Turkey in the Straw."

When they got to Hansen Dam, Ramis, Daniels, Celotta, and much of the crew worked from underneath a tent. Everyone else was exposed to the elements for hours and hours on end.

Brian Baumgartner: This episode for the actors should have been called "Temperature Day." The whole week was all about temperature, whether it was ninety-eight degrees on the bus or freezing at night.

Jen Celotta: It was so hot during the day and everyone was dying. We had these little fans and then at night there were heat lamps. The temperature change was crazy.

Brian Baumgartner: We had tents pumping air-conditioning that didn't work all day long, and it's in the Valley so everything becomes frigid at night and there were heaters everywhere.

If that wasn't uncomfortable enough, Leslie David Baker, Rainn Wilson, John Krasinski, and Ed Helms all had to wear enormous sumo-wrestler suits for one of the competitions. And everyone had to stuff their face with hot dogs for an eating contest that required many, many takes.

Kate Flannery: The hot dog–eating contest was probably the toughest part of the day.

Brian Baumgartner: There was a deleted scene. I don't know how this was cut. But when Michael said, "Dip the hot dogs in the water so it slides down your gullet," I think there was an improv of "That's what she said" from about five or six of us. I don't know if it was standards and practices or Harold or Greg, but that was so funny.

Ed Helms: What I remember is eating tons of hot dogs and spitting them into a bucket. For me, the act of spitting chewed food out of my mouth activates my gag reflex. It is so upsetting. The worst part is the prop folks are walking around with a big plastic bucket and like four people are spitting into it. You have to spit out, but you're looking at other people [doing the same thing]. It's just disgusting. . . . The suits were so profoundly uncomfortable. You had to lean against things. We did take against take. In one of the scenes where I'm fighting Rainn, I broke a fingernail really bad. I was like, "Stop stop stop." And everyone was like, "Big deal, he broke a nail. Jesus."

Randall Einhorn: I remember Leslie got sand in his eyes. I think he had to go to the hospital.

The key moment of the episode comes near the end when Pam gathers up the courage to walk across hot coals. She then triumphantly walks over to the rest of the gang and unloads months' worth of frustration and agony. "Why didn't any of you come to my art show?" she asks. "I invited all of you. That really sucked. It's like sometimes some of you act like I don't even exist. Jim, I called off my wedding because of you. And now we're not even friends. And things are just weird between us and that sucks. And I miss you. You were my best friend before you went to Stamford. I really miss you. I shouldn't have been with Roy. There were a lot of reasons to call off my wedding, but the truth is I didn't care about any of those reasons until I met you. And now you're with someone else and that's fine. It's . . . whatever. That's not what . . . My feet really hurt. The thing that I'm just trying to say to you, Jim, and to everyone else in the circle I guess, is that I miss having fun with you—just you, and not everyone in the circle. Okay. I am going to go walk in the water now. Yeah . . . good day."

Jen Celotta: She did this speech a bunch of times and was so amazing take after take after take.

Brian Baumgartner: Her progression, her journey in this episode is so fantastic.

Gene Stupnitsky: We kept talking about empowering Pam and her growing as a human and not being so weak.

Jen Celotta: Jenna is just brilliant in that episode because you feel her. You feel her watching Jim with Karen. You feel these moments where she misses that. She misses that joy and she misses that fun and she misses playing. And then to have her be able to have this brave moment where she just—not for anybody else's sake but just for her own sake—just proves herself. She was strong and she was confident that she owns herself now and that she's brave enough with the thrill and the adrenaline to give this speech and say, "I miss you."

Kate Flannery: Jenna is a really good actress. She just makes believe that she really is that person. Pam has failed at so many things by that point. I thought it was really brave to show her like that. I just think it's great when they sort of show full sides of somebody.

Randall Einhorn: That speech is an instance where I was like, "I know they're actors, damn it, but I'm still caught up in this moment."

chapter 13

WHO IS MICHAEL SCOTT?

("Loneliness is the most universal emotion.")

Michael Scott made a somewhat radical change from the first season to the second one when the writers made him more sympathetic and less abrasive, but he continued to evolve as the show went on. Each writer on the staff had to constantly ask themselves a crucial question: Who exactly is Michael Scott?

Justin Spitzer: On a whiteboard in the writers' room, Greg Daniels wrote a "running from self-awareness diagram" about Michael. Picture this big hill with a big slope going backward, and Michael was running sort of up it. It was like Michael is always sprinting away from self-awareness. If he looks back and he sees how pathetic his life is or what people think of him, he'll get swallowed up. So his whole drive was fleeing from that self-awareness because he just can't face it.

Steve Carell: I think he's a man who clearly lacks self-awareness. I always said if he caught a glimpse of who he really is, his head would explode.

Jason Kessler: If you tried to describe Michael to somebody, you would never want to get within ten feet of him. But when you see him in action, and you realize his motivations, it opens the character up so much to being a real person who just wants to fit in.

Alan Sepinwall: Basically every writer on the show had a different vision of who Michael was. So there is Michael the unbearable oaf. There is Michael the guy who's somewhere on the autistic spectrum, who just doesn't understand how to relate to people. There is Michael the largely well-meaning and talented guy who's just sort of socially clumsy. Like there's a lot of different Michaels in there and sort of from episode to episode it really varied. Basically it's a testament to how good Carell was that these all felt like the same guy.

Caroline Williams: I sometimes felt that to each writer Michael Scott represents a version of themselves that they're most ashamed of. I saw Michael Scott as just socially desperate and yet good-hearted, which is probably how I would, in my darkest moments, describe myself.

Lee Eisenberg: Paul [Lieberstein] would write the dumbest version of Michael. Michael Schur would write the most humane version, decent Michael. Mindy would write the most gay version of Michael.

Jason Kessler: Gene and Lee liked when Michael embarrassed himself. They liked when Michael had to sit in whatever mess he made. Jen was able to put a ton of heart into Michael. She puts a lot of heart into everything. I think that was really her superpower as a writer.

Justin Spitzer: Mindy's Michael was more feminine. I probably saw him as a little more pathetic early on. That's obviously coming from loneliness, but he's responsible for a lot of his own loneliness, too, by being pathetic. As the show went on, he became more and more likable and more and more relatable. In season two, they dealt with the fact that he wanted a family so much, and that was a big part of it. That always became a big part of his drive, and I think increased his loneliness.

Caroline Williams: For me, Michael was just lonely. Loneliness is, at least for me, the most universal emotion. And I think he captured that so well. And then Steve Carell brought this sweetness to some things that would otherwise be so dark. And it came together in such a funny way that it was delightful for me, as opposed to pathetic. It couldn't have been done better and that character is so delightful for so many reasons. It's this social desperation combined with sweetness.

Anthony Farrell (Writer, Seasons 4 and 5): I saw him as a lonely, powerful man. There's that scene where you see young Michael and he's a little kid and he just wants to make friends.

He's referencing a particular cringe-inducing scene in "Take Your Daughter to Work Day" from season two where Michael shows everyone a tape of him appearing on a puppet show as a child. Young Michael is asked what he wants to do when he grows up. "I want to be married and have a hundred kids," he says, "so I can have a hundred friends and no one can say no to being my friend." Even the puppet can't hide his sorrow after hearing that.

Anthony Farrell: That's who he still is. That's who he still was to me. He comes to the office because that's where his friends are.

Jason Kessler: I think you get such insight into Michael when we do any sort of a scene that involves him as a little kid. You see this is an only child that grew up not knowing how to fit into the world. I think it's hilarious that once he gets a little bit of power he uses it to try to be a friend 'cause that's the opposite of how most people wield power. But that's what Michael wants more than anything else in the world. He wants to be liked, and he wants to be loved, even if it's with the wrong person, as we see with Jan.

Jenna Fischer: Ultimately, he's just a man who wants to be loved. And as annoying as he could be, you don't want to kick him while he's down. You know where it's coming from, and so you tolerate it. That's what's so brilliant about that character, and what was so brilliant about Steve.

Warren Lieberstein (Writer, Seasons 5–9): He's truly someone who's yearning to love. He does want to be the object of attention. He wants the world to revolve around him, to be noticed and seen. He wants to be the puppet master of everything that's happening. And I think in less capable hands it could have failed miserably, but Steve was so nuanced in his portrayal of Michael. He could show a lot of things at once. He's like one of those athletes who you watch and you're like, "Oh, that's easy. I could easily go out there and do that." But it's so impossible. He just makes it look effortless.

John Krasinski: I think if he wasn't lonely and there wasn't this horrible sadness to him, then the dynamic between Jim and Michael would've been much different and [it] would've been a lot harder to play me defending him or me trying to be nice to him, because if he's just hateful that's sort of a hard place to be in.

Halsted Sullivan: I saw Michael as someone who was desperate to be liked and desperate to be included. And in that desperation, he would sometimes push people away. And he wouldn't quite understand why because he feels like he is doing everything right. And he always wanted to be at the center of the action. And if people around him were having a good time, then he was having a good time. I don't see him necessarily as a tragic figure. But if you're the life of the party, even if you're the self-declared life of the party, you're at least at the party, as opposed to not being at the party.

Justin Spitzer: He doesn't have much family and he doesn't have any friends. He views himself as the fun boss. He views himself as a fun guy, but the only people that are around him are his coworkers, who have to be there because they need the money and that's mandated. So how does a guy like that, who the only people who want to be around him are there because they're being paid, justify to himself that he is actually popular and well liked? He has to make himself believe that they are there because they love him so much.

Tucker Gates (Director): The heart of the matter is that Michael has the best intentions. He just has no sense of how to make those intentions work in a way that's correct.

Steve Carell: I really like "Gay Witch Hunt" because it shows that he's not intrinsically racist or homophobic or sexist. He just doesn't have a frame of reference. He's not capable of understanding. Once he does glean some understanding, he misinterprets it and it becomes something else altogether. At least the way I feel about the character, he has a decent heart. He's a decent person and he's just trying his best.

Rainn Wilson: One of the details I love about our show is that Michael is an excellent salesman. He's a terrible manager. He's just been promoted to an entirely wrong position. He should just be the top salesman in the office. He'd be fantastic.

Jen Celotta: We spent time reminding ourselves that he's actually good at his job a lot because he can be a little bumbly, but if he's not good at his job it doesn't make sense. That was a reality that was very important to Greg and every once in a while we'd cross that line and then we'd pull ourselves back because it's like he needs to be good at his job for any of this to make sense.

Jason Kessler: I think with Michael, the fact that he was a great salesman is a cautionary tale of American working life because he was such a great salesman that they made him a manager, and he's a terrible manager. And I think that happens over and over again. It happens in TV itself. Every showrunner got that job because they were an incredibly good writer, and that doesn't mean that they're great managers.

Gene Stupnitsky: It was very important to Greg to show that Michael was a good salesman. It's the Peter Principle. He was promoted above his capability. He was really good at closing the deal, which is odd when you actually go back and think about it because he is an idiot in many ways so he really wouldn't be a good salesman. Good salesmen have a lot of qualities that Michael didn't have. But it was a good idea in terms of explaining his longevity at the job.

Brent Forrester: By the time I got there in season three, there was this mantra in the writers' room of "Remember, Michael's good at his job." They would say it like they were exhausted from it. They'd say, "Don't make the mistake of going, 'This is a dumb guy who's a buffoon and he isn't good at his job.'" Of course, if this were a goofy sitcom, the buffoonish boss would be just truly an idiot and terrible at his job. Of course, in reality, no one could long remain a manager of a company if he was truly bad at his job.

Paul Lieberstein (Toby Flenderson/Writer, Seasons 1–9): To me, it's all a comment on what I've seen at real places. They will make every excuse in the book for someone who's bringing in a lot of money. And the second you stop bringing in money, it doesn't matter if you're the nicest, most PC guy in the world. Sometimes I feel like that's why Toby's there, because there's a guy who brings in lots of money that needs full-time handling. It's one of the big switches we had to make from the British show because David Brent was a character designed to get fired. He had no redeemable qualities.

Lee Eisenberg: We wrote something that we never filmed, though I wish we did. Basically, Jim and Michael are going to take a client golfing. Michael closes the sale on the first hole and then Jim is just terrified that over the course of the next two and a half hours he will ruin it. Michael is one of those guys, if he comes in and makes a few lame jokes you're like, "He's harmless. He's fine." Then he gets the sale and he gets out and he knows the business well enough, but if you sit with Michael too long then you're like, "What is with this guy?"

Jen Celotta: We had a lot of discussions about how quickly to evolve Michael. Sometimes the nonevolved Michael was the funnier Michael and sometimes the more evolved Michael was the one you were rooting for.

Brent Forrester: The writers were intimidated to write Michael scenes. I don't think they were really intimidated writing for any other character. It was fun to write for everybody and fun to write for Steve for sure, super fun. But we never presumed to fully understand Michael Scott on the level that Carell did. When writers would give him material, you never were able to know whether it was good or bad until Carell read it and approved it or did something with it. It was unlike anything I've seen with writers and actors. You frequently would try to under-write Michael Scott's lines. That was better. Don't write too much of a joke in there because Carell is better at finding the joke in the way he's performing it. Often we would just get it a little bit wrong. You would just see Carell's almost disappointment that we had made his character too silly. Of course the temptation is just to write Michael dumb. That was never the wrong way to go with him, I think.

Steve Carell: Michael is hyperaware of the camera crew in his office. Everything he does is influenced by the presence of this documentary crew. When he screws up, you can see the wheels turning as to how to dig himself out of the mess he has created, but that never ends up happening.

Greg Daniels: I like that he's trying his best. He's not trying to be mean-spirited. He's trying to show everyone how cool he is, and when we were auditioning actors for this, it was very hard for me to give notes to the actors to audition, so I set up a little video camera. I decided I would tape myself auditioning for the character. I'm not an actor, but I tried, and I found that the note that I would give myself to get as good an audition as I could possibly get out of it was that I was hoping that the documentary about this would one day be seen by Jennifer Aniston, and I was just trying to impress her any way I possibly could. So that's what I think is part of it. He's in Pennsylvania, but he's hoping that all of America is going to see this and he wants to look as good as he can. It's like when you leave an answering machine message to someone that you're trying to impress and you start to stumble on it and you stumble more and more because you know that it's being recorded, and there's nothing you can do to get it back, and that's what I like about him.

John Krasinski: Loneliness and being misunderstood is probably the deepest fear for a lot of people. I think that's what made it so universal. You could really see yourself in Michael and see yourself if you ever told a joke that didn't go over well or if, you know, you dressed up for a work day or a dance that nobody dressed up [for]. It's just one sort of small nightmare after another with him. I think that's what made it so fun.

Anthony Farrell: The great thing about Steve was that he could say such terrible things as Michael, but his eyes were so empathetic that you would let it go. You put that dialogue and some of the stuff that Michael Scott did into any other actor's voice, it would not play as well because they would not have the vulnerability and the empathy that Steve had when he was playing the character because he just felt for him. A lot of times, when he would mess up, you'd feel like you do when you watch a kid mess up. You're like, "Oh, well, he's just a kid. He's just trying his best. He just doesn't know things." And that's what, I think, what happened a lot with Michael Scott when Steve was playing him, because he just felt like, "Oh, he's doing terrible things, but I just don't know if he knows that they're terrible. He's just a lost little soul." Instead of being angry at him, you feel for him. I think that was Steve Carell's magic superpower.

chapter 14

FILMING *THE OFFICE*

("They perfected the art of shooting us like animals in the wild.")

By the end of the third season, The Office's *camera crew had their unique method of shooting the show down to a science. It came out of the world of reality TV, which became a part of the American network television landscape just a few years before* The Office *came on the air, with shows like* Big Brother *and* Survivor. *Those shows not only influenced the look and feel of* The Office *(i.e., the use of handheld cameras and the cast's talking directly to the camera) but also gave them a talent pool to draw from when looking for a director of photography who would build on Peter Smokler's work in the pilot and create a unique aesthetic destined to be copied by lesser shows for years to come.*

Greg Daniels: I wanted to find someone to DP from reality television, and Ben Silverman had worked with this brilliant guy, Randall Einhorn, who was a camera operator on *Survivor.*

Randall Einhorn: I came from an outdoor adventure background. I was a white-water kayaker and I was filming white-water rafting trips. And then I started filming expeditions and I started *Eco-Challenge*, which is Mark Burnett's precursor to *Survivor.* And then I went on and did the first season of *Survivor.* I had DP'd some horrendous piece-of-shit reality TV for Ben Silverman and I was in Jackson Hole filming extreme sport stuff with

Shaun White and Jeremy Jones, two legendary snowboarders. Ben was in the tent one night watching me filming these guys and he's like, "That's the guy we've gotta hire." He totally sold me to Greg and said, "This is the guy we need to hire to DP this series."

Ben Silverman: I knew we needed somebody who understood reality television.

Randall Einhorn: I met Greg at a Starbucks in Santa Monica. I was forty-five minutes late because I was new to LA. He said, "We'll meet at the Starbucks on Santa Monica." I'm like, "Okay." I didn't realize there was a hundred of them. So I went to two of the wrong ones and I showed up forty-five minutes late and Greg was just, "Nah, it's cool." But I said to him, "The show is a tofu hot dog. It's good food disguised as junk food." In other words, we took something and rewrapped it in a different type of veneer that sells it. And Greg's like, "All right, so, you've got the job." That was all from tofu hot dog.

Greg Daniels: Randall brought in other great operators like Matt Sohn and Sarah Levy, and the three of them DP'd the series between them.

Matt Sohn: Randall and I had worked together as camera operators for years on shows like *Survivor* and knew the dance. And we were brought in to give this sitcom a documentary feel.

Doing that meant throwing away five decades of standard practices for shooting sitcoms and basically starting from scratch. Not only did the laugh track go, but also studio audiences and enormous cameras affixed to dolly tracks. Instead, Einhorn and Sohn strapped Sony HDW-F900R cameras onto their shoulders and shot the show just like they would any episode of Survivor. *This is known as a "single camera" setup even though they actually used two cameras.*

Matt Sohn: On most any kind of scripted show, the camera operator is using a dolly and he has what is known as a "cowboy shot," which is a shot that goes from just above the knees to the top of the head. That operator is going to get a beautiful shot and hold it steady. He also might have a tight shot that is just of the chest and head and it's going to be a beautiful shot too. Whereas for us, we would go from our wide angle to our tightest shot in a matter of seconds just to find those reactions and to keep it moving, which is something you kind of quickly learn and pick up when you're shooting documentaries. You don't have the time to do multiple takes in documentary, you have to get all of your coverage as it's happening in front of you. Shooting it like that helped make it feel even more like the people watching are part of what's going on at that moment.

Randall Einhorn: I work on a show now with ten camera operators. Our camera department in *The Office* was Matt and I and the two guys who put cameras on our shoulders. That was it.

Matt Sohn: Because both Randall and I were on the floor, we would kind of do a zone defense and break the floor up. For example, if I was in the accounting area, he might take Michael's office and we'd work our way around and just get our generic working shots. And if Brian Baumgartner or someone would get up and walk over to give papers to somebody else, it would give us a transition to go from one group to another. Our thing was to kind of follow the bouncing ball and tell a story.

Randall Einhorn: The way that Matt and I shot that show is we just observed it. We just reacted. We didn't premeditate, and if we found ourselves premeditating, we would do stuff that would undermine knowing where we're going. I would always try to get something too late. I would see Jim and Pam about to go in some place and I could have caught them going into that room, but instead, I would just be late or we would put somebody in the way and I'd get there just late and you'd just get a glimpse of them going.

Paul Feig: The genius of Greg Daniels is the fact that he hired the guys that shot *Survivor,* so he hired an actual documentary crew to shoot it, knowing that they knew how to follow the action and when to zoom. Greg's whole thing is he didn't want anybody to be aware of the camera. He'd rather the cameraman not see any rehearsal and just do it.

Kate Flannery: They perfected the art of shooting us like animals in the wild.

Creed Bratton: When you're with guys who've gone down in canoes in Borneo being chased by cannibals, you know you're in good hands. You're not going to get hurt with these guys. They were revered, those two guys, truly. They still are.

John Krasinski: You could see why Randall did *Survivor.* He would appear next to you and you had no idea that he was there.

Greg Daniels: My goal was to direct the camera operators as if they were actors, since they were really in the scene too since it was a documentary. For instance, instead of saying, "Start wide and then pan left and push in," I might say [while shooting "Dinner Party"], "You know that Jan is jealous of Pam so look for evidence of that, and make sure to check in on Dwight's weird date, I think she is doing something with her fork," and then let them decide when it was interesting and appropriate to find the action, using their instincts from covering reality. Sometimes I would tell them to close their eyes and spin around so they didn't know where they were, and then on *action* open their eyes and try to find the scene.

Ken Kwapis: One of the things we did early on was decide that the camera wouldn't necessarily be on the right character at all times. So that if the camera's looking at Dwight, for example, and Pam makes a comment, the camera would quickly pan over to find Pam, but by the time the camera got there her line was finished, and we'd land on her for a deadpan reaction. We'd pan occasionally to find nothing but dead air. At the beginning at least, there were times when we tried to not be in the right place at the right time, to create the illusion that we were catching this by accident.

Greg Daniels: [The camera operator] became a character in the show because Randall had a lot of judgment and leeway about where he was looking. And often that adds a tremendous amount of comedy, choosing to look over here to see what this person thinks and [going] back and forth. He was definitely a hidden character in the show.

Melora Hardin: Randall and Matt became characters in the show. Even though you weren't really seeing their faces, you were feeling their presence. That was a very decided purposeful thing that gave the show that personality.

That personality was also shaped by tiny details few viewers noticed, like where exactly certain characters were placed when they filmed talking-head segments.

Matt Sohn: Jim was the only talking head at the beginning [of the series] that had a view to the outside [through a window] when he filmed his talking heads. All the other talking heads of everybody else in the cast, besides Michael, who did his in his office, you'd see into the bullpen with Stanley behind them. Then when the relationship finally blossomed between Jim and Pam, her talking heads also became out the window. And I think the theory was always that these were people that had more possibility of escape than some of the others.

Paul Feig: Any character who was hopeful and had a future in front of them would have a window behind them. We believed that Pam and Jim had a little more hope in their lives and they would go to more blue skies.

Matt Sohn: It was slight, and I don't know how many people ever noticed it and I don't know if it was anything that anybody ever really talked about, but it was something that we had always kind of kept in the back of our minds.

Getting into the mind of the documentarian that was supposedly filming all the action occupied more of their mental energy.

Randall Einhorn: I thought heavily a lot about what the attitude of the documentarians [was]. What are the documentarians thinking? What are they knowing? And you always had to think in terms of, what are the documentarians witnessing? They cannot be ahead of the action. They have to be slightly behind the action of what the audience is seeing.

Ken Kwapis: When Ryan makes his entrance in the pilot, he's very thrown by the idea there's a camera watching him. I think at first most of the characters are trying to avoid the fact that there's a camera crew there. They just want to get through their day. And then a few people started to become curious, like Jim. He is one of the characters who starts to feel more comfortable glancing at the camera.

John Krasinski: I remember the first time reading the script that I had to look in the camera. That's very stressful, because you don't want to blow it and overdo it. And I always joke that there's a number. My favorite thing was our DP Matt Sohn was like, "So on this scene when you look to Jenna, give me the number four." And I always loved thinking that I had somehow got it down to a catalog of four different looks.

Matt Sohn: It became a thing that you would know a certain Michael Scott line was coming and you would want to throw to John and he would throw you that little look, which was gold. He was truly the only character that truly played to the camera. There were other times that other people kind of tried and failed, but John was the everyday man of the show. He was the one that was saying, "Do you see what I have to deal with every day at work?" And I think it was very relatable for the audience, and it was something that became sort of an iconic thing for the show.

Ken Kwapis: For Michael Scott, obviously, having a camera crew at work is a dream come true. This is preparation meets opportunity. A man who fancies himself a star suddenly has a team of people documenting his every move. So he couldn't be happier. But I think a part of the big story arc of the whole series is just the idea that over time, not only are the characters comfortable with the camera, but they begin to get more acquainted with the actual people operating the cameras.

Jenna Fischer: As an actor, I loved knowing the difference between when we would talk about "does Pam know the camera is on" or "Pam doesn't know" and how there are little differences in how we act.

Matt Sohn: Whenever you have something blocking the frame, it becomes a dirty shot. And the great thing is we not only had those blinds, but we also had the partitions between the desks or just a bookshelf or something. And what's interesting is that with other shows, you might move stuff in front of the camera to find those dirty shots, but we never did. We would make it feel truly authentic, and we would really be where we would have to be jammed on the floor into a corner behind a bush. We had some potted plants that we would get kind of behind and crouch to make it feel even more spy than usual.

Ben Patrick: We'd do this thing where we'd sort of catch someone in a vacant moment just playing with their gum or something and then all of a sudden had camera awareness. It was a great trick and it worked for all those years. It never got tired.

Dean Holland: Because it's a documentary, they're not going to behave the way they really would when there's a camera in their face. So the further the cameras go back, the more real and open they become. We found that any time you wanted to do something heartfelt and emotional or romantic or whatever it was, we were like, "Let's just bring those cameras further back."

J. J. Abrams: There's sort of this passive agreement with the audience that you understand it's meant to be a documentary, but that it's also not literally treated that way when you think about where certain cameras went. You know when the characters would be aware that a camera was there.

It was never really consistent with what a true documentary would be. When I directed, it was never a thing I focused on.

B. J. Novak: I think a lot of people watching never stop to think that it's a documentary. My dad when he watched the British series, it never occurred to him that it was a documentary.

There's also an incredibly widespread misconception that The Office *was largely improvised.*

John Krasinski: People always ask me, "Oh, man, how much of *The Office* is improvised?" and I go, "Ninety percent of the time it was exactly what the writers wrote." Nobody ever believes me.

Andy Buckley: It's 98 percent scripted.

Robert Shafer (Bob Vance, Seasons 2–7 and 9): Every now and then, Steve or John or Rainn would do something different to make each other laugh. People always ask us about how much improv was there, and I'm like, "Uh, zero," because it's network. They had to approve every word in it, so you're not deviating. That's why they're paying twenty writers to sit around. You're not there to revise it, you're there to execute it. I remember I changed up a line one time, and Greg looked at me and said, "Do you mind saying this the way I wrote it?" I'm like, "Absolutely not."

Oscar Nunez: The whole thing was scripted, and then after a couple takes [using the script] if people wanted to improvise, they would. The leads would improvise more than we would, but we would improvise. Some of my lines got in, but for the most part, it's a scripted show.

Amy Ryan (Holly Flax, Seasons 4, 5, and 7): My memory is that we did a few takes where the writer was following you around, like "No, you said 'of' and it's 'and.'" It was very exact. And then after we got those takes in, we would do another pass, and Steve would generally be the first to go off script. And then it was like once he did, others would follow. And I feel like there was just so much respect for him that that was just an unspoken rule.

Tucker Gates: In the first two or three takes we'd do the script, and then we'll start throwing in alternate lines and then we'll start playing, and very quickly we'll be into the tenth or twelfth take, and it will have become something much different than what it started out with. Oftentimes, when it gets into the editing room, it goes back to something more original, but every once in a while you get something that's really great, quite funny, or quite extraordinary in that process.

Matt Sohn: Everybody besides Steve Carell pretty much stuck to their lines. But sometimes we would do a thing called a fun run where we would just let people go and say whatever they wanted. Every once in a while there would be nuggets that came out of that, but I feel like 95 percent of the time the stuff that we got was all truly scripted and it just felt like it was improvised.

Greg Daniels: They start with the lines as written. Then they improvise a version of them. And then they look back at the original lines with a new understanding of them before improvising them and then wind up doing the lines as written, but more naturally.

Kate Flannery: Steve and Rainn probably improvised more than anybody but still it was within the confines of the scene. I always say the writers laid out this beautiful track and if you kept going then it was really like kind of you were led there in a great way.

Jason Kessler: What's amazing about the entire cast is that everybody comes from an improvising background. But how do I phrase this? Just because they come from an improvising background doesn't mean that they brought an improv sensibility to the roles. But what they did bring from that background is that when you're an improviser, you say yes to everything and you're open to every situation. And even though the entire show was scripted, they brought an openness to everything. So to watch them play off of each other was incredible. And that's from Steve Carell all the way down to everybody in the cast.

Mark Proksch: They would write the first part and you always got that down. And after that, you were allowed to just come up with stuff. There was one I came up with on the spot where I give my résumé to Dwight and I tell him I need it back because on the back side it has my mom's chili recipe. That one made it in.

Mindy Kaling: What's interesting is that when people improvise, there's comedy and then there's story. Most often, 100 percent of the time actually, actors will improvise on comedy. But when you have to edit it, [the actor is] not usually like, "The reason I did this was because . . ." You don't have a lot of improvisation on stories. So even when it's hilarious, it's cut out.

Melora Hardin: I'd never seen writers so close to set as they were on *The Office*. They sat in the greenroom literally on the other side of the wall. They would come in and out of the set, and Greg would go in and out of the greenroom. We would all have conversations about how things are working or not working, and what's funny and what's not funny. Sometimes they would go off and just say, "We're gonna rewrite this. Here's some of the beats we need to hit. You need to talk about this, and we need to get to that. Why don't you guys just improvise it and we'll film it, and then we'll go work on it and we'll come back and we'll give you a scene." There was a lot of, I would say, play, and a lot of valuing of the fact that we're actors and we know how to do this and we know how to improvise and we do it well together. It was like, "You're capable of doing some stuff, hit these beats. We're writers, and we're good at that, and we are gonna go and write this. Then we'll put those together and we'll create something."

Creating the illusion that this was a real paper company also meant using minimal makeup and dressing the actors in clothing their characters would likely wear.

Carey Bennett: Hair, makeup, and wardrobe were never allowed on the set, which was something I had to really unlearn. Because we were used to going in and doing little touch-ups and keeping things on track and looking good. They didn't want that. They wanted it to be really real. So we were never allowed to go in there. The actors would get sweaty and they had their own little powder, little mirror and powder in their desk drawers so they could touch themselves up.

Kim Ferry: This is a reality show. It's supposed to be very natural and they didn't want everyone to look like well-groomed actors. They wanted them to look like regular people who might have a pimple or might have a hair misplaced or might have clothes that are kind of crinkly. It was fun to do that. Greg would often say to me, "Make sure you're not making them too pretty."

Lisa Hans-Wolf (Makeup Artist): It was like the cushiest, strangest job that I had ever done. They wanted them to look so very real, and they wanted them to really look like they weren't done or even wearing makeup at all. Sometimes we would send them in with little powder compacts and they'd do it really quick, boom boom boom, because literally we really were not allowed to go in there. I think maybe Greg thought it might ruin the whole vibe.

Jenna Fischer: I liked not having people fuss over me.

Richard Gonzales: When season three came around and the show was a hit, NBC wanted to make sure that Jim and Pam always looked good, so there was a little more touch-up time between setups. So even though it was supposed to be this office documentary and some people weren't supposed to be beautiful, they wanted to make sure that Pam looked great and that nobody was sweating badly.

One thing that caused the actors to sweat was the stress it took to not laugh in the middle of a scene.

Brian Wittle: A lot of times it didn't feel like we were working. It just felt we were all just goofing around.

Kelly Cantley: At one point during season two I was like, "What happened to Greg?" He had been right next to me and then he was gone. It turned out he was under John Krasinski's desk with his face in a couch pillow trying not to wreck the shot because he was laughing so hard.

Randall Einhorn: We laughed a lot every single day and that became a hard thing because the actors would break. I'd try really hard not to break because if I broke, I'm the guy holding the camera and if I'm laughing my ass off they don't have a chance.

Brian Wittle: You just laugh. I did it all the time. I ruined takes multiple times, but everybody does it. There's nothing you can do. I learned to bite my tongue or the inside of my cheek. The only thing that really eventually saved it is we'd just do it enough times that we're desensitized to it so it's not funny anymore.

Ben Patrick: There were times when Steve Carell would have to do something pretty heinous to another character and he'd be like, "I'm so sorry. I'm so sorry." He would always be apologetic before he did it. And at those moments, a lot of times people couldn't keep their faces straight. Some people were famous for breaking. One of them was definitely John Krasinski. The other one was Brian Baumgartner off in accounting. Sometimes you would just hear them dying in the back of the office because something's happening. And then the camera people, Matt and Randall, would pan off of them immediately trying to save the scene.

Ed Helms: Oscar Nunez was legendary because he was unbreakable. He never, ever broke.

Oscar Nunez: That's because I was in the Groundlings for a long time and

I learned how to hold it in. But the person who would break me was Ed. His facial expressions and his character reminded me a lot of Floyd the barber from *The Andy Griffith Show*. He was grounded in reality but so bizarre. He would make these faces and gestures with his hands and his face together. He did, like, a steeple where he'd put his forefingers on his chin and that cracked me up every time. Steve would make Krasinski laugh like shooting fish in a barrel. He would just stare at him and make him laugh, and once Krasinski fell, the dominoes would fall. Angela would laugh and then Jenna would start. . . .

Ed Helms: Me and Krasinski and Angela, we were just like giggle maniacs. If something tickled us, it was over. And we would ruin take after take after take and burn a lot of film.

Oscar Nunez: One time Ellie Kemper peed a little bit. We were in that stupid mobile home driving around ["Work Bus" in season nine]. Krasinski and I did this stupid bit that wasn't even on the show, but she started laughing so hard that she peed. But the person who made everyone laugh the most was Steve. When he did that Santa Claus bit with Brian sitting on his lap ["Secret Santa" from season six], you see Ed Helms in the back, he couldn't even stay in frame. He had to keep walking off the set because he was laughing so hard.

Brian Wittle: The hardest I ever laughed was that Christmas episode where Brian sat on Steve's lap and tells him what he wants for Christmas. Everybody was just dying. Brian is like three hundred pounds and he was sitting on Michael's lap. Michael's struggling and is like, "Just tell me some toys you want!" We had to do that so many times because we couldn't stop laughing. What made it even funnier was that Steve didn't want to do it again because this big fat guy was sitting on his lap. It was like, "Well, we ruined that one. We have to go again. Well, we ruined it yet again. We have to go again." It was just this perpetual hysterics. That's one of my best memories ever from that show.

Randall Einhorn: Steve could always hold it together when everybody else was dying. When we filmed Prison Mike [in "The Convict" from season three] everybody was dying. I was crying. We were all crying and he just had to keep it together and muscle through. When somebody else breaks it's so contagious. And then there were times it was just like, "Let's just take fifteen minutes. Everybody go get a pee and come back because we're not getting anything because it's just too funny."

Creed Bratton: When we shot Prison Mike, I'd go home with the insides of my cheeks bloody because I would chomp on the inside of my jaw and grab that fleshy stuff inside there and hold on to it, because he was killing. People were howling, just howling.

chapter 15

SEASON FOUR

("I would never have gotten them together till the end.")

The fourth season of The Office *was a very stressful time for nearly everyone involved in the production. Not only did the growing movie careers of the leads create endless scheduling headaches, but there was a looming strike by the Writers Guild of America that threatened to take the show off the airwaves for an undetermined period of time. Meanwhile, the writers had to find a way to rip Michael and Jan apart, squeeze as much comedy as possible from the Andy/Dwight/Angela triangle, figure out what would happen to Ryan after he got Jan's former corporate job in New York, and, most important, find a way for Jim and Pam to come together without ruining their chemistry. The season begins with "Fun Run," where the audience learns they've been secretly dating for the past few months.*

Jen Celotta: As a fan of other shows, you know that once romances get consummated, there's a magic that is hard to keep. I was on the side of keeping them apart as long as we can make it believable for these two characters, who we were trying to get inside and understand. What does Pam want to do? What is she lacking? Does she need more confidence? What is Jim doing? Why is he at this job? Once you understand why he's there, why she's there, and once you get those questions answered, then you feel like both of them have gotten to a certain place of growth on their own personal journeys. Then it feels like we're stalling. Once we feel like we're stalling, I feel like as an audience member you feel like you're being cheated.

Jenna Fischer: Traditionally when you have relationships on television, whatever the relationships are, they don't tend to necessarily evolve from the formula that made the show successful in the first place. And I feel like *The Office* took a lot of really great risks in deviating from formula and letting characters do things that might seem contradictory to their sort of archetype, if that makes sense. One of the most obvious examples of that is allowing Jim and Pam to get together, rather than waiting for the end of the series for the ingénue couple to finally realize their love.

John Krasinski: In the writers I trusted. I know Jenna probably did, too. They had done such a good job of keeping us apart that I only assumed they would do a good job in getting us together and keeping it detailed and layered. It was sort of a foregone conclusion that we had to go there at some point. I just remember it feeling really organic to get us together. And if we had gone a little longer, I worried that it was going to get sort of, I don't know, slightly annoying.

Larry Wilmore: You and the audience have both made a pact that this will happen. You just haven't agreed on a time.

Jason Kessler: People were afraid of what happens if you keep them apart for too long and then, also, about what happens if you get them together too soon. And I think we toed the line really well in having them get together at just the right time.

Kate Flannery: It's sort of like *Who's the Boss*. You don't want Angela and Tony to really get together. But I felt like if any show was going to figure it out, it was going to be ours.

Justin Spitzer: Two people longing for each other is such a huge place to get story and scenes. Once we got them together, are people not going to be as interested? Are they not going to have chemistry anymore? Fans always say that they want you to get them together, and writers, we always believe, "No, you think you want them to get together. As soon as they get together, you're not going to be happy anymore." That was that fear.

Lee Eisenberg: All you're doing in keeping them apart is creating all these false obstacles that you know are gonna be surmounted. But we did have huge debates because we worried that when you do bring Jim and Pam together, you're letting the air out of the balloon in some way. But at the same time, in real life, people do get together. No one longs for somebody for ten years. That feels less realistic.

Jenna Fischer: The approach was always that these were real people. The early seasons had this "will they/won't they" tension. But we all ultimately agreed that it was going to start to feel manufactured if you pushed it after a certain point. This was a documentary documenting these people's real, authentic lives. It felt like we had to let them be real people rather than characters, and if these were real people, they would get together at this point. And so we took the leap of faith that we could do that and then it would be okay.

Anthony Farrell: The change from the "will they/won't they" to the "now they're together" situation, I think, was good. I liked them together. When you are writing it, you're asking yourself, "How do you keep the people invested who are just watching it for the Jim and Pam love story? How do you keep them coming back to see more?" The thing that we did was make them teammates. So now it became Jim and Pam versus Dwight, and Jim and Pam helping Michael. It made them like a little duo. I think that worked for most of the episodes.

Justin Spitzer: The question became, "How do we keep it exciting?" And not just exciting but romantic. It's not like romance dies once two people get together instantly, or even once they get married. But the fact that this is a mockumentary within a workplace. When they couldn't be together, their entire relationship had to be at work. That meant it was all in longing glances or flirtation, with subtext. As soon as they're dating they're going home together, then that's where the romance is, right? I don't want to see big romantic gestures at work. I don't want to see them making out at work. It would be like, "No, guys, do that at home on your own time, when we're not watching." Any time you get a couple together it's tricky, but especially in a workplace mockumentary.

Brent Forrester: In truth, I think, my experience was that we basically proved the old adage, which is once the couple gets together there isn't a lot of obvious story material. It is harder to find stories between a couple once they've had the resolution of coming together like that.

Ricky Gervais: I would never have gotten them together till the end. It's nauseating. Two people in love in an office, fucking nauseating.

Season three ends with Ryan getting the corporate job in New York after Jim turns it down. Within seconds of learning the news, he dumps Kelly and an evil grin comes across his face. It was the start of a new, powerful Ryan. When we first see him in season four, he's had the job for the past few months and is reveling in his new role. He also has a closely cropped beard and a designer suit. It's no coincidence that this took place not long after Office *producer Ben Silverman, who had the exact same beard and love for expensive suits, took over for Kevin Reilly as the cochair of NBC Entertainment. The writers only hinted at the parallels back then, but now they're all willing to admit that Ryan's new persona was a way to gently make fun of their boss.*

Brent Forrester: I can't deny it. Silverman definitely influenced the portrayal of Ryan there.

Ben Silverman: It's true. Ryan was moving up and being ambitious. He was like, "I'm going to do it like Silverman." So he grew the scrubble shadow beard and started wearing a tighter suit. I love B. J. and of course he talked to me about it and teased me and I teased him back. Also, Will Arnett did a little of me at *30 Rock* too. [*Tina Fey has admitted that Arnett's character of GE executive Devon Banks, who also had the scrubble beard and enormous corporate power, was modeled after Silverman.*]

Jason Kessler: In both cases, it was a younger person ascending to this powerful position. I don't know if every element of that character was like Ben. I hope not.

Anthony Farrell: We really enjoyed taking the piss out of Ben a little bit because when I met him it was like, "He's the smoothest, coolest, jet-setting-est guy." He was like young Richard Branson. So of course if we have a character like that at our disposal, we're going to take advantage of it.

Lee Eisenberg: B. J. is hilarious in the early episodes because his character doesn't want to be there and he's always put-upon. It's hard to, every day, every episode, have a moment where that guy is just not psyched to be there. Writing for Ryan was hard until he became Ben Silverman, until he became this douchey guy who was pretentious.

It doesn't take long for New York Ryan to become a cocaine addict who defrauds the company and is ultimately arrested.

Anthony Farrell: We wanted to take it even further than Ben had ever gone and just see if we can have this character, who is a young man from this small town but now living in the big city, go through the wringer. It was playtime for a lot of the writers. It was kind of like, "Okay, we're gonna get to do something silly with this guy. Let's take him all the way down." A lot of that was because it was just funny to us to watch him implode because he was such a douche, and also, to give him a reason to crash so we can bring him back.

By this point, NBC's ratings were in a state of absolute free fall. Their big ideas for that season were a remake of The Bionic Woman *(canceled after eight episodes), the time-travel romance saga* Journeyman *(canceled after thirteen episodes), the Brooke Shields–led* Sex and the City *clone* Lipstick Jungle *(canceled after twenty episodes), and the horror anthology series* Fear Itself *(canceled after thirteen episodes.)* ER *was on its last legs and ratings for* The Apprentice *and* My Name Is Earl *were down precipitously.* The Office, *meanwhile, had been growing its audience for three years and was now NBC's biggest sitcom. As a result, the network wanted as much of it as possible and gave a green light for the first four episodes of season four to be an hour each.*

Gene Stupnitsky: I don't think, creatively, doing four one-hour episodes was the right move.

Lee Eisenberg: I think an hour-long episode needs to feel important, feel significant. It began as an experiment in how would an hour-long comedy work. From a writing perspective it's really fucking hard because you kinda want to leave the audience wanting more.

Michael Schur: They couldn't just be one-hour episodes. They had to be episodes that, when they're shown in repeats, can be broken up neatly into two half-hour parts, [and it] was very hard to tell stories that would arc individually over two episodes but would individually work as just one episode.

Justin Spitzer: Those episodes were a bitch. Greg was aware that at some point we would want to divide them into two for syndication. So that meant that with our three-act structure we were doing at the time, act three had to end in a way where it felt like that was a perfectly good, serviceable episode all on its own, and also have a throw forward to the next act. Those four episodes took much more time to break and figure out than eight standard episodes because of that challenge.

One reason NBC was racing to create as much content as possible was because a writers' strike was on the horizon that threatened to shut down all of Hollywood. It began on November 5, 2007, and stopped production on The Office's *fourth season after just twelve episodes were shot.*

Creed Bratton: We all got together and went down and joined the writers with their placards. We got in front of the studio and marched with them and sang "We Shall Overcome" and songs like that. It was solidarity.

Angela Kinsey: It was kind of a really wild time for us in this town. A bunch of our writers would go hit the picket lines and a few of us actors went with them to support because the Writers Guild and the Screen Actors Guild are so interconnected in our contracts. One can often influence the other, so it's in our best interest to all support one another.

Ben Patrick: A big issue for *The Office* in particular during the strike involved streaming rights and streaming royalties for the writers. One of the reasons *The Office* survived the beginning is that it was one of the first shows you could get, other than *Lost,* that you could watch on your iPod, because there wasn't an iPhone at the time. The writers had to put their foot down, because there was a lot of revenue there. I mean, *The Office* must have made NBC so much money. And the writers were not getting their due part. The agents and the managers for the writers hadn't caught up to speed of how to negotiate that stuff, so they went to the labor union.

John Krasinski: My take on the writers' strike was really in support of our comrades. To me, they were the most important part of the show and I wanted them to feel like they were completely and totally supported. It was less about feeling weird whether I was going back to work in a day or a week or whatever, but more just wanting to come back whenever they're happy. I didn't want to put myself or anybody else in a position to be upset. So, I was just waiting for them to feel good about it because, obviously, they were the lifeblood of our show, so I wanted them to get whatever they wanted.

Kim Ferry: Steve was amazing because he said ahead of time, "I will not cross that line. I won't."

Jenna Fischer: It was really crazy. I remember that Steve didn't come to work. There was a script that had been already written and I remember there were certain rules. One was that you can't have writers actively working on a project, but if you have a script you can film it, but you can't have a writer on set to help it along, which is really typical in television. Steve was a member of the WGA and he's also a member of Screen Actors Guild, but as a member of WGA, he wouldn't cross the picket line. And we all really respected him for that.

Justin Spitzer: Actors were still expected to show up and still act, even if the writers weren't there. This could be apocryphal, but I heard that Steve called in sick and said he had come down with "giant balls" because it took balls to sit out on the strike.

Matt Sohn: It was a little depressing. During the actual first days of the strike it was fun because we all went into work and sat around with all of our writers who were protesting at the time. We all just hung out and talked and didn't work because the cast didn't come in. By this time we were all friends with the writers, and everybody was supporting everybody else, but we didn't know how long it would go on. It was always a little nerve-wracking because you never know. We were like, "Is this going to go on long enough that it could potentially kill the show? Is this going to slow down the momentum?"

Gene Stupnitsky: I thought the strike was pretty good actually because our life before that was just totally *The Office,* so we actually had a little bit of time to live. We would picket every morning for a couple hours then [Lee and I] would work on [our movie] *Bad Teacher* in the afternoon. We had nothing else to do. We also went to New York for a while. I imagine it was not as nice for people who weren't making money and had families to support.

Ben Patrick: The day after the writers' strike happened, I went to Costco and bought the ten-chickens-for-ten-dollars deal. My wife got really sick of roast chickens.

Carey Bennett: We were probably relieved to have a little time to breathe. But, in any show, we're all freelancers. So something like that totally can potentially really mess up your life. And you worry that we won't come back at all. There were of course all kinds of rumors going around, like "If we have a long enough break we won't be able to come back." It was nice that we were the family that we were, so everybody was very supportive of each other. I found it to be really sweet actually that the writers did talk to us about why they were doing it, what they were trying to achieve and their hopes that it would trickle down to what we all do.

Justin Spitzer: The first week it was exciting to be a part of that. It felt like it was very much bonding with the staff. But then after that, any writer at the time will tell you it was just a grind, months and months. I wasn't personally nervous financially. I felt terrible for the writers who were. It was just picketing for four hours a day, holding a sign, and a bunch of people with bad backs. Sometimes I think the strike could have gone on even longer if all the leads said to the writers, "Just go take a break. We'll be back." People wouldn't have been as anxious to come back if they didn't have to walk around holding signs.

Kim Ferry: They basically notified us that they are closing production down because of the strike. They were like, "We don't know when it will resume again, but you should consider yourself free to take other work." And then, I will say, much to everyone's appreciation, Greg Daniels wrote out a personal check to every single crew member for, I think it was either $1,000 or $1,200. It was literally just from him and his wife, Susanne. And they said, "We are very sorry about what's happening. We really are looking forward to being together again. This is probably a small amount, but we want to say thank you so much. And we want to try to help if this could pay your rent or bills or . . ." It was incredibly, incredibly generous and kind. He literally paid every single crew member out of his own pocket. Who does that?

Brian Wittle: I think it was $1,000 a person, if I recall. Then I think the cast, I think, pooled their money together and gave each person two grand or something, if I recall.

Kelly Cantley: I think Steve may have had something to do with it too. We all got $2,000. If you talked to anybody else during the writers' strike, nobody else did that.

Angela Kinsey: We were fortunate because we were on a show that we knew had legs and had a following and that the writers' strike would definitely derail our season, but that we probably after the fact would not be out of a job. I had friends that when the writers' strike happened, their shows folded and that was it. It was really devastating for a lot of people. It was a time for us where we weren't able to work, but we were really supportive of our writers, but I think we all knew that our show would be coming back.

Ben Patrick: Some series did not survive it. And I think there were movie projects that did not survive it either. It was brutal. At the same time, as somebody who worked with the writers, and I recorded everything that they wrote, it did seem like, yeah, you've got to stand up for your right. So I supported them as much as I could. I mean, I had no work. But Greg and Steve, they were very generous to the entire crew. They wrote checks that were big enough to make a difference.

The Writers Guild of America strike ended on February 12, 2008. The cast and crew of The Office *immediately went back to work, but they only had enough time to make six additional episodes before the season ended. One major plotline they wanted to continue focusing on was Dwight and Angela's secret relationship, which had been a major element of the show since early in season two when the camera crew caught them making out in Jim's backyard during his house party.*

Rainn Wilson: They both have an obsession for structure and discipline, and I imagine that there was some incident at the copy machine that first brought their eyes together—like someone putting legal-size paper in the letter-size drawer.

Angela Kinsey: Dwight and Angela are that couple that you're like, "WHAT? NO WAY!" and then you start thinking about it and you realize, "Oh my God, it totally makes sense!" because they're both these militant, carry-a-clipboard, aggressive people in the workplace—they take it all so seriously.

Jen Celotta: I loved their relationship and how different it was than Jim and Pam, which was slow burning and unconsummated. Dwight and Angela were not going to wait around very much. They both are go-getters and they're so unusual, and they yet somehow just perfectly fit together. They're both so strong, but they don't want to show their feelings. But then there was a softness every once in a while when they reached out for each other, which I absolutely loved. I really loved that dynamic between the two of them. They both were such strong actors that they pulled off this relationship and made it feel very real.

At the start of season four, Angela breaks off her secret relationship with Dwight after he euthanizes her sick, elderly cat Sprinkles and then lies to her about it. She begins dating Andy even though they have absolutely nothing in common and she can barely stand the sight of him.

Angela Kinsey: What's great about a show that's on for a long time is you can take these characters that we get to know so well, pair them up with another character within the show, and all of a sudden that character opens up a whole other side to a character you thought you knew so well.

Michael Schur: Pam and Jim had finally gotten together and we wanted to replace a little bit of the longing in the show, and so we decided that Dwight and Angela would break up and we'd flesh out Dwight's character a little bit by showing that he was truly in love with Angela and missed her a great deal.

Jen Celotta: I loved the outside threat of Andy. I wrote an episode where Andy and his buddies sang a cappella to Angela over the speakerphone. It was so much fun because there's this kind of earnestness about Andy that is very different than Dwight. I thought that that was an appealing contrast and such a mismatch. You knew that Dwight and Angela were just meant to be, but what was it about Andy that was at all appealing to her?

Angela Kinsey: I felt like Dwight broke Angela's heart and then she revenge-dated Andy, but then also ended up kind of thinking, "Well, maybe he'll do." It's like that moment in life where you settle. Of course, she didn't love him and poor Andy was just one of these people who is lost and is always searching, searching, searching. And so to me it kind of made sense how the two of them ended up in this odd relationship and neither of them were happy, but they were both in it for different reasons. I liked what it sort of showed of my character; she was hurt by Dwight and then she kind of took it out on poor Andy.

Ed Helms: There was definitely something sweet and puppy dog about Andy at that time in the show and that was some of my favorite stuff with the character. He just wears his heart on his sleeve and his pursuit of Angela was so unabashed and just straight from the heart and so passionate and full of big, big, grand gestures. The only heartbreaking part is how blind he was, to the lack of reception from Angela. That was kind of what made it beautifully and comedically tragic. But my favorite story lines for Andy were the ones where he was really passionate about something.

At the same time, Michael and Jan's toxic relationship finally ends after the events in "Dinner Party." Melora Hardin would occasionally appear as Jan in future seasons, but this ended her run as a main member of the cast.

Jen Celotta: When we had Michael together with Jan, he grew past her at a certain point and it was very difficult. There were a lot of discussions in the room of what to do about that because there was so much comedy in his dynamic and his relationship with her. So as a comedy show, you want to mine that for everything you can, but if you're trying to make very real characters, it's sad. It's sad if he has evolved past someone, and to keep him there because it's comic doesn't feel very truthful and doesn't feel very relatable and doesn't feel very real.

Melora Hardin: I remember Greg saying to me, "We have to commit to Jan's unraveling, and that that probably is gonna end your time on the show." I was sad about it, but at the same time, I was moving on. I did think it was really sweet that Greg told me himself as opposed to me finding out some other way. He's such a great guy and he's such a sweet man. But I made peace with it, though I didn't really keep watching after I left. My husband and I specifically had turned our TV off when we started having kids. Fans come up to me and tell me things about the show all the time. I'm always like, "Wow, you've seen way more of *The Office* than I have."

KEY EPISODE 6

"Dinner Party"

The writers' strike kept The Office *off the air for five months in late 2007 and early 2008, but they came back with what's arguably the greatest episode they ever produced: "Dinner Party." There had been a slow buildup to it throughout the season as Michael tries to get Jim and Pam to a dinner party at his condo, but when he finally gets them there in this episode he's unable to hide the sad and outright toxic state of his relationship with Jan. Written by Gene Stupnitsky and Lee Eisenberg and directed by Paul Feig, it's* The Office *at its most brutally cringey and its most hilarious.*

Gene Stupnitsky: We kind of talked about "Dinner Party" as *Who's Afraid of Jan Levinson-Gould?* That was the inspiration for it. And just the world's worst dinner party, the most awkward dinner party—with your boss. We had set it up earlier, where Michael kept asking Jim and Pam for plans, and they kept having excuses.

Lee Eisenberg: We set it up so in the cold open Michael pretends there's an emergency. They're all gonna have to stay late that night, so everyone has to cancel their plans. Michael Scott is always the fool, but in this moment he outsmarts Jim and Pam because he so desperately wants to hang out.

Greg Daniels: In the very beginning, the episode was called "Virginia Woolf" in my notes, and the idea was to have Jim and Pam have this super-uncomfortable night seeing all the awkwardness of Michael and Jan's relationship and watching it melt down in front of them, in a comedy version of the Albee play. From Michael's point of view, he and Jan are the central romantic relationship and Jim and Pam are the funny sidekick couple. There was an early talking head where Michael says: "Things are good with Jan, but not as much fun as when I'm hanging out with everybody at the office. I want Jim and Pam to be in my life. They are my Rubbles or Mertzes. I want Jan and Pam to be friends."

John Krasinski: Because the writers had written such good stuff for "Dinner Party," it was like tons of gunpowder being in one room.

Ed Helms: It's such a crucible for the relationships. It's a tight, contained space where so many relationship issues are bubbling around between Jim and Pam, Andy and Angela, and of course Michael and Jan. That pressure-cooker aspect and the decorum of the dinner party, the sort of need to rise to a different sort of social construct, as opposed to just being coworkers in an office, just kind of heightens everything. It's just a boiling-hot crucible of comedy.

Gene Stupnitsky: The table read started off very slow. Not a lot of laughs. Little by little, it just starts building, and I never experienced that before. The laughs kept getting bigger and bigger and bigger and bigger. I remember I was just sweating through my T-shirt. It was the greatest feeling I've ever had.

Lee Eisenberg: There's nothing more satisfying than having Steve Carell barely able to get through his lines. It's like a live show. You're seeing someone experience it right in front of you for the first time, which is great.

Angela Kinsey: When we read it, we were laughing hysterically, *hysterically.*

John Krasinski: There were definitely episodes where I remember the electricity that went through my body in the form of laughter, "Dinner Party" being one of those episodes for sure.

Mary Wall: One of my favorite parts of my job is that I basically just kept track of the laughter at the table reads. Any time there was a laugh in the room, I put a check mark next to where it happened. The bigger the laugh, the bigger the check mark. During the one for "Dinner Party," the check marks were going off the page.

Ed Helms: Sometimes table reads are quick and easy and sometimes they're a bit of a slog, and that one had just so many laughs already built into it. Gene and Lee just had such a grasp of the voice of the show and of these characters that we knew that, yes, we're onto something special here. This is going to be a blast.

Gene Stupnitsky: Most scripts get rewritten, and I think this was the only one ever done that didn't. The only thing that was changed was that in our first draft Jan hits the neighbor's dog and kills it on purpose.

Lee Eisenberg: We decided that maybe that was going too far.

Greg Daniels: It did better at the table than anyone had expected considering we were pushing the characters hard, and I remember thinking, "Wow, people love these characters so much they are willing to go with them anywhere." The cast really sold the script and protected the characters. Starting with Steve and Melora, they brought so much humanity and depth behind the comedy that you never felt the characters were being laughed at or disrespected.

Lee Eisenberg: We always got notes from the network, and sometimes those could be really contentious, but Greg Daniels always handled them really well and at that point we had a pretty good trust and a good shorthand with the network. So the writers got called in to the office to hear the notes. Greg gets on the phone and the executives are on the other line, on speakerphone. Only the writers have read the scripts so far and this is, you know, before the table read, and they get on the phone, and they go, "This script is really, really dark." And Greg said, "Yeah." And there's a pause and they said, "It's really dark." And Greg said, "Yeah. It is." And they go, "It's really dark." And he goes, "Yup." And then he goes, "Okay, anything else, guys?" And they said, "Uh . . . nope." They hung up and that was it. They didn't offer any other notes.

Greg Daniels: By that time we were the number one comedy on NBC, so we had earned some leeway. I maybe had to use up some chits to protect this episode, but I had a bunch of chits in the bank. I think we did a little to redeem Jan, like she didn't intentionally run over a dog, she spray-painted it, but other than that I was pretty confident it was going to be a great episode. Jan and Michael were never supposed to work out, so I think there is an element of relief and hope that they break up. There are some nice moments, like Dwight taking to Michael at the end, or Jan trying to glue the Dundie back together or Michael trying to take the blame with the police, so it wasn't too dark in my opinion.

Jim and Pam are the first couple to arrive and they get a tour of the house. Andy and Angela come next, followed by an uninvited Dwight and his elderly babysitter Melvina, played by Beth Grant.

Greg Daniels: [The idea was] Jim and Pam would stumble across all these things like the camcorder on the tripod by the bed that would be reveals of what Jan and Michael are like in private. Then we opened it up by including another dysfunctional relationship in Andy and Angela, and after initially thinking the comedy with Dwight would be how upset he was at being excluded, we found a way for him to show up in the most weird couple of all. One of my earliest ideas about Michael's character before the pilot was that he would refer to Target as "Tar-jay," and one of the early ideas about Michael and Jan's relationship was that they were the kind of people who called each other "babe" all the time. We tried to figure what was in character for Michael and Jan, knowing that this was a star-crossed, opposite-of-soul-mate type of thing from the beginning.

Lee Eisenberg: Michael so wants to be friends with Jim and Pam, and the idea of having people over at his house for a dinner party is something I feel like he's dreamt about for years, with having a girlfriend and being proud of her and all that. He still tries to push through in spite of the fact that Jan is clearly on the edge and in spite of the fact that their relationship is crumbling. He's trying to put on this façade. At the beginning of the episode, you kind of know that the relationship isn't great, but then, as you continue to watch it, it's like, "Oh, my God. He's trying to get investors in her candle company. Oh, my God. They hate each other! Her assistant wrote a song about her." That's the peeling-of-the-onion of it.

Beth Grant (Melvina, Seasons 4 and 9): I had just done *No Country for Old Men* and I'd worked with Greg Daniels on *King of the Hill*. When the strike ended, he called me and said, "We want you to play Rainn Wilson's date and former babysitter." I was like, "Oh, my God, from the beet farm?" Needless to say, I said yes very quickly. I heard they improv'd a lot, but when I read the script I was like, "My goodness, they don't need any improv on this. This is just fabulous." It almost read like a [Harold] Pinter play because it was so literary.

The interiors and exteriors were shot at an actual condominium located at 7303 Bonnie Place in Reseda.

Lee Eisenberg: When Paul Feig came aboard, we scouted the location with him and it was this pretty nondescript condo. Paul said, "I want to paint the walls here, I wanna do this and I wanna do that." At the time, we had pretty much just been on the office set, and when we did locations, we were on a location for half a day. You know, at a grocery store or something. We never knew that you could kind of transform a place like that.

Paul Feig: My first episode was "Office Olympics," which, ironically, involved finding Michael's condo. It was fun making it look the way that it would look when he was buying it. And so I always felt very connected to the condo, because we shot a lot of episodes in there. It's around Woodland Hills, where we shot a lot of *Freaks and Geeks*, and so I've already had a really great connection with the Woodland Hills area, just because it looks kind of Midwestern.

Lee Eisenberg: We talked a lot about the decor. There's that kind of Andy Warhol picture of Jan. What does the bedroom look like? You don't want to point to the jokes too much. You try to kind of throw away as much as possible. There are just little touches, like the beer sign in the garage, and Michael having that hand-shaped chair. We talked about this idea that Michael buys a lot of things that he sees late at night on TV, so he has a Bowflex and he has a Soloflex. He has an Ab Roller. He never uses any of them, but his garage is filled with that stuff. We talked about him having a tiny, tiny flat-screen TV that's fourteen inches. That was written in the script. He's very proud of it, because it's a flat-screen.

Paul Feig: It was such a rich story line to play with, production-wise, because of all this stuff. The whole candle business was just so funny to us. It was also the challenge of "How do you get the joke across that the room just absolutely stinks of candles?" Krasinski was so brilliant at conveying just how badly the room smelled. You can't put a big flashing red light on and so it really came down to a ridiculous amount of candles and then John's performance.

John Krasinski: Paul was always and still is one of my favorite collaborators to work with because he just so understood the idea of using us as the tool to help him get wherever he needed. He is such a brilliant director, and one of the things he knows how to do is get the best out of everybody. So he's very nice for saying that, but I'm sure that part of it was him telling me to do that.

Jenna Fischer: We loved any time that we got to go on location, because we spent most of those ten years in [the main *Office* set]. I mean, we were excited every time we filmed in the parking lot. So the fact that we actually went on location was super-duper exciting. It was like the kids got to go to Disneyland.

Ed Helms: It's always fun to kind of go on field trips, especially if it was a little bit of a smaller group. Those locations are always a little more social because you don't have your same comforts to go back to, your trailer and the lot. You just wind up socializing a bit more, and those group scenes are the same way. You wind up just sitting there at the dinner table with all these wonderful people and you're just kind of killing time between setups and shots and making each other laugh. They were fun bonding experiences, in a way.

Melora Hardin: It was a tiny condominium deep in the Valley, and so it really was uncomfortable. You really couldn't get away from anyone. You had your dressing room, but it was, like, a block away, because they couldn't park it right there. It was perfect for the episode, it really was. I kind of used that a lot and used the heat. It was just scalding hot, I remember. I mean, the place was air-conditioned, but it was hot outside. It was just scorching.

Paul Feig: Since the episode all takes place at night, we had to tent the place so that it looked dark outside. So that just adds an extra layer of insulation. You can have air-conditioning hoses running in, but, you know, we do long takes. When we start to shoot a scene, 'cause it's the mockumentary style, we turn on the cameras and then we never turn them off until we finish the scene. So it was a little bit of an ordeal in that way.

Greg Daniels: Yes, I remember that too. The condo is pretty cramped just for four couples, but you have to consider all the crew right behind the cameras and the hot lights. I remember the camera operators getting jammed in the tight halls. Plus we often had air-conditioning ducts running in to cool stuff off, but you couldn't run them during the takes because of sound, and we had long enormous takes with very little breaks between.

Angela Kinsey: It was a very small condo, which I thought was great. It was a very small living room, and we were all sort of wedged in on the sofa together and more people kept arriving. It was definitely a great foundation for this awkward comedy setting. You know? This very awkward dinner party in this very small space.

Paul Feig: To shoot the testimonials, they had to be crammed inside this little bathroom. We just shoved a camera in there that we could barely fit in the room. I was, like, up on the sink and the cameraman was sitting back on this tiny countertop. It just gave it that feeling of there's no escape, like they're just trapped in this place. Also, our director of photography and cameraman had come from *Survivor.* That's the genius of Greg Daniels. We'd set the scene up and then they would just shoot it the way they would shoot a reality show.

Breaking was always an issue when filming The Office, *but they rarely blew as many takes by laughing as they did during this one.*

Jenna Fischer: I couldn't stop laughing when we shot the scene where Jan catches me eating. It was insane. There's a scene where they're giving us a tour of the house, and Steve explains that he sleeps on the little chaise longue at the end of the bed, and we could not get through that scene. Every time he went to explain that that's where he slept, the way he delivered that was so funny, and then he would, like, curl up. . . . We couldn't get through it. The biggest one was when he's showing us his flat-screen television. And it's so tiny. We laughed so hard, like, tears were streaming down our faces.

Melora Hardin: I don't remember that there was anything particularly funny, but we just got on a laughing jaunt, and we literally could not stop. Every time they turned on the camera, either [Fischer] or me would just be absolutely in fits of laughter. It probably took the longest of any of the other scenes, because we had to literally take a break and walk away to stop laughing. And I don't even know what we were laughing about. I think we were hot and exhausted.

Beth Grant: When I first arrive, I'm standing in the doorway holding a cooler. Steve went on this wild riff that just killed me. I was trying so hard not to break. Especially as a guest star, you don't wanna waste everyone's time and money. The dinner scene was one of the hardest things I've ever had to do. I was physically dying inside from holding back laughter. I had to hold a beet on my fork and suck on it. I put everything into that.

Paul Feig: The thing with the bench on the edge of the bed was based partly on an experience I had when I was an intern working for a producer. I became friends with one of the women in the office and I would go kind of hang out with her occasionally. One day she took me to her house. She was living with a guy, and she was showing me around the house, and we look in the bedroom and there's a little cot next to this king-size bed. I was like, "What's that?" and she was like, "Look, you're a single man. You should learn from this. This man I'm with has issues with someone being in his bed." And so basically, after they had sex, she had to roll off onto this cot. I was like, "That's the saddest thing I've ever heard in my life." I can't even remember if it was in the script or not, but we just had that bench and Steve had to roll off onto it. My favorite thing that I've ever contributed in the editing room was as we were editing I said, "Don't cut when he gets on that bench. That has to last as long as it can before everyone [breaks]." And so we stood there with him curled up on that bench way longer than you should. Jan was just like, "See, he fits, he's comfortable." That just destroys me.

Melora Hardin: In the sequence where I sort of dance inappropriately, I purposefully did not do that in rehearsal, just so that John Krasinski could be particularly uncomfortable [when I tried to dance with him]. I waited until we were filming to do that so that he would be completely surprised and have to deal with it on camera, which is why it's such a great, ridiculously uncomfortable moment. And he doesn't get up from his seat. I'm a dancer, but I really tried to just dance a tiny bit off the beat. It was so much fun to just be a little bit wrong.

John Krasinski: That's where the 10 percent of us getting to improv comes into play. The writers were always so supportive of those tiny decisions being up to you. I totally remember that moment. As soon as she started dancing, it was that thing, you could feel the energy in the room, and we were already at maximum, and it just felt ridiculous. It was amazing.

Nothing made them laugh like Steve Carell proudly showing off Michael's tiny plasma-screen television.

Ed Helms: I had never laughed so hard as I did during that scene. I had my little trick: If I was really laughing, I would began to look at Steve's ear. That was my trick. I couldn't make eye contact with him because I would laugh, so I would either look at his chin or his ear or even something behind him and just focus on that, just so that I could get through something and keep a straight face. There was probably plenty of scenes where I'm stiff as a board, not even acting, so to speak, but just trying not to laugh.

John Krasinski: I think that's probably the hardest I've laughed during the entire run of the show, and it's very evident. I was not professional enough in those scenes because I cracked every time one of those jokes happened. One of the funniest things I've witnessed in my life was Steve showing us that flat-screen TV and saying, "When . . . when people are over you can just do this" [pulling the screen out from the wall]. The TV only moved, like, a half an inch. Sometimes Steve would get frustrated when we couldn't keep it together because he didn't think he was as funny as we thought he was and also he's more professional than all of us. But on that one, he couldn't come back. There was something in the room there that was like an untamed animal, and we were just getting demolished by laughter.

Ed Helms: Then there is this little side table that Michael hand-built that looks like it was built by a three-year-old. There are little throwaway jokes, but they say so much and they're so dense. There are just so many beautiful elements like that.

Another great moment comes when Michael reveals that Jan has forced him to undergo three vasectomies because she kept changing her mind about whether or not she wanted children.

Paul Feig: We shot that exchange, like, four or five times, and it was really good but it was super heavy. I remember we were all like, "This is a little . . . this isn't as fun as we wanted it to be." So I went over to Steve and said, "It's awesome, we just need to make it a little more fun." And so that was the take that's in when he said, "Snip-snap, snip-snap, snip-snap." That all came out of Steve being such an amazing actor and going, like, "Okay, I know how to take it and make it Michael craziness." [The cast] were just laughing so hard and going, like, "God, this guy is such a fucking genius."

Melora Hardin: There's that scene when we're all sitting in the living room and I'm telling this story about Michael running through the glass because he heard the ice-cream truck. He said something like, "Well, you know, she put the glass there," and I said, "Yeah, I'm the devil," and I put my fingers on my head like little horns. I just thought of it in that moment. Steve's reaction, he almost cracks up. If you watch him, he's laughing and saying, "Yeah, yeah, you are the devil!" He was sort of simultaneously almost losing it, because it was funny. When we cut, we all burst in laughter. It's just one of those really alive kind of moments, and that kind of stuff happened all the time, where we're just always improvising.

One of the great musical moments in Office *history comes when Jan plays a folk song by her young assistant Hunter where he's clearly singing about losing his virginity to her. Everyone at the party appears horrified when they pick up on this, though Michael looks pretty oblivious. It was written by New Pornographers guitarist Todd Fancey.*

Gene Stupnitsky: We liked the idea that Michael was clueless and it was clear to everyone else that Jan took her ex-assistant's virginity. He wrote it clearly about Jan and how she made him a man, and it was a terrible song. Watching Carell, just kind of looking like there's nothing in his eyes, just kind of bopping his head along slightly. He likes the song. He has no clue.

Lee Eisenberg: I have a different read on the Carell thing, which is I think he does know and he's just hoping against hope that he's wrong. When he's listening to it, on some level he does know that [Jan and Hunter] had something. We couldn't remember exactly how it got to Todd. Basically, we wanted it to sound good. We had some relationships with some musicians, and some other people on the show did, and we sent out the lyrics to a bunch of different people. People we had actually heard of and bands we had heard of took the time to record it, kind of on spec, I think?

Gene Stupnitsky: There were some crazy versions. There were some metal versions.

Todd Fancey (New Pornographers guitarist): I got a call from my friend Alicen Schneider, who was vice president of music creative services for NBC. I was a huge fan of the show, and she said, "Do you want to give this a shot?" I said, "Sure, I'll do it," and the producers sent me the lyrics. I was living in Vancouver. I just went downstairs to my other apartment—I had two at the time—and boom. It came really quick. I wrote it on acoustic guitar. I went into a studio in suburban Vancouver and recorded it. My direction was "Make it sound kind of amateur. He's a struggling musician."

Lee Eisenberg: Todd's version just made us laugh the most. We ended up going with that one.

Todd Fancey: A few months later, after the writers' strike, the New Pornographers were on tour in Houston. I had almost completely forgotten about the song. I got a call on my cell from a production assistant on the show. They were like, "We really liked your version, but we want it to be smoother, more polished. And we need it to be Tuesday." It was a Saturday. I hang up the phone and was like, "Shit. How am I going to do this?" So I booked a studio in Denver with these complete strangers and did a more polished version. I got it in by Tuesday and then they called and said, "We're going to use the original one you sent. This new one is too polished." I got a lump-sum payment, and every quarter I get money wherever it's played.

Most important for the broad picture of the series, the episode marks the end of Michael's relationship with Jan.

Greg Daniels: Once Jan had gotten together with Michael, I always felt like it would play out like some kind of Greek tragedy for her. She was so together and superior to him in the beginning, and this one weakness that got her entangled with him would eventually destroy her and drive her mad. That was the arc for her, and for Michael we were enjoying the comedy while protecting him where we could, like his strong desire to have children and his romantic yearnings, so that one day he could find someone else more appropriate.

chapter 16

THE WRITERS' ROOM

("I've watched grown men cry when they're being rewritten.")

The writers' strike dragged on for months through season four and cut it considerably short, but the cast and crew never even thought about crossing the picket lines. They knew that the writers were the lifeblood of the show and that nobody worked harder than they did. In the beginning, it was just Greg Daniels, Mindy Kaling, Michael Schur, B. J. Novak, and Paul Lieberstein working full-time, with Larry Wilmore and Lester Lewis there three days a week. But as the show grew, so did the team that wrote it. With the hindsight of time, it's clear that The Office *had one of the most talented writers' rooms in the history of the medium, right up there with* Seinfeld, The Dana Carvey Show, Roseanne, In Living Color, Your Show of Shows, Golden Girls, *and the early seasons of* Saturday Night Live *and* The Simpsons. *Overseeing everyone was Greg Daniels.*

Larry Wilmore: When we were pitching ideas, Greg had a system where we'd just write the idea on a three-by-five card and we'd just put it on the board. In no time, we had tons of cards on a bulletin board.

Jen Celotta: It sort of looked like *A Beautiful Mind* in the writers' room. There were note cards everywhere. At first, it was just random cards that were fragments of stories or fragments of jokes. Then it kind of divided into characters and episodes, so there was a little bit more order to the note cards as the seasons went on.

Brent Forrester: It looked like a family of graphomaniacal Unabombers lived in the writers' room, because every single inch of every wall had a three-by-five card with an idea for a story. There was a really big office wall like twenty feet long [that] was entirely covered with cards in categories like "A story," "B story," "C story," "runner," and stuff we called cover stories.

Justin Spitzer: The "cover story" was Greg's concept. That's because you imagine that the cameras don't come to the office every single day. It was especially true early on that we thought the cameras probably come just on big days, like the day of the sexual-harassment seminar or something. So we'd be like, "What is happening in the office that makes it a little different than a normal day?"

Brent Forrester: Pretzel Day was something that you would call a cover story. [The] blood drive was a cover story. It meant an event that a documentary crew showed up for, but it isn't the actual drama of the episode.

Justin Spitzer: As the series went on, we came to just believe that the cameras were just kind of always there.

Aaron Shure: During my tenure [seasons five, six, seven, and eight] we had around fifteen writers, usually three rooms going, and we had inherited the Greg Daniels style of idea generation, which focused on manifesting and externalizing ideas in a physical way, usually in the form of three-by-five cards that came to festoon the walls of the writers' room if they were worthy enough by Paul and Jen's estimation. We also had a process called "blitzing" where the writers would hunker down in their offices for an hour or two and come up with as many ideas as we could on a given topic. For instance, a few blitz topics I have in my notes: "Obstacles to Erin and Andy dating." "Ways Andy and Kelly can try to subvert Gabe."

"What happens with Hay Place?" We'd come back with as many ideas on those topics as we could, read them aloud, and put the promising ones on the wall. Out of those ideas a few would be selected to move closer to a storyboard. It was a big bubble-sort played out on the walls. While writers would campaign for and champion various cards, it was hard for there to be specific ownership of any given idea, with plenty of duplication and accidental repitching. Similarly, stories were broken in rooms with five or so writers all working on the beats. We'd come back to the room and pitch those boards.

Jen Celotta: There's a lot of working in a writers' room that's similar to improv, where it's like "Yes, and . . ." You want to be able to keep your mind incredibly open and think of all the possibilities. Greg actually called it "blue-skying." Let's take an example: "Michael is being broken up with and he's going to handle it like a fourteen-year-old boy because he's at the emotional level of one. What does he do to process it? How does he deal with something like that?" Sometimes there's a tendency to just go for the first good idea, but we would spend a lot of time trying to find the best version of something. We would send people off to think and say, "Let's keep in the blue-sky zone. Don't put restrictions on yourself. How would a person deal with that?" And every once in a while, something just brilliant would come back and out of that because you have five writers thinking of just this point for an hour.

Aaron Shure: I was in a "story-breaking room" that was being run by Jen Celotta, and we had the story beats up on a corkboard, three-act structure, maybe fifty cards. Jen squinted at the board and said, "C'mon, story, show yourself." I really liked the idea of the story being a thing that was out there. It makes it hard to attribute specific ideas to specific writers, which was partially the point.

Jen Celotta: There are seminars and books that you can read about story, and I think that there are certain things that most or all stories have in common. But also I feel like there is a magical element to story that cannot be quantified, can't be explained. There's a part where you're breaking the story, where you know when you have it, and you also very much know when you don't have it. On *The Office,* we were always trying to tell a different story, one that we haven't seen before, or tell a story, maybe, that you've seen a little bit before, but in a different way, and through a different lens, with different characters. It can be incredibly frustrating when you're working on a story and you feel like there's a story there, but you just don't have it yet. And then when you have it, there's just no better feeling.

Justin Spitzer: I remember one moment when we had tons of cards up of different story ideas, different pieces. Greg was just sitting there. It's that part of the season where he's burned out. He's staring at all the ideas and he's like, "We don't have enough ideas. We need good cards. We need *good* ideas." Then almost in the same thought he's looking at all the cards and he's like, "There's just too many. There's too many ideas here. There's too many cards. We have too many cards." We're like, "You're saying opposite things." He'd go, "We need fewer bad cards. We just need more good ones." Then he came up with this idea that maybe he needed to try to see things three-dimensionally, so he started taking Dixie cups, poking holes in them with pencils, and taping cards to them so that he could create depth in how he was organizing the cards. Some of them were just off the wall, made no sense, but it was entertaining because you knew in the end he was going to find it.

Owen Ellickson: Greg not only was interested in what we would put on TV, but interested in the process by which we would put it on TV. It seemed like sometimes he would make a point of running the room in a different way to see how it worked. One night he printed out a script and put each page out horizontally aligned in the hallway, and then we had to sort of go down crawling and read the script, as though somehow reading it in that fashion might generate new insights or something like that. He liked splitting the room in surprising ways, like sometimes he'd just send two people off on their own. It felt very experimental in a way that I found exciting. He created a lot of the formative comedy in my lifetime, so I was definitely excited to undergo whatever experiments he wanted to do. Would I have been willing to do that for multiple years on end? I don't know, but I enjoyed it immensely.

Halsted Sullivan: Greg always talked about "stuffing the sausage," as opposed to, "Let's all build to one big joke." A show like *Frasier* would build a huge set piece at the end. We would have jokes all along the way.

Jen Celotta: We'd try to "stuff the sausage," and if we are throwing out great things, that is a good position to be in. We were like, "We don't want to just kind of get by with the bare minimum. We want to try to find a lot of fantastic things and put them in." What would end up happening is that our scripts would be long and we would shoot long episodes and our editing process would be way more involved because we stuffed the sausage. It required more patience in the process of editing because we would have to take out great things. We'd have to decide, "Do we pull out a little bit of every scene, because we can't possibly make the final cut? Do we take out a little bit from every scene, or do we have to pull full stories out?" That could be really challenging, but it ended up, I believe more times than not, having great stuff air because we spent a lot of time stuffing the sausage.

The process of creating the final script changed very little throughout the entire run of the series.

Jason Kessler: Over the years, I've come up with a pretty good way to describe it. Think of it like an hourglass. All of the writers start at the bottom of the hourglass, where everybody is just pitching ideas. "Wouldn't it be funny if this happened? Wouldn't it be funny if this happened? What if there was a story where Jim did this?" As that progresses, as Greg and the co-eps decide, "Okay, this is a story we want to focus on," you narrow the hourglass a little bit. You start focusing on that story, you pitch specific jokes, specific beats of that story. Everybody has a say in that. And then one writer is then assigned that story, and they take all the notes that the writers' assistant has compiled, which could be pages and pages. Sometimes I'd send fifteen, twenty pages home with somebody. And they'd cull through everybody's joke pitches and create a first draft. So that's the middle of the hourglass, which is one writer. And then, as soon as that first draft is done, they submit it to Greg and then everybody gets to read it, and then it opens back up again as the entire group rewrites it.

Caroline Williams: Greg would assign episodes to writers for various reasons. Sometimes it was your turn. Sometimes it was an episode that you thought of. Sometimes it was an episode that he thought you would do well with. Generally, it seems to me that it did go in order of who was up next. But somebody would be chosen as the writer. They would go off—meaning go home for two to three days—[and] write an outline based on the bullet points on the board. And sometimes that would include joke pitches. You would take the writers' room notes with you. You would bring the outline doc to Greg. He would go through it. If it didn't work, he would bring it back to the room and say, "What can we do to fix this?"

Jen Celotta: There's story everywhere, it's just about finding it. When you're a newer writer it is all about getting out of your own way in order for it to be there. If you've set it up, and you have interesting characters, and interesting situations, you will find the story.

Caroline Williams: Then the writer would take all this and have about a week to write a draft that would be presented to all the writers. That would be a very stressful day when it was your episode because it would be e-mailed to all the writers. You would come in that day knowing everyone was reading your script at the same time. And if nobody was laughing, you were fucked, because you wanted to hear laughter in the offices, knowing they were reading your script. That was a very stressful hour. You would just sit in your office, shaking, hoping somebody would come by and be like, "Good job." And then sometimes they did and sometimes they didn't. Sometimes it was just a great script, and the writer had nailed it. And sometimes it wasn't the writer's fault that it didn't work. That's when everyone would gather around and they'd talk about what worked, what didn't. Sometimes the writer would get another pass to go back in, and sometimes they would just stick it into the computer and everyone would sit around while they went line by line through your script.

Anthony Farrell: When a script came in the writers' room, we'd tear it apart like a bunch of wild animals, basically. Writing is a competition in some ways. Everyone wants a part of them in the script, so you're always trying to think of a way to one-up a thing that's already in there. There were no slouches on that show, so everyone always had great first drafts. But we'd get to the room and we'd just start hammering it like a bunch of blacksmiths, just pounding at it. That's the process because that's how a show gets stronger.

Peter Ocko (Writer, Season 7): We would go through the script and basically you would try and beat the lines that existed. But instead of working on it in the room, at least when I was there, you would take stuff away. You'd go back to your office and come up with several versions of the same line and then come back. And then Paul, or whoever was running the room at the time, would go through and pick the ones that worked. And it was very much survival of the fittest in that sense. And it felt way more competitive in the moment than rooms that I had been in previously. And to good end, it worked.

Jen Celotta: I've watched grown men cry when they're being rewritten. You just learn that it's not a personal thing.

Lee Eisenberg: In season five, Gene and I wrote a draft that we were really happy with of "New Boss." And for whatever reason it got dismantled a week before the table reading, and not to our liking. I remember the table reading didn't go well. There's nothing worse than when you felt like your work was good and it got rewritten, probably made worse. I remember after the table read I was seething. I was so angry that I was like, "I think I might just walk out and then I'll never come back to the show." Greg came up to us and was like, "What do you guys think?" And I said, "I think we should go back to the first draft. I don't know why we're here. I don't know how we got here." I was furious. We had spent all this time rewriting the script and now we had to rewrite the script again. The next day, Jen and Paul brought us a cake with our names intentionally spelled wrong to defuse the tension. It was their version of an apology. They were like, "Not saying you guys were right and we were wrong," but I think they were acknowledging that they could have handled it better. It defused the tension of a shitty rewrite. There's nothing worse than being at work until midnight and then it not working.

Anthony Farrell: One of my old teachers used to say, "Writing is rewriting," and I didn't really get that until I started working regularly on TV and I was like, "Oh, okay, yep. This is it. This is the gig. Writing is rewriting."

Lee Eisenberg: You would learn in a writers' room that if you pitch something and it's not funny people don't explain to you why it's not funny or why it's not going to work. You're just met with silence. It was like, "Do you want us to say it again? Are you thinking?"

Gene Stupnitsky: That's what would happen. I would pitch something. No one responds and I'd be like, "Oh, they didn't hear me." I would say it again louder. It would just make it worse.

Lee Eisenberg: This was not a casual room where people were punching a time clock. Every single person—and this is a credit to Greg in terms of staffing—every person on that show felt a major sense of ownership of the show for a lot of reasons. You were editing your own episodes. You were getting to help cast it. You're on set. Greg would ultimately cut what he didn't like, but I felt, very very early on, from Greg's perspective, that it was a meritocracy and the best idea won.

Halsted Sullivan: One of the best things I learned from Greg Daniels is that when an episode isn't working, you go back to four things: What are the stakes of the episode? Is there escalation, meaning are we going from a small organic place to a huge funny place? What is the consequence of what these characters are doing? And then there's motivation. Are the characters acting in a motivated way? There were a lot of times where you would write a story where you're like, "Oh, it would be funny if this happens." But then you'd be like, "Well, Dwight would never do that." So then it's like, "Okay, maybe it's not a Dwight story. Maybe it's a Phyllis story." At no point were characters ever interchangeable. Only certain characters could react in certain ways. And that is how we built the story and that is why the ensemble worked so well. It may have been a seventeen-headed beast, but it was one beast and it moved in unison. You were never like, "Oh, this is so disjointed." There were never factions in the office. There might have been cliques like Ryan and Kelly, but they were still a part of the whole. They weren't off on their own.

But there were far more ideas pitched than ever had a chance to make it to the air.

Caroline Williams: Did Michael ever have clear braces? No? That was on a card. It was just, "Michael has clear braces."

Justin Spitzer: There was one whole episode in season one that Greg wrote that they never shot. We always would talk about it as our "break the glass episode" that we'd do if we ever were totally in trouble. It was called "Pet Day," where everyone took their pets to the office. I can't remember much about it, but it was funny. I think Michael had a parrot named Jim Carrey. There was a moment at some point in the run where we realized, "Okay, the characters and their situations have changed so much now that we can never, ever do 'Pet Day.' The show has changed too much now. It wouldn't play." There were a few seasons where we were like, "There's always 'Pet Day'!" whenever we'd get into trouble.

Halsted Sullivan: We talked about maybe there's another company that moves into the building. They had done [the meeting of the office park leaders] the five families [in the fourth-season episode "Chair Model"] before, but it was like, "What if there's a rebel in the building?" We had tried to break what it could be. Is it like a high-end stationery company or something like that? But it just didn't really gain that much traction.

Warren Lieberstein: We thought of one called "Premonition." It was really an interesting story about someone having a dream that someone died on the way home from work and no one wanted to leave the office because they started to believe that it was going to come true. So everyone kind of stayed late, but we never figured it out.

Jen Celotta: I wanted to do an episode where it started at the beginning of the lunch break and everybody just went off and we followed everyone, what they did for lunch. It would almost be a real-time episode. I wanted to see them outside—I mean, we do see them outside of the office, going on a job-related mission, or at a party, but I wanted to see the reality of the everyday lunch.

Aaron Shure: I had a crazy pitch that never got in but I kept pitching. It was that Michael Scott gets accidentally crucified. I had a whole thing where he was playing basketball at his house with Jim and the garage door opens up in such a way that his shirt gets caught in it and he gets pulled up by the garage door, underneath the basketball hoop, which is like the crown of thorns. And no one notices and they leave him there overnight, so he comes into work feeling Christlike because he spent the night kind of, somewhat crucified. But obviously no one ever took that one on.

Jen Celotta: Another one that I was a little bit passionate about in an annoying way, because I kept pushing it, was Phyllis goes through menopause. I really wanted to tell that story. I remember thinking that Phyllis made it so cold in the office that it led to thermostat debates that every office has. And maybe Angela actually freezes at her desk for a tiny bit.

Maybe that was a little bit broad. Oh, and I was always fascinated with the idea of Michael coming down with ennui. Some stories are hard to tell, but you take a main character and he's in a funk and he didn't understand what it is and he couldn't point to the thing causing it. He's just very lackadaisical and just kind of blah. I imagined the office having to deal with a blah Michael and getting everybody else involved in putting a focus on why he felt kind of blah that day. Then maybe it would get into a philosophical area of, what's the point of all this?

Owen Ellickson: I wrote an episode called "Here Comes Treble" about Andy's old a cappella group and [Stephen] Colbert ended up playing his friend Broccoli Rob. Early on, Carrie Kemper and a couple other writers and I were talking about Andy's old buddies coming back and him sort of bragging and peacocking around all smirky with his guys again. Then they mention that one guy who was in the group died when they were in school, and it becomes clear to Andy that he and his friends killed that guy, but Andy was so drunk that he didn't remember it. Basically, Andy unwittingly had been part of sort of a murder silence pact. I always wanted to find something that Michael didn't do, and that certainly fit the bill for me. [*"Here Comes Treble" aired in season nine, minus the murder-pact subplot.*]

The writers also took many incidents out of their real lives and put them into the scripts.

Lee Eisenberg: The writers were incredibly stressed [even by season three] as they're watching their portfolios shrink to nothing and so therefore everything was being called from your life experiences. It's like, you go on a bad date, you go in to work the next day and you write about it. Call of Duty was something that we started playing in the writers' room and then it was like, "What if the people in Stamford start playing Call of Duty?"

Halsted Sullivan: They needed a Dwight story at one point. Growing up I just remember that at Christmas there's always a toy that everyone wants, like Cabbage Patch Kids. Then there's a run on the toy and they become very expensive when people start hoarding them. So that was the genesis of the Princess Unicorn story in "Moroccan Christmas." And since I'm African, I always remember that whenever I wanted a doll, I'd always get the African American version, which turned out to be the punch line for that as well.

Jen Celotta: My parents had a Honda Odyssey minivan. One day I was in the backseat looking at the GPS manual. I opened the first page and it said, "No matter what your GPS tells you to do, don't drive into a body of water." I'm like, "Who the fuck would drive into a body of water?" And then I was like, "Michael Scott would drive into a body of water!" So then I looked up who does this and I found all these articles all over the place, including a town in England where there was a bridge, but now the bridge is gone and the local people charge forty pounds to get your car out of the water because so many people listen to their GPS.

Halsted Sullivan: Warren [Lieberstein] and I, before *The Office,* we were going to an important meeting with an executive. We walked in this building, which is basically like a converted bank.

Warren Lieberstein: It was a fancy office building with a marble floor and the reception is across the lobby. And it was one of those open atrium buildings where everyone can come out of their office and look down into the lobby.

Halsted Sullivan: Warren is chewing some gum and I'm walking straight ahead to the receptionist. He goes off to the right to throw his gum into a trash can.

Warren Lieberstein: It's a sunny day out and when I first get into the office my eyes were having trouble adjusting so I couldn't even really see, but I'm looking for a wastepaper basket. I throw my gum out and I turn. What I don't see is how close I am at that moment to a koi pond. I do not see it at all, and I turn, and when I turn my back foot I think it's going to land on ground, but it doesn't and I start falling backward. And the scary thing for me is that I don't know how far I'm falling at that point. In that moment I don't know if I'm falling to my death. So I'm like, "Ahhhhh!"

Halsted Sullivan: And as I'm announcing ourselves for the meeting, suddenly I hear a huge splash and like, "Oh my God! Oh my God!" And I turn around, and Warren has fallen into a koi pond, like Nestea Plunge fallen into it, not just like up to his ankles. He fell backward into it.

Warren Lieberstein: I'm absolutely 100 percent drenched. It's not just my legs. I Nestea Plunged into this koi pond. And I've got to say, as embarrassed as I was in that instant, I was like, "I'm not dead." But then I was like, "Oh, but is there a shark in here? What the fuck is happening?"

Halsted Sullivan: They had removed all of the koi for cleaning. The koi pond had the same marble as the floor, so it just looked like the floor at first glance.

Warren Lieberstein: We're there for a meeting and I'm drenched. And I'm like, "Oh my God." And Halsted is like, "Warren! Warren!" He had a very high pitch to his voice and I'm like, "Oh my God!" I'm sopping wet on this marble floor.

Halsted Sullivan: I was like, "Oh my gosh! My fortunes are tied to this person."

Warren Lieberstein: The first person to come over and try and help is someone with a tissue. I'm like, "You need like seven beach towels to clean this." Then everyone of course hears the commotion and all of a sudden people start popping out of their offices and looking down. I'm as embarrassed as you can possibly be in that moment, as well as weirdly thankful that I'm alive. But also like, "What am I going to do now? Do we cancel the meeting?" And I was like, "Yes, definitely." And Halsted's like, "No, definitely not. We're keeping this meeting." And I'm like, "Really?" He's like, "Yes," and I'm like, "Okay, well I need a change of clothes then." So I walk down to this athletic shop just a short little walk away. I walk in there and I remember there were two salesladies and they just look at me. And they were like, "Oh man, this guy. What happened to you? You pathetic schmuck." And I was like, "I just need a tracksuit please." I walk into the meeting and I just look ridiculous. I look like Vanilla Ice or something. Everybody at the meeting got a big kick out of this. Even our agents texted me afterward and said, "I heard you made a big splash at the meeting." It was all very punny after that.

Halsted Sullivan: So, lo and behold, it just became this really funny story that we told a lot. And then it's like, "Okay, what if Michael falls in the koi pond?"

Warren Lieberstein: We were able to turn it into an episode of *The Office*. I remember when we were shooting Steve Carell didn't get it on the first take and he had to do it again. As he was drying off I was with him and he was like, "Is this even believable? Can anyone possibly believe that I fall into a koi pond?" And Paul was there and he was like, "It happened to Warren." And I was right there. I was like, "Yeah, happened in a meeting. So sorry. That's why you're falling in a koi pond." Steve's very sweet. He's very kind. But I could tell in that moment he did not want to fall in a koi pond for a second time. He was like, "You! You're who I have to thank for this!" But that's a classic case of how life can become art.

Jason Kessler: Remember when Jim puts Andy's cell phone in the ceiling and calls it all day? That's a prank that I did when I was a personal assistant to Angie Hamilton, the associate producer that had hired me. We were out in trailers outside of the office in that first studio we were in and one day I just took her phone and hid it in the ceiling and I kept on calling it. She did not punch a hole through the wall like Andy. That luckily came just with the script. But when we were pitching on what would make Andy crazy, I told everybody the story of putting the cell phone into the ceiling and it made it into the episode.

Halsted Sullivan: My sister will hate me for telling this story, but she called me from New York one time and was like, "I just won this seventeen-thousand-dollar Italian sofa." I'm like, "That's amazing." But then she's like, "In this contract, it looks like they want me to pay for it." I'm like, "Well, send me the contract." And I look at the contract. I had gone to law school and it wasn't that hard to decipher. Basically, she thought the silent auction was to guess the price. So, she guessed the price of the sofa. So, they had this contract where it's like, "Okay. Now sign it and then you're gonna owe $17,000." I'm like, "No. You absolutely are not gonna sign this. You will be buying the sofa, it is not guess the price." So, that became a Dwight episode ["Fundraiser" from season eight].

Mindy Kaling: Greg used to do this thing where he'd get hot in the writers' room and he'd try to take off his outer layer, his fleece, and he'd do this thing where he'd [accidentally] pull off all of his layers and you'd see his naked torso for a moment and we'd be like, "Oh, this is so weird." Later, with Michael and Pam, when he accidentally said come into [his] office, [she] saw his penis, in "Fun Run." So we'll take an event that is just mildly awkward and exaggerate it into something that is truly horrifying.

Aaron Shure: When I was writing for *New Adventures of Old Christine* and there was a speed radar gun out front of our offices, I ended up running past it once and then got the rest of the writing staff to run with me to see how fast we could run. It was surprisingly fast. For a sprint everyone can be like Usain Bolt for a few feet. We ended up using it in a cold open.

Melora Hardin: Greg and [his wife] Susanne had me and my husband over for a brunch along with Steve and Nancy Carell and their two kids one time. My daughter, Piper, was just a few months old at the time. We all sat down at the table and she was hungry, so I just pulled my shirt down and breastfed her because I was very committed to this idea that I don't really like putting a thing over my baby's head when they're breastfeeding. I also feel like we live in a country where people can have a gun rack in the back of their car, but you can't breastfeed your baby in public when that's what your boobs are for. But Greg and Steve got all nerdy and were like, "Oh, oh, oh, okay . . . so that's happening." I said to them, "I believe that I should breastfeed whenever my baby's hungry and that's what I do. If it makes people uncomfortable, then they can leave." I think the discomfort of that moment for them and maybe watching Steve squirm inspired the scene where Jan comes in and breastfeeds the baby in the office and they pixelate out my boob and the nipple.

Halsted Sullivan: When Jim and Pam are interviewing for day care they walk in on the guy sitting on the toilet, that was basically my interview in high school when I went to Williams. I was waiting for the interview and was like, "You know, I should go to the bathroom before this." And then I walk in and this guy is sitting in the stall and I'm like, "Oh my gosh! Sorry." Close the door. And then, lo and behold, that's the guy who's interviewing me. And as a high school student, that was the most mortifying thing of my life. And I did not even fill out the application to go to Williams because I was like, "Well, that's the end of that."

Larry Wilmore: "That's what she said" began as a joke in the writers' room. We could not stop saying that. I think it was a whole year where we did that joke to ourselves. It was so *hilariously* funny that we'd be crying laughing. We were like teenagers doing this joke. And even when we stopped saying it in the writers', we still couldn't stop doing the joke, even though we were sick of it. We still couldn't stop using it. It was so ridiculous. I was always impressed by how fast Jen [Celotta] was with a "That's what she said." I think her father was a physicist or something and she comes from this genius-level family. Her brain was so fast. I'd be like, "Damn it! Jen got that one so fast!" People would break you down in the middle of a pitch with "That's what she said, that's what she said!" The attention to language was so intense that you could not get an entire sentence out without at least three "That's what she said"s, and they were completely accurate and funny. They absolutely made sense too.

Caroline Williams: It was a typical writers' room, meaning people use coarse language and humor tends to go blue pretty quickly. And Jen Celotta had this sort of angelic persona where she was so positive and smiley that when she would go blue, it would seem incredibly incongruous and therefore very funny. The fact that she would be the one making a dick joke just made it so much more funny. And then "That's what she said" took on a life of its own on the show. I don't know even how that happened.

Jen Celotta: I made a lot of "That's what she said" jokes, and some of them would get in the script, but it got to the point where Greg said to me, "All right, can you be slightly more selective in your 'That's what she said's?" Greg since then has mentioned that he thinks there was a separate part of my brain always constantly on the hunt for "That's what she said"s. I wish I could use that part of my brain for curing cancer or something. All that said, I don't think it was me that first brought back "That's what she said." I think it was B. J.

Aaron Shure: We would shoot in our own offices, so a lot of what we would go through ended up in the script. All those dynamics on the show were present in the writing staff. There was ageism and romance since there was a little bit of romance in the writers' room. And then there's the question of, "Does competence win out or does self-promoting work better?" All those issues, we were living it like any group of people would and then they wound up on the screen. There was also the issue "Who is running the company?" With us, it was first Greg running it and then Paul and Jen were running it. So all these things, we would feel them and then we would write them.

Nearly every writer admits that they always kept an eye on the fan website OfficeTally's episode recaps and the fan comments section.

Halsted Sullivan: These were truly die-hard fans and they made us know what is not working. Sometimes it was like, "Oh, it's making them uncomfortable? Then that's exactly what we wanna do as well." It's also just great to see what played. And often, your most well-crafted joke doesn't get a mention. But then a throwaway line that you didn't think about as you were writing becomes huge because of the way the actor delivered it. The reaction, just the time and place in which it happens, became a huge moment.

Mary Wall: Everyone on that show went on OfficeTally. It was the pulse of what the people who were fans of the show were feeling about it. I also think that Jennie Tan had just a great way of moderating it. She was really down-to-earth about it but still a fan. There are times now if you go on Twitter, things can get crazy opinionated. But I think she did a really good job of moderating so that it was really informative to the people who worked on the show.

Brent Forrester: I never really got into any of that stuff, but the other writers were always reading that site and the show, in part, became more Jim-and-Pam heavy because of the comments they were reading. I think it was Greg who said that it took him a while to realize that the kind of person who is online writing comments is most likely a lonely, love-struck, heartbroken person, so that the demographic was really skewed. It wasn't really an accurate representation of viewers in general.

Gene Stupnitsky: All of the writers were obsessed with OfficeTally. We'd still be at work when the episodes would air on the East Coast, so we'd go onto OfficeTally and we would go on to look at the comments, all just wanting approval.

Lee Eisenberg: It was also the first time you'd have instant feedback. It was really exciting. You would constantly be refreshing it and you would see how it rated versus other episodes.

Gene Stupnitsky: Those people had so much influence over us.

Lee Eisenberg: There were probably only about four hundred people on OfficeTally, but they did wield so much power. They'd say something like, "Dwight is so broad!" We'd be like, "He is broad!" and try to address it.

As on almost every sitcom of the era, the writers' room was often overwhelmingly white and male.

Anthony Farrell: I was the only black guy there in season four, and then Halsted Sullivan, who was a cowriter with Warren Lieberstein, was there for most of season five. I knew I was a diversity hire, but I didn't feel out of place because of race in that writers' room at all. If I felt out of place, it was mostly because I came from a single-parent house in Toronto and grew up working as much as I could because I didn't have any money. So I felt out of place because I didn't go to Harvard and I didn't go to any fancy schools.

Halsted Sullivan: There were a lot of *Harvard Lampoon* writers. I went to Harvard Law School, but I don't consider myself "Harvard" because I went to the University of Virginia undergrad and I have much more affinity to that. It's clear that I was not a Harvard guy when it came to the *Lampoon* guys. It was never like, "Oh, let's hire another white guy." I just think a lot of people stayed. We would add one person at a time. And it just sort of naturally became a very male *Harvard Lampoon*–type room. But the same is true for *SNL* or *The Simpsons*. And that's where Greg had come from.

Anthony Farrell: My first day meeting the cast when they introduced the new writers, Craig Robinson came to me. He was like, "So, they brought you in to write for me?" And I was like, "I don't . . ." I was taken aback by it and was like, "No, no, I'm writing for everybody." But it's the kind of thing that you think about 'cause you're kind of like, "Oh, maybe they just needed a black voice in the room to back up whatever they want us to do with Craig," 'cause I know they had Larry Wilmore for a little bit, season one. But Ryan [Koh] was Asian. Mindy was Asian. There was always like a healthy mix. For me, I do feel like whenever I am putting together rooms, I think it's important to have a fifty-fifty male/female mix just because I feel like that was something that I'm sure *The Office* could have used a lot more of just because it's good to have that diversity, just because you just can't put words into someone's mouth without knowing where they're coming from, and I feel like having a room that has more diversity will get you better stories.

Claire Scanlon (Editor): One thing I took issue with [about] the writers' room early on was that there were no women aside from Jen Celotta and Mindy Kaling. You've got like fourteen writers and only two of them are women and one of them's a cast member, so she's oftentimes acting, so where's your women in your room? So in season eight, Paul [Lieberstein] was excellent about really looking for women and bringing them in. So Carrie Kemper, Amelie Gillette, and Allison Silverman came in. And then season nine, Niki Schwartz-Wright came in. That was great. And that is squarely on Paul's shoulders, for bringing more women into the room.

Jen Celotta: Before I joined *The Office*, I was often the only woman in the writers' room. Mindy Kaling was the only woman for the first season, and then I joined second season, and because the room was so small I was like, "Hey, cool, there's another woman!"

Larry Wilmore: Mindy Kaling was an Asian-American woman in the writers' room and she was a major voice on the show. That was a breakthrough.

Claire Scanlon: It's not that showrunners are not trying to hire women. It's that showrunners are writers and they're weirdos. They just like the people that they know, so it gets incestuous. Look, Justin Spitzer and I worked together on *The Office* and he's [producing] *Superstore* now, so he knows me, so I'm good people. It's the same thing with Danny Chun and *Speechless*. It's not like, "Oh, I don't wanna hire that woman who's just getting started." It's more like, "Oh, I know Claire, let's go with the devil I know." It's not some master plan of keeping women out of directing or out of the writers' room. It's just like, "Oh, I need to make more friends that are women and feel comfortable working with those people in a work environment." And if you look back when Greg was starting, if you were coming from Harvard, odds are the landscape was mostly men. And the fact that Greg hired Mindy Kaling was pretty special. I don't think there were many other Indian-American women in the writers' room and on-screen. I would argue she was one of the first.

The writers from The Office *have gone on to run shows themselves all over Hollywood. Nearly every one of them looks back at the experience with incredible joy and nostalgia.*

Jason Kessler: I feel like I got to go to the best comedy-writing grad school in the world.

Jen Celotta: At the time, I knew it was unusual because I'd been in other rooms, and I'd been in other great rooms. But looking back on it now, I see even more how unusual it was to have so many talented people in one room. I credit that to Greg. I heard that he read two hundred or three hundred scripts to find that original group of people.

Justin Spitzer: It was amazingly intimidating to be in that writers' room. I was a young writer and all of a sudden I'm stuck in this room on my literal favorite show. It felt like *Laughter on the 23rd Floor* [Neil Simon's play about a writers' room stacked with amazing talents]. Everyone was so talented and so insanely funny. I was thinking every day, "How do I not fuck this up? I'm never going to have an opportunity like this again, surrounded by these people."

Caroline Williams: To learn among these geniuses was really exciting and intimidating. I look back on myself in that situation and I cringe. I cringe at what I said. I cringe at what I wore. I cringe at what I did wrong.

I cringe at what I pitched. I remember one day I came in wearing these Adidas track sweats and Mike Schur was going through what we had to do that day. He turned to me, and he was like, "So, Caroline, what was it like at Eight Mile last night?" You could not get away with anything, and yet it was always so smart that you had to give it credit. But as a newbie, it was terrifying and incredibly instructive. It was also just so funny.

chapter 17

GREG

("My image of him is of the absentminded professor.")

Greg Daniels led the writers' room throughout his entire time as showrunner, and even when he took time off to launch Parks and Recreation *his methods remained their guiding lights. Ricky Gervais and Stephen Merchant may have created* The Office, *but they'd be the first to say that the true genius behind the American edition, beyond even Steve Carell, was Daniels. He began his career at Harvard, where he wrote for the* Lampoon *alongside his good buddy Conan O'Brien. They moved to Los Angeles together after college and got jobs writing for HBO sketch series* Not Necessarily the News *before moving over to* Saturday Night Live. *Brief stints on* The Simpsons *and* Seinfeld *led to* King of the Hill, *which he ran with Mike Judge from the beginning of the show in 1997 through 2005, when he left to adapt* The Office *for American TV.*

Alan Sepinwall: Greg is one of the underrated geniuses of the last twenty-five years in television. If you go back to the early stuff he did on *The Simpsons* to *King of the Hill* to *The Office* to *Parks and Rec,* who has a better batting average than that?

Brent Forrester: There are many, many things that make Greg an extraordinary television creator, but one of them is his insistence on setting a naturalistic tone on his shows, which is a hallmark of the tastemakers in comedy. Judd Apatow, to my knowledge, has never met Greg Daniels, but both of them point to the same TV show as their favorite show: *The Larry Sanders Show*. Why? Because it was this great naturalistic comedy. Greg loved the comedy of Bill Murray, stuff like *Stripes* that just really struck a naturalistic tone. It's just *real*. It's funny, but it never tries to be *surreal*. And in animation what he did was amazing. Look at the difference between *The Simpsons* and *King of the Hill*, where he imported naturalism into animation, which had really never been done on this grand a scale. He then took it to another level with *The Office*.

Jeff Blitz: As a storyteller, he's just brilliant and he intuitively understands that when the heart of a comedy is in the right place, it lands in a different kind of way. He was always trying to capture something that's real about who people are and how they live and feel and love and want and mourn.

Jen Celotta: Greg was always reminding us that the characters need to be very real. If you pull out of the story as a viewer because you feel like you're not engaging or relating to the character, or understanding the character, then you're not going to be laughing. If you really understand where the character is coming from, and what the character wants, it's easier to make everything funny.

Robert Shafer: He's very quiet. Like all good writers, he's an observer.

Kate Flannery: Greg is a very understated guy. He doesn't have a lot of bravado and he never even had a publicist. I feel like some of these showrunners go on talk shows and they become a personality. Greg was never like that. I remember one time we went to the Golden Globes and Greg rode his bike because he only lived like a mile and a half away. I was like, "I liked you before, but I love you even more now." It was hilarious.

Mindy Kaling: Greg's a very low-key guy, with the bearing of a gentle, athletic scientist.

Kelly Cantley: He drives a normal car. One season he was in a Mini Cooper, which he loved.

Creed Bratton: Greg is a cerebral man. If you know him for a long time, you know how kind he is and loving he is to people. But when he's working, the cards are close to his chest. It's all business, and he's got a ship to keep on course. He launched everybody's career when you think about it. The only one that was off and running already was Steve.

Caroline Williams: It's funny how many of us owe our careers to him. There is such a culture of attention-getting in our business, but also just in the world, and the fact that he is not like that seems counterintuitive. Like, "Why wouldn't he want to have all this attention?" But I just think it's because he is better than that. In my mind, it's just not important to him to have that kind of adulation. He just is a very, I would say, humble person. And private. He wasn't an oversharer.

Kim Ferry: Greg, he's amazing. He's an interesting man because you don't always know what he's thinking. He had these thoughts in his head and you don't know where he's going. Sometimes in the middle of the day I would be in the trailer doing a haircut for somebody and he would kind of just walk in. And I'm like, "Hi, Greg, how are you?" And he's like, "I'm good . . ." And he'd just walk around and look. I'd be like, "So like . . . you want a haircut?" He was just so random, but I loved it. I think he had a million different things going on in his head at all times. Probably the nicest producer I've ever worked with.

Melora Hardin: If you were to meet Greg Daniels and not know that he was a show writer, you might think he was a lawyer or an editor, 'cause that's the energy he gives off. You'd never guess he was this visionary.

Alysia Raycraft: Jesus, what a gift to be able to be around that guy. He didn't present to you his personality. You either got it or you didn't, and I was lucky enough to get it.

Larry Wilmore: Greg is very nontraditional in the sense that I couldn't tell sometimes if he had a story in his head or if he was finding the story as he went along. I think it was a combination of both. He's the kind of showrunner that would overshoot. Many showrunners have a film in their head and they know exactly what they want and they probably won't do more than exactly what they need because a lot of it's already cut in their head. Some people are at the opposite. They know what they want, but they need to see a lot of examples in their heads to help shape that to that final product. Greg kind of worked like that.

Jen Celotta: Showrunners, in general, can be control freaks. I mean that in a good way. As a showrunner, you're supposed to put things through your filter. But I found that there's control freaks with egos, and control freaks without egos. Greg cared passionately about what he did, but it was without ego. When you would pitch something in a room with Greg, whoever pitched it, if it was a great idea, it would go in. And there are other people that I've worked with, where they kind of wanted their stamp on everything. The best idea won, and it didn't matter who it came from, even if somebody was kind of just starting out, or a lower-level person who he was just kind of showing a scene to see what they thought. Any idea that was great would win. I just thought that that was a fantastic way to run things.

Jason Kessler: Greg is a genius, he really is. He knows exactly what he wants. He knows what's funny. He knows the tone of the show. And what made him a good leader is that he's a good manager, as well as a good writer, and that's rare to find. But I think he knew how to get the best out of people, and I think he had such a clear vision of what worked on the show that it was easy for him to bring everybody along.

Kelly Cantley: I've done several projects with Greg. He's my favorite showrunner and one of my favorite people in the world. He's super stealth and super quiet, but he knows more about comedy than I'll ever know. Occasionally, I'd say, "Hey, Greg, I'm having a hard time with this script."

Greg would say, "Well, let's look for the hidden weakness." "What do you mean?" "It's the thing where, if you pull one thread, you later discover you've unraveled the whole sweater, but you didn't realize it when you were doing it." His comedy is brilliant and the way he approaches it is super logical, but I'm not in his brain.

Jason Kessler: He does not have a big personality. I would go as far as to say it was difficult for me, as a young kid trying to work my way into this industry, to have Greg as a boss because I had no idea how to talk to him. It wasn't easy for me to connect with Greg, but I was always in awe of Greg, with how smart he was about everything. That's really what I think made the show so wonderful, is that everything was guided by intelligence. It wasn't guided by a sense of, "Here's the cheap laugh." It was, "What's the smartest thing we could do in any single moment?" And I think Greg looked at that across the board. It wasn't just in the scripts. I think it was in the sets, in the costumes, in the props, in the people he hired. I think that there is a level of intelligence in the show that's really rare to find in Hollywood.

Ken Kwapis: Greg I think is both incredibly intuitive and highly analytical. I think one of the reasons I'm so admiring of Greg is he knows exactly when to rely on his guy instincts, but at the same time, he really breaks things down and really analyzes and tests things out. It's almost like he's both a scientist and he's also someone who can shoot from the hip. I'm not one of the writers, so it'd be better to talk to the writers about this, but clearly he created a space that allowed people to do their best work.

Justin Spitzer: My image of him is of the absentminded professor, that's him. He's just so smart and analytical, but also a little crazy in a way that helped the show. I think creatively I've taken that from him, that you want to follow the story and track it, but you can't forget to have those moments that feel a little more dangerous or off the beaten path. He would always surprise me with his ability to be able to track that and to make those calls about things that feel both true and unexpected.

Paul Feig: He's never been one of those showrunners—and I've directed a lot of shows in my day—where it was like, "They've got to say this joke just like this," and "They can't change this word. If anybody wants to change any words, you have to call me." They make it really difficult and there would be all these layers, which basically meant the showrunners just didn't want to deal with the actors, didn't want to deal with any kind of any deviation from the words that the writers wrote. That's like the worst way to do a show if you have talented people. Greg was just always about, "Cool, let's just make this work."

Carey Bennett: How do I explain Greg? Oh my gosh. Totally lovable. But possibly living on another planet. Very cerebral, but he never really understood the practicality of production. It was something that completely eluded him. When the show got going, we were trying to re-create the haircuts from the pilot and we were talking about doing some new ones. And he said, "Can I see what the haircut is gonna look like before we do the cut and then after?" I'm like, "In the animation world you can, yes. Not with real people."

Briton W. Erwin (Post-production Supervisor): There's an episode ["Murder"] where Jim convinces Dwight to fight himself because he's such a karate master that nobody else could be a match for him. The way it was scripted was at the end of the fight Dwight ends up sort of defeating himself by kicking himself in the crotch and essentially falling to the ground. In the pre-production meeting, Randy [Cordray] asked Greg, "Has Rainn seen this? Is he physically able to do that?" And Greg said, "Oh, you get one of those things that does it." And everyone looked sort of perplexed and Randy was like, "What sort of thing are you talking about?" And Greg said, "Oh, I've seen them before," and he draws this little doodle that just looks like kinda chicken scratches on the back of the script. He insists that there's a contraption that is made that somehow you can harness someone into it and it will allow them to kick themselves in the crotch. And Randy said, "Someone makes this thing?" and everyone kinda has a bit of a laugh and of course nobody makes that sort of thing. He was absolutely convinced that he had seen, at some point, this contraption somewhere. And it ended up with him just punching himself because we could not find said contraption, because of course it doesn't exist.

Justin Spitzer: There are so many Greg stories. He's the guy who will wear the same thing a bunch of times in a row even though he's a very rich guy. He was always eating at little diners like Norms. None of this is really conveying much. . . . I don't know what else to describe about Greg. He just has the ability to just see things. Sometimes you didn't really understand where he was headed. I don't know if he was always able to explain where he was headed, but finally when you got there, it made sense. That's not even to say that he always knew. There was a lot of him that felt like it was out of control, in a good way. It's not like he always knew what was going to happen. He didn't have it all planned. A lot of times things felt like chaos, but he was so smart that you knew you were going to wind up in a good place. But he was always figuring it out, too.

Andy Buckley: He's obviously super smart, soft-spoken, and a serious guy who is obviously one of the funniest guys around. But it's not like he's standing there trying to tell you jokes or make you laugh or anything like that. He was just a calm presence. I remember I had a conversation with him at some point about hiring writers. One of the things he said is that when you're looking to staff up a show, you really want people who aren't necessarily trying to tell jokes all the time because A) you're gonna be in a room with them all the time and B) that tends to be disruptive. You just want people who are there to kind of quietly make the show as funny as it can be without showcasing their own jokes.

Dean Holland: If you ever do get to meet or talk with Greg, he's such a wonderful human being, but he does things far differently than almost anyone I've ever worked [with]. In our initial interview, gosh, I don't even know if we talked about the show. We talked about what we liked in comedy and what our inspirations were, all that kind of stuff. Where do you come from? Always his first question is, "Where are you from?" And he's from Connecticut and I'm from Connecticut near Longshore. And he's like, "Longshore? My brother was a bartender at Longshore."

He loves that sort of thing because he's a smart guy and is like, "I have to sit in an edit room for hours and hours and hours with these people." So maybe he's looking for someone who he can do that with and not be annoyed by. And at the same time it's like, "What are their instincts? What are their guts?" I used to be like, "I gotta be an editor. I have to learn how to edit because I have to have some sort of skill that someone's going to hire me for." And Greg was the one who kind of taught me that people are going to hire you for your brain.

Kelly Cantley: I talked to Greg for about ten minutes when we first met. He asked me what I liked to do besides work and I said, "I like to go sailing." And he said, "Oh, tell me about that." And we talked about sailing for five or ten minutes and then he got up and left. I said to Ken [Zbornak], "Is that the end of the interview?" And he said, "Yeah, usually." I was like, "Okay, great. Now what?" He said, "Oh, I'll call you in a couple of days," and then I got the job.

Jeff Blitz: His philosophy, for the most part, was that you get the right people and then you stand back and you let them do their thing.

Rusty Mahmood (First Assistant Director): Greg knew that the way he operated frustrated the assistant directors because we can't get off the starting mark until we have a script. We're supposed to get them on a Monday, but there were times I didn't get them until Saturday afternoon. And we'd shoot Monday so I'd have to work all weekend. Then it was always a struggle because I didn't have answers. I'd be like, "I don't know if we can build this. The prop guys can't work this weekend. That prop can't be available. We can't shoot that Monday because Jenna's not available that day." It would become ridiculous. For us as ADs it was like, "Oh my God. Hold on! We just locked in that location, so that's gone now? Okay, so . . . we're doing a koi pond? We need to build a koi pond!? Oh my God!" For us, it was a nightmare. He's the nicest man though.

Brian Wittle: Greg was the kind of guy who on the first day of every season he would have his assistant Mary Wall go around and take Polaroids of everybody and write their name on the Polaroid so that he could just memorize everybody's name. He had a whole book in his office strictly just to help him remember everyone's name. I don't know any showrunner that's ever taken that step. It was just important to him that he know everyone's name, and that's cool.

Shelley Adajian (Standby Painter): My first day there his assistant came around and she said, "Do you mind if I take a picture of you?" And I was like, "No, no problem." And she explained to me, "Greg likes to put names to faces," which I thought was amazing because he's our glorious creator, and normally a lot of them don't have much to do with the likes of someone like me. I was just the standby painter. But every time he saw me he would say, "Hi, Shelley." He made it a point to try and know who everybody was on that crew.

Oscar Nunez: Everyone respected him because he respected everyone. He's super funny and super professional. No drama. No ego. We got lucky with Greg.

Claire Scanlon: To this day, I need his blessing on everything that I do. I call all of us graduates of the University of Greg Daniels.

chapter 18

SEASON FIVE

("I feel like I'm in a horror movie and I'm the only one that sees the monster.")

The great television shows of the modern era are expected to make just about ten episodes a season, and audiences are forgiving if they take an occasional year off to make that happen. But back in 2008, The Office *was forced to make up for a strike-shortened season four by grinding out twenty-eight episodes in their fifth season. Making matters worse, they had to do that while building in a long break to allow Steve Carell to film a movie. It was a brutal slog of a season for everyone involved, even though they miraculously pulled off a stellar run of episodes. They got the season off to a nice start by bringing Amy Ryan onto the show as Toby's HR replacement Holly Flax. She quickly became Michael Scott's love interest.*

Anthony Farrell: We were in a place where the Jan thing had run its course and we wanted to see Michael in a better place. Jim and Pam were together and so we were trying to figure out another love story, another way to keep people invested. When we were discussing people to replace the Jim-and-Pam thing, Michael came up, and, I think, rightfully so. We were like, "Yeah, let's do it with Michael. We just need an amazing person to put up against him." Everyone at the show was a huge fan of *The Wire*, so any time we had another character, it would be like, "Well, what about so-and-so from *The Wire*?"

Brent Forrester: The *Office* writers were obsessed with *The Wire*, Mike Schur in particular. They couldn't believe how great the show was.

Amy Ryan: I had just been nominated for an Oscar [for the gritty thriller *Gone Baby Gone*] and I knew I was going to get a bit pigeonholed with playing hard-drug-addicted-mom kind of roles. And I said to my agent, "If there's any chance that people would take our phone call, it is now. I want to do comedy. Can we call *The Office*?" There was a little bit of coincidence in [the] timing since I'd known Paul Lieberstein from years earlier when we both worked on *The Naked Truth* with Téa Leoni, but [we] hadn't really been in touch in between that show and *The Office*. But a lot of the *Office* writers were fans of *The Wire*, so I think my name was being thrown around in that time. It just happened to sync up with my agent calling them saying, "Is there anything that Amy's right for on the show?"

Brent Forrester: We were asking ourselves, "What actress could come in here and be the great love interest for Steve Carell in this incredible character of Michael Scott that he's created?" I remember Paul Lieberstein and a couple other handpicked writers were being shown a tape of Amy Ryan in the main conference room. It wasn't even an audition for *The Office*. It was an audition for some other show that they had gotten their hands on. I saw everybody just standing and staring and just riveted. I don't even know to this day what the scene was, but I remember she had her back to the camera and she kept looking over her shoulder. She was delivering lines out of context. In just that, it was one of the most riveting auditions I'd seen. It didn't surprise me at all when everyone just went bananas for her and cast her in the show. I remember she was instantly riveting to all of the writers and Carell as well. There was no testing period for her that I recall. It was just like instant home-run casting.

Amy Ryan: They didn't have me read for the role. They invited me and I think hoped for the best. It's flattering, but at the same time, not auditioning is sometimes stressful because you're hoping nobody made a mistake, including yourself.

Michael's instinctual aversion to human resources initially causes him to despise Holly, but as soon as they begin speaking he realizes she's the perfect match for him. She's goofy, lovable, and shares his juvenile sense of humor. A look of pure rapture comes across his face when he breaks out his Yoda voice while helping her fix a chair and she responds with a Yoda impression all her own.

Brent Forrester: She had the thing that you saw in Michael Scott at his best, which was a big heart, and to some degree she had the same bad taste that Michael has with comedy. She was just exactly on his level. That Yoda moment by the chair was it. That was the moment where you're like, "Oh my God. These two are perfect for each other."

Amy Ryan: I did not have a Yoda voice. *Star Wars* is not my chosen movie that I would go to in terms of quoting things. I probably had to Google Yoda. I knew who Yoda was of course, but I'm sure I Googled scenes of Yoda just to make sure I could somehow get it in there.

Justin Spitzer: For Holly, we talked about creating the perfect woman for Michael without it being the paint-by-numbers perfect woman. You don't want it to just be Michael as a woman, but someone with like a goofy sense of humor feels right.

Aaron Shure: After he'd had such a hard time with Jan, who was kind of a cold fish, we thought it would be great to give him a sort of a kindred spirit. Someone who would have similar nerdiness to him. Amy is so guileless in real life too. She really is that sweet and nerdy. And so it was to have Michael Scott have the same reaction that the audience had of like, "Oh my God, she gets me." She was just a total pro and played off of Steve beautifully. That chemistry seemed real to me.

Brent Forrester: You never really were rooting for Michael and Jan to be together. It always felt like a toxic relationship. What was fun about it was how awful she was to him. But with Holly, of course, you really did root for them to get together. You just really felt like suddenly Michael Scott is in an actual romantic comedy and you want him to find happiness with this woman, which was an incredible achievement by the two of them.

Jeff Blitz: How could you find someone who felt like a partner to a guy who felt like he shouldn't be partnered with anyone? Her approach to the character was she has such a good heart that she sees that Michael is coming from a place where the things that he wants are good, and that when he fucks stuff up in the world, that's not the important stuff to her.

Amy Ryan: She's a great dork. I mean, I think there's a lid for every pot. She's not like Michael Scott, but they definitely are cut from the same cloth in many ways. I think she's good at her job, but she is a playful dork. And honestly, this isn't an exaggeration, I would come home feeling like I had worked out in the gym every day 'cause my abs were sore because I laughed so hard during filming. Getting to laugh at work just made me so happy. I've been literally crying for my supper all these years in these heavy dramas. It felt so good to go home happy.

Behind the scenes, however, major changes were coming to The Office. Parks and Recreation *was picked up by NBC as a six-episode test run late in the 2008–9 season. It was created by Greg Daniels and Michael Schur, and they both left to work on it midway through season five. Schur would never come back beyond brief cameos as Dwight's dim cousin Mose, though Daniels ultimately found a way to divide his time between the two shows. In the early days of* Parks and Rec, *however, it ate up most of his time. Paul Lieberstein and Jen Celotta became co-showrunners of* The Office.

Jen Celotta: Greg is obviously phenomenal, and he created the show, and the show was always better with Greg around. He's just fantastic. But I felt confident when Paul and I were made co-showrunners. We'd been there for a while, and we were excited, and we were ready for this challenge. When we started doing it, we had the awareness that Greg was still involved and he'd hear what we were doing, and give us notes, and give us thoughts, and so it didn't feel scary.

Kelly Cantley: We called Paul and Jen "the Committee." With Greg, you could say to him, "Hey, Greg, I need you to think about this thing and I don't need an answer now, but I need an answer Wednesday to save money or Thursday to make it possible." And then you'd circle back and he'd give you an answer. With Paul and Jen, it was different, and I can't tell you how it's different. I have worked with both of them since, and I really like them. I like them as much as I like Greg, they're just different to work with.

Jen Celotta: For the most part, Paul and I did similar things. There would be two rooms; Paul would run one room and I'd run another room. I think he was in editing a little bit more than me, but both of us spent a lot of time in the writers' room, a lot of time in editing, and kind of a decent amount of time onstage as well. He was a little bit more savvy about the kind of produceral budget and money things, where I wasn't. I was happiest in the writers' room, but there was so much work to be done that we were both doing too many things all the time.

Aaron Shure: Greg would float in and out and he would often be in editing. It was always exciting when he would show up.

Randy Cordray (Producer): Greg had been grooming Paul Lieberstein and Jennifer Celotta to take over the show when he left for *Parks and Recreation*. Greg was still around sometimes though. That meant that to get anything done I had to get three people to sign on it. I needed three people's opinions on everything. I had to go chase down Greg. I had to go chase down Paul. I had to go chase down Jen. And frequently I'd see Paul and he'd say, "Well, what does Jen say?" I'd say, "Well, I haven't seen her yet." He'd go, "Well, go ask her." I'd go ask Jen. "What does Paul say?" I'd say, "Well, he said to ask you." She'd go, "Well, you'd better check with

Greg." So this went on and on and was a bit of a difficulty for me, but it's all in a day's work. It's what you do.

Jen Celotta: That's hilarious to hear now, though it must have been frustrating at the time.

At the same time, longtime Office *director Paul Feig was hired to work on the show full-time.*

Paul Feig: I actually thought I was going to direct at least half of the episodes, but what ended up happening is there were so many people that had it in their contracts that they could direct an episode by that season that I became the guy who was on the set making sure that the new people knew how to direct the show, which was fun.

Randy Cordray: Paul Feig was there to supervise these new directors to not make mistakes or not go into areas that were not *The Office*, to be on the set and maintain the overall quality and style and look of the show, and make sure that newcomer directors were not departing from that style.

Brian Wittle: I think Paul was hired as an extra person to fill Greg's shoes. Greg trusted Paul in that way.

Oscar Nunez: Paul Feig ran our show for a little while.

Justin Spitzer: I wouldn't say that Paul Feig ran the show. I think the idea was that he would be an on-set producer. And so he was on set all the time, which was great. Usually the writer would be the sort of on-set producer. But I'm sure if Paul was there he was able to make those key decisions that especially a lower-level writer couldn't have made. He'd be in the writers' room sometimes but I don't think that was his main role.

Kate Flannery: I don't know what Paul's title was at that time, but he was definitely running the show. And then Paul Lieberstein and Jen Celotta later that year. It was about as comfortable as it could be with Paul Feig. Greg was really smart about not bringing in someone from the outside. Everything was very insular in a great way.

The cast and crew needed all the help they could get to churn out twenty-eight episodes.

Randy Cordray: We shut the show down from December twenty-second that year, 2008, through February second of 2009. And this was to give Steve Carell basically six weeks to go honor an obligation to be in a feature film.

Mary Wall: We went from getting six episodes to barely knowing if we were getting picked up to doing like twenty-eight. It's a privilege to be in that position, to be trusted to do that. But yeah, that's a lot of work.

Jen Celotta: That schedule meant we had to do nineteen episodes in a row at one point. This is when Paul and I were running things. I told Paul at one time, "I feel like I'm in a horror movie and I'm the only one that sees the monster." Then later, halfway through the season, he's like, "I see the monster, I see the monster!"

Paul Feig: It was grueling on the writers. I just remember being like, "Holy shit. How do we get through this?"

Lee Eisenberg: Looking back at seasons two through four of *The Office*, to me, they're pretty perfect for comedy. There's episodes I like more than others obviously, but I think that that's as good to me as network comedy can be. But if you were to task those same writers to do thirteen, I do think the quality would've been higher. It's really hard to put together a show. You're breaking an episode. You're rewriting an episode. You're editing an episode and you're shooting an episode. That's all happening concurrently. There just aren't enough man-hours.

Aaron Shure: There were a few times that season where you'd be driving home listening to *Morning Edition* on NPR. We made pacts in the writers' room to all work out and just keep our physical selves going.

Halsted Sullivan: I joined in the middle of that season. It was like being thrown into the fire. There was no freshman week where you're beginning to know your dorm-mates and putting up posters. It was brutal from the second I got there. And I think for people who had been there from the beginning, it was extra brutal. But I will say these twenty-six-episode seasons, especially in a world where I've been on thirteen-episode shows ever since, the idea of twenty-two right now is crazy. And then, adding four more when you don't have any more pre-production in the beginning, it becomes exponentially harder.

Gene Stupnitsky: At first you're like, "I would do anything to be hired on this show that I love so much." We were obsessed with it. And then by season five you're just like, "I don't have a life. I wanna go on a date. I want to see my friends or meet them for dinner. I want to go home." You can't do anything and you start to resent it. At first you're like, "I would give my pinky finger to work on this show. . . ."

Lee Eisenberg: But then it becomes a job. I think that even for all the actors. The coolest thing about the show was it broke a million actors. It broke a ton of writers. But then at a certain point, you're not basking in the gratefulness that you were hired five years ago. You're resenting the fact that somebody wrote a bad script and now it's midnight on a Friday and you're like, "We might have to come in on Saturday?"

Ken Whittingham: Everybody started to get a little tired because they were doing so much, especially Steve. I remember Steve asking me at one point in season five, "Ken, how long do you think this show is gonna go?" And I said, "As long as you wanna do it." And he just kinda had this look like, "Oh man!" I could just tell that he was very tired just because everybody was pulling him on so many levels. They were pulling at him for movies and God knows what else. I think he was really starting to be drained by about season five. He wanted to finish out and he loved the cast and didn't want to let anybody down. But I could see that it was starting to wear on him a little bit.

Justin Spitzer: It was hard. It was a lot of crazy-late nights. I remember that point where we figured out the whole Michael Scott Paper Company was really exciting because we latched on to an idea that generated four episodes and they weren't super hard to break. Season five, at that point we're at the place in the run where it feels like, "Okay, we've done every story there is to tell, every available story." So we're like, "Oh my God, there's this whole new thing, and it's generating a few different stories!" We would always talk about that afterward. We'd be like, "We've got to find another arc like that."

Halsted Sullivan: It was a grand experiment that worked. And we were able to breathe life into the middle of a very long season. The way for us to make it manageable was to sort of take off chunks and make them mini arcs.

The six-episode Michael Scott Paper Company arc began with Dunder Mifflin hiring a strict, no-nonsense vice president named Charles Miner. He was played by Idris Elba of The Wire.

Anthony Farrell: I remember sitting in Greg's office with Paul and Jen and me pitching, "I think Michael should have a black boss, someone he can't mess around with. Someone he tries all of his jokes with; nothing works. He just cannot get any traction on this new boss." And then Paul goes, "Yeah, like a Stringer Bell type," and I was like, "Yeah!" And I could see his wheels turning from that moment and then he made it happen.

Idris Elba (Charles Miner, Season 5): I didn't even have to audition. They were all really big fans of *The Wire* and they were like, "Please come and do it." I was like, "You know I don't do much comedy." They were like, "Oh, no, you'll be fine."

Jenna Fischer: Idris was so awesome, but unfortunately I was in the Michael Scott Paper Company most of the time he was on set. But he is really handsome. All the girls were aflutter.

Kate Flannery: He was so interesting because he was always in character and he spoke with an American accent the whole time so he wouldn't accidentally slip out of it during a scene. And I loved how tough that character was on Jim. I thought that was hilarious.

Brent Forrester: One thing about bringing in Idris Elba was how funny John Krasinski was able to be once we brought him in. It was Mindy again who really identified this before anybody. She was like, "Watch how funny it is when Jim eats it in front of Idris Elba and looks like the jerk and the goof and he's not the funny guy. He's just seen as a jerk." I thought it was super effective. It was a gear that I had not seen from John, usually who's always great but Mr. Cool. He was suddenly not Mr. Cool. It was just so fun.

Gene Stupnitsky: Everyone loved Jim and we were really into the idea of a guy who just didn't get him and put him on the back of his heels. He cannot win this guy over no matter how charming he is and no matter how hard he tried.

B. J. Novak: What I love about this arc is you get to see Jim play comedy stories because he's just a guy whose boss hates him for some reason. John is a really gifted comedy actor and we've come to think of him as a romantic lead because of the Jim/Pam story, but when he's allowed to be funny he's just so excellent. And then Michael/Pam are such a good pairing. Instead of Jim/Pam and Jim/Dwight and Michael/Dwight, now you get this Michael/Pam dynamic and this Jim/Idris dynamic and some Dwight/Andy.

Ken Whittingham: Idris stayed in character the entire time, which I was very impressed with. Every once in a while you could hear a little bit of his English accent, but almost never. I never have seen anybody do it that well.

Andy Buckley: I'm one of the few people who still hasn't seen any of *The Wire.* Even back then people were talking about how it was one of the greatest shows ever. That day I got to the set people were saying, "Stringer Bell is here! Stringer Bell is here!" I walk in and he's actually in Michael's office doing his vocal warm-up exercises because obviously he's doing that American accent as a guy from Pittsburgh and he's not that. It was pretty darn impressive.

Idris Elba: I loved working with those guys, John Krasinski and Steve Carell. It was the height of the show's popularity when I came on. I wasn't really there to do the comedic role, I played pretty much the straight guy, but I really enjoyed that. I learned a lot about the process of how they make those shows. There was a script, but there was a certain amount of improvisation and they were always trying to trip each other up and make people laugh. It was like, "I'm going to say something that's really ridiculous and it's not on script and it's going to be a surprise," and then you have to keep a straight face. They were the best of the best.

Michael also doesn't get along with Charles Miner, and he quits after going to the corporate office in New York and complaining to David Wallace.

Lee Eisenberg: We'd been building up to this. Michael applied for the job that Ryan ultimately got and he felt undervalued. Putting in Charles Miner was this type of thing where it's like, "Is Michael gonna go out on his own? Is he going to stand up for himself?" When he quits he says to David Wallace, "You have no idea how high I can fly." Which is such a cheesy line, but it worked. David Wallace was saying, "Michael, you're a nice guy. . . ." He was placating him. He was like, "I'll be your fake friend but you're not gonna get this other thing." Michael had the agency to stand up to him. Dunder Mifflin was his life and the fact that he had enough self-worth to say fuck off felt very satisfying, at least to us.

In a scene straight out of Jerry Maguire, *he makes a grand exit speech and asks for someone to join him in starting a new paper company. Much to Jim's shock, Pam agrees to join him. They recruit Ryan from his new job at the bowling alley and start a rival paper company down the hall from Dunder Mifflin.*

B. J. Novak: It was a big challenge making it funny that Michael would have his own paper company and still making it realistic that Pam would believe in it.

Halsted Sullivan: The Michael Scott Paper Company run is probably one of my favorite times at *The Office*. It was a great mini arc. And I feel like that's another thing I learned at *The Office*. What happens if you actually move the star outside of the office? It's not like killing Ned Stark [on *Game of Thrones*], but on other shows, you would never do that. You'd never take your main characters and take them out of the heart of the show and put them on their own planet.

Warren Lieberstein: It was a lot of fun because it was another way for us to show that Michael Scott was a smart guy and not just a buffoon. He could go out and start a company all by himself that could be successful. Weirdly, we probably spent too much time researching how he could do all this: How much money would he need to start this up? What kind of investment could he get? Where could he get the suppliers from? We figured out all these mechanics of how he could do it and then none of that got onto the show.

Brent Forrester: It took us a while to realize how vital the boss character is in an office comedy. Michael Scott was a great boss for an office comedy because he could create chaos by his personality. Then similarly, to bring in a boss who's more powerful than Michael was a great story generator.

Halsted Sullivan: With a character like Michael Scott, who's sort of in everyone's business and a very nontraditional boss, what happens if you bring in a very traditional boss? When Michael is in the office, everyone else seems like . . . I don't wanna say the sane ones. But everyone else seems like the well-behaved ones. But then you realize, when you have a very strict disciplinarian boss, how Michael has pulled them toward his own way of thinking and goofing off and having fun at the office. What happens when Michael's not there?

B. J. Novak: We were worried about this arc since we struggled sometimes with Pam in New York and Jim in Stamford for the episodes to feel whole and not just have people itch for it to go back to the office. When we started this arc we were more confident because we knew we had Michael and Pam and Ryan [together]. It just wasn't one character going off to a new place, but we were still nervous shooting so many people out of the office. . . . [But] I think it's the most successful of the arcs, in my opinion, where we move people around.

The Michael Scott Paper Company manages to undercut Dunder Mifflin and steal many of their biggest clients. That means selling paper at a huge loss, but it does force David Wallace to buy the company rather than compete with them. All of this is happening while the US economy and the stock market are in a state of free fall. That led to chaotic days for Andy Buckley as he tried to balance his fake responsibilities as the head of Dunder Mifflin with his real-world responsibilities as a financial consultant at Merrill Lynch, where he continued to work despite being on The Office *for the past three years.*

Andy Buckley: The day the stock market was down 750 points just happened to be a day where I was in scenes from seven A.M. to seven P.M. It was the whole negotiation where we're gonna buy the Michael Scott Paper Company from Michael, Pam, and Ryan. They would say, "Okay, let's cut. We're gonna take five minutes." I'd then pick up a phone and call as many clients as I could to try and calm their nerves over the market crash. It was an absolutely crazy day where both worlds were colliding. And of course I can't sit there and say to them, "I'm sitting here all day doing scenes with Steve Carell and Idris Elba. I wish you guys were here," when people's world was collapsing.

Another major plotline of season five was Andy's finally learning that Angela is having an affair with Dwight. In the end, she loses them both.

Brent Forrester: We all just delighted over the Andy/Angela dynamic. Back in "The Merger" when Andy and Dwight had their first scene together, I was like, "This is the funniest, greatest thing in the show, just these two, their rivalry." I think everybody felt that. Pitting them against each other was just one of the funnest comedy battles ever. Of course, to put Angela between them in this rivalry was endlessly funny.

The penultimate episode of the season is "Cafe Disco," where Michael turns the former Michael Scott Paper Company office into a combination coffeehouse/dance hall. It's wonderfully surreal, even though it's straying from the naturalistic tone of the early seasons.

Warren Lieberstein: We had this space where the Michael Scott Paper Company used to be and I remember we wanted to do something with it. We were talking about, "What should it be? Should it be a café? Does Michael open up a small café? Or is it like a dance club?" And I think at that point it was me and Halsted and Brent Forrester. . . . It was just the three of us trying to figure out what the fuck we were going to do. And then Paul [Lieberstein] came out of B. J.'s office. We're like, "We're trying to figure out if it's going to be a café." And Paul just pauses and then he just looks up and then he's like, "It's a café and a disco." He goes, "Michael, there are two things that he loves: coffee and dancing. Write that." And then he goes back into his office. And then the three of us just look at each other and we're like, "Okay, that's it." And then we were on our way.

Halsted Sullivan: I love "Cafe Disco" because everyone had their moment. There were lots of subtle jokes in there, like Angela walking under the limbo stick. We just had a blast writing it. Warren [Lieberstein] and I just sort of swung for the fences with that episode. And we were just like, "Really? He's gonna have a disco downstairs and there's coffee?" We had to think about the whole puzzle. It's like, "Oh, what if there was a vent where it goes up through the bathroom and then Michael wants to restore order?" This was after Michael Scott Paper Company and Michael was like, "I need to reset this office and get everyone back to their old self." And then we said to ourselves, "What are the stakes so it's not just people dancing downstairs?" It then became, "Can he get Angela to dance?" He spent an hour trying to get that little foot tap from Angela because she was just not going to do that.

Jennie Tan: "Cafe Disco" is one of my favorite episodes. That had such a great ending when they're all in there dancing in that tiny room and Bob and Phyllis are dancing. I think that is the hallmark of the best episodes of *The Office*, where everyone gets involved and they're somehow supporting each other, rooting each other on.

The season ends with "Company Picnic." It's a packed episode where Michael reconnects with Holly, Pam demonstrates surprising volleyball skills, and Michael inadvertently tells the Buffalo branch of Dunder Mifflin that their office is about to be shut down. At the very end, Pam goes to the hospital to mend a sprained ankle and finds out that she's pregnant. The audience doesn't get to hear the dialogue, but you see Jim turn to the camera with a look of absolute shock and joy on his face.

Ken Kwapis: It's an emotional moment for Jim, and John and I were discussing the right way to play it. I reminded John that Jim has now had this relationship for a few years with this camera operator. This is a guy, or woman, we don't know who's behind the camera, but Jim has developed a relationship with this person. So suddenly the way John played it, the reaction was very personal. It was very much about sharing this news with somebody who's been in his life, this off-screen camera operator.

It's a great episode, but it was also the twenty-eighth one of the season and by that point Jen Celotta and Paul Lieberstein were completely fried.

Jen Celotta: I crashed a little bit before the table read for "Company Picnic." I was lying under the table in the conference room and only my feet were visible. All I could pitch were Creed jokes because my brain was gone. But Paul got us through the finish line and then we went to the table read and it went really well. Steve started telling Paul how great it was, but Paul said it felt like this shell came down over him. He saw like Steve's mouth moving, but he couldn't hear a word. It was like the end of finals at school. We had been running on adrenaline for so long and now that it was over, we just both completely crashed.

KEY EPISODE 7

"Weight Loss"

"Weight Loss" is a double episode of The Office *that kicked off season five, introduced the character of Holly Flax, sent Pam to New York to attend art school, and had the entire Dunder Mifflin staff group-weighing themselves on an industrial scale as part of a fitness competition with other branches. It's a packed forty-two minutes, but it's a thirty-three-second scene where Jim proposes to Pam in front of a gas station during a downpour that created the biggest headaches for the crew. It's also the scene that stirred up more heated debate than any other scene in the history of the show.*

Randy Cordray: Greg wanted the proposal to take place halfway between New York City and Scranton. Pam was off at art school and they decided to meet halfway at a rest stop. The dialogue said, "Meet me at that rest stop. Do you remember the one where the soda exploded all over you? We'll meet for lunch there." That was all Jim had told to Pam. You had no information that he was going to propose to her whatsoever. Greg insisted that this be shot at a rest stop during the day, in the rain. I kept trying to pick his brain as to why he wanted it like that. He said to me, "Momentous events can happen to us in a place that we least expect it." That's why Jim proposed to Pam at a rest station gas stop in the rain. He couldn't wait another minute, and the place wasn't important. It was the event that was important to him.

Matt Sohn: Funnily enough, it was a gas station that Greg once saw.

Randy Cordray: What he had in mind was an actual rest stop that he and his family visit when they visit his in-laws in Connecticut. They would fly into LaGuardia and hop in their rental van and they would always stop at this one ExxonMobil station along the Merritt Parkway to use the bathroom and get a bite to eat and get a drink, and then go on to Connecticut. So this was his archetype of what he wanted for a rest stop. After 9/11, we learned that ExxonMobil had put a moratorium on filming any of their locations. They did not want the hassle and the security issues of a film crew on that location. And they're obviously a big enough corporation that they don't need the money, and they don't need the hassle of having a film crew. So it was an absolute no, there was no negotiating around this. We could not shoot at that location.

Finding a similar one proved to be nearly impossible.

Randy Cordray: I tasked our locations department to go find this location. He kept bringing back various photos and Greg was rejecting them one after another. I learned that rest stops back east are typically gas stations with fast food. Out west, they are usually provided by the state department of transportation and they include a grassy spot to walk your dog, a couple of bathrooms, maybe some vending machines, a big kiosk with some maps, and places for trucks to park and places for cars to park. That's not what Greg Daniels had in mind. Now, this is my first episode on the show. I'm scared to death that I'm going to fail on my first episode for Greg Daniels. I don't want to fail him. I want this to work. I want him to be pleased with what he gets on film. And obviously, this is the most significant event in the history of Pam and Jim, this has to be right.

Michael Gallenberg: After six weeks of searching all over LA and in fact the western half of the country for a suitable rest stop where we might find or make rain, Randy Cordray comes into my office and informs me they were sending me on a red-eye Friday-night plane and I would be picked up by a PA from Conan's show and driven to the rest stop on the Merritt Parkway.

Randy Cordray: We sent Michael on a stealth junket. He drove out there to that particular rest stop and without identifying himself he took a bunch of stealth measurements and photos of the place. And came back armed and prepared to build this location.

Michael Gallenberg: We had nine days to scout, design, build, and shoot a rest stop with a four-lane parkway.

Building it near an actual four-lane highway wasn't an option.

Randy Cordray: We contacted the California Highway Patrol and they said that the filming crew was creating a hazard and they would demand that we slow traffic down to five miles an hour through the rain zone. Well this was completely unacceptable.

Jen Celotta: I think it cost $300,000 to build it on an airport runway or something.

Randy Cordray: There's five acres of black asphalt behind a Best Buy store in Glendale, California. It is completely barren, unstriped and unpainted. They built downtown Tokyo there when they shot *The Fast and the Furious: Tokyo Drift*. Michael Gallenberg, clever, brilliant man that he is, designed that gas station to merely be a façade. It was only eight feet deep. When you see the shot in that episode, and you see activity behind Jim in the minimart of the gas station, that's only eight feet deep. There's just enough room for a person in there to walk up to a cashier. It was all done with photographs. The colorful cases of sodas, those were photographs that Michael took and printed and laminated them onto foam-core backing. They were merely planted on the back wall of that set.

Brian Wittle: We built a gas station. It was totally unnecessary, way overboard.

Randy Cordray: Then we built a four-lane freeway out in front and we used colored tape to mark the lanes. And we built a median strip with Astroturf and guardrail. This was designed in a giant dog bone shape so that cars and trucks could pass through the shot at fifty-five miles an hour, and then go way out into the distance, arc in a big circle, and come back through the shot the other direction. I hired thirty-five precision drivers.

Michael Gallenberg: I also shot stills of the trees in Connecticut for the digital backdrop to hide the rolling hills of Los Feliz. And we had three crane rain rigs.

Randy Cordray: The nearest water was a fire department hydrant in front of Best Buy, which was several hundred yards away, so we had giant construction cranes holding up water tankers over the whole set so that we could rain [on] four lanes of freeway and the whole top of the gas station.

The scene begins with an establishing shot of the fictional Fairview gas station. The cameraman is positioned across a four-lane highway as cars whisk by in the rain.

Randy Cordray: The concept was that the documentarians had followed Jim to the lunch date and missed the exit. Jim made the exit and made it into the gas station, but the documentarians missed the exit and therefore they pulled off on the shoulder and they were shooting across the four lanes of traffic, through the rain. We see Jim arrive. Pam is already there.

Pam playfully complains to Jim that the gas station isn't halfway between New York and Scranton and that she had to drive more than halfway. Without saying a word, he gets down on one knee and proposes. "I couldn't wait," he says. "Pam, will you marry me?" She agrees and they passionately kiss. They only had time to film a few attempts before the sun disappeared behind a mountain and ruined their light, but they emerged with a perfect take. When they got to the editing suite back in Van Nuys, however, a whole new problem emerged.

Jen Celotta: There was this massive debate about whether the proposal should have sound or not have sound. *Massive.* We were in two camps and I think we were just divided down the middle.

Dean Holland: That was my fault. We had the scene and there was dialogue and we cut it and everybody loved it and everything was great. And I said, "Greg, I did another version for you and I just want you to see it." I showed him a version where you're hearing the traffic and everything and he pulls up. And what I did is, I just took all their dialogue out. It was as if they didn't have their mic packs on.

Halsted Sullivan: Greg pulled me and Warren [Lieberstein] into the editing room and showed us both takes. He said, "Do you want sound or no sound?" And I said sound. And Warren said no sound. The debate was, "Is it a cooler move for Jim to turn off his mic and make this a truly personal moment between him and Pam?" And [on] the other side, not as a writer of the show, but really as a fan of the show, I've waited so long for this moment and we haven't turned off the mic yet. I wanna hear it. I don't want to leave unsatisfied.

Jen Celotta: Greg felt like, we've waited a long time for this. You want to sort of hear it. A lot of the writers felt differently and we enormously respect each other, so fighting was encouraged because everybody was so passionate about what we were doing. And the writers were so wanting it to be, like, messed up and muddied.

Brian Wittle: I told him I think he should leave the sound on, and the reason is because the shot is in close-up. If we're really there, we would hear something. We would at least hear rain. If you wanna do a romantic thing where all you see are the gestures and you can tell that he's proposing to her, and you can tell that she says yes and you can tell all that, then I would play that from a wider shot and only hear the rain. I said, "If you're gonna do it like that, then yeah, take the dialogue out. But otherwise, I think you need the dialogue."

Randall Einhorn: I would have been definitely no audio. If we're doing a documentary, they would have taken it off, right? Greg entrusted me with being the documentarian and if somebody tells you to do something you wouldn't do, tell them to fuck off. What you imagine might be even more romantic than what you actually hear.

Jen Celotta: I sent Greg my pro/con list for sound/no sound. I found a legal pad in his office with people who wanted sound and people who didn't want sound. His wife and one of his kids was one side, his other two kids were on the other side. We went back and forth to the point where one night I was coming from a trailer late at night and I walked up to Greg as he was getting into his car and I was like, "Did you make a decision?" He's like, he said, "No, no, no, no, no. We don't have to lock till tomorrow!" It was like I was cornering him in a horror movie.

Halsted Sullivan: Greg began pulling in all sorts of crew members to hear their opinions. He brought in the guards from the gate to A and B it. It just became one of the most debated things ever on the show.

Jen Celotta: At one point a guard came in to see both versions while Greg was on speakerphone. This guard was a lovely, lovely man but it didn't appear that *The Office* was a show that he watched and I didn't want to call him on it. We show him the scene with sound and without sound. We're like, "Which one do you prefer?" And he goes, "I like the one with sound." We ask why and he's like, "Oh, 'cause I can hear it."

Dean Holland: It wasn't just the security guards. He also showed accounting and the cleaning crew.

Brian Wittle: Greg is so sensitive to other people's opinions. He's this super-talented amazing guy, but if you tell him, "Oh, I don't think this part works," he'll take your comment really seriously, no matter who you are, which is pretty amazing, but it's also gotta be torture for him.

Dean Holland: We had two versions mixed and ready to go. And Jake Aust, who was our post producer, he called me at like eight forty-five in the morning and said, "I can't get in touch with Greg. And he hasn't decided yet. You got to call him. He has to decide." So I called Greg in his car and said, "Let me tell you how I proposed to my wife. I didn't say anything fancy. I didn't say anything special. If I could go back now, it was probably the lamest proposal ever. But that's what my wife and I will always remember." Both of us were talking about our proposals and at the end of it he's like, "I've pulled my car over. I have tears in my eyes," and says this is the way it should be. And then we went with dialogue, [because] people are going to want to hear it even though it's not elegant and articulated perfect. They're going to want to hear it. So he chose the dialogue version, but I think both would have worked. I hate saying that, but either one would have been fantastic.

KEY EPISODE 8

"Stress Relief"

On February 1, 2009, nearly one hundred million Americans sat down to watch the Pittsburgh Steelers squeak out a 27-to-23 victory over the Arizona Cardinals in Super Bowl XLIII. The second it ended, the action went from Raymond James Stadium in Tampa, Florida, to Dunder Mifflin for a special double episode of The Office. *The show was already NBC's most popular comedy with upward of nine million viewers a night (even though it never came close to* Friends*-like numbers), but this was a chance to introduce it to a new mass audience.*

Ben Silverman: I was running the network at the time and I was talking to everyone about what we should put on after the Super Bowl. They're like, "Should we put *The Apprentice* on?" I'm like, "No, *The Apprentice* is fine and it's got that audience already. It'll do well, but it's not gonna do that much better there. What asset do we have that can also grow, sustain, and help really drive the night?" Everyone came around to the idea of it being *The Office* and said, "Let's do this and let's figure out how we stunt it and make it big."

Jen Celotta: We wanted people who didn't know about *The Office* and who were watching the Super Bowl to enjoy it. That caused us to think a little differently than we normally would about the show. We ended up throwing out a bunch of story ideas and we never did that before or since.

Halsted Sullivan: We were tasked with making it a stand-alone episode, but making it something that fans who have been along for the ride all five seasons could enjoy, but also people who tuned in to the show for the first time would be able to enjoy. It was very important. We were given a lot of mandates and they didn't even come from NBC. They came from Greg. He was like, "Look, this is our opportunity to sort of re-pilot the show and introduce a whole new group of people to *The Office*. It's very important to have a really grabby opening."

Warren Lieberstein: It needed to be an electric opening because we were concerned about channel switching.

Gene Stupnitsky: That was a very stressful time because Greg came in one day and he had a big idea inspired by some French film he saw. Basically the idea was that Jim loses Pam in a poker game. He was like the father of us all and we were like, "Dad . . . Your idea . . . We're not so sure about it."

Lee Eisenberg: But we started breaking the poker game episode.

Gene Stupnitsky: We went pretty deep into it.

Lee Eisenberg: It was a show that needed to be small, real, and relatable. And then it was like, "Okay, he loses her in a poker game. . . ."

Greg eventually came to his senses and approved an idea where Dwight stages a mock fire to test everyone's safety response time, causing Stanley to have a heart attack. The fire drill took place seconds into the episode and was a scene of absolute mayhem, complete with Angela desperately hurling a cat into the air, Oscar crawling through the ceiling for help and falling to the ground, Kevin breaking into the snack machine and stealing all the candy, and everyone else desperately trying to find a way out.

Ben Silverman: The fire drill was insanity. Greg and I talked about it and were like, "Okay, let's make this one hundred percent like a movie, like a stunt. When it happens, how do people not change the channel?"

Kate Flannery: That scene was a big deal. It was so fun, but I also knew that it was expensive, so it's like, "Don't fuck this up." It was definitely like a little nerve-wracking because you just didn't want to be the one that messed it up for everybody else.

Anthony Farrell: Greg was like, "It's the Super Bowl episode. We need it to be big and crazy and wild and this is the first thing they're gonna see, so we want people to stick around." He said to me and [fellow writer] Ryan Koh and some of the writers' assistants, "You guys work on this cold open." We knew it would start with Dwight setting off the fire alarm and Greg was in a place where he was like, "We need it to be bigger and crazier." So we just started adding all sorts of crazy shit happening with the mayhem and the melee, like them using the photocopier as a battering ram and cats falling out of the ceiling. A lot of it wound up getting shot.

Randy Cordray: All of the characters think they are going to die. Oscar jumps up on his desk and climbs up into the drop ceiling and Angela pulls out a cat from her file cabinet and says, "Save Bandit!" And she throws Bandit up to Oscar, who doesn't want anything to do with Bandit. And then moments later the cat crumbles through a panel of the drop ceiling and falls back down. This was a big sequence that Greg really wanted in the show. Well, you can't injure an animal, and so we had to figure this out. We had to build a stuffed animal to match Bandit. It was about $12,000 because seamstresses have to match the coat of the cat, they have to meticulously paint furry fabric and create the exact shape and size of Bandit.

Jeff Blitz: In the original script, Oscar was already in the ceiling when Angela threw up the cat. They had thought that it would just be like a stuffed cat. Oscar would extend his leg out from the ceiling to kick the cat back down. I thought that that would seem really mean-spirited. I thought it would just be really funny if the throw is just a little too strong and so the cat went too far and then came down. And then I was convinced that we couldn't use a stuffed cat because it would look like a stuffed cat being thrown. We ended up using two real cats. There was one trainer who was standing in the ceiling to catch the first cat and another trainer to throw an identical cat back down. Then there was a cat thrower who had an Angela wig and Angela wardrobe on that we had to bring in for that.

Randy Cordray: I worked with a wonderful animal training company at that time that provided us with the cats. We talked at great length with them. They absolutely will protect their animals. The animals are their livelihood. And you just don't want to hurt an animal in filming. It's illegal, it's a felony, it's unethical, and none of us want to do that.

Jeff Blitz: The trainer had said that she was comfortable with us only doing it like two or three times. Greg wanted to know why that was and she was like, "Well, because the cat gets scared of doing stunt work and can't do this kind of work anymore and then it will need to be retired." Then Greg wanted to know what the lifetime income of a cat like that might be so that if they wanted to do more takes they [would] just buy it out forever. When Greg floated it, Randy was like, "No way, can't do that."

Randall Einhorn: That whole scene was pandemonium to shoot, but really fun.

Jeff Blitz: There's a moment when they start to run and the camera goes down. I think that's an actual take where Randall didn't mean to fall, but we just used it.

But a zany fire drill scene wasn't enough for NBC. They wanted the episode to feature big-name guest stars to draw in a bigger audience.

Lee Eisenberg: The network was insistent that we get celebrities, and that was really complicated. I remember wanting Matt Damon or Ben Affleck to be on it. I was like, "Okay, we'll get somebody who has a blue-collar feel to be running a warehouse or they're gonna go up against Michael somehow. It's Matt Damon or Ben Affleck versus Michael Scott." For a lot of reasons, people just decided that putting someone like that in just takes you out of the reality of the show.

Randy Cordray: Greg was really at odds with NBC over this. His point was, "How does that fit into a show based in an office in Scranton, Pennsylvania? What would celebrities be doing interacting with a paper company office in Scranton, Pennsylvania? Why would you pitch that idea? That makes no sense. What would celebrities be doing in Scranton?" His way of doing that was to make a movie within the movie. Andy had access to stream a movie on his laptop and so we created this movie. That was our way of satisfying the network creative people and putting promotable star talent into the Super Bowl episode.

Halsted Sullivan: *The Office* always shied away from stunt casting. At the time, *Will and Grace* would have someone like Cher or J.Lo on every episode, and the episode [would be] about that person. What we didn't wanna do is have some stunt casting in our opportunity to showcase *The Office* as a new pilot to the world and say like, "Oh, you're gonna get Jack Black every week if you tune in." So, instead we had Jack Black and Jessica Alba in that stand-alone movie so we could promote them. They were in the show, but at the same time, at no point did our characters get outshone by these big movie stars.

The pirated film that Andy shows Jim and Pam, Mrs. Albert Hannaday, *is about Jessica Alba taking her boyfriend (Jack Black) to meet her grandmother, played by Cloris Leachman. Black falls madly in love with Leachman and they furiously make out in a bathroom.*

Jeff Blitz: In one of the early drafts of it, the movie itself had a martial arts spin to it. But then they landed on this weird Mrs. Robinson thing. The day we shot it felt very un-*Office*-like. Jack Black was very into it, but nobody was ready for the energy that Cloris Leachman brought to it. At the time we shot that, Cloris Leachman was in a frame of mind where whatever was on her mind, she would say. In no way was she restrained and she let everyone there know she was excited about the idea of making out with Jack Black.

Warren Lieberstein: I love the *Harold and Maude* dynamic. Just knowing the two of them were going to be making out, it was worth the price of having that in there.

The second half of the episode centers on Michael's thinking it would be fun to stage a Comedy Central–style roast of himself in the warehouse, but he grows deeply depressed when everyone takes the opportunity to viciously insult his intelligence.

Halsted Sullivan: This was probably the most difficult episode to write that season. It took longer than any other episode because it had to be an hour and it had to be stand-alone. I remember for a long, long, long time we did not have an ending. And I came up with the idea for the roast. That's because I grew up in Atlanta and my father was president of a medical school. Every year, they had a follies where all the students would make fun of the professors and we would go to that. It was a fun evening, but it was also like, "Oh, is this really what you think of me?" And that turned into the roast of Michael, where he was able to bring the office together again and restore order after all this chaos by becoming the victim. Of course, it did really hurt his feelings, but in the end it brought the office back together.

On a more serious note, Pam's dad decides to leave her mom after having a private talk with Jim. Pam is freaked out and wonders what Jim could have possibly said to him. She finds out in the end. "He said that you told him how much you love me," a teary-eyed Pam tells Jim. "About how you feel when I walk in a room, and about how you've never doubted for a second that I'm the woman you want to spend the rest of your life with. I guess he's never felt that with my mom, even at their best." The Jim-and-Pam scenes are as dramatic and heavy as the rest of the episode is goofy and absurd.

Jeff Blitz: There was a lot of talk with Greg about whether Jim and Pam's emotional stuff should play with as much drama as it does. I remember Jenna and John felt strongly that the truth of it meant that they had to go to a place of drama and that seemed so right to me.

Warren Lieberstein: We definitely were aware that there's a certain part of the audience that very much likes the Jim-and-Pam stuff. And there's a huge swath of people that liked the antics of Dwight. We knew in that particular episode we had enough time, an hour, to really satisfy and hit all different kinds of viewers that we could possibly hit that enjoyed our show.

Twenty-two million people watched the full episode and 37.7 million people watched at least some of it. It was the highest-rated NBC show in nearly five years in the coveted eighteen-to-forty-nine-year-old demographic.

Paul Feig: My greatest regret from *The Office* is that I so badly wanted to direct that one. I had just directed the Meredith's-intervention episode that I don't think the network liked, so they wouldn't let me direct the hour-long episode, and then that ended up winning an Emmy for Jeff Blitz. I always feel like, "Oh, I almost had an Emmy." Jeff did a great job though. It's a really good episode.

Ben Silverman: That really propelled the show. It exposed it to a whole new audience that showed up and kept watching and grew.

chapter 19

13927 SATICOY STREET

("You wouldn't want to walk around there at night, for sure.")

The brutal shooting schedule of the fifth season meant that the team behind The Office *often spent more time on set than at their homes. By that point, they'd been operating out of Chandler Valley Center Studios in the gritty LA neighborhood of Van Nuys for four years. They'd remain there until the last day of shooting. Most TV shows filmed on enormous soundstages on cushy Hollywood film lots, but* The Office *was created in a radically different place.*

Randy Cordray: Chandler Valley studios is in an industrial area that is not glamorous by any means. It's an area of warehouses and potholed streets.

Aaron Shure: Van Nuys is the Scranton part of LA.

Carey Bennett: It was on a middle-of-nowhere street that you would probably never go down. There was a car repo place across from us and a crematorium we had to drive past every day.

Paul Feig: It wasn't like you walked out and said, "Hey, we're in the commissary. Oh, look, there's movie stars. There's extras walking around dressed as centurions." It was like, you walked out of there and saw some sort of machine shop that makes gun parts. It was so remote.

Lisa Hans-Wolf: It was a really shady neighborhood. I mean, I wouldn't want to park off-campus and walk to my car, you know?

Creed Bratton: It could be dangerous going up that street. You wouldn't want to walk around there at night, for sure.

Rainn Wilson: There was a junkyard with a junkyard dog right across the street from us.

Jenna Fischer: He got out once. He got loose in the cul-de-sac.

Ken Kwapis: This scrubby area in the San Fernando Valley—which did have a Scranton, Pennsylvania, vibe to it—was probably frequented by people in the porno industry more than anything else. We certainly had the kind of creature comforts that you get working on a show or a film, but it just wasn't within the kind of entertainment-drenched atmosphere of a studio. I think this was due in part to Greg's desire to create an atmosphere that felt different than doing a TV show.

The set itself was a near-identical re-creation of the Culver City set from the first season, though there were some minor changes that most viewers wouldn't notice.

Michael Gallenberg: The entrance and elevators were new, the kitchen was enlarged and the bathrooms added, and if you walked through them you would go to the real bathrooms on the soundstage. Ryan's closet office was added, the annex was enlarged, and [there was] a fake stairwell that matched the practical stairs by the writers' offices and an exit from the set by Mindy's desk. Paul Lieberstein's office was built out to match Michael Scott's office on three sides so we could shoot the parking lot out the window. We made our backing from the view across the street from that office so it would match. We redesigned the warehouse to work in the new stage and walled off half of the stage for swing sets, and we added fake steps to match season one.

Jason Kessler: It was strange to come in second season when we moved up to Van Nuys and see that they had completely re-created those offices.

Matt Sohn: We were very excited because we were building the set and we felt we were going to have some ability to have some walls that could move to give us some extra space to film and some ceiling pieces that weren't there to allow us different styles of lighting. But Greg was very specific that he wanted everything to be just like we were the first season, meaning no walls were wild. They couldn't be moved. A lot of that stuff is done so you can light it easier, so you can get cameras to places where they couldn't be, but Greg wanted to make it feel like it was a true environment where if a camera was there, it was jammed into a corner and you could tell from the shot. The one thing that we did manage to talk him into was giving us a little more space in the kitchen area, because the original kitchen area was so tight that we couldn't do anything in there. I think he allowed us to get another foot or two to widen that area out, but that was pretty much it.

Kate Flannery: It was crazy. It felt like a dream. It felt like it was sort of pushed out some parts a little bit so there was a little more space. But it was so identical to the previous set that it was crazy.

Matt Sohn: Greg liked that we didn't have executives popping in because we weren't on a lot. They would have to come a certain distance to find us. We were just on a crappy street down at the end of a cul-de-sac.

Justin Spitzer: A lot of these executives wouldn't come out even for table reads. It was just a trek. And so it felt a little more like Greg's fiefdom rather than just another show on the lot.

Brian Wittle: It's just two really large buildings with a parking lot in the middle of the two of them and in the front of them. If you're standing on the street staring at them, the building on the left is the main set. When you walk inside, the office set is there. That probably took up about half of that space. Then the other half was where we ate, with tables and chairs set up. The other building was the warehouse set. The writers' offices and the edit team were there.

Randy Cordray: We used to say, "We use every part of the buffalo here at Chandler Valley studios." The writers' parking lot became the parking lot for Dunder Mifflin. The front of the writers' building became the front of Dunder Mifflin. Greg Daniels's office was Michael Scott's office. If we needed an exterior where Michael was looking out the window, we used Greg Daniels's office. Now, Michael Scott's real office was onstage. That was a set with a photorealistic backdrop out the window that approximated what you saw if you went in Greg Daniels's office and looked out the window.

The first person on set most days was caterer Sergio Giacoman.

Sergio Giacoman (Caterer): I'd usually be there at three A.M. to start making breakfast. It was a big cast and my job was to make them whatever they wanted. Steve Carell, for example, wanted a turkey burger on a wheat bun for breakfast every single day. John Krasinski always wanted scrambled egg whites with tomatoes. We called it the Johnny K. Jenna would usually just order a small portion of scrambled eggs. Rainn liked breakfast tacos with eggs and beans. One special that became real popular was called the Rashida after Rashida Jones. That was black beans, egg white scramble, turkey bacon, avocado, and green salsa. Everybody liked that. I'd make it all day.

Randy Cordray: It was a massive show with sixteen series-regular cast members, and that translates into a huge amount of support crew on the show each day. A typical sitcom might have a hair-and-makeup crew of four people. *The Office* needed a hair-and-makeup crew of eight people, because frequently you had to get all sixteen people ready for the first setup of the morning. So people had to come in at four thirty, five o'clock in the morning.

Richard Gonzales: It took a lot to get all those people through hair and makeup. The girls came in first and then the boys would follow later.

Kelly Cantley: Many of the women would have to come the earliest, because the women would take an hour to an hour and a half, and then you need to get a guy into their chair. Phyllis and I got to be friends, because Phyllis would get ready and come on in and sit at her desk, and so we'd be there all by ourselves on set, and just chat while she was sitting at her desk. Most actors know in their heads that it is a business of hurry up and wait.

Kate Flannery: We had our own parking spaces with our characters' names and they said Dunder Mifflin. So I was parking in Meredith's space every day. They were right by the trailers. I don't even think it was two hundred yards from the gate. I'd be one of the first in hair and makeup each day. I was usually in by five A.M.

Kelly Cantley: We would have a crew call at seven A.M. and we'd get our first shot at about seven thirty.

Kasia Trojak (Second Assistant Director): The first thing that you would see when you would walk onto the stage is this big whiteboard where the PAs would write which scene we're on, what we've completed, and which cast members are in which scene. Then there was an area where we had all these desks for the crew with big monitors to see what's happening on set because most people weren't allowed on. There was this corridor that would lead to the set. You could either enter through the kitchen or the hallway right next to where the conference room was.

Kelly Cantley: Within the walls of the office, the only people that were ever there were actors, director, camera operators, boom man, camera assistants, me, and the script supervisor. We would move and hide behind file cabinets, walls, and desks to stay out of the shot.

Kasia Trojak: We'd break at one o'clock for lunch.

Sergio Giacoman: Lunch was served buffet style and there was a salad bar. Steve Carell was often first. He just walked right out the office into the line. Everyone would just eat and talk and sometimes have birthday parties there. It was very cool to see all that.

Briton W. Erwin: The entire crew, post, the writers, the cast, everybody is kinda jammed into this one little area. You're eating lunch together every day with everybody. The cast is there and you're sitting with Craig Robinson and Leslie and Kate and the DP, and the editors. You're all just at banquet tables onstage having lunch together. So it very quickly created a familial atmosphere because so many of the people there had been there pretty much since the beginning.

Halsted Sullivan: Just by having lunch together every day, which does not happen at most shows, you get to know the actors as people. It also became another organic way to find stories. We were doing a Halloween episode once and Creed said to me, "What if I bring back that blood bag I had in an earlier episode?" I was like, "Oh my, that's great!" And then I added it in.

Jason Kessler: It felt a little bit like we were all away at summer camp. We're all on the same lots, eating the same catering. Everybody had lunch together. It was a self-contained thing, and I think that gave people a little more pride of ownership in a way.

Steve Burgess (Producer): We didn't have distractions of other shows going on right next door. It was kind of like being on location, but not being on location.

Creed Bratton: People couldn't come on the lot, so we got more work done. I think it was a great benefit to that show.

Kim Ferry: I've worked at Universal. I've worked at Warner Bros. I've done this for a long time. And it was actually really nice to just have it be us. No one else was there. We're on this private lot and only our family and friends would come. I would have my kids come over for lunch back when they were really young. Pretty much every lunch some of the actors would walk over and start picking up my kids or take them to craft service. They were really sweet about it.

Claire Scanlon: I went through some really hard times in my personal life while I was working on *The Office* and it truly was a home away from home and so enveloping, so warm, so supportive. I got divorced right when I was cutting "Niagara"; my marriage blew up, like, literally when I was cutting the marriage episode. It was shocking and just crazy. Paul [Lieberstein] was like, "You need to go to therapy, go." Jenna came in and talked to me about her own experiences and about priorities and making sure you have a healthy selfishness. Rainn was like, "This is what it's like to be a good, caring husband. You have to make work sacrifices to make your personal life work." I think he had just turned down doing a movie with Jennifer Garner, just to be present with his family. There was nothing wrong with his home life, but he was just like, "I'm gonna be home, I'm gonna be around."

Kate Flannery: We were cocooned. We were lovingly guarded and cared for in a way that we didn't even notice completely at the time.

Claire Scanlon: It was such a good group of people in the way that everyone kind of had each other's back. They were like, "Yes, you're never going to get through life obstacle-free, and conflicts are gonna happen. Let's talk about it. Let's work through it." There were things that were tricky, like Angela Kinsey got divorced from Warren Lieberstein, who was Paul's brother and also a writer on the show. It all happened during the course of the show and they handled it so well. That's representative of how classy people were on that set. That was from the top down. You start with Greg Daniels and Steve Carell, two of the kindest people I know, and good things are gonna flow from that.

Paul Feig: There was such a routine to the day that it sometimes felt like we all worked at Dunder Mifflin.

Oscar Nunez: The leads had their own trailers. The rest of us shared. We had like half a trailer or something, which was fine.

Creed Bratton: Now, of course John, and Jenna, and Steve of course, and Rainn, had their own trailers. They were the stars, but everybody else had three-bangers, they call them. When people like James Spader would come on or Idris Elba or Kathy Bates, they would give them their own trailer. But we were never there that much anyway. It was just a place to go to have breakfast if you didn't want to eat with everybody else and glance at your script. You're on the set all day long anyway. If you weren't, you were glad to just pull in, crawl onto your couch, put your pillow out and blanket, and take a nap. We had some long hours there.

Kate Flannery: I had a triple-banger trailer I shared with Phyllis and Angela.

Creed Bratton: Ed and I would play music in our trailers. I'd go to his trailer. He'd come to my trailer and we would jam in between.

Ed Helms: Typically, we were in each other's trailers all the time just hanging out and teaching each other songs and making music. It was a really fun way to pass the time and I think we learned a lot from each other.

Shelley Adajian: Creed and Ed Helms would have bluegrass jam sessions out in the parking lot, just sporadically, and we would all gather around to watch. It was just a different vibe than a lot of shows that I've worked on.

Richard Gonzales: We basically had a gigantic base camp around the set with about twenty trailers. I was in charge of running everyone to set and making sure they were ready. I never had to worry about Carell. He was always ready. It was the other ones that got a little . . . they'd be on the phone with their agent or manager or whatever trying to get other deals going. In season two everyone was happy to just have a job. By season three, I'd knock on a door and hear, "Okay, well, did Leslie walk [to set]? Did Steve walk?" If you look at the episodes, you don't have as many people in the background by the third season because they didn't necessarily want to be in the background of somebody else's shot. Rainn and Jenna in particular would say, "Well, we're in an office, right? I'll be in the bathroom for that scene." Or they'd say, "My character is in the snack room during this scene."

Rusty Mahmood: They brought me on because some of the personalities from some of the people . . . I won't mention any names. . . . But there were certain people that started to get egos. They started demanding things. I'd hear, "I don't want to come in that early," or "You have to schedule all my things together." But there were fifteen of them who wanted that. It was impossible. Someone gets pregnant and that person doesn't come in before ten o'clock and they have to leave at three o'clock. But they're in every scene, and we shoot from seven o'clock to seven o'clock. How do we do it? It was a real juggling act for me. This actor has a shoot with *Shape* magazine and this actor is flying out early to New York and they're in the same scene together. How are you going to make that work? It was a scheduling and logistical nightmare for me.

Randy Cordray: A call sheet is the daily plan of the shoot. It tells everyone when they have to be there. And there is a pecking order on that call sheet. All the cast members have a negotiated number, like Steve Carell was number one on the call sheet. Rainn Wilson is number two on the call sheet. John Krasinski was number three, and Jenna Fischer was number four, and so on.

Rusty Mahmood: Steve Carell was number one on the call sheet; no one had a problem with it. Steve was the perfect actor to work with. He was professional. He was on time. He was kind. He was fun. He was incredibly talented. And he kept to himself, really. He was friendly with the rest of them, but he was there to do a job. When the other cast started to get to be too big for their britches, as an AD it made my job harder. I just wish the others would've looked to Steve's example a little more. Steve was a consummate professional. By the end, some of the others really got on my nerves. I'd think, "No one knew your name three years ago and now you cannot seem to make it in on time? And the entire crew, about seventy-five of us, we all seem to make it here. And not just on time, but we get here early to have breakfast and prep. We're ready. We're on set, ready to rehearse, at seven o'clock. But when you roll in at seven thirty and then you have to go see hair and makeup, you put a cog in the wheel." That just messes with everything. Then we have to reschedule the day because we can't start with this actor.

But even though the days were long and scheduling got to be tricky at times, everyone felt at home on the Saticoy Street set and missed it when the show was over.

Creed Bratton: I called Steve Carell on his birthday not long ago and he told me that he'd just gone over to the old set just to see it. They were shooting a different show over there. I told him a few months after the show was over I was heading to the market and all of a sudden I found myself driving toward Woodman to work. I went, "Wait. God, the show's over." My body went into autopilot. I guess I just missed being there.

"THE OFFICE"
Monday, October 27, 2003

<u>ROLE OF "DAVID BRENT"</u>

PAUL GIAMATTI (END)

PHILIP SEYMOUR HOFFMAN (PARADIGM)

CHRISTOPHER GUEST (CAA)

JOHN C. REILLY (WMA)

~~EUGENE LEVY (WMA)~~

RIC MORANIS (CAA)

~~DAN ACKROYD (CAA)~~

~~MATTHEW BRODERICK (CAA)~~

~~OWEN WILSON (UTA)~~

~~OLIVER PLATT~~ – Not avail; "Huff"/Showtime

JASON LEE (UTA)

~~STEVE BUSCEMI (END)~~

STANLEY TUCCI (CAA)

JON FAVREAU (END)

WILLIAM H. MACY (W&A)

GARY COLE (ICM)

~~HANK AZARIA (END)~~ – Not avail; "Huff"/Showtime

ANDY RICHTER (UTA) – Deal at NBC.

~~ROBERT TOWNSEND (INNOV)~~

JOHN CARROLL LYNCH (ABRAMS)

10/27/2003 11:46 AM

DAVE KOECHNER (WMA) – Not avail; "Why Blitt"/FBC mid-season

STEVE CARELL (WMA) – Likely doing another NBC show… (Tom Pappas)

PETER MACNICOL (ICM) – ~~Avail~~

ALAN TUDYK (END)

ENRICO COLANTONI (INNOV) – Avail

JEFF GARLIN (ICM) – "Curb Your Enthusiasm" likely exclusive…

KEVIN HEFFERNAN (UTA/3 Arts)

IAN GOMEZ (METRO) – Avail

DAVE HERMAN (GERSH) – Avail

STEVEN COLBERT (James Dixon NY)

JIM WISE (BRILSTEIN GRAY)

~~DAVE THOMAS (GL)~~

DAVE FOLEY (UTA) – Avail

BOB ODENKIRK (WMA) – Avail

LOUIS CK (UTA/3 Arts)

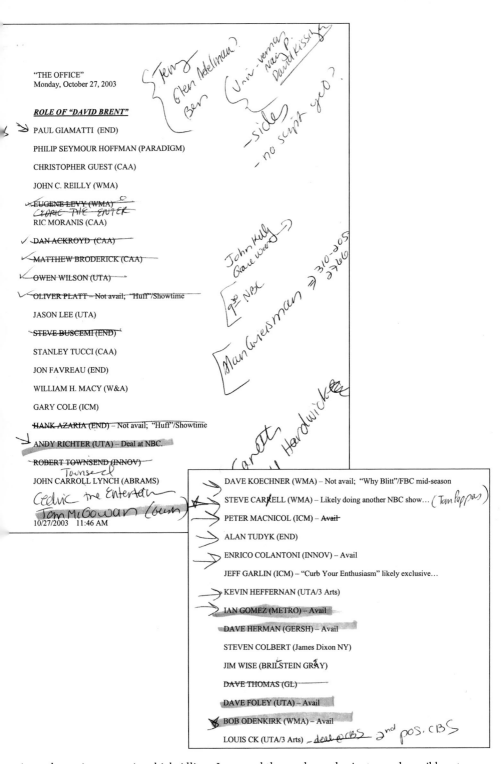

An early casting memo in which Allison Jones and the producers brainstormed possible actors for the role of Michael. Steve Carell has a star by his name, but they indicate that he was tied up with the NBC sitcom *Come to Papa*. *Allison Jones*

"THE OFFICE"
Thursday - November 6, 2003

Pilot
Producer Session
Universal Studios
Bldg. 5170 Conf. room

TIME	ACTOR	ROLE	AGENCY
12:00	RAINN WILSON	MICHAEL OR DWIGHT	END 310/248-2000
12:10	ADAM SCOTT	JIM	GERSH 310/205-5862
12:30	MARY LYNN RAJSKUB	PAM	END 310/248-2000
12:40	HAMISH LINKLATER (HC)	JIM	UTA 310/246-6052
12:50	BEN FALCONE	MICHAEL	ACME 323/954-2263
1:00	ALAN TUDYK * FF -"Underdogs" until Jan. 04	MICHAEL	END 310/248-2000
1:20	ENRICO COLANTONI	MICHAEL reschedule	INNOV 310/656-5113
2:00	MATT BESSER	DWIGHT	UTA 310/246-6052

The audition schedule for the pilot. Note that Rainn Wilson was trying out for both Michael and Dwight. *Allison Jones*

Dwight Schrute

Dwight is the team leader and Scott's sidekick. He actually admires Scott, although it is unclea this is due to Scott's personality or Dwight's officious inclination to look up to whoever is abo him in the hierarchy. Dwight is obsessed with survival, personal security tactics and other grandiose nerd action fantasies, probably because he got his ass kicked a lot as a kid. A volunt policeman on the weekends, he takes any excuse to go on a power trip in the office. Yet his survival training appears to be more Gilligan's Island than Green Berets.

Although aggressively horny, he has no idea how to behave with women. His unpleasant perso habits and annoying personality suggest an unsocialized loner, a sort of Caliban or Gollum. If stuck in an elevator, he would probably start drinking his own urine after ten minutes. His lack social skills render him the butt of office jokes and thus bearable. If Scott is redeemed by havi the heart of a nine-year old, then Dwight can perhaps be pitied for his interior teenage geek.

We need: someone who can look a little grotesque or at least be believable as a geek. Someone who has no desire to be likeable or please an audience, except through total identification with character. Someone who can seem reasonable to himself while saying insane things, who understands the comedy of playing it straight.

Jim Nelson

Jim is a sales rep in the office, who has to share a workspace with Dwight. He is an ordinary, decent person with good taste leading a life of quiet desperation. He likes people, is a good listener and wanted to be a psychologist. His clever sarcasm and takes to camera are little defe against the vulgarity that surrounds him, although they make Pam the receptionist laugh. You wish he would be more assertive in love and at work. After playing with Pam, his chief enjoyment in the office is using his superior social and emotional skills to prank Dwight, altho you get the sense that when he indulges his immature impulses he is letting the environment defeat him.

We need: someone likeable, around 30, who can get laughs by raising an eyebrow or doing a t to camera. He needs to be pleasant-looking enough for you to root for him to get the girl, with being a hunk in any way. Although hidden by his ordinariness and bad haircut, Jim is the romantic lead.

Pam Beesley

Pam is the receptionist and Jim's friend. Pam is decent, reasonable and friendly. She has the manner of a nice kindergarten teacher or future mom. She is an ordinary woman with a sense c humor. She allows her loutish boss and fiancé to push her around some, but can exhibit flashes

The original character descriptions from the files of casting director Allison Jones. This was early in the process and featured characters who were eliminated before filming began, including a little person named Anton, a "bland stupid nice girl" named Kirsten, and an average guy named Bennett. *Allison Jones*

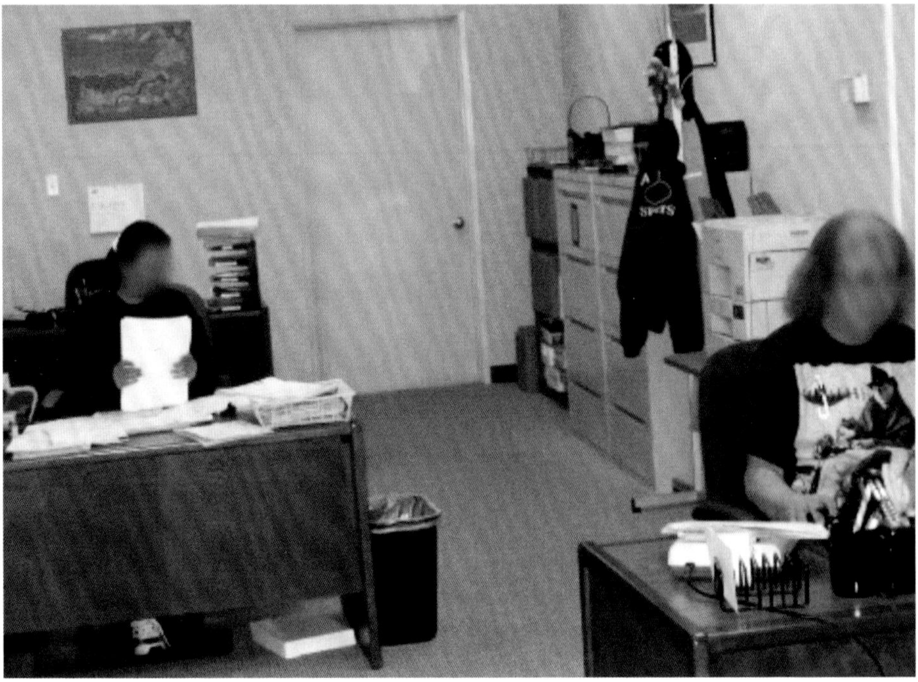

Employees at Economy Office Supply in Glendale, California, that costume designer Carey Bennett observed while creating the looks of the characters. The man in the John Michael Montgomery shirt was one of the inspirations for Dwight. *Carey Bennett*

The Economy Office Supply character in the chair here provided the inspiration for Dwight's mustard-yellow shirt. He's even wearing the striped tie that Dwight often wore. *Carey Bennett*

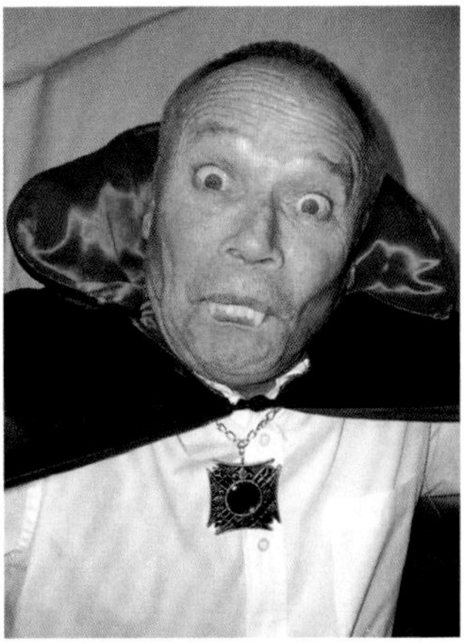

Left: Greg Daniels (right) with Ben Silverman during the NBC 2005 Television Critics Association Summer Press Tour, right before season one premiered. *Frederick M. Brown/Getty Images*

Right: Creed Bratton during the filming of "Halloween" in season two. This was the episode when he was finally given a chance to prove that he had comedic chops. *Carey Bennett*

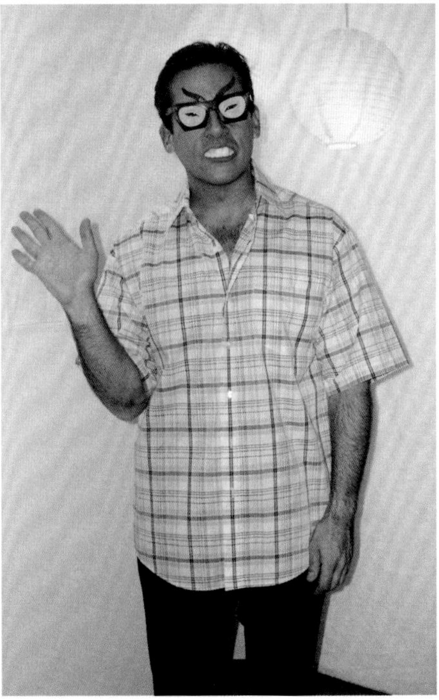
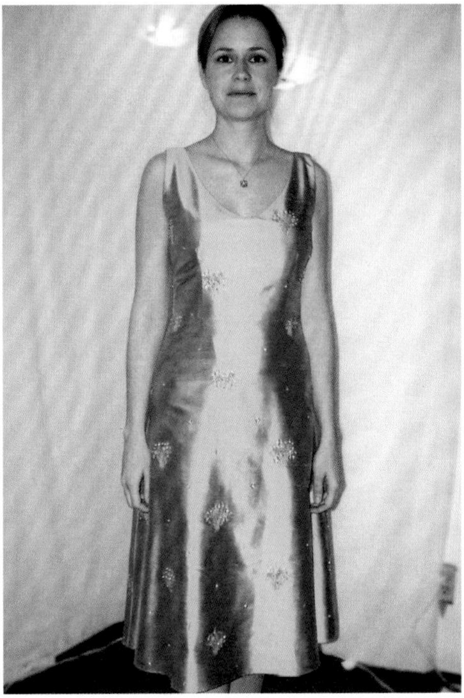

Left: Michael's offensive Ping character, shown during the shooting of "The Dundies" in season two. *Carey Bennett*

Right: Jenna Fischer first trying on the dress she wore in "Casino Night." Costume designer Carey Bennett spent weeks trying to find the right dress for the big scene when Jim finally kisses her. They found it at David's Bridal the day before filming. *Carey Bennett*

Rainn Wilson and Steve Carell on the roof of Chandler Valley Center Studios during the making of “Safety Training” in season three. *Brian Wittle*

Left: Angela Kinsey at her cubicle during the filming of the season three episode "A Benihana Christmas." *Carey Bennett*

Right: Kate Flannery with Brian Baumgartner during the filming of "A Benihana Christmas." *Carey Bennett*

Left: Angela Kinsey and Jenna Fischer on the set of "A Benihana Christmas." They became extremely close friends throughout the run of the show. *Carey Bennett*

Right: Phyllis Smith on the set of the third season episode "Diwali." *Carey Bennett*

John Krasinski sitting between his two on-screen romantic partners: Rashida Jones and Jenna Fischer. *Carey Bennett*

The fake gas station manufactured at enormous expense for the Jim/Pam proposal scene. The cranes are tied to tanker trucks full of water that they used to simulate rain. *Brian Wittle*

Leslie David Baker battles John Krasinski in a sumo competition on the season three episode "Beach Games." *Brian Wittle*

Left: Angela Kinsey and Jenna Fischer on the "Fun Run" set in season four. *Carey Bennett*

Right: Oscar Nunez, Creed Bratton, and John Krasinski on the set of "Fun Run." *Carey Bennett*

Above: Paul Lieberstein and Mindy Kaling on the set of "Fun Run." Writer Anthony Farrell is in the background in a red hat. *Carey Bennett*

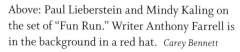

Right: Rainn Wilson and Angela Kinsey on the set of "Fun Run." *Carey Bennett*

Left: Michael Schur as Dwight's dim-witted cousin Mose with the raccoon he brought to the office in "Goodbye, Toby" to frighten Holly. *Lee Eisenberg*

Right: Greg Daniels during the 2007–08 Writers Guild of America strike. He wrote personal checks to members of the crew to keep them afloat while the show was on hiatus. *Lee Eisenberg*

Left: Mindy Kaling with writer Lee Eisenberg. *Lee Eisenberg*

Right: Ellie Kemper and B. J. Novak goofing off. *Warren Lieberstein*

Brian Wittle booms Rainn Wilson and Steve Carell during the filming of "Survivor Man" in season four.
Brian Wittle

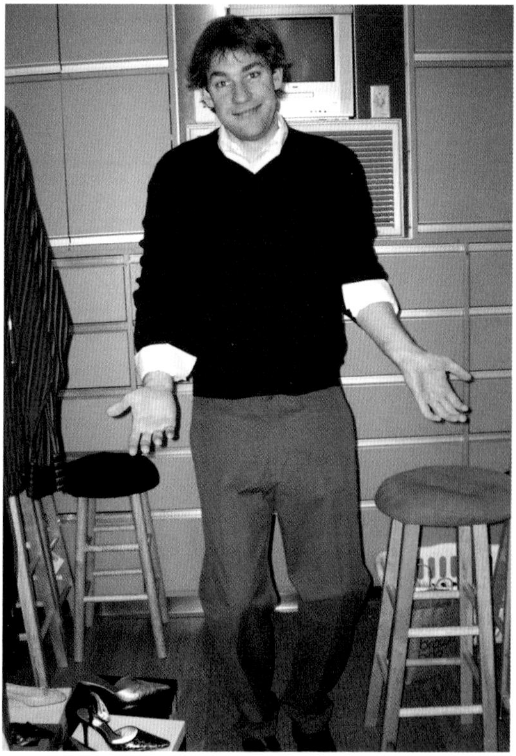

Above: Hairstylist Kim Ferry preparing Kate Flannery's bald wig in the season nine episode "Lice," when Meredith shaves her head. *Edward French*

Right: John Krasinski in the wardrobe trailer. *Carey Bennett*

Real boom mic operator Brian Wittle with the actor, Chris Diamantopoulos, who essentially played him in season nine. *Brian Wittle*

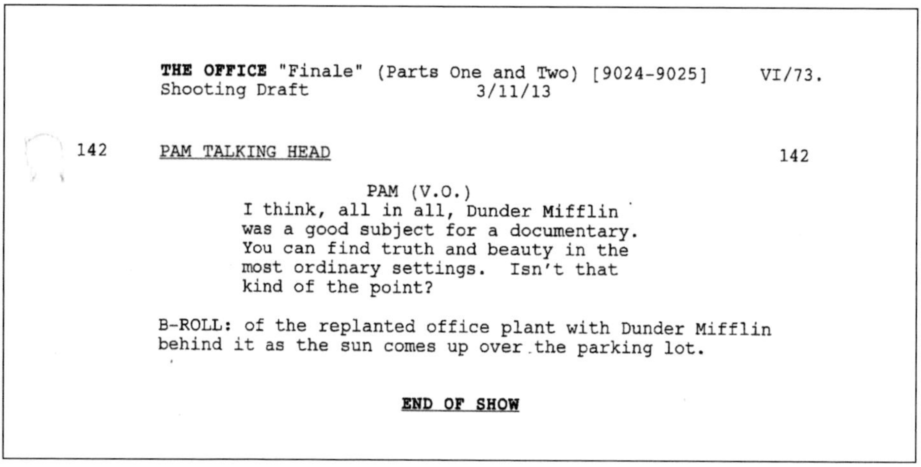

THE OFFICE "Finale" (Parts One and Two) [9024-9025] VI/73.
Shooting Draft 3/11/13

142 PAM TALKING HEAD 142

PAM (V.O.)
I think, all in all, Dunder Mifflin
was a good subject for a documentary.
You can find truth and beauty in the
most ordinary settings. Isn't that
kind of the point?

B-ROLL: of the replanted office plant with Dunder Mifflin
behind it as the sun comes up over the parking lot.

END OF SHOW

Above: The last page of the "Finale" script.
Roxxi Dott

Left: The official invitation to the finale wrap party at Unici Casa in Culver City, California.
Roxxi Dott

Below: Schrute Farms, which is actually a house at Disney's Golden Oak Ranch in Newhall, California.
Brian Wittle

The Office set stripped of the carpeting and the cubicles during a hiatus between seasons.
Brian Wittle

Chandler Valley Center Studios in 2018. *Courtesy of the author*

chapter 20

THE TROUBLE WITH MOVIES

("You made it work for Ed Helms. You need to make it work for me.")

The Office *was the biggest comedy hit on NBC during the fifth season, which led to many of the leads' getting offers to star in movies. Scheduling had always been a problem since* The 40-Year-Old Virgin *turned Steve Carell into an A-lister shortly after the show began, but now that Rainn Wilson, Jenna Fischer, John Krasinski, and Ed Helms were landing major parts as well, finding the time to create the show that made them famous in the first place became an enormous challenge for the producers.*

Randy Cordray: Agents and managers were constantly calling me and saying, "My client needs out for this job. He's being offered a guest spot on this particular show." Or, "He's being offered a cameo, or a role, in a feature film during these dates. Can you accommodate?" So my job was to build the calendar each year taking all of this into account.

Ken Whittingham: I remember an executive even saying one time, "We'd do a movie about a lampshade if Steve Carell was involved."

Randy Cordray: Greg felt that it was essential to try to accommodate these actors in these various roles and their scheduling conflicts, as best as our ability. Now, we had first position on all of these people, mind you. They were contractually obligated to *The Office,* so it was a courtesy to try to spring them from our shooting schedule, to go do these other projects.

Ken Kwapis: There were definitely points where production really had to bend over backward to accommodate cast members wanting to work on a feature.

Rusty Mahmood: A couple of times we had to shut down production because Steve did a couple back-to-back movies. This is how much he was loved: The crew was fine with it. Being laid off for six months is a hard thing to do. You have to find another job, but you don't want to do another job that's going to jeopardize coming back to *The Office,* so a lot of people just were out of work. But it was like, "It's for Steve. And Steve deserves this." And then, "Okay, we're gonna do this."

Randy Cordray: We made the show easy for Steve. It was an unwritten rule that we always gave Steve three-day weekends. This was not in his contract, this was something that I worked out with the assistant director. We always gave Steve a Monday or a Friday off so that he could have a three-day weekend with his kids and his family. Steve is a very strong family guy, loves his children, loves to take them to school and participate in activities with them. And so it was an unwritten rule that we would always give Steve a three-day weekend. These were the perks of being number one on the call sheet.

Kate Flannery: It had to be tough for Steve. He's such a trouper though, but he was always doing award shows and things like the Kennedy Center. It was crazy. He was always doing something wonderful.

Randy Cordray: They set Steve's yearly schedule a year in advance and they told us what that schedule would be. We built our schedule around that and it never varied. There was almost never a situation where at the last minute [his manager] Steve Sauer would call me and say, "Hey, can you spring Carell for this or that?" That rarely happened. It often happened with the rest of the cast, but Steve, almost never.

Carey Bennett: I remember Steve being so exhausted when he was making that movie about Noah [2007's *Evan Almighty*]. I look back at those episodes [near the end of season two] and he looks so tired to me. They once made him go through a four-hour costume fitting before he came into work. He actually slipped down the stairs of his trailer one time and tore his suit just out of sheer exhaustion. He was working at such a fever pitch and it just broke my heart, really, that he had to endure that moment.

Oscar Nunez: In the third season, Comedy Central wanted to buy a show that I did, which I would be in, but I didn't want to leave *The Office*. I asked Steve Carell what should I do, and he said, "Oscar, do everything. That's not your problem. Let your managers and agents take care of the scheduling and all that stuff. Work as much as you can. Do everything that you can." And we said yes to both things, and then Greg Daniels was so cool that he gave me [time] off. And the way he gave me [time] off was "Gay Witch Hunt" [where Oscar's character is given a paid vacation so he won't sue the company after Steve outs him to the entire office and forcibly kisses him].

That same season, John Krasinski was offered a leading role in the George Clooney 1920s football movie Leatherheads. *It was his biggest movie offer up until that point and he was dying to do it, but there was one problem.*

Kim Ferry: It would have meant cutting his hair into a 1920s hairstyle. But continuity-wise and contractually-wise, actors are obligated to keep their hair how it is for a series unless they get producer approval, of course. But it would have been cutting his hair super short, which would mean getting rid of the wings on the side and his long hair. He came to me and said, "Could we do a wig?" He went to talk to them and said, "I really want to do this project." And they were like, "I think it would be obvious that it was a wig." Greg really felt like it won't look like him.

If he couldn't get a haircut, he'd have to tell George Clooney that he couldn't take the part. Desperate for a solution, he gave Kim Ferry money from his own pocket to make an elaborate wig without telling any of the producers.

Kim Ferry: Hiring a wig maker is not inexpensive. We did the fitting in his trailer and when it was done it looked amazing. It looked exactly like him. We were shooting him playing basketball at David Wallace's house ["Cocktails"] and no one knows that I have this wig hidden in my side of the trailer now. He comes in. I put the wig on him, glue it down, take care of everything. And I go, "Okay, let's do this, right?" And he's like, "Let's do this."

J. J. Abrams: I have no memory of any of this.

Kim Ferry: The next day he was going to go in and watch dailies with them and then basically say, "Hey, guess what? That's a wig. It does look like me." But he didn't do that. The plan shifted. John just vanished when the scene finished filming and I heard he drove back to the set. I jump in my car and I'm like, "Oh my God. Oh my God. What's he gonna do?" So I run over and I remember running up the stairs because the writers' office was up on the top level. I walk down the hallway and my heart is pounding. I'm like, "Oh my God. What is happening?" I walk in the room and Greg Daniels is sitting at his desk. I look at John and the wig is off. It's sitting on Greg's desk. John told me later that Greg said to him, "John, I'll know if it's a wig. You can't fake that kind of thing." As he's staring at him with the wig on. And then John's like, "Really? I don't think you would," and he takes it off right in front of him. And then Greg said, "You win, I give you full permission to wear the wig." When I came in [Greg] said to me, "You guys have a lot of balls." For a minute I really thought I was going to get fired.

About two years later, Ed Helms was offered one of the lead parts in The Hangover.

Randy Cordray: It was being shot in Las Vegas. And Greg Daniels had the opinion that it was good for *The Office* that our cast would be out doing these other projects, because it would bring eyeballs back to *The Office*. I negotiated with Ed Helms's management a couple of months on this. How it ended up shaking out was that basically all during October and November of that year, we only had Ed Helms on Tuesday, Wednesday, and Thursday. They would fly him to Las Vegas on Friday, and on Monday night he'd catch a red-eye and come back to us. It caused an enormous amount of scheduling difficulties to not just slot any Andy scenes into just Tuesdays, Wednesdays, and Thursdays, but whatever scenes Andy played with other actors, you had to cross-check the calendar to see if there were conflicts. It made the show infinitely more complex and difficult to schedule and I can't say it did not affect other people's schedules.

Making huge allowances for Steve Carell was one thing, but Helms didn't join the cast until the third season and was therefore number thirteen on the call sheet.

Randy Cordray: If there were conflicts people would say, "Hey, why can't I have that day off? I need to do this project." I'd have to say, "I'm very sorry. That's a day that we only have Ed Helms. And you perform with Ed Helms in this scene, and that's the day we need to shoot it." They'd go, "But Ed Helms is number thirteen on the call sheet, and I am higher than him." I want to tell you I didn't have a lot of these arguments, but occasionally I did, and it presented scheduling difficulties. Nothing was compromised about that, but it opened the floodgate for subsequent seasons. When other actors would do projects, they would go, "Hey, you made it work for Ed Helms. You need to make it work for me." And that was a valid argument. I couldn't very well shoot that down.

chapter 21

SEASON SIX

("Are we jumping the shark? It shouldn't be this slapsticky.")

The sixth season was a time of transitions for the gang at Dunder Mifflin. Jim and Pam finally get married, Jim and Darryl both get promoted, the company nearly files for bankruptcy before it is purchased by the Florida-based paper and printer company Sabre, and Pam gives birth to a baby girl named Cecelia. This was also the season where new receptionist Erin Hannon, played by Ellie Kemper, joined the cast full time after appearing a few times near the end of the previous season.

Ellie Kemper (Erin Hannon, Seasons 5–9): I spent about seven years in New York [after graduating from Princeton] and I got really lucky since I was able to book a string of television commercials. I also did a lot of improv comedy, which forced me to perform three or four nights a week, and really that's the only way to get better.

In 2008, she auditioned for Saturday Night Live *alongside Aubrey Plaza and Kate McKinnon. She didn't get the part.*

Ellie Kemper: I can say with confidence that I would not have been good on that show. Strong characters and impressions are not my forte. Lorne

Michaels made a very good decision in seeing that. The timing was very lucky because I think that auditioning for *SNL* [even though I didn't get on the show] got the attention of some agents, who I didn't have yet. And then stuff comes from that and you meet new people.

Less than a year after learning she wasn't going to be on Saturday Night Live, *she tried out for a role on* Parks and Recreation. *She didn't get it, but she impressed Greg Daniels, and within a few months he called her back to read for the role of a wide-eyed receptionist to replace Pam late in season five when she leaves with Michael to form the Michael Scott Paper Company.*

Anthony Farrell: Greg was really good about trying to hire really funny people, and Allison Jones was great at casting. They had seen her YouTube video where she was talking about giving a guy a crazy blow job and clearly she was just hilarious.

Allison Jones: She had great energy and was different than Pam, but still felt like the kind of a girl next door that would work in a job like that and be happy to do it.

Ellie Kemper: My first day literally felt like walking into a television. It's a weird feeling that I can't totally describe knowing people that you feel you sort of already know because you watch that TV show. I think television does that more than a movie because you visit these people every week and you feel like you're sort of in their world. And then to physically be in their world is really surreal. That was especially true the first few days. I had very early calls and I had not been up that early in a long time and I was so nervous that I wasn't sleeping much. Then to have Steve Carell there as Michael Scott in the flesh as I'm operating on no sleep was very dreamlike.

Halsted Sullivan: Ellie was so great. She was not coming on as a series regular at first, but she did so well that we thought, "What a great organic way to bring new life into the office by having her stay."

Ellie Kemper: It was supposed to be, I think, just four episodes, and they extended it until the end of season five. And then Pam became a saleswoman, and so the position as receptionist became permanent. So that was lucky for me.

Halsted Sullivan: And then it was like, "How do we create a different character who is not Pam at the desk?" She was very effervescent. She was a lovable kook. She wasn't smart, but she strove to be smarter. I feel like people rooted for her. We definitely did.

Danny Chun: We thought she was the sweetest, nicest person, but also extremely funny and surprising. She also had a real weird streak and that really informed what the character became. That's what you see on the screen. We also felt that this is a person who's really talented, we think we can throw a lot at her.

Justin Spitzer: I love Ellie. She's amazing. I don't know with that one that we had that much of her character in mind before we cast her. I think we initially wrote her a little more straight and then she just brought so much to the part and then we followed that. I think that's always the case, that characters get more depth once you cast them and once you're with them, but it was more true with her than with others since we did not have a fully fleshed-out character at first. I think that is kind of the best way to bring in a character like that. You have a little bit, bring someone in, and then start writing to that performer.

Brent Forrester: I'm such a fan of Ellie Kemper. I will never forget her coming into the show, because this was another example of, "Hey, we're six seasons in and it's refreshing to add another character." But at this time it was so difficult to come into the show of great performers who knew their show so well. It was very challenging for Ellie, I think, to step into that cast. But I do remember that all the writers were so excited and wanted to write for her immediately. It was like her energy was like a shot in the arm for the writing staff. Writers can get very mopey and morose and depressed. You could feel that writing bits for her was like Prozac for the writers. It just carried over to the actors as well. I thought the scene where Andy and Dwight play this dueling thing on guitar and banjos for her, to me, is like the coronation of Ellie on the show.

Ellie Kemper: I think the key to the character was that she was naïve. Because every now and then we see a glimpse where she does something sort of sharp or she gets it when you expect she wouldn't.

Brent Forrester: She absolutely fit in this world. She's just this great spark of comedy. I also remember seeing her do her first scene with Steve Carell where he brings her in to fake-fire her and it was an echo of the pilot. I remember watching them shoot it. It was great. It was like Carell, this titanic improv actor, doing a scene where they're going to improv and riff, and Ellie was just right there giving him exactly what he needed. It was like, "Wow."

Rusty Mahmood: She was such a breath of fresh air. I remember telling her, "You are so talented. You're fun. You're effervescent. You're like one of the crew. You're just awesome. If you ever change I'll hunt you down, because it's such a pleasure to work with someone like you."

Brent Forrester: We were always aware of the Pam-being-replaced-by-Erin element being volatile and a good source of conflict. There was an episode where we filmed a whole subplot when Pam was in art school and Ellie tries to clean the office and she cleans Pam's painting of the office and the water runs in and destroys the painting. Then she tries to fix it. And of course you can't fix a ruined painting. She tries to. I thought it was just funny and delightful.

Ellie Kemper: The writers kept unpeeling my character layer by layer, like an onion. There was one where we see who Erin's roommate is and it's her foster brother and they're sort of romantically linked and it's really weird. There was also a whole side story of an episode that got cut where Erin had epilepsy. We learn that she has a very colorful past. Mindy Kaling wrote her line "In my foster home, my hair was my room" [from "Secretary's Day"]. I love that line. In a few words, that's sort of how you can sum up Erin.

Erin was also unique in The Office *for being the only character who looked at Michael with incredible awe and respect.*

Danny Chun: A lot of the decision making when we brought in characters was the question, "What are the dynamics that we haven't seen yet?" That's because it's such a huge cast that you've got to have almost every base covered in terms of different attitudes and dynamics, so that was one that we hadn't done and we felt could be very funny for the character and also for Michael.

Warren Lieberstein: The concern off the bat was that she was going to be too much like Pam. We didn't want that, so we had to figure out how she'd be different. What we came up with is that she's a huge people pleaser and sometimes she's just a step behind everyone else in figuring things out. Also, she's so impressed by Michael and no one else in the office is. Everyone just kind of sees him as a fool or a schmuck or somebody who tries too hard or is a nut, but she just absolutely adores him.

Gene Stupnitsky: When Pam comes back from her honeymoon she gives Puerto Rican candy to Erin and she's like, "Oh, coco leche!" And Pam's like, "I got them for the office." And Erin is like, "I need to ask Michael." And Pam is like, "I think it'll be okay." Because it's literally just putting candies out, but she's like, "I'll just ask Michael." It's so small, but clearly there's a memo that Angela or Dwight had put out at some point about sharing gifts. It's like the tiniest thing. It's really hard to come up with those ideas that feel so real to what working in an office is actually like. It's about things like bagel Fridays.

Andy develops a crush on Erin shortly after she arrives and they have a long, awkward courtship throughout season six.

Danny Chun: We had this really funny, oddball new character and so we tried to hang some more substantial stuff on her. That's how the Andy/Erin stuff started, which became sort of a fun house–mirror version of Jim and Pam. We didn't really ever feel that it was going to be the exact same sort of soapy thing as them. We felt like it was these two goofy oddballs, weirdos who have never really had anyone understand them, let's see what happens if they sort of work in the same place and have interest in each other.

Myles McNutt (TV Critic, AV Club): You can't do that. You can't do a huge will they/won't they relationship, play it out, and then decide you're gonna do another will they/won't they relationship that's basically just the same thing. And . . . particularly not with characters that don't have the same sense of groundedness. I mean, I love Erin's character in many ways, but they could never decide how dumb she was and it was always really uneven.

Right before taking off to Niagara Falls for his wedding, Jim gets promoted to comanager and gets his own office.

Danny Chun: That was coming out of a bit of affection for Jim. We like Jim and we want him to keep advancing in life. We don't want him to feel like he's stuck at the same desk for his whole life, so let's give him a promotion. It also felt real. If a manager came into the office, they would probably realize Jim is one of the few truly competent and intelligent people there, so it felt [like] also there's a reality to it. Also, it felt very stupid and wrongheaded because corporations and businesses do stupid things all the time because a bunch of people in a conference room talked themselves in circles and then came up with this as their best idea. We all liked the comedy of how weird of an idea it was to have two equal comanagers.

Warren Lieberstein: There was some discussion of, "When you give Jim authority does it cut out what makes him so likable? Does it take away some of his comedy power when he looks at the camera and goes, 'Oh no, now I have to do *this*?' What are his looks to the camera now that he's in charge?" But it makes sense to advance him. Someone as bright as him would not be content to just stay in the same position for that long. There would come a point where something would have to give.

After fourteen episodes as comanager, Jim was demoted back to salesman.

Danny Chun: Taking Jim, who is sort of the point-of-view character of the show, and putting him in the power position did sort of fundamentally change some of the dynamics that were central to the show. I think a lot of people were sort of missing the original dynamics.

Just as Jim was demoted, Darryl was finally promoted from the warehouse up to the office. It finally allowed Craig Robinson to be a full-time presence on the show.

Danny Chun: That came out of affection for the character and wanting him to kind of have a win and have ambition and see that through.

Warren Lieberstein: We did that for the very same reason as Jim moving up. Someone who's bright and capable would want to make that kind of jump. It was also an effort to give Craig Robinson more screen time because he's so funny. He is the kind of comedy guy where it doesn't matter how straight the line is written, he's funny. Whenever you have an opportunity to have that kind of an actor in your scene, you want it.

Myles McNutt: Darryl in the warehouse was an outsider. He had a different perspective when he wasn't part of the office culture. There was an upstairs/downstairs perspective that he brought. When you bring him into the office, you lose that. And I think that ultimately it was an unfortunate decision. I still liked the character, but they no longer could tell a story about him being an outsider. And then you have to figure out, "Who is this character now that he's gained this goal? What are his new goals? What is he trying to accomplish?"

Danny Chun: We did see there was a downside and it was all part of the discussion during the pre-production of the season, when we have lot of arguments and debates. And then ultimately whoever is running the show just decides, "Okay, let's do it this way and we'll have to try to mitigate or find some way around the cons."

Midway through the season, Zach Woods joined the cast. He played Gabe, a gangly, awkward representative from Dunder Mifflin's new parent, Sabre, who yearned for more power than he was actually afforded.

Zach Woods (Gabe Lewis, Seasons 6–9): Gabe was just ego. The only thing that mattered to him was supremacy and dominance and power and popularity, and he was so ill equipped to attain any one of those things.

Kate Flannery: He was so young and didn't have much experience, but he was so brave. He was so beautifully fearless, so dry and so terrific. He always seemed to have five completely different takes on what he was doing. He always gave choices immediately when we shot a scene.

Justin Spitzer: He used to go on these riffs that were just shockingly funny. It couldn't have been easy for him to come six years into a show, but I don't remember him ever having difficulties. If he did he kept it to himself. And he wasn't a selfish actor at all. He would just find ways to give people things, improv gifts and things like that.

Halsted Sullivan: Zach Woods was like an ace in the hole. He was a brilliant improviser. He was brilliant at talking heads. He was brilliant at just making an inference that you didn't think about before he said it.

Danny Chun: He was one of the most amazing improvisers I've ever worked with. When we were shooting talking heads, we'd have like five of them already written and he would do them all and then he'd be like, "Can I try something?" And you'd be like, "Sure," and he'd just rattle off ten more that were as good or better than what we had written. It seemed like he was just coming up with them off the top of his head.

Rusty Mahmood: He was an amazing improv. Steve even said, "That guy keeps me on my toes." What a great compliment. Zach would come in and he would say his lines that they gave him, and then when he had a little more feel for the show, he started really going for it. The only bummer is that the direction of the show wasn't there to feature him. He had the Ichabod Crane role and it was just a small role. But he made that role great. He's just like Ellie, the nicest guy, down-to-earth. I told him just like I told Ellie, "Your star is going to rise. You're going to hit it. You're too talented. And unfortunately, this show has too many big stars now to nurture a new one this late in the game." But thank God he found *Silicon Valley* and he's just killing it.

Brian Wittle: They couldn't have picked a better guy. He's not just funny, he's super sweet and ridiculously nice. He's gonna be like Steve Carell, I think. That's his disposition. He was really good at improvising, one of the best ones I've ever seen. I can't remember the scene, but one time I was laughing so hard that they had to cut the shot. Mindy was there and she was like, "I've never heard sound break the shot before."

Along with Zach came Kathy Bates as Sabre CEO Jo Bennett.

Kate Flannery: Kathy Bates was intimidating initially. I'm a huge fan, so in my mind I was trying to get the movie *Misery* out of my head; my God. But eventually she did warm up and was lovely, but I think it was daunting on both sides initially.

Teri Weinberg: I remember her coming in and doing the first table read and all of us just sat so quietly, because we were so in awe of who she is. We were so intimidated by this aura that she'd brought in. It was really fun to be able to be fans of some of these people that came in and be able to see the incredible work that they did.

Claire Scanlon: I remember when Kathy Bates spoke her voice was trembling at first. We were shocked. We were so excited to be working with freaking Kathy. I knew that she would be intimidated by coming into that group. She said, "You guys are like a well-oiled machine, it is daunting coming into this group."

Jeff Blitz: It felt like people were a little intimidated by her, but her presence on set was that of a total pro and she got the humor of it. Sometimes they would bring people from a world of drama that just didn't quite get the rhythm of the comedy of it; she did. When she would blow a take she would often say something along the lines of, "Oh fuck a duck." Everybody would start to laugh and then feel real chill about it.

Randy Cordray: When Kathy Bates arrived a lot was going on and I felt very bad because occasionally I had to go to Kathy Bates and say, "Kathy, the schedule does not favor you for tomorrow." "Oh really, how so?" "Well, we have you in this upcoming scene, and we need to shoot that first thing in the morning, and then there's a scene that will probably be right after lunch that you're in, and then you're not going to work again until the end of the day, which would probably be seven P.M. So basically I need you for three different scenes, but they are interspersed." And she was like, "Randy, don't turn yourself inside out on my behalf. You're paying me for the day, you're giving me a nice comfy trailer, I've got a book, and I'm happy." That was pretty cool. She was a total professional and a dear, sweet woman.

Aaron Shure: When Kathy Bates came she would ask questions like, "Can I change this *and* to an *or*?" She'd ask permission for tiny, tiny little script changes. I do remember thinking that was good for the rest of the cast, to hear the degree to which she respected the script. Because I think she could have just done it her way without even asking, so the deference she showed to the script was really nice.

Dunder Mifflin's dire financial situation and the transfer of power to Sabre was the main story line of the season.

Danny Chun: We had a lot of conversations about what would it feel like if a company bought Dunder Mifflin. That would add an infusion of completely new people and corporate dynamics and the power structure would change. It also felt vaguely representative of what was happening in the news and in the world of the economy. There was this feeling of, "Hey, this could be interesting. Let's see what happens if an entirely new company comes in. That's obviously a real thing that happens to companies, they get taken over, they get bought out, whatever, so let's explore that."

Halsted Sullivan: What happens when we dig ourselves into a hole and explore this new world? What happens if the company gets purchased? 'Cause in real life, companies get purchased by other companies and there's consolidation. And how does Michael deal with this super-powerful woman who is Kathy Bates? Sabre was just a new world to explore, and bringing in Gabe created a real different dynamic because he's not an employee of Michael's, so their dynamic is very different.

Justin Spitzer: You can only tell so many small, relatable workplace stories and it just seemed like it was one of the kind of beats we had in the back of our mind that could sort of subtly change things, give things a new flavor.

Danny Chun: People got really excited about sort of the depiction of this extremely bland, really terrible sort of tech/computer company, Sabre. It was fun to pitch on how bad that company could be. We were basing it off of all these different computer companies, many of whom don't exist anymore, like Compaq and all those places.

Aaron Shure: We were looking for more drama. It was also something that was going on in our world too with the Vivendi and NBCUniversal sale, and we just sort of felt like part of the zeitgeist with mergers and new management.

The ratings were still quite strong for an NBC sitcom of that time, but this was the first season that didn't begin with Greg Daniels at the helm and many on the creative team were starting to feel severe burnout.

Ben Patrick: To this day, I kind of think that five seasons of anything is about as much as you ever want to do. It started to be muscle memory after a while. By season six, it started to feel more cartoonish at times. Greg was such a stickler for everything being based in reality. Paul and Jen are friends of mine, but they just have different comedy styles.

Kelly Cantley: I think the reason that the show was so funny in the first four or five seasons is that when there was a choice between reality and comedy, they always picked reality. That meant the comedy was super grounded in relatable, true characters.

Anthony Farrell: *30 Rock* was happening and there was a little bit of a push to kind of go broader, and I was always like, "No, let's not do that!" I was always trying to pull things back to more realistic. My favorite season of *The Office* is the second season. I wanted more of that. I wanted more of the painful reality of the show, so I'd always be championing that stuff.

Brian Wittle: There were times when stuff felt too jokey. I remember one episode where they dress up with mustaches and they think they're dealing with the Mafia ["Mafia" from season six]. The guy from *Goodfellas* [Mike Starr] was in the episode. Everybody just thought that episode was so stupid and so ridiculous, even Steve. While we were shooting they were like, "This is so silly. Are we jumping the shark? It shouldn't be this slapsticky."

Ben Patrick: I love Jen Celotta's scripts and I love Paul Lieberstein's scripts, but they definitely ran it a little differently. I also know that when Greg left, John and Jenna started to feel like they needed to have more control over their story lines. They started pushing their weight around more.

Briton W. Erwin: I think Paul was exhausted a lot of the time. That's a massive amount of stuff to take on. It's hard enough being the showrunner, but being the showrunner who's not only the head writer but is also part of the cast and ultimately the one deciding which episodes get locked . . . He had no breaks whatsoever. When Greg was in charge he was on the set a lot, but we could also get his attention when we needed to lock an episode. When Paul took over and was a cast member and a writer and the showrunner, you caught him when you could. It led to a lot of long nights, but we got to play a lot of Call of Duty.

At the end of the season, Jen Celotta decided to leave.

Jen Celotta: It was the best job I ever had. It doesn't get better than that. Back when I was leaving one of the people who worked there was like, "What are you doing? Have you lost your mind? What else is there?" I agree with that, but I also got to a place where brain-wise I needed stimulation. Those were the best characters I've written for, but they were created by other people and after a while you want to create your own thing.

Lee Eisenberg and Gene Stupnitsky—the writing duo behind many of the show's best episodes, including "Dinner Party," "Weight Loss," "Women's Appreciation," and "Scott's Tots"—also quit.

Gene Stupnitsky: Greg was barely around by that point and I think we were just ready for something new. We worked seven days a week for five years and by the end you're just exhausted. You're burnt out. I had nothing more to give. We were ready for a new challenge. I couldn't come up with any more stories about a stapler missing.

KEY EPISODE 9

“Niagara”

Most sitcoms facing a wedding between two of the main characters would build up to it throughout the course of an entire season. But on The Office, *Jim married Pam in the fourth episode of the sixth season. It was a double episode that required a trip to Niagara Falls and endless debate in the writers’ room about how to pull this off without jumping the shark.*

Halsted Sullivan: We kept asking ourselves, “How do you make a wedding just not about the bride and groom and how do you also service the wedding so it’s special?” That’s because Jim and Pam were anything but traditional. There was a lot of talk of, “Would they invite the office to the wedding? Would they truly? There are young people in Scranton. Wouldn’t they have their own friends? How do we make them real characters without the show feeling too claustrophobic? But then, at the same time, how do we make the episode feel like an episode of *The Office*, with all of these characters that we love, and everyone has their moment?” That’s why the wedding itself is really just one act. But leading up to the wedding we have all of these different stories that we’re servicing. There’s Kevin and his shoes and his toupee, Dwight and Michael being this fun combo trying to pick up women and then, lo and behold, he hooks up with Pam’s mom.

The idea of having them get married three hundred miles away from Scranton at Niagara Falls came from Greg Daniels.

Randy Cordray: That summer, on their vacation, Greg and his family had gone to Niagara Falls. And whereas Greg saw that parts of Niagara Falls are commercialized and tawdry, it is still a significant natural phenomenon that has an incredible power over people. As crazy and full of Ripley's museums and thrill rides and vendors hawking silly trinkets and wares [as it is], it still has some magical mysterious power over people that causes romance. People still go to Niagara Falls to get engaged or to get married. This was Greg's idea, that a significant event could happen in a place that had been completely commercialized and taken over by the money grubbers in the temple, as it were.

Greg Daniels: When I was a kid in New York there [were] a lot of advertisements for Mount Airy Lodge, the "Host with the Most in the Poconos." It was really kitschy, and I always wanted Roy and Pam to go there on a trip and we were all set up to do it and we found out it had just been sold. Niagara had that kitschy sort of feeling, but also an amazing thing at the center of it that we could hide all the way to the end and expose this beautiful, dramatic thing.

Having the wedding at Niagara Falls was a great idea, but Daniels had another one that proved to be less popular.

Paul Feig: Originally, it was supposed to be that Pam and Jim are in the middle of their ceremony and Roy has been haunting around and regretting that he let her go and wanted her back. When they were in the middle of the ceremony, it was supposed to be that Roy rides into the church on horseback dressed like a white knight to win her back.

Randy Cordray: Roy had decided that this whole episode with Jim was really just Pam trying to make Roy jealous to get her back. He thought Pam was really in love with him all along and that he needed a grand gesture to get her back. And so in the story outline, Roy goes to a horse-rental facility, a stable, and rents a beautiful white horse.

Paul Feig: When he rides in Pam is like, "Ugh, get out of here."

Randy Cordray: When she turns around he sees that she's pregnant and he realizes, "Oh, I am deluded. This is crazy. She doesn't want me, she wants Jim. She's having a baby with Jim." And he would slink away in disgrace.

Paul Feig: He then has to turn the horse back around and ride back out, which was super funny. And then Greg came up with an idea where Dwight has an obsession with the falls and some sort of suicide gene to go over them. He fights it the whole episode.

Randy Cordray: Dwight Schrute, horseman and beet farmer that he is, would then come along after the wedding. He's walking outside the church and he sees Roy despondent, sitting on the curb, holding the reins of the horse. And he says, "Tough luck, buddy, that didn't work out like you wanted it, did it?" And Roy would be, "No, and I'm stuck with this stupid horse. I paid for the horse for the rest of the day." And Dwight says, "Hey, I'm a horse person. Let me take care of it." He takes the reins of the horse and he's taking it ostensibly back to the stables, but Dwight somehow finds himself riding along the banks of the Niagara River.

Paul Feig: He then rides it into the water.

Randy Cordray: They're riding along through the white water of the river and Dwight realizes he's gotten too close to the edge of Niagara Falls and the horse is looking fearful and Dwight is looking fearful. Dwight finally realizes he's gotta bail off the horse and swims safely to shore. We cut to Jim and Pam having a romantic moment on the bow of the *Maid of the Mist* boat, and in the background we see this white horse go tumbling over Niagara Falls, plunging six hundred feet.

Paul Feig: I remember all the writers were coming to me like, "We can't do this. You can't kill a horse. It's crazy." Everybody was all over Greg, and Greg was just like, "I'm telling you this is going to work." He was digging in and everybody was just freaking out about it.

Brent Forrester: Greg just thought this was super funny. I think many people felt that it was in violation of his own rule of keeping the tone naturalistic, a horse going off the falls. They fought him, many of the writers, aggressively on this. I think some people also felt that Greg didn't love animals enough.

Randy Cordray: I needed to find a church that had doors big enough to accommodate a horse and a rider. And trying to capture a white horse going over a pure white waterfall is a job for Peter Jackson. This was a gag that, to be done right, would require a feature film's worth of digital effects. I thought it was going to look cheesy and shitty.

Gene Stupnitsky: I never understood if Greg was serious about certain ideas or if he wanted to push to see as far as he can go and to see how we would react. He's so smart and so brilliant. Sometimes there would be a left-field idea and you would be like, "Is he fucking with us?"

Danny Chun: If felt to me felt like a proxy for a lot of the sort of intra-writers'-room conflicts that had taken place over many years. I was a newcomer at that point and I didn't know what part was bit and what part was real. I didn't even understand if Greg himself actually liked it. My vantage point on the whole thing was, "Does he want to do this or is this the longest, most deadpan bit?," which I also would have completely believed.

Justin Spitzer: It just seemed so crazy. Oh my God, it's such a broad idea. I think that's some of what Greg's genius was though. This show was generally a very grounded show, and every now and then he'd put in these totally absurd moments. And because the rest of the show was so grounded you could actually buy them. But that one I remember a number of us felt like maybe we were pushing it too far.

Brian Wittle: It would have been stupid.

Warren Lieberstein: I'm one of the few people who trust that Greg could have made it work, but so many people were against it, including Steve. And I just think Greg is one of these people who, he can make it work. I do remember people at the table read being were very, very concerned about it.

Danny Chun: I wasn't in favor of it, but I felt like Greg liked the reaction he got out of the writers over stuff like this because there was a real sort of family dynamic between him and Mindy and B. J. and Paul. I think there was a lot of meta entertainment value in this debate.

Randy Cordray: A week in advance of going to Niagara Falls, we had our table read for that episode. The network is there and the studio is there. The actors all read the parts, the director reads the stage directions out loud, and then afterward, the network and the studio give a few notes, and then you are left with just the writers to discuss the episode. Steve Carell stays behind because he is a producer on the show and he has some say over the writing of the show. Steve was the first one to speak up. He said, "Guys, I love the episode but you can't throw a horse over Niagara Falls." And Greg and Mindy were like, "Really? But it's so funny." And he's like, "Yes, it is funny. I love your writing. I love all of you, but this is really an animated joke. This is a cartoon joke. This is a joke we might see on *The Simpsons*. I know many people think that *The Office* has already jumped the shark in many different ways, but let me just say, throwing a horse over Niagara Falls is really jumping the shark. I'm not in favor of this." And with that, he took his leave and we were left to discuss this.

Paul Feig: Everyone just attacked Greg so much that he finally very angrily said, "All right, forget it! We're not going to do it!"

Greg Daniels: Luckily, I was persuaded not to do [it].

This didn't give them much time to come up with an alternative scene for the wedding.

Gene Stupnitsky: We watched a lot of YouTube during lunch and there was this viral video of a couple dancing down the aisle at their wedding. We decided to go with that.

Paul Feig: I remember the writers coming up with that and thinking it would be fun to have a dance number. The day we were shooting in the church was just a really packed day. We had so many things we had to shoot and we were running way out of time. I saw the end coming and I thought, "Oh my God, we have to shoot this entire dance number. We're not going to make it." We had time to do maybe two takes of it. I was like, "Oh my God, what's going to happen?" We shoot it the first time and it's so fucking great. Everybody just nailed it and the energy is fun and everybody's joyous. I was just completely in tears. It was so moving. It's still, to this day, it will choke me up when I watch it.

But the joyous wedding dance wasn't even the emotional peak of the episode. Prior to the ceremony, Jim and Pam are seen running away from the church. The guests begin to get restless as they wait, but suddenly they come back and the ceremony begins. It's only during the wedding dance that we flash back and see that they actually got married on the Maid of the Mist *boat by the captain so they could have a private moment away from their crazy coworkers. Unlike every other scene in the episode, it was actually shot at Niagara Falls. Randy Cordray pulled double duty as the line producer on the shoot and the captain that married them.*

Steve Burgess: Randy felt really strongly that we couldn't do that with a green screen on a fake set onstage somewhere. He fought really hard for NBCUniversal to send him, Jenna, John, and a splinter crew to Niagara Falls.

Randy Cordray: When I prepared that budget, one of the comments from the studio was, "You're not taking John Krasinski and Jenna Fischer to Niagara Falls. You can go there and shoot on the *Maid of the Mist*, but you're gonna shoot them in a digital composite here on a stage in Hollywood and you will plant them on the front of that boat. We're not spending plane tickets and hotel fare and putting our actors out on that boat. You're gonna digitally composite that." Well, I knew that was gonna look like crap. I knew creatively that we had to have John Krasinski and Jenna Fischer getting actually wet under the spray of the actual Niagara Falls on the actual *Maid of the Mist*. I was not about to give that up. When the horse went away, I knew we could do it. I knew we had the money to do it.

Randall Einhorn: The digital cameras I was using then wouldn't have looked good with the glare of the falls, so I used a Super 16 millimeter film, which is a really expensive thing to do.

Paul Feig: It was pretty misty on the boat, so Randall had to get this attachment for his camera that spun this piece of glass in front of the lens so that the water would fly off.

Randy Cordray: We go through the scene and I recite the vows and Jim pledges his undying loyalty to Pam and Pam recites her vows. Jim puts the ring on her and the boat is so deep into the water of the falls that we are drenched. I look over at Jenna Fischer and it's all I can do to control myself because I'm looking at her. It's like someone dumped the Gatorade bucket on her after a pro football game. She is drenched. Her hair, her makeup, her eye makeup. Everything. John has kind of got a wry smile on his face in that take too because he's looking at Jenna just melting in the spray. We're just all drenched.

Paul Feig: At one point during the shoot the mist was so bad that I think Randy's Bible blew off and blew into the water.

Randy Cordray: We have a powwow with Paul Feig and he's like, "Boys and girls, it was too wet. We couldn't understand the dialogue. There was so much water on the camera. The spinning device was working quite well but Randall was concerned that you couldn't really see them." And so we're like, "We've got to do this again. We have to do this again. And maybe we'll recite the vows a little earlier than in the spray of the falls." We went back to the hotel and it took three hours to get everyone dried off and back together with hair and makeup.

Cordray was only able to get the Maid of the Mist Corporation to let them shoot on the boat if they didn't even speak to the captain, let alone ask him to change the course of the journey.

Randy Cordray: But when we got back on boat the captain turned to me and said, "Boy, you guys got really soaked last time, didn't you?" And I said, "Yeah, we did." And he said, "Do you want that?" And I said, "No, actually we don't want to be." And he said, "Well I don't have to go so deep." And I said, "Really?" And he goes, "Yeah, I'll do anything you want." And I said, "We want to stay out of that fray." And he said, "Hell yeah, buddy. We'll do that. We'll just keep it backed off. The tourists don't need to know that they're not getting the full-ticket ride here. They won't care. They're getting to see an episode of *The Office*. I'll do anything you guys want. You tell me." I was like, "God bless you."

Paul Feig: Claire Scanlon was the editor on that. I remember us working on that and just cutting back and forth between the dance number and Pam and Jim on the boat. It was just so emotional.

Claire Scanlon: So there was this one shot where Jim looks to the camera with his arm around Pam at the very end while they're on the boat. He's like, "I did it, I did this. I got the girl."

Greg Daniels: Claire found this shot. That was totally unexpected and wonderful.

Claire Scanlon: And when I found that I was like, "Okay, that's the end. That'll be the last shot that you see in this whole montage." And so Jenna and John came into my bay to watch it when it was done. I turned around after they saw it for the first time and they were crying. And I was like, "Yes, I made them cry." It just felt really good. That's always the goal, by the way. Even though it's comedy, you always want to make people feel. That's the highest compliment you can get, is to make someone feel something, whether it's laughing, feeling kind of anxious, or anything.

Paul Feig: I was sad because when Emmy time rolled around it wasn't nominated. The show had been on for so long by that time that people were past voting for it. I always felt that episode really got short shrift because I think that's one of the best episodes, to me, that I've ever seen.

chapter 22

SPIN-OFF BLUES

("Parks and Recreation *should have been a spin-off.*")

The pilot for Parks and Recreation *aired right after the fifth-season* Office *episodes "Dream Team" and "Michael Scott Paper Company." But even though it was a mockumentary created by Greg Daniels and Michael Schur and featured Rashida Jones in a major role, it wasn't a spin-off. And despite endless debate and one very noble attempt, there never was an actual* Office *spin-off.*

Justin Spitzer: Greg was always talking about what a spin-off could be and there was a lot of stress about it. I remember even at one point I had that one line as the doctor [in "Fun Run"] and he looks at me and he's like, "We'll spin off the doctor!" That was obviously a joke, but he was just kind of searching for what characters have we had that we could spin off.

Ben Silverman: When I took over as the chairman of NBC [in 2007] I was like, "We should be doing a spin-off of *The Office.*" And *Parks and Recreation* should have been one.

Justin Spitzer: One of Michael Schur's favorite books was *The Power Broker,* [about] Robert Moses. He was essentially head of the parks department in New York in the early twentieth century. I think some of *Parks and Recreation* came from that.

Teri Weinberg: And at that time when *Parks and Rec* was developed, Ben and I were at NBC, and so we were a part of the birthing of *Parks and Rec* with Greg and Mike Schur. We made the decision to create a whole new world around Amy, and take the relationships that we had with Rashida and Amy and the cast that we'd built around that show, to create something new and let that be its own organism.

Ben Silverman: I wanted it developed as a spin-off and I'm annoyed that my voice wasn't heard. They initially wanted to call it *The Big Dig.* I was like, "Government bureaucracy is not that great unless you make it a spin-off." I went and got Amy Poehler for the network and she was open to doing a spin-off, but then Greg Daniels and Mike Schur didn't want to do a spin-off. I would have had Amy come on and start a relationship with Ed Helms or someone and then they would have kind of spun out into their own show. They wanted to do their own things. I was like, "You're wrong." They could have aired together back-to-back. This would be like the biggest thing. It would have been incredible. It just was shortsighted. Everyone would have loved it. It would have been better for both shows.

Kate Flannery: I thought *Parks and Rec* was a great testament to what we were doing and I felt that it was part of the change of television. It was definitely an affirmation for everything we were about. I don't think it weakened us because it was so different. Of course, I missed Greg and Mike Schur since it took them away from us.

Justin Spitzer: I think in the casting of Rashida Jones as a different character on *Parks and Rec,* that was them saying, "This is definitely not a spin-off. We have the same actor playing two different parts. These two shows can't even exist in the same world."

Teri Weinberg: We knew we were comedy gold and we knew that we had so much talent in our characters. In this business, you always get the question of, "Are you strong enough to take a relationship out of your show you can spin that off? Is there a way to take the success of a show and turn it into a spin-off?" And I think that we were smart enough to not fall into that, because we cared about the show so much, and we cared about keeping it intact, and we didn't really want to steal from ourselves. We made the decision to keep it intact.

Five months after Parks and Recreation *came on the air,* Modern Family *debuted on ABC to enormous ratings. It used the same mockumentary format as* The Office.

Justin Spitzer: Greg had in mind to maybe do a family mockumentary show, but I don't know if that would have been a spin-off or its own show. But I know Greg had that idea. Then *Modern Family* came along.

Alan Sepinwall: *Modern Family* shamelessly copied *The Office.*

Ben Silverman: I was really bummed about that. It annoyed me. *Modern Family* is about a family the way *The Office* is about an office. All I'd wanted to do was a family spin-off. I was so bummed not to be able to pull that off.

Aaron Shure: We always put so much thought into why a camera would be present for certain scenes. And then *Modern Family* came along and did all the same stuff we did with zero justification about why the camera would ever be anywhere and America just loved it.

Oscar Nunez: *Modern Family,* which I love, doesn't even have a documentary team, but they still do talking heads.

Teri Weinberg: Interestingly enough, I was at NBC at the time when [*Modern Family* creators] Steve [Levitan] and Chris [Lloyd] pitched the show. I recall at the time, it was about an exchange student doing a documentary about their experience staying with this family. I was really honest with them and I said, "I think you guys are brilliant and it would be a gift for us to be able to work with the two of you. But with all due respect, we're respecting the property that we have in *The Office*. There are conversations about what the future of that show is and that's where my attention is, that's where my focus is." So we passed on it. I don't have any regrets about it though.

As The Office *was winding down in season nine, a final attempt at an* Office *spin-off was made. They called it* The Farm *and it focused on Dwight's life on his beet farm with his previously unseen family members. NBC ordered a pilot, which was spearheaded by Paul Lieberstein. Thomas Middleditch was cast as Dwight's brother Jeb, Majandra Delfino was his sister Frannie, and Tom Bower was his uncle Heinrich.*

Brent Forrester: Paul shoots it. It's great. We all love it. We're like, "Oh my God. This is a spin-off! Dwight's going to be the star of his own show!"

Steve Burgess: The thought behind it was how much fun it could be to see the rest of the Schrutes. We had only gotten a little glimpse of them with Mose, and obviously Mike Schur wasn't gonna be available to do a lot about it since he was the showrunner on *Parks and Rec.*

Brent Forrester: NBC decided not to pick it up.

Briton W. Erwin: Creating a family out of full cloth just didn't work. The cast didn't have chemistry and none of it fit together. It was very clear when we were doing the pilot that it just was a little rushed and the casting was off. Paul was not very clear in what he was going for. I think it would have been better to wait until *The Office* ended and then spend some time with it, really develop it and give it a chance to be its own thing. Pilots are hard enough to do on their own, but when you're trying to kinda do them simultaneously while you're doing a huge hit show, you're not giving yourself great odds for success.

Claire Scanlon: It wasn't good. Sometimes there are great pilots that don't get picked up. This was not one of those. It just didn't have a point of view. It was a mess.

Briton W. Erwin: Suddenly introducing a long-lost sister and a long-lost brother to Dwight and having it kinda revolve literally around the farm didn't really play to strengths that *The Office* had built up. It was gonna be much more of this kind of condensed world of these few family members sort of bickering with each other. What you could have done was have an *Office* anywhere, in any city. If the spin-off had been about Dwight moving, opening a new branch in some small town in the Midwest, I think you could have gotten something from that.

When NBC didn't go with the show, they took much of the footage and folded it into the ninth-season episode "The Farm."

Claire Scanlon: Doing that almost ate the cost of the pilot.

Brent Forrester: Greg and NBC decided, "Well, we're just going to do it as an episode of the show." I remember thinking, "Come on, no one will buy that. It doesn't have any of the cast, right?" They were like, "No, we can shoot some new material and a new cold open. Oscar can be there." So we did it and it's just one of the episodes. To my knowledge, no viewers rebelled. Nobody really figured it out. It's just considered to be this unusual episode. To people who didn't know the backstory, it must have just seemed like the most surreal, biggest swing ever taken by a TV show, where it's like, "None of the principal cast will be in this episode. It will be all guest cast and they will never be seen again."

chapter 23

STEVE

("He would stand there and help every single person out of the van.")

The pressure on Steve Carell to find time for his family and growing film career along with all his work on The Office *became greater every single season. As the sixth season wound down, many* Office *insiders feared his days on the show were numbered. It was a frightening thought since he wasn't only the boss on the show; when the cameras turned off everyone continued looking at him for guidance.*

Kate Flannery: I knew Steve in my days at Second City in Chicago. He was hilarious, very shy and very kind. He was so committed to his character that watching him work was like taking a master class in acting. We all knew he was number one at that show, but he didn't accept that. He made it seem like there was no hierarchy. He was really just all about the work and that was totally who he was on the show as well. He never changed. The show did not change him one bit.

J. J. Abrams: Steve is a brilliant comedic actor. He brought a different color to the character than Ricky Gervais did and made Michael Scott relatable and heartbreaking. At his core, the character is so unbearably sad, and Steve really brought that out. He's also so gifted at improv. When

I directed his testimonials I was looking into the eyes of Michael Scott, not Steve Carell. It was the most surreal thing.

Lee Eisenberg: When you'd engage with him before a take he'd be talking and he'd look at you clearly. But when they would say *action* his eyes glazed over and it was a subtle transformation, but in that moment his IQ dropped fifty points.

Kate Flannery: I feel like people don't acknowledge the level of mastery that he's giving each character that he plays. I don't know if he still gets enough credit for what he did with Michael Scott.

Ricky Gervais: He's a great actor . . . a brilliant actor. There was no ceiling there for a comic performance because he was great. He's so likable. I teased him and said that he's *nearly* handsome. He gave such gusto to that role. It was just great. And fucking hardworking. Jesus Christ. Unbelievable. He'd have a week off and go and do a movie.

Teri Weinberg: Steve is one of the most dedicated, grounded people that I think I've ever met. He was always a leader on set and he was always the one who set the tone. He was always the one who showed up to everything, every table read. He was the first one on the set. He cared so much about the show, and he cared so much about what we had all built. We knew in time he would make the decision to leave the show and have the incredible career that he has. But you would never know every time he stepped foot on that set that he was a gigantic movie star, because it was all about the work, and it was all about the love and the respect for what our family had built, and how much he loved the character and how much he loved being on the show.

Amy Ryan: Steve is strangely generous for an actor of his caliber. A scene would finish and he'd compliment me. He'd say, "What you did there was really funny!" I'd be like, "Really?" It's not that you doubt it, but it's just so rare that the star of a show, or star of anything, just turns the light on the other person. He's also brilliant at putting other people at ease. After years of working in a company, he's comfortable sharing the joke or the spotlight. He did from day one. He was just very complimentary and incredibly playful.

Dean Holland: Steve Carell's takes were never the same. That was also true for Chris Pratt and Amy Poehler [on *Parks and Recreation*]. Very often we would sit in the editing room and I'd play eight takes in a row of other actors for Greg and every single line in each take would be the exact same. But Carell would give you something different with each take. It was just a plethora of options from him.

Melora Hardin: We really just had a similar instinctual understanding of the craft and we just clicked. He was really good at making room for me to do my stuff, which is rare. Sometimes you feel like people are sitting on you energetically, but never Steve. He made our scenes a big play space where I could come in with surprising moments. He let us both be in the moment. In a perfect world as an actor, you just want to be giving and receiving all the time. You want to be tossing out the softball, and you want the softball to be caught, and then you want it to be thrown back to you. That's what makes a great scene. Nobody was better at throwing the softball back to other people than Steve. He was so generous.

Briton W. Erwin: Steve is one of the nicest human beings on the planet. Around the time of season five, he's one of the biggest movie stars on the planet and he's also in every scene of every episode. We'd work sixteen-hour days for weeks on end and I never once saw any kind of diva mentality. He set a really high bar for everyone on the show. Because if anyone had the right to complain about conditions or the length of time it took to do stuff or whatever, it would've been him. He never did.

Stacey Snider: He's one of those actors that always makes the work better, and that the people that he's working with go out of their way to give him that extra push. I always say that writers, and directors, and actors know that studio executives can pull certain levers that they don't even know they can pull when they care about the person. We work across all the films to make them as great as they can be, and to market and structure them to the greatest impact. That extra secret sauce is just reserved for certain people and you're not even aware that you're using it. For someone like Carell, people go out of their way. He's just that good.

Andy Buckley: He's just such a magnificent guy, but he's also such a magnificent actor. And every time you would do a scene with him, he would always try something different. Not different lines, but he would just do it in a different way, so that was fantastic because you just have to react to whatever's coming at you from him, which just makes it super fun to do that.

Jen Celotta: There was never a false note with Steve because you believe that he's true in everything he does. He has his own set of rules and he plays by them. Even when he's doing ridiculous things, there's such integrity to him. He protected his character and he knew his character. He would be up to go to the edge of the line we needed him to go [to] for comedy, but he did it so smartly. We trusted him enormously.

Alysia Raycraft: Nothing disparaging about anyone else with regards to fittings, but if I had a fitting at five A.M., five A.M. on the dot Steve would walk in with nothing but a can-do attitude. He was just the greatest.

Carey Bennett: Steve Carell is truly the loveliest man in Hollywood. We would go on location and we'd all be jammed into a van. He'd be in the front seat and he'd hop out first, open the door and help everybody out of the van. He'd help the crew out of the van! I've never seen that before or since.

Randall Einhorn: Steve, every day, would open the doors of the van, grab the ladies' chairs and their makeup and hair bags, and he would walk them to where they would sit and he'd put them down and then he'd go run his lines. He would carry their chairs because they were older women and he's a gentleman.

Kim Ferry: He would stand there and help every single person out of the van. Then if you have a chair, he would grab your chair and walk it over to the trailer and put it outside the trailer. He always was such a gentleman. So kind. I don't remember, in the almost ten years that I was on that show, [that] he [ever] said a bad word about anybody. He was so gracious and so kind. I've never worked with someone as kind as him. He's just a class act.

Randall Einhorn: Steve was amazing and always a treat to watch in that he would give you different levels each take. He would try a different thing each time. He's the perfect improv actor because he's not throwing a pass that's gonna hit you right in the gut each time. He's throwing a pass where you have to go "Whoa!" and catch it as you're flying through the air. He would set you up to look like a hero because he wanted everybody to be funny. He didn't want to be just the funny one. He wanted everybody to be funny.

Claire Scanlon: I remember watching the very first episode I cut, which was "Golden Ticket." I remember watching all the takes and being like, "Oh my God, he's so much better than people know. He's just doing something great in every take. How do you make the choice of which one to actually commit to and work from?" He could do vulnerability, deflection, and then a pathetic take, and then just pure broad comedy. His range was just so broad.

Mark Proksch: Steve was the only one that wouldn't jump on his cell phone when we finished a take. He would go off and run his lines and try different things. I learned a lot from being around him because he worked so damn hard and would try little changes with each take.

Richard Gonzales: Steve became a big sorta movie star, during the course of it, and nothing changed. He was still the same Steve.

Ben Patrick: The guy will pretty much do anything to make the scene work or the shot work. I always used to joke, like, you could tie two concrete blocks around his feet and ask him to deliver his line with his head turned sideways so that he saw the camera and [would] still be able to be mic'd. He would do all those things. He would contort himself to make it work.

Randy Cordray: To this day, in my long and varied career, Steve Carell is the most wonderful and most professional actor and the best human of anyone I ever worked with. I hold Steve Carell to the highest level of anyone I ever worked with. He was such a professional man. What was so amazing about Steve was that as Michael Scott, he could make your skin crawl in one scene by being such a jerk, and such an asshole, and in the very next scene you would weep for him. You bled for the man because he was so blind to his own faults.

B. J. Novak: He is the greatest actor alive, I think. My God, I don't know if Russell Crowe or [Robert] De Niro or anyone you go to as the greatest actor could do what Steve does.

Robert Shafer: I don't think people understand what a grinder he is. He's in every scene, pretty much, and he's driving every scene. When he's in between takes, he is looking at those pages and working. That guy's a stone-cold worker, and you have to be 'cause it's your show, so you're shouldering the responsibility. Not only that, but you're setting the tone. The star of the show sets the tone. I recently did a *Criminal Minds* episode, and believe me, the difference between Thomas Gibson setting the tone and Steve Carell setting the tone is pretty huge.

Kim Ferry: There was only one time where he told me about being really upset. It was because on the weekend he was trying to teach his daughter,

Annie, how to ride a bike and he had a lot of paparazzi that started showing up outside his house and started taking pictures of her. They were saying "Hey, over here." They were kind of heckling and at one point as she was trying to ride the bike she stopped, started crying, got off the bike, and she ran into the house. He was livid. At that point he walked across the street and he told me he said, "Look. I'm right here. You wanna take pictures of me, take pictures of me. You want to take pictures right now I'll stand here for an hour. But do not ever hurt my daughter like that. She didn't sign up for this. She just got born into my family and I'm famous." He was trying to explain to them she didn't deserve that just now. "Why can't I have an experience with my daughter, private?" And there was one paparazzi that literally stood in front of all the other guys and said, "You know what, guys? He's right. We should go. We'll all go. We should go."

Amy Ryan: He's such an approachable, warm person. And he's somewhat shy. I think a lot of people might think Steve is one of those actors who is constantly on, and doing bits and keeping everybody entertained. But it's quite the opposite.

Paul Feig: Working with Steve caused me to ruin so many takes because I'd always just burst out laughing. He'd go off in a tangent or an unexpected reaction and I'd just lose it. I will go to my grave saying that one of the biggest injustices in show business history is that Steve never won the Best Actor Emmy. I think the problem was that he made it look easy. Alec Baldwin is obviously funny too, but that's a very showy role. People didn't realize how hard Steve worked to create that character. If there's any justice, they will retroactively give him an honorary Emmy for that performance, because that's right up there with Carroll O'Connor as Archie Bunker.

Randall Einhorn: What everyone else did was not even in the same ballpark as Steve. I thought, Alec Baldwin's character, no discredit to him at all, but it was a much broader character, which is real easy. If you're going for funny, that's easy to do. You make it silly and wacky. And Tracy Morgan's character was all wack-a-doodle crazy. Steve tried to be a real guy. He's trying to be a boss of a paper company who ruled as far as the eye can see. He played such a small man trying to take such a big credit. It was just really interesting and really funny. The fact he never received Best Actor, that's just crazy.

Creed Bratton: How could someone like Steve Carell not win the Emmy for best actor? It's a travesty, a joke. One time, we were all at the table together and Angela said, "This is bullshit!" We went, "Yep!" At that time, I didn't even care what people thought, because we'd had it. We were behind him. He was our captain. I was very upset. I wouldn't even want to talk about it afterward. For a character you dislike to make you laugh like that? And in the bat of an eye he gives you heart? Come on! That's depth. That's some acting chops. His humanity as a person shines through his eyes.

Jenna Fischer: I can't believe that Steve did not get an Emmy for that character. It's one of the greatest performances in television history, in my opinion, and I feel like he should be given just honorary Emmy award for Michael Scott.

chapter 24

SEASON SEVEN

("Somebody didn't pay him enough. It was absolutely asinine.")

The sixth season of The Office *still had four episodes to air when Steve Carell went over to England to promote his new movie* Date Night. *Near the end of an interview, he was asked if he might stay on the show after his contract expired at the end of season seven. "I don't think so," he said. "I think that will probably be my last year." It was the first time the public heard that Carell was likely to leave the show, but his departure from the show was much more complicated than anyone knew at the time.*

Brian Wittle: I sat with him one time and he told me the story. He was doing a radio interview and he haphazardly mentioned, almost unconsciously, that it might be his last season. He didn't plan on saying it out loud and he hadn't decided anything. He was kind of thinking out loud, but he did it in an interview in public and it created news. Then what he said was the people connected to the show had no reaction to it. They didn't call him and say, "What? You wanna leave?" He said he didn't get any kind of response from them. When he realized he didn't get any kind of response from them, he thought, "Oh, maybe they don't really care if I leave. Maybe I should go do other things." So I think that made it easier, because when the news broke that he was considering it, the people that are in charge of keeping him there didn't make a big effort to do so until afterward.

Ben Silverman: The executive at the network who managed it, managed it so poorly, but I think they could have kept him even longer. He wanted to stay on the show and it was totally blown. The network boss at the time didn't go see him, didn't talk to him, didn't listen to him. This was when the network lost its ability to manage talent for a while, whether it was the Conan/Leno situation or losing Carell on the show. None of it had to happen. All of it could have been managed, but no one would talk to the talent.

Jeff Zucker: I vaguely remember having conversations [with Steve about staying], but I don't remember any details around it.

This took place just as Zucker was about to step down from NBC following Comcast's purchase of NBCUniversal. Bob Greenblatt replaced him.

Randy Cordray: NBC management had changed and there was a gentleman in charge of NBC programming by the name of Bob Greenblatt. Speaking in general terms, when a new head of programming takes over a network, the first thing he does is attempt to develop new comedies and new dramas under his watch. He's been hired for a reason. He or she has been hired to revamp a network's programming. We all believed that Bob Greenblatt was not as big a fan of *The Office* as we wished he would've been. He took *The Office* for granted.

Bob Greenblatt (Chairman of NBC Entertainment): I can't remember the sequence of events, but I think Steve was already departing the show when I arrived. I couldn't do anything about that since it preceded me.

Teri Weinberg: I think Steve made the decision to leave on his own. Of course, Bob [Greenblatt] would have wanted to have Steve, and we all wanted to have Steve. But I think he felt like he had seen his character progress in a way that was incredibly satisfying to him. And he felt that it was time and the story had taken him to a place where the character was ready to make that move, and we respected that.

Rusty Mahmood: I think he was ready to leave. I think he was ready to leave after six and was persuaded to do seven. That's from what I heard. And he was so busy. He had expressed to me how exhausted he was on multiple occasions.

Kim Ferry: He didn't want to leave the show. He had told the network that he was going to sign for another couple of years. He was willing to and his agent was willing to. But for some reason, they didn't contact him. I don't know if it was a game of chicken or what. That part I don't know because I couldn't believe why they wouldn't want Steve Carell to stay on the show. Maybe they were just trying to wait it out and then they were going to offer him something lesser. I have no idea. But I'm telling you that Steve wanted to stay on the show. He planned on staying on the show. He told his manager and his manager contacted them and said he's willing to sign another contract for a couple years. So all of that was willing and ready and, on their side, honest. And the deadline came for when they were supposed to give him an offer and it passed and they didn't make him an offer. So his agent was like, "Well, I guess they don't want to renew you for some reason." Which was insane to me. And to him, I think.

Allison Jones: As I recall, he was going to do another season and then NBC, for whatever reason, wouldn't make a deal with him.

Kim Ferry: His manager [Steve Sauer] basically manages three people: Steve, Julie Andrews, and Carol Burnett. I know he would have done anything to keep him on the show. He tried. It really was disappointing.

Randy Cordray: I think Steve would've stayed had he been given an offer by the network. Steve loved the show. We always tried to schedule his conflicts so they didn't affect the show. And he loved the people on the show. He loved all of us and I don't think he was ready to leave. I really think that he would've stayed on longer, but if you're not respected and don't even get offered a contract or a discussion of a future contract, then you move on.

Kim Ferry: We literally had this conversation in the trailer. I will never forget it because I was incredibly sad that he was leaving. He was like, "Well they didn't pick up my option." I'm like, "How do they not pick it up? What? What are you saying?" I couldn't believe it. He was like, "Look, I told them I want to do it. I don't want to leave. I don't understand." It just is mind-boggling how that happened. And I feel bad because I think a lot of people think he did leave the show on his own merit and it's absolutely not true. I'm telling you. I was there. I was *there.* He really wanted to stay. And it devastated all of us because he was the heart of our show.

Roxxi Dott (Hairstylist): How much money did NBC waste on everything when they could have just paid Steve what he wanted or given him what he was worth?

Allison Jones: Somebody didn't pay him enough. It was absolutely asinine. I don't know what else to say about that. Just asinine.

This put the writers in the difficult position of having to find a way to write Michael Scott out of the show by the end of the season.

Paul Lieberstein: For a while we had been talking about firing him, and we were going to do it in a way that nobody would [think of]—that when it finally comes to firing him, it's about money and it was a business mistake that he'd made. A small business mistake that had blown up. And all his behavior was excused, and everything over the years was excused, when the money was right. But as soon as he's not the earner, he's out. . . . I don't think it's as much fun for the viewers.

Peter Ocko: There was a sense that he had to achieve a certain amount of maturity before he left, but I think everyone understood that had its limits and that we had to respect who he was. You couldn't just heal the guy and then make him a fully functioning member of society and send him away.

B. J. Novak: The whole season we would approach by letting Michael grow a bit by the end of each episode, which we generally never did.

Paul Lieberstein: Up until this season, Michael would just find a new level of denial to end an episode.

B. J. Novak: And that would be funny, but we could start firing off our Michael self-awareness gun because we knew we only had a few bullets anyway.

Amelie Gillette: There were definitely a few big things that we wanted to hit with Michael in terms of all the relationships that he had built. And this wasn't just Holly, but we wanted to bring Todd Packer back and have that relationship have a form of closure. There were a few sort of tent poles that they identified and we as a room sort of identified, like, moving into it. They definitely wanted the whole season to be a farewell to Michael.

Warren Lieberstein: We wanted to make sure he had an iconic goodbye.

Danny Chun: Steve was such an amazing actor and it felt like, "Okay, we can really push him in every direction and just let Steve be just amazing." And so the bad-boss thing we had done a lot. We were like, "Okay, we love this guy. Let's let him really sort of experience different things, and let's see him learn and grow and change and then send him off with really good vibes."

B. J. Novak: This was a very strong season because we knew going in what we had to work with and where we were headed toward and we could just have fun along the way without inventing any big moves or anything. What are the great last Michael stories?

This led to episodes where he confronts all his ex-girlfriends after fearing a cold sore was an STD ("Sex Ed"), makes peace with his longtime nemesis Toby ("Counseling"), comes to terms with the fact that Ryan isn't quite the stand-up guy he thought he was ("WUPHF.com"), and finally finishes his dream movie ("Threat Level Midnight"). Most important, Holly returned to Scranton midway through the season in "Classy Christmas."

Aaron Shure: We wanted to send him off like he's going to have a better future. I wrote "Baby Shower," which is a pivotal moment between him and Jan, where he still has this odd attachment to Jan's baby and tells Holly that while Jan's in the office he's going to be mean to her. And then when she leaves he hugs Holly. It's a step toward the right relationship and a step away from the wrong relationship and a step away from the delusions. I think his trajectory starts there.

Peter Ocko: Holly gave Michael a reason to evolve. And I think without that, there was no believable way to get him to change. She offered a direction to point him in that was believable. You understood why he would give up some of the things that both seemed intrinsic to his character but also beloved. And yet you could forgive him for moving away from some of those as a viewer, because I think you were so rooting for that relationship. I think it gave him permission in the audience's mind to change, which I think is a difficult situation when you have someone who's beloved for their flaws. You have to give the audience a good reason to change that.

Danny Chun: When Holly was introduced, it did feel like she loved him for who he was, so it didn't feel like, "Okay, he's got to completely get rid of all his flaws and you've got to transform in order to end up with Holly." A lot of it felt like he had found his person, but the stars were not aligned at first. What we loved about Holly was that she did love him for his goofy weirdness.

Halsted Sullivan: Leaving to go be with Holly felt so right for him. I wanted him to end on an up and not on a down because we always wanted people to leave with a positive feeling about office life. And Michael had been through so much, especially with Jan, that I feel like once the Holly idea came up it just really trumped all the other ideas. And he had grown, especially in that season. We worked hard to give him the tools for what he needed to cope in the world outside of the world of Dunder Mifflin.

Warren Lieberstein: We weren't going to leave him in the woods and have everyone be like, "Oh no, this guy can't feed himself. How are we going to leave this little baby Michael in the woods?" We had to make sure the audience was not going to be worried for him, that they were going to be happy for him.

In "Garage Sale," Michael proposes to Holly by her desk in the annex surrounded by so many candles that they set off the smoke alarm and leave them completely soaked when the sprinklers go off.

Randy Cordray: You can't run the sprinklers on a set without destroying the floor and ruining everything else on the set. So we tore the annex down and moved it off the stage. We then lined the whole floor with Bituthene and rebuilt it on top of that. And, by the way, you don't want to douse your actors with icy cold water, so we used a big boiler and we brought the water up to a kind of swimming pool temperature so that Holly and Michael would not be chilled to death by the frozen water. Now, add to that, bring in a couple of hundred candles. Well, how do you light them all for a take? Well, we had a crew of special effects guys, like six of them, with barbecue lighters, going around to light all the candles. It takes a while to light that many candles, and by the way, all of those candles are putting toxic wax fumes into the air. So I had to rig an air-purifier system to drag the toxic fumes up and out of the annex so that we weren't gassing the actors and the crew.

Amy Ryan: They told all of us the water was going to be warm. Well the sprinklers go off and it's freezing. It was a shock. And our faces are totally showing an honest reaction, but it doesn't look very pretty. I kind of have a horse-face-looking expression on. We finish and they say cut and the producers are like, "Okay, we're going to dry everybody off and start all over and do another take," because I think they wanted something a bit prettier looking and romantic in there. Steve was the director on this one. He said, "No, I really want to keep this take because it's just so real, because it's not pretty and it's not romantic and that should be how Michael and Holly's romantic life is represented." I was glad he stuck with it. It was great.

Michael was the focal point of season seven, but a lot of airtime was also devoted to Jim and Pam's new role as parents to baby Cecelia.

Peter Ocko: When I first started they had the idea for a christening episode, which is as unsexy an episode as you can possibly pitch. And when they brought it up, the entire room looked at me 'cause I had a lot of kids. And I think the thought was, "Well, let him write it." And I felt acutely a sense of, "How do you keep what we all loved in Jim and Pam in this post-marriage, postbaby world?" And it was honestly very difficult. We had to live in that space, and I think it was to the actors' credit and to the writers' credit it managed to keep people's attention. But it was definitely a difficult stretch, I would say.

Halsted Sullivan: I wouldn't say we struggled. But we definitely had to work extra hard to make it work because for so long Jim and Pam were the heart of the show and people on the message boards were always talking about Jam. But as opposed to seeing them constantly vying for one another, let's now see them grown.

Peter Ocko: We tried to lean into it and just acknowledge that the office was as much a family for Jim and Pam in season seven as it was for Michael. So when you do this christening episode, you bring the office into that story. And yeah, it felt a little artificial and I think it certainly stressed the weakest parts of that setup, but it still worked.

Warren Lieberstein: It was challenging because you had to do relationship stuff and tell believable stories so people were like, "Oh yeah, I've sent my kids to day care and done all this." So you send Jim and Pam on these little excursions or believable journeys and show the hiccups that happen in everyday marriages. Doing that was challenging but fun.

Danny Chun: We wanted to honestly portray their arc as a couple and as a family. We understood that we had spent the real drama of them getting together. And at least I personally didn't want to kind of keep recycling that and keep rehashing it over and over. It seemed we were past it.

Alan Sepinwall: Once Jim and Pam became a couple, the show had some problems writing for them and about them. And there's a point at which they become the smug popular kids, which is not what they were at the beginning.

The Andy/Erin dynamic was still going strong in season seven, though it began with her dating Gabe.

Danny Chun: That came from us feeling like we're doing a comedy version of a will they/won't they as opposed to the Pam and Jim. And that relationship was very funny but was also at times very dramatic and very soapy and very emotional. So I think once we leaned into the idea of, "Let's tell the funny version of this and the less soapy version," that led us to "Who's the last person in the world, but still believable, that Andy would sort of go nuts, go crazy about Erin dating?" That's where that idea came from.

Erin finds Gabe pretty repulsive, but she says she agreed to date him because he is her superior.

Ellie Kemper: Please, take this with a grain of salt, but I think Erin is me at times. I understand that instinct of like, "Oh, I'm supposed to do this. I don't want to hurt his feelings. He's the boss. I have to." And I sort of get that. I mean, I would never act on that, but I understand her unique reasoning behind it.

The obvious move would have been to bid Steve Carell farewell during the season finale, but he actually left with three episodes remaining in the season.

Danny Chun: The idea was, "This is not the Michael Scott show, this is a show about this office. The people in the office might change, but it's ultimately about the place and sort of the spirit of the place." So we ultimately decided that, if Michael leaves on the very last episode then it does feel like we've said, "This is the Michael Scott show."

Shortly before Michael left, Will Ferrell came on as new boss Deangelo Vickers.

Will Ferrell (Deangelo Vickers, Season 7): I was over at CAA in a meeting with my manager and my agents, and we were just going through projects. And at the end of it I just said, "Hey, I know it's Steve's last year. I'd love to go on and just do a cameo." It just popped into my head. I was watching [an episode] on an American Airlines flight or whatever. I just thought, "God, that'd be fun." My TV agent was like, "What? Oh my God. Really?" I was like, "Yeah." "Oh, they'll go crazy. They'll flip for that. Now, the only thing is, would you want to do more than one?" Sure enough, they responded in kind and were like, "Would he do, like, a whole character arc?" Yeah, let's do it.

Danny Chun: He really did just volunteer. We were so stressed out about what do you do the next day after Michael is gone; that was the most sort of stressful and intimidating episode to think about. And really Will was like, "What if I came in for a few episodes? Would that help?" And we were like, "Yep, of course it would help."

Halsted Sullivan: By bringing in Will Ferrell we wanted to say, "Look, the show is still continuing." It was also just a great way to energize that ending and not make it feel maudlin.

Danny Chun: It really felt like a gift that he gave us. What it allowed us to do writing-wise was just to have a bridge, a really interesting and different bridge, so that the first episode after Michael wasn't simply the Michael-less episode.

Will Ferrell: It was a little intimidating at first because that cast is like a well-oiled machine and they know each other so well.

David Rogers: Will really came in with positive energy, happy to be there. I think everybody was happy to have him there.

Warren Lieberstein: It was really such a nice generous gift of Will to give us because it was a bittersweet time. Everyone was so sad about Steve leaving that the presence of Will Ferrell there was like a soothing balm to put over the situation of everyone's sadness. Everyone felt like it took some of the sting off.

Greg Daniels: He couldn't do anything that wasn't really funny. I don't see how he could have if he tried.

Randy Cordray: Will was just a wonderful man. This was another one who I would have to go to and say, "You know, Will, we need you first thing in the morning and then we're not going to need you until last thing in the evening. If you want to disappear for six, seven hours, just sit near your cell phone and let me call you when we need you." And he was like, "Ah, heck no. You know you guys have provided a nice trailer for me and I saw a basketball hoop out there. You got a basketball?" I said, "Sure, props has a basketball." "Hey, I'll go up to shoot hoops." So Will Ferrell would hang out for hours behind the warehouse set just shooting hoops with some of our crew people who weren't busy at the moment, like electricians or camera guys or grips. I said to them, "Go shoot hoops with Will. We'll call you if we need you."

Basketball played a key role in extracting the Deangelo Vickers character from the Dunder Mifflin universe. In the episode "The Inner Circle," Vickers tries to slam-dunk a basketball in the warehouse but winds up getting a horrific injury when he falls and lands on his head. That set up a cliff-hanger where nobody knew who would become the boss in the next season.

Randy Cordray: It was strange not having Steve around, but the show went on and the writers were trying to figure out how to gracefully end the season. So after the final episode was "Search Committee," where we went through all the various cameos of people coming by and applying for the job.

Brent Forrester: What you see there is this interesting move that we tried, which was to do a story arc about searching for the new boss that should also seem to the audience like we're casting a bunch of new actors here and one of whom will become the boss of the office. Now, that's kind of what was happening behind the scenes. All the actors you saw coming in—Ray Romano, Catherine Tate, James Spader, Ricky Gervais, Jim Carrey—were meant to be creating interest in the audience's mind of like, "I wonder who's actually going to become the new boss?"

KEY EPISODE 10

"Threat Level Midnight"

In the second-season episode "The Client," Pam finds a script that Michael wrote in his desk drawer entitled Threat Level Midnight. *It's about Michael Scarn, a James Bond–like spy who battles a deformed foe named Goldenface. When Michael steps out to pursue a new client, a meeting is called in the conference room, where the script is read aloud by everyone in the office. At Steve Carell's urging, B. J. Novak penned an episode near the end of Michael's time at Dunder Mifflin where he screens the movie, which he's been filming slowly over the past seven years using the entire office as his cast. It meant not only bringing back old characters like Karen, Roy, and Jan, but carefully deaging the main cast so they'd look period appropriate. It was an enormous undertaking.*

B. J. Novak: We did a greatest hits of Steve Carell before he left. "What do we want to see?" And this was one of them.

Amelie Gillette: That was a dragon the writers wanted to slay for a long time, doing *Threat Level Midnight* as an episode, and we finally got the push to do it because it was Michael's last season.

Peter Ocko: You knew that you weren't going to have him around much more and we wanted to check that box of, "God, if I could do one more thing with Michael Scott, what would it be?" And being able to do that in particular was a lot of fun.

Steve Burgess: We brought everybody back for one day or a half a day to do their little pieces as if Michael Scott had been doing this throughout the whole thing. B. J. wrote the script.

Halsted Sullivan: That was really B. J.'s baby.

Randy Cordray: Hair and makeup and costume had to match the look from earlier seasons. We had a lot of research time where we would go to editing with the department heads and we would print off stills so that they had matching stills to match from for hair and makeup. We tried to maintain the integrity of the joke that this had been shot during the previous seven seasons.

B. J. Novak: They glued sideburns on me and put Pam in old outfits and Jim in his old hair.

Initially they thought about just showing the movie without any scenes at the actual office.

Amelie Gillette: That was a big discussion for a while. It would have been very cool to have it that way, but it's hard to do something that breaks the form so much in a network television show.

B. J. Novak: I think it's a very entertaining and substantial work on its own, as Michael Scott's film, but it simply felt out of context to simply air that the way we normally air *The Office,* without including any background reactions, or consequences to the characters.

Tucker Gates: I wanted to ground it in the world.

Rashida Jones, Melora Hardin, David Denman, and all the old warehouse workers came back for tiny roles.

Randy Cordray: We tried to get Amy Adams [who played Jim's girlfriend Katy in seasons one and two]. I worked with Allison Jones on this and we were even willing to shoot her stuff completely out of order, on another week if necessary, but we just couldn't make it work. Her feature schedule was just too busy. And she sent a very nice note thanking everyone and wishing that she could participate.

B. J. Novak: I had scripted a scene in which she is a "floozy" in bed with Michael Scarn before Dwight wakes him up with a mission from the president. In the scene, Michael is unsatisfied from their empty lovemaking because no one is as good as his wife was, and Michael explains to her what love feels like. Then, in a talking head, Katy explained with embarrassment how she had some interest in acting back then, and we catch up with where she is in the present day.

The basic plot of the movie is that Michael Scarn is trying to stop Goldenface from blowing up the NHL All-Star Game.

B. J. Novak: I always liked that he saved all-star games, which to Michael Scott would be more important than championship games but most sports fans know are kind of irrelevant.

One challenge was making a watchable movie that could conceivably have been made by Michael Scott.

Tucker Gates: Some people said, "Well, the production values were too good for a Michael thing. He would've shot on a phone." But I really looked at it like it was his life's project. He watched all these James Bond films and he would have wanted to try and re-create those things. He may not have had a dolly, but he would have made something that could have given him a dolly feel. I really wanted to see the aspiration and the heart that he put into it and the homage that he was trying to play with however awkward or amateurish it was. Michael had an aspiration to make something great. This was his opus.

B. J. Novak: We didn't want the joke of the episode to be how bad he was at filmmaking, which would be a little too easy and actually a little out of character; we wanted it to be more about how he actually did a heartbreakingly good and diligent job on doing something completely ridiculous.

Perhaps the greatest scene takes place at a bar, where Michael Scarn meets a bartender with a ridiculous Boston accent played by Ed Helms and does a line dance called "the Scarn" with Karen, Phyllis, Meredith, Angela, and the entire warehouse staff.

Steve Burgess: Mary Ann Kellogg, who started working with us on the "Cafe Disco" episode, and did the wedding dance and the lip dub that began season seven, choreographed it. A big problem was people laughing when they weren't supposed to be because it was just so funny.

B. J. Novak: [That] would have been filmed right after Karen transferred to Scranton, so she would have been a brand-new employee in a new city, eager to fit in; you can even see her going the extra mile to play along pretending to "learn" the Scarn dance the first time Michael demonstrates it.

Tucker Gates: I was so nervous about that scene because I can't dance to save my life, but it's Michael's choreography, so we're not doing something too technical.

Calvin Tenner (Lester/Calvin/Glenn, Seasons 2–9): We rented the next building over and we choreographed this whole dance. It probably took maybe thirty minutes to learn.

For no clear reason, a little boy in overalls that looks like he just wandered over from a farm joins them.

Tucker Gates: It's an Opie character [from *Andy Griffith*]. I think it's a reference to probably some older movie that he saw. We just wanted to make everything as referential as possible. The bar scene has a *Cheers* element to it. When he works out, it's shot like *Rocky III* even though he's using a Bowflex. Then there's the noirish moment when he's out in the rain. Michael has seen a lot of movies, but not necessarily good ones.

Throughout the episode, we return to the conference room at Dunder Mifflin, where everyone is watching the movie and trying to hold back their laughter. Michael is initially very offended, but after a talk with Holly he's able to see the ludicrous nature of his own film and laughs along with everyone else.

B. J. Novak: This was Paul's idea, that Michael has a very active fantasy life and as his reality becomes more fulfilling, he has to let go of it.

Kate Flannery: That whole episode was odd and could have been so mishandled, but it wasn't. B. J. is just such an amazing writer and I feel like he's so wise beyond his years. I never ever questioned any of his choices, ever.

KEY EPISODE 11

“Goodbye, Michael”

Everyone working on The Office *knew they were building up to Steve Carell’s last episode throughout the entirety of season seven, but when the week finally came to film it, none of them were emotionally prepared. Paul Feig was brought in to direct and keep everyone on task throughout the process. Greg Daniels wrote the script himself, which revolves around Michael’s secretly leaving a day earlier than planned and trying to have a little moment with each character that they don’t realize is his goodbye.*

Brent Forrester: In the opening shot of the episode, Michael is up on the roof of the building in a folding chair. At first, you just see him from the waist up and above him is the sky and the clouds. That was, quite deliberately by Greg, a symbol of death. Here he is in heaven, and the whole energy of that episode is really that of a funeral. It was very, very serious and difficult for Greg to wrap him off the show. I think it was very, very serious for Steve and all the other actors as well. It is a little bit corny to compare it to a funeral, but at some level for all the people involved, that’s exactly what it is. It’s like, “Oh my God. I can’t believe this is ever going to end. Now I’ve got to say goodbye.”

Greg Daniels: This whole experience [of making the episode] had a lot of sadness in it.

David Rogers: [Steve is] pretty incredible. [Look at] his range in this episode alone, you see all the highs and lows.

Brian Baumgartner: I think the episode encompasses pretty well what was going on in real life in terms of leaving a workplace that had become pretty much a family and choosing to move on to other things. [There's] some excitement and happiness in that and some sadness too.

David Rogers: Paul Feig directed this episode and he did a really great job handling everyone's emotions on the set.

Paul Feig: I'd kind of moved on from the show at that point and was just working on other stuff, but they called me up and asked me if I wanted to do it. And I was, of course, "How can I not do Steve's last episode?" The biggest thing about that one was that everyone loves Steve Carell. Steve Carell is one of the greatest people on the planet. Every scene was about him saying goodbye to people. And the cast was just devastated, so we'd go to each scene, and everyone would be tearful and falling apart and I had to keep going, "All right, guys, you've got to remember one thing. We love Steve Carell, but the workers of Dunder Mifflin don't really like Michael."

Greg Daniels: Paul was the only director that spent an entire year with the cast on every episode, in season five, and there was no other person the cast would be as comfortable with for something like this.

Paul Feig: I kept being like, "Okay, now, remember, it's just like, 'Okay, I'll see you later.' You actually don't really care if he leaves, except for Jim, who has some kind of connection to him, and obviously Dwight, who also has affection for Michael." I also had to keep saying, "All right, everybody's got to pull it together. We've got to get makeup in here. We've got to get the red out of everybody's eyes. Everybody's got to act completely disinterested in this."

At one point, he takes his World's Best Boss mug and throws it into the garbage.

Rob Sheffield: It's a really beautiful moment that reminds me of the end of Shakespeare's *The Tempest,* when Prospero breaks his wand and almost indicates that his charms were all artificial the entire time. And for Michael Scott to very explicitly surrender this authority, which was never anything more than this really petty pissant little authority that was just plugging up emotional holes for him, was very, very moving.

Near the end, Jim figures out that Michael is lying to everyone and it is actually his last day. With tears in his eyes he says that Michael is the "best boss [he] ever had."

Greg Daniels: They were bawling.

David Rogers: It was Steve Carell and John Krasinski, not Michael and Jim. They were very emotional.

Paul Feig: That was really tough to get through. It was just us in that little office, and John was really having a hard time holding it together.

Greg Daniels: We finally made a suggestion of, "Play it more like guys going off on suicide missions in an old movie about the Royal Air Force."

Ellie Kemper: I was sitting in the back while all this snot kept spilling out and I was like, "Don't ruin the take."

Oscar Nunez: Thank God Will Ferrell was there to sort of keep us laughing with his craziness, because it was really sad.

Paul Feig: When we were shooting his last scene in the bullpen area, I looked over, and there's a couch where people would wait for their appointment or whatever. Greg Daniels was just lying on it facedown. He was so emotional, but that's how everybody felt.

Michael spends much of the episode waiting for Pam—who secretly ducked out to see The King's Speech *at a movie theater—to come back to the office before his cab arrives to take him to the airport. He's eventually forced to leave without saying goodbye. We then see him actually speak to the camera crew at the airport ("Hey, will you guys let me know if this ever airs?"), take off his mic, and make one final "That's what she said" joke before he walks off. Pam then races into the shot and gives him a hug, and they exchange words we cannot hear.*

Paul Feig: Greg was always really hung up on wanting his last scene to be that Michael takes off his microphone and we don't get to hear the final thing with Pam. Just talking about that now, I get really emotional.

Jenna Fischer: I told him all the ways I was going to miss him when he left our show. Those were real tears and a real goodbye.

Rob Sheffield: It's so emotional because it's a moment where they step back from jokiness and have a very raw, unmediated moment of affection between two characters that was very beautifully done, very elegantly done, understated in a way. It was also a very beautiful callback to the last episode of the UK *Office* where Tim takes off his mic before confessing his feelings to Dawn. It was a moment that we weren't eavesdropping on and that there was nothing shticky about it or jokey about it, or even comic about it. It was very, very moving. I've watched that many times since the night it aired and I always cry at the end.

Danny Chun: Michael and Pam had a special dynamic and Greg felt they were sort of the core familial dynamic of the show. I don't even remember there being a lot of debate about it. We knew Greg was going to write it and it was going to be awesome.

Warren Lieberstein: Greg wanted his final scene to be with Pam because Greg always said they had this strange emotional connection between them. It was a loving connection. I think of all the people that Michael Scott counted on, she was maybe the most important.

Owen Ellickson: I feel like the soul of *The Office* is Michael Scott, and probably the show should have ended with him. But I think the protagonist of *The Office* is Pam. The pilot was the verbatim UK *Office,* and it basically ends with Michael being shitty to Pam, and Pam sort of unmanning him by talking about how he shitty he is in a way she knows he won't respond to. I feel like the great thing about the American *Office* was they realized that this was a nice guy, and this was a nice enough woman to see past that stuff. That was the core friendship of the show.

Peter Ocko: I think it made sense to have Pam say goodbye to him last because she was capable of getting to Michael in a way that certainly Dwight or Jim weren't. He was able to connect with her on a level that we weren't even privy to, but we imagine potentially it was more genuine than we'd seen previously. I think that's what made it believable, is that she had the capacity to cut through the bullshit with him and let him grow in a way that the other characters couldn't.

Rob Sheffield: In the last couple seasons of *Mad Men* they were trying to re-create that airport scene with Don and Peggy over and over again, and they just couldn't do it because it's hard to step back and do that scene understated. So with Don and Peggy, they have to dance to Frank Sinatra singing "My Way" on the radio and Don says, "Let's dance." They had to shtick it up a bit. I love *Mad Men* with a passion, but it's almost impossible to do a scene like that without making it shticky, and *The Office,* as Bruce Springsteen would say, just stood back and let it all be.

Brent Forrester: What was unforgettable to me was hearing Steve Carell say more than once, "I will never do a television show as good as this show." He said that early on, like maybe in season four. That's how much he loved the show and how much he respected it and believed in it. Leaving after seven seasons was the opposite of dramatic. I think it was really just him going, "This is a work of art I've always intended to bring to a completion at seven seasons, and now I have done it."

The preparations for his goodbye party in the warehouse started in secret weeks earlier.

Randy Cordray: I became the de facto planner of it and had to wrangle all of the various elements and make sure that everybody that needed to be there [was there], like Steve's wife, Nancy; [his manager] Steve Sauer; Bob Greenblatt. We wanted it all to be a big surprise. We scheduled his final scene to be in the office with everyone so that we could say, "Ladies and gentlemen, this completes Steve Carell's work for now on *The Office,* but the party's really just starting. Can we have everybody please escort yourselves over to the warehouse, where we have a party prepared, so let's all go to the warehouse."

Oscar Nunez: There were wonderful speeches. John Krasinski did a video for him, and John McCain was on it. All these people he got to say bye.

Kim Ferry: Everyone was in tears, I'm not kidding. Everyone.

Randy Cordray: Rainn Wilson gave a speech on behalf of the actors. Greg Daniels gave a big speech on behalf of himself and the writers. Bob Greenblatt gave a few words on behalf of the network. We decided that we weren't killing off the Michael Scott character, he was merely moving to Boulder to be with Holly, so we decided to retire the number one designation on the call sheet. I said something to the order of, "Steve, we will never forget you, and we're hoping that you never forget us, and this is a small token of our affection toward you. We are retiring your number on the call sheet. It will never be used by anyone other than Steve Carell from this day forward on *The Office.*" And I revealed this hockey jersey we all signed and I said, "From now on until the day you return, all of our call sheets will begin with number two." And that had never been done as far as I know in the history of Hollywood, as far as I know. After that every call sheet began with number two, which was Rainn Wilson.

Randall Einhorn: After the party in the warehouse, we had a party at the Soho House and it was great. It felt like a big moment.

Randy Cordray: John Krasinski threw together this party, and he did it somewhat at the last minute as I understand. It was in this beautiful penthouse room at the Soho House with an incredible view of the city. It was just a lovely party. John's wife, Emily Blunt, was there, along with a lot of the famous directors of the episodes, like Paul Feig and Jeffrey Blitz. People were roaming and having drinks, and sharing moments with Steve Carell. It was a very really generous and special thing. Prior to that, I helped Steve to his car after he literally cleaned out his dressing room and he said, "I have something for you too," and he gave me this Rolex. I burst into tears. I loved the guy so much, and I didn't expect or need a gift from the guy.

Creed Bratton: Everyone got a Rolex from Steve. I still wear mine all the time. It just says on the back, "To Creed, Love, Steve." I got so emotional when he gave me mine. You want to be able to give back as a human being, but how can you give back something like that? I mean, that just shows how amazing and unselfish he is. He's a caring guy. No one else is going to do something like that. Still to this day, I'm still stunned by that generosity.

Randall Einhorn: When it was all done, you're just wondering, "What's going to happen? Can the show sustain? Who's going to take his place?" Everything felt uncertain.

chapter 25

MEET THE NEW BOSS

("What if Queen Latifah becomes the manager?")

Season seven wraps up without resolving who will be named Deangelo Vickers's replacement as the new regional manager. This was partially to incentivize viewers to tune in to the next season premiere, but it also gave the writers time to figure out which character was up for the task. Opinions were all over the place.

Brent Forrester: How are you possibly going to fill these gigantic shoes? There's just no easy answer.

Teri Weinberg: We knew we were never going to fill that void. We knew that we could never replace Michael Scott, nor would we try to do that. For us, it was, "How do we serve the story? Who do we bring in and create some disruption now that Michael is gone? And how do we keep the level of comedy at a place that it was and how do we have some fun with who becomes the new manager? Who holds this group of people together?" And so, we threw around a million names.

Paul Lieberstein: One of the important aspects is that the boss puts something on the [relationships in the] office that's not just totally professional. They have to see it as a lot more than it is.

Amelie Gillette: My God, there were a ton of debates. "Should it be an outsider? Should it be someone internal?"

Danny Chun: There were so many different opinions. I don't recall anybody particularly having one opinion that they held to the entire time. I feel like everybody kept changing their minds, everyone was arguing, debating, and really it just was like an exciting but scary conversation to be having.

Warren Lieberstein: I think the lessons we gleaned from Jim being made comanager made the decision tougher. We didn't want to lose what made people funny by putting them in a position of power.

Owen Ellickson: In retrospect, I feel like Craig Robinson actually would have been a good pick. The ways shows go, characters get broader over time. If you want to oversimplify it, in season one it was crazy boss, normal employees. By this point you had crazy employees, so actually picking a normal boss would have been a good inversion of the dynamic. It just would have been fresh and it would have been more of a change from Carell.

Ben Patrick: I would have loved if Craig Robinson could have gone there. He's like the most delightful person in the world. Every day we had something that featured Darryl was kind of the most fun day to shoot because he is just a very charming and lovely person. Somebody had released "Darryl for Manager" T-shirts at the end of the seventh season. At the time, the cast and crew were actually kind of wondering what the writers were going to do.

Ricky Gervais's David Brent character did apply for the job in "Search Committee," and at least for a second the idea of bringing him in was brought up in the writers' room.

Paul Lieberstein: When we talked about it, my biggest problem was that David Brent is a version of Steve Carell. That's a big coincidence. There's also two people outside his office who are exactly like the two people he worked with. And then it just so happens that a documentary crew happens to be following them around? It wouldn't have made sense.

Halsted Sullivan: I pitched the idea of, "What if Queen Latifah becomes the manager?" Slowly, one by one, she starts firing all the employees. And you just bring in all these black comedians. It becomes a black office, and you'd just go from there. But, you know, that didn't get that much traction. It would have been fun though.

Peter Ocko: I felt very strongly that you couldn't replace Michael with another member of the ensemble. I thought he occupied a very particular position in the office dynamic and it would be better to pull somebody in from the outside and just own that, rather than simply saying we'll just fill it from inside. I wasn't alone in that, but there were definitely different sides.

Danny Chun: One of the big debates that took place was, "Should it be someone inside the office or should it be someone new?" That was a really big one. On a meta level it was like, "Do we want to bring in a brand-new actor, a big star, or do we want to sort of cultivate the people that people already know and love?" There was also a real aspect where we asked, "What would be happening at the office itself?" Ultimately what we decided to do was have the process play out in the office because that is what would happen. "Should it be someone from the outside or someone from the inside? Who should it be? Who's the best person on the inside?"

Amelie Gillette: There was ultimately a big Dwight camp and there was a big Andy camp.

Justin Spitzer: I remember a lot of discussion about what we should do. I did not think it should be Andy. I loved the character of Andy. I loved Ed. I don't think I could see yet what Andy would bring to the table that felt distinct with him being the boss. He's such a people pleaser, but Michael is a people pleaser. I think people would have been more excited to see Dwight as the boss because he'd been wanting it for so long. It just seemed like it suggested more stories to me.

Danny Chun: We love them both and were so fortunate to have talents like Rainn Wilson and Ed Helms. I could see both of them working. But maybe if there was a gun to my head, I was coming a little bit more to the Dwight side because I saw that version a little more clearly than Andy in charge. But I think that's partially why some people liked the Andy version. They liked the possibility that it could go in multiple directions, and it ultimately did kind of go in surprising directions, whereas it felt like the Dwight version, there was a lot of inherent comedy, but maybe a little less of a sense of surprise.

Mark Proksch: I think if Dwight had become the boss it would have opened up a lot of interesting doors and story lines.

Aaron Shure: I did not think Dwight should be the boss because I think Dwight is not as benign as Michael Scott. He's like this weird amalgam of Mennonite and *Star Trek* nerd. There's just so many candy bags to draw from that he carries around that I was worried that if we gave him the boss position it would just be disastrous. I also didn't want Dwight to be empowered because I was afraid he wouldn't be funny anymore with power. It's funny if he sets the office on fire and blowtorches all the doorknobs. But if he did that all day long without any sort of check on his behavior, it would be terrifying.

Danny Chun: I understand that, but my counter to that would have been Michael also did a lot of things early on that were preposterous and inappropriate and awful. And then also part of what we were dramatizing was that person's progression, humanizing the boss character and understanding their perspective and having them learn to understand the perspective of the people that work for them. And I always personally felt that Dwight was a really deep and kind, ultimately good character. I've chimed in on

Twitter multiple times when people think that Dwight would have voted for Trump because I don't think he would have. To me it felt like he was going to do some insane, inappropriate, horrible, and cruel things, but he may now suddenly be forced into a position to contemplate what he was doing a little more, and that seemed intriguing.

Amelie Gillette: I wanted to be Team Dwight because I always liked Dwight a lot and the pinnacle of what he wanted was to become the boss and it would be interesting to give him that comedically and to see where he would go from there. Also, Rainn was just so good. I do think that Andy was an interesting choice too, and believe me, I switched camps a lot. I think a lot of us did because you don't really know until you do it. But we felt like we could still get some juice out of Dwight not being number one, but being a foiled number one. We thought that might be a good comedic engine. I think that's ultimately why Andy won out.

Halsted Sullivan: Dwight was probably the expected choice and Dwight would have been an excellent manager. Andy was more the unexpected choice. I feel like I was on both sides of the debate because there were strong arguments for both. It was not a black-and-white thing. We tried out Dwight in that role and in the end, we went with Andy. It was a photo finish. I think everyone would have been happy with either person in that role.

Brent Forrester: The writers and the cast, generally speaking, were really excited about Dwight becoming the boss. It just felt correct, and that was our creative thrust. Mostly it was pushback from the network saying, "Well, is there someone more famous that we can put in here?" Of course, the creators always bristle at that and just want to do the right thing creatively. That was a big thing. But Ed Helms had this giant advantage because of course he was in *The Hangover.* Not to completely read the minds of the network, but that was my understanding of how that decision got made.

Owen Ellickson: I think the *Hangover* calculus sort of shifted things toward Andy pretty quickly.

Justin Spitzer: It felt with Andy that we were substituting someone in for Michael that might feel like just another version of Michael. It's not about the actor or anything, just that people are gonna inevitably compare it, and you're always gonna compare unfavorably with the original. Whereas Dwight would have been his very own energy if he were a boss. That might have gone horribly and been broad and stupid. So I don't want to make it seem like I'm in any way questioning the decision we made, but at the time I was on the Dwight side of things.

Amelie Gillette: There was an episode where Dwight was boss ["Dwight K. Schrute, (Acting) Manager"], and I think a lot of writers thought that Dwight had the farm stuff and might not be as office-y as Andy.

Owen Ellickson: All of this was happening just as the 2012 election was starting to take steam. I feel like making Andy the boss right around the time that we were all choosing not Mitt Romney to be the president, there was just an awkward fit to it socioeconomically. It was not a moment when we were all like, "Let's care more about these types of people."

Kate Flannery: I was not consulted, but I thought it was a great idea to make Andy the new boss. I thought it made the most sense how they did it. And once again, interesting that he had just had a hit movie with *The Hangover*, much like Steve with *40-Year-Old Virgin*. It was kind of kismet.

At this same time, Kathy Bates became the lead character on the new NBC legal drama Harry's Law. *With her no longer able to commit to the show, it created a great opportunity to bring in another big-name actor who could help fill the void of Carell's departure and generate excitement going into a season that everyone knew would be very difficult.*

Peter Ocko: A lot of names were tossed around and I won't list them all, but the sky was the limit honestly. Because it was such a well-regarded show, I don't think there were names that came up that we would think, "Oh no, they'll definitely say no." I think there was always a bit of hope that you could go anywhere and say, "Come do it for a season," and they'd do it.

Brent Forrester: Paul went and met James Gandolfini, who was really the one that we were super excited about. It was like, "Wow, that would be crazy having him as the boss."

Owen Ellickson: I was excited about the idea of Gandolfini. I mean, that's not a unique opinion for a white guy in his thirties, but I loved him. I thought he was a brilliant actor and would have given us a million colors to play with.

Danny Chun: Paul and B. J. and I went to go meet James and talk to him about it. I remember him being really, really complimentary, but he wasn't super familiar with the show. He had watched a few episodes and he was really unsure about comedy. He was like, "I don't one hundred percent know how to play this."

Alan Sepinwall: Jim was really funny and he would've been menacing as hell because he's James Gandolfini. They could've done a lot with him and it would've been great for him too, because he was really desperate to not be Tony Soprano anymore at that point.

Danny Chun: Obviously we all know he was an amazingly talented person. I think he was good in anything he ever did, but I think he felt a little . . . I don't know if I want to say he was ever intimidated by anything, but I think he was just unsure of the idea of helming what was one of the biggest comedies on TV.

Justin Spitzer: We all worshipped Jim. I don't know whatever happened with that, but he would have been great. I don't know long-term if that would have been good though. That would have been an amazing arc and then at that point you just have to see how he is in that world. *The Sopranos* was something very specific, somewhere between a drama and a comedy.

And it was written kind of as a comedy, but you didn't focus on that part of it. So I don't know if people would want to see that guy in their living rooms every Thursday being the boss. But just as a presence he would have been an interesting element in the show.

Danny Chun: We were still very early in the process of developing his character. We hadn't opened up the full conversation of it, but I remember feeling like we were excited by this idea of this really sort of salt-of-the-earth, intense, passionate guy who could be your father figure and your biggest supporter and the most sort of wonderful person to have on your side, but also turn around and be the scariest person you've ever seen in your life, and just bite your head off about something. We just felt like the sort of range that James had was very exciting to us.

Brent Forrester: I think Gandolfini said yes and then hesitated or something. But it was really, really close to him being the boss.

Teri Weinberg: This is a hard subject. Boy, I miss that actor. That was definitely a conversation though. I think Greg had a conversation with him. I don't think that we stopped talking to him. I mean, that conversation went on for some time, but he had also had some shows that he was developing for himself and that was just part of what his focus was, so I don't think that he was necessarily ready to just jump into this role. And I think some people, I don't know that they wanted to take on something that Steve had essentially stepped out of, to try to step into.

Brent Forrester: I remember at one point it came down to James Spader and James Gandolfini.

Spader was a tertiary member of the Brat Pack who had his start in teen comedies like Mannequin *and* Pretty in Pink *before moving into more serious films like* Sex, Lies and Videotape *and* Stargate. *He came onto the eighth season of legal drama* The Practice *in 2004 and breathed new life into the show before spinning off his character onto* Boston Legal, *which ran for five successful seasons.*

Teri Weinberg: We just were big fans of his and he created such an incredible, delicious character in *Boston Legal* and he had such an incredible dry sense of humor. He's such a super-talented guy, and we'd just fallen in love with him. I think just over the course of having a lot of meetings, it just worked out that way and he said, "I love the show." And we loved him.

James Spader (Robert California, Seasons 7 and 8): When this all started I didn't have much money left from [*The Practice* spin-off] *Boston Legal*. I'd done a big renovation on my house and then I did a David Mamet play [*Race*] in New York for a year, which was a perfect antidote to doing a television series, but when it was done I knew I was going to need some money because I was hemorrhaging cash doing the play. And then all of a sudden I got the call from *The Office*.

Halsted Sullivan: James Spader was more of a surprise during the process, but he just really popped. It was like, "Wow, he's a huge star, he's really funny, and he has a different energy. What happens if we add him into the mix as well?" Greg Daniels's mantra for this was, "If there's someone who can hit home runs, let's add them to the cast and see how things develop." Our ensemble was so strong that it felt like you could try those experiments.

He initially came onto the show for a quick couple of scenes during the final episode of season seven, where Jim and Toby were interviewing potential hires for the regional manager job.

James Spader: I said to them, "Okay, but there's no obligation, right?" They said, "No, no, it's a one-off. It'll be great. And you can come over whatever time you want. We know you're not a morning person, so if you want to come during the afternoon or whatever you want to do, we'll just shoot it quickly." And I said, "Great, this will be great fun." Anyway, so I went over and did it and it was, it was a ball. We really had a lot of fun and that was the end of that. But then it aired.

Even though he was up against the likes of Jim Carrey, Ray Romano, Will Arnett, and even Ricky Gervais reviving his David Brent character, Spader stood out as the clear audience favorite. He played the Robert California character as a suave, cocksure mystery man, almost as if Don Draper from Mad Men *had an evil twin. Even critics who felt* The Office *had jumped the shark by that point were impressed. "Wow!" wrote* New York *magazine's Megh Wright in her review of the episode. "I instantly fell in love with his creepy psychological tactics and love for pregnant pauses, and his stare-down against Dwight was one of my favorite parts of the episode."*

Owen Ellickson: Spader was brilliantly funny in that scene, almost funnier than he ever was in season eight.

James Spader: Apparently they were following the audience reaction to their shows in real time through social media. They told me people just loved the character and they said, "Is there any chance we can convince you to come back as that character in any capacity?" And I said, "Do you have an idea where the show is headed?" And they said, "Yeah, we have a basic framework for what we're thinking about for next season, and this character could be plugged in anywhere along the line. It's very flexible."

Ben Silverman: I didn't like the Spader idea. That came from Bob Greenblatt. They could have done better.

Danny Chun: It's completely possible that Greenblatt pushed Spader early on in that process, but I remember us being really sort of taken by the energy that he brought that was just so different than anyone else's energy on the show. And I think we felt like there's something very, very interesting about this really really specific, strange character. We were kind of drawn to exploring that a little bit more.

Right around this time, Spader was approached by Steven Spielberg about taking on a prominent role in his upcoming movie Lincoln.

James Spader: I really wanted to do it, but they were doing it at a greatly reduced budget. Everybody was cutting their fees for the picture because they really didn't have any idea about whether this was going to have a broad audience or not and it was a fairly expensive picture to make in terms of the production values. There wasn't much money up front, but we were all getting a piece of the back end. But it wasn't going to shoot for eight months and by this point, I was broke. Really, I was *broke*. I had enough to last me about a year or less, and I didn't really find anything I wanted to do over the next six to eight months. And so I was in a real pickle in terms of *Lincoln*. I was terrified I'd have to tell Steven I couldn't take the part if something that pays well came along that was shooting at the same time.

As he was pondering this, the Office *producers called up his agent.*

James Spader: They said, "We'll take whatever we can get from James." Those were their words. I said, "All right, how about call them back and say, 'You know what? Forget about an arc. If you want me to do the show, I want a whole season. But if I'm going to do the whole season, I need a couple of months off to go do this picture. So how about that for a deal?'" And you know what? Everyone agreed.

chapter 26

SEASON EIGHT

("It was Cheers *without Ted Danson.")*

The Office *went into season eight facing enormous headwinds. Not only was Greg Daniels devoting much of his time to* Parks and Rec *and key writers from the past like Michael Schur, Jen Celotta, Gene Stupnitsky, and Lee Eisenberg were all gone, but now Steve Carell had bolted as well. On top of that, they were facing the sort of creative issues that sitcoms begin hitting when they've been on the air for the greater part of a decade. All of this came together to create an extremely rocky season.*

Kim Ferry: When Steve left it was really hard. Things changed a lot and were just never quite the same afterward. And it wasn't Greg's show anymore. It wasn't his writing. There wasn't one set leader that had always been there. It wasn't the same voices that we heard. Everything was different.

Rob Sheffield: They saw this coming years in advance. They had plenty of time to prepare for it. Up until then, every prediction ever made for any kind of failure that they'd ever had was proven wrong. So speaking as an American who expected the show to suck from the get-go, I was always shocked at how many good, against-the-odds creative decisions they made, from Jim and Pam getting together to Michael and Holly getting together. I had absolute faith that they knew what they were doing at that point. It was only once the eighth season was under way did I go back and think, "Wow, they just went into this without any kind of Plan B whatsoever."

Karly Rothenberg (Madge Madsen, Seasons 1–8): Once Steve left, everybody sort of felt like it was *Cheers* without Ted Danson.

Rusty Mahmood: When Steve left, the heart of the show went with him.

Ben Patrick: It felt like a different show. Some of us were saying that the days were numbered, but we also liked each other so much and we were sort of hoping that Ed could pull it off or the new characters would really work. But the writers really had to step it up to make all this stuff happen.

Andy Buckley: I kind of thought, "Oh, they'll be able to keep it going. It'll just be interesting to see how they do it." Think of when *ER* lost George Clooney. Shows you love lose people and it becomes a different show to a large degree. But there are still many many of the same elements. You still have Dwight Schrute and you got Jim and Pam and you got everybody else in the office and Andrew Bernard and all that. It kind of gives other people a chance to shine a little bit more perhaps.

Matt Sohn: It was always discussed that Steve was the linchpin that held it all together. There were a lot of viewers that once he left, they quit watching, I think, because that was their version of *The Office*. But I still feel like there were great episodes after Steve left.

Randall Einhorn: It was a very different dynamic with James Spader. I don't want to speak ill of anybody, but Steve just set the bar so high and it just changed so much for me at that point. It felt like he was the anchor. It just never felt the same for me.

Creed Bratton: I thought there [were] moments where the focus drifted and you weren't sure what was going on. There wasn't the commonality that there was when Steve was on the show.

Oscar Nunez: It was funny enough, but it was a different show. We were very sad when Steve left. For me, that was the end of the show, and then we did two years without him, which was a different thing.

Melora Hardin: I don't know if I can get into it, but it didn't have a great feeling [when I came back for guest spots after Steve left]. I was happy that I wasn't around all the time. I was like, "Wow, I don't mind being here today, but I'm glad I'm not here every day."

Brent Forrester: Greg Daniels anticipated what was going to happen in season eight and told the staff before we wrote a word of it. He said, "Look, the buzz on shows has cycles. Look at the way people have talked about *Saturday Night Live*. It starts out with a golden age, right? Then comes that second wave that's still trying to keep it together. But at a certain point, the narrative has to be, '*Saturday Night Live* has lost its mojo.' Then if you're lucky and you stay around long enough, the narrative will change and be like, '*Saturday Night Live* is back.'" He was like, "The same thing is going to happen on *The Office*. We've been praised as this great show. We had our golden years. The next stage of the narrative will be, '*The Office* has lost its mojo,' but if you stick around long enough we can maybe get to, '*The Office* is back.'"

But despite the promise of his first appearance at the end of season seven, it quickly became clear that Spader wasn't clicking with the rest of the cast. And judging by the awful reviews and sinking ratings, the show was rapidly losing popularity.

Claire Scanlon: Someone like Ellie Kemper was able to come from UCB and be quick on her feet and be like, "Okay, well they're not giving me enough, let me work on this, let me improv and ad-lib, and try to find my character, because they're certainly not helping me find it." I don't mean that in a bad way. It's just that they had eighteen people to service. But with James Spader, it was different. He liked the writers and respected them and thought, "Write me well and I will act well." He didn't want to find the character himself.

James Spader: The characters on the show were constantly treating my character like this sort of enigmatic guy who they couldn't quite figure out. And I realized partway in that the writers couldn't quite figure him either. I mean, the same relationship that the other characters had with Robert California, the writers had with him as well. But I felt that worked to my advantage. They wrote some really strange, eccentric stuff that I loved goofing around with. Now, whether it was successful in terms of the greater context of the whole of the show, I don't know. That really wasn't my concern. My concern was to try and play this guy and commit to him. And to me, he was just this very strange, totally eccentric, enigmatic guy.

Creed Bratton: He didn't seem comfortable. That wasn't because he's not a great actor, because he is a great actor. But not everyone can play what Steve Carell can do.

James Spader: It was a fantastic experience for me. It felt like TV camp. I had a ball.

Ben Silverman: Spader is a good guy and he's smart, but we needed brilliant comedians and James Spader isn't funny.

Mark Proksch: In the early days of the show, they were so rewarded by bringing in unknown talents. And when it got to the point where everyone wanted to be on the show, it took away from what the show was. When you have Jim Carrey and Will Ferrell and just a bunch of stunt cameos, I think it takes away to a certain extent the original documentarian feel. I know it took me out of the show when that occurred. I think Spader was a holdover from that and the natural documentarian style breaks when you bring in famous people to play these everyday ordinary people. And I think with Spader, for whatever reason, they decided that he was going to click, and it just didn't. You could just feel it not working when we were doing it. But you're on the eighth season of the show; how do you continue to make it fresh and make it interesting without redoing the same story eight times? And so you bring in new cast and new characters. And some are going to work, and some just aren't. I think they would have been better served by bringing in an unknown again.

Alysia Raycraft: He didn't fit and we worked our damnedest to make it happen because if anybody can make something funny, that group could.

Claire Scanlon: He did one thing and one thing well, which is creep you out, which is what he's kind of famous for. He needed to be on something like *The Blacklist,* which plays to his strengths.

Owen Ellickson: I think the main problem was that he was the head of Sabre, but his job was amorphous based on the sort of universe of the show. The show drilled into you over and over there's the regional manager, there's the assistant to the regional manager, and that's your universe. Then there's a Jan type, sort of above and distant, but you never saw that person hold sway in the actual office itself on a day-to-day basis. I think it was never clear how much or little authority Robert California had, so giving him a murky position in addition to the murkiness of his personality, it was just too much murk total.

Aaron Shure: I understand what they're saying. That sort of inscrutable, mind-fucker boss is like an amazingly good plot driver, but you don't really crack exactly what his motives are too closely.

Owen Ellickson: The best use of him would be as a villain, but there was reticence about taking a new famous guy and making him a villain. So, it felt a little bit like there was just this weird guy who was almost apathetic to the goings-on of *The Office*. So we never quite got anything. We had trouble finding the edge that he had at the end of season seven.

Warren Lieberstein: His character was this trickster character who comes in and shakes things up. And then when it was clear that he would only be there for one season, his character started to become darker. He became an agent of doom and chaos as opposed to how he was initially written as a person who comes in and shakes things up. When it turned I think is when he was like, "Well, what's going on? Why am I now all of a sudden this agent of chaos?"

Briton W. Erwin: James is an unusual guy. His trailer was right next to ours and he had a very different working style than everybody else. He was much more meticulous, more actor-y. Things had to be very clear to him why he was doing these things and he wanted to know the backstory to explain why he was doing this or that.

Halsted Sullivan: I think it probably did take him some time to adjust, because he was the star of all the other shows that he was on. And *The Office* is an ensemble. I think there were probably seventeen characters at the time. And if you're servicing all of those characters, it's hard to have a lead as having 50 percent of the lines. So, I think he wanted to make the most of his lines, and just had a lot of thoughts about how to do that.

James Spader: I liked the size of the ensemble. It was very well balanced. The last show that I had worked [*Boston Legal*] was on a very heavy workload. And on this show, no one had a very heavy workload because they had the balance to work between so many different characters. The cast was incredibly welcoming and hospitable. I thought they were lovely to work with. It was a pleasure to work with them all. I had a great time that year.

Rusty Mahmood: James Spader is a very unique dude. He's a little out there. I remember one time he had a six-page soliloquy almost that was crazy and hilarious and he had it memorized. But by that point, some of the others in the cast wouldn't even read the scripts. They would come in in the morning and wouldn't even look at their lines when they were in hair and makeup. Not everybody, but certain people would come in and we'd start rehearsing and it would be somebody's line and they'd all look at this person like, "Oh, what? Can I have some sides?" They had their characters down so well that they just looked at the lines they could memorize fast. But James had a real hard time with it. He was like, "Hey, man, I studied. That's what we do. We study our lines, we prepare." And he definitely had some troubles with some of the cast members later in the season.

Alysia Raycraft: The squaring off between James and Paul [Lieberstein] was a little difficult at times. He could have tried harder to be directed. It wasn't the James Spader show and that's what I think he was ready for.

Halsted Sullivan: Paul and James would indeed have long conversations about the character. I think it was an effort on James's part to really understand the character. It wasn't like, "Oh, my character wouldn't do this." It would be like, "Okay. You've written this. Why would my character do that?" It was an effort to give the best performance and the best of his method. He just wanted to do the best job possible. And for him, his process is asking a lot of questions. But yeah, they'd have long conversations about his motivation.

James Spader: I sometimes would pull Paul aside and talk to him, but I wouldn't say it was to talk about my character's motivations. It was more contextual so that I could have a sense of where we were moving toward or what was happening. More than anything else my conversations with Paul were really more about me thinking out loud about how I wanted to play the character.

Rusty Mahmood: Every discussion with James was a long one. He liked to dive in deep.

Brian Wittle: He wasn't happy with what they were writing for him and the speeches they wrote for him were just too long. He would do these big, long, funny speeches, but they were three minutes long, four minutes long. The whole episode is only twenty-one minutes. Three minutes of it is gonna be Robert California's speech? So they'd always end up getting chopped down to hardly anything, so I can see from his perspective if you're handed this big long thing to memorize and this big long thing to act and do, and then one-tenth of it ends up in the episode, that does seem like maybe what they wrote didn't matter in the first place.

James Spader: That sounds like an exaggeration to me. A majority of the stuff that I did on the show was in the show. To be frank, if that was how they were operating, then I would have gone to the writers and said, "Write less, because I'm not going to just act on the set for it to continually every week end up on the cutting room floor. Just write less. I can just do it less. If that's what you want, then simply write less." That's what I would have done if that was what the pattern was, but that wasn't really the pattern.

Kelly Cantley: Spader is super meticulous and I think probably classically trained, although I don't know that. But his training is regular film and TV where you shoot five shots of five different angles of the same scene, but you shoot five angles, one after the other, and keep repeating it verbatim. And Spader always matches. Spader says a line and on the word he picks a pencil up, he'll pick that pencil up in the exact same way every time, which editors love because it's super easy to cut together. That is what all actors in movies and television should be trained to do. But on our show, because we were handheld doc style, we shot both sides at the same time, [so] it was not a strict requirement that you match. Everybody was more interested in the funny. So Spader was trying to find his footing and he'd say to the script supervisor, "They never do the same thing twice. How do they cut this thing together?"

Mark Proksch: James was very relaxed and I didn't see anything really faze him at all during his performances. He's the type that he doesn't look at his lines really in between takes because he has them down. And that's that old-school memorization that he had to have to be able to rely on for the bulk of his career. He didn't improvise at all that I saw. And I think that goes back to when he was young, they weren't allowed to really improvise. They were told, "Get the damn lines right." And so, I don't think he had that muscle, or has that muscle. And if he does, for whatever reason he chose not to use it.

Jeff Blitz: Spader's style of working was not improv heavy at all. Spader wants to know the script and know it cold. And if there is a word that isn't right to him or that seems off, Spader wants, prior to the shoot day, to sit and to make sure everyone is cool with the script being changed like that. I don't think there was anyone else on the cast who came from that same school.

James Spader: Certain actors were more improvisational than others and I had been trained in improvisation, but I also have great respect for material. And I didn't ever see any fully improvisational scenes ever on the days that I was working. It wasn't like the scripts were handed out in outline form. The show was fully scripted.

Kate Flannery: We didn't really have to deal with too many stars suddenly hijacking the show and here was a new character who would have very, very long monologues. His work was so different from ours and Michael Scott's. I mean, it was just written so differently. And it was just interesting because I just felt like he's not really a comedy person so it was just odd. It felt like taking kind of a heavy turn. I mean, I think it worked out. But being in the room I was like, "I don't know about this . . . he's got the baby . . . don't drop the baby . . . don't drop the baby." That was always in my head.

Myles NcNutt: The character is such a wild card and his presence was basically just to unnerve people. He had no other motivations. There was no effort to flesh out his character. There was no effort to make him seem like a more grounded part of the show. He developed no interesting relationships with the main characters. And to be fair, the show had this problem with Jo, the Kathy Bates character. I think they were already struggling to figure out how to create authority figures that operate in this world, but there was no reason for him to be in Scranton. There was no good reason for the character to really exist, except that I think they felt like they needed to add something, but they couldn't [make] him feel like a natural part of the world. I personally prefer my *Office* to be very grounded and realistic. I felt like Robert California threatened that in a way that was exciting at first, but then the longer he stood around, you realized that that was it. That was all he could do.

James Spader: I think that the nicest thing about that character was how enigmatic he was and how he didn't explain himself to anybody, and he just was who he was, and you had to take him at face value. I was perfectly comfortable with that dynamic. As far as reviews? I don't use the Internet or social media. I really truly do not have any idea how you even access those things.

Complicating matters even further, Andy's transition from salesman to regional manager didn't generate a lot of laughs. And to fit him into the new role, the writers rid the character of many of his quirky, easy-to-anger edges and made him rather dull and uninteresting.

Amelie Gillette: Andy was a goofier character before that season. I feel like we tried to rein him in a little character-wise, make him more boss-like. But I think that that's what anyone who rose to that position would do.

Myles McNutt: I think they didn't quite realize how much they were moving away from that previous character, how much it felt like that character almost didn't exist anymore. It felt like a retcon. It's also hard to like Andy when he's the boss and they've neutered any meaning in his character and left it largely instead with just, "He's a well-meaning guy, but he messes up sometimes." There was no real desire there.

Owen Ellickson: Ed Helms is brilliantly funny and Andy Bernard was a pure comedy character. In the last episode before he was made manager, there was a runner about how small his dick was by his own definition. These are characteristics that you don't usually give to your quarterback on a show. It felt a little bit like the way we try to three-dimensionalize him in season eight, but we just kept running into ways that they had three-dimensionalized Michael. It felt to me like we were having trouble breaking out of a Michael-shaped mold for the manager. That, to me, was one of the biggest problems.

Danny Chun: Part of it was realizing we had Ed Helms, who was an amazing actor, and we wanted to present a three-dimensional version that people can really sympathize with. I guess you can say that was a retcon, but I feel like it was also just a very natural thing to happen with a lot of characters on this show, and on other shows, where the more you get to know them the more three-dimensional and sympathetic they become.

Alan Sepinwall: Andy became just a watered-down Michael, that's all it was. He was a Michael who the people already liked, so there's no tension and there's no comedy. He was also really annoying. They already established that people did get along with him and then he becomes the boss, so they were just rehashing an old dynamic.

Jeff Blitz: I think that the show with Andy as the boss could have worked. That the idea was that Andy was a bad salesman and would be a good manager. That took the comedy engine out of the show. Michael was the exact opposite, a good salesman and bad manager. When you flip the formula it doesn't work as well. The whole sense that the office is off balance couldn't come from the top down anymore.

Justin Spitzer: There was always the knowledge that we were trying to be the Steve Carell show without Steve Carell.

The Steve Carell show without Steve Carell shed viewers with almost each pass-

ing week and the critics tore it to shreds. The writers tried to shake things up by moving a bunch of characters down to Florida for a long arc where they opened up a Sabre store, and they briefly tried to threaten Jim and Pam's marriage by bringing in Lindsey Broad as a new character with a crazy crush on Jim, but nothing seemed to work with fans or the press. The AV Club, where writer Amelie Gillette had worked until Mindy Kaling hired her to work on The Office, *was particularly critical.*

Amelie Gillette: Before I joined the show, Nathan Rabin was doing the reviews, and Nathan was a huge *Office* fan and would always rate the shows very well. Then when I joined they hired a new reviewer [Myles McNutt], who seemingly hated the show. I felt very responsible because they took Nathan off of the *Office* beat because of a conflict of interest, I guess.

Myles McNutt: I'm not shocked they felt that way. If I were a writer reading some of those *Office* reviews I would've been pissed, but I didn't hate the show. I loved that show. My response to that season was entirely based on how much I liked what came before. I loved those early seasons so much and I just felt like it was no longer working.

Owen Ellickson: I loved reading Myles's reviews on the AV Club. My frustration with them was outweighed by my morbid fascination with them. I'd been in the business for eight or nine years, and I had never seen any real scrutiny of any episode that I've ever worked on. So, I sort of loved it. I remember disagreeing with him a decent amount, and agreeing with him a decent amount. But it was quite a thing to see this kind of real anger underlying his review.

Amelie Gillette: You don't think, as a person that's writing reviews of the TV episode, that the writers from that episode or that show might read your review during lunch, but sometimes they do. I totally understand that criticism of thinking that James Spader didn't click. It's hard to bring in a big celebrity into an existing show. That is always going to be a hard adjustment, but at least initially, I do remember it being a fun character to think about and write for. I totally get people having soured on him as a character though.

Owen Ellickson: I understood where critics were coming from. I did feel like some of the key elements of the show were missing, and we had a million pieces, and we were moving them around kind of frantically. Even though a lot of fun stuff came from that, I could understand people feeling a little bit of whiplash.

Paul Feig: It was just the end of an era when Steve left, the end of just something wonderful. Him, and just the cast, and all those writers, and how wonderful they all were. And since Greg was so smart, they were able to keep it going. But for me personally once Steve's gone, that's sort of the end of it for me. It's like a body, and you rip the heart out of it and you can either be Iron Man or have a new nuclear heart; it isn't your real heart.

Danny Chun: By season eight, no matter what, your show's going to get a lot more criticism. People are going to say—and I'm not saying it wasn't deserved, but I'm saying it's also just inevitable. And I had come from a show [*The Simpsons*] that was in like season nineteen when I left it. So I think maybe I understood that a little bit more. But we were certainly feeling really creatively challenged and figuring out how to keep things going just for our characters. What are the next steps for these characters? How do we tell stories that we haven't already told?

Myles McNutt: The core of the issue at the end of the day is that Michael Scott leaving changed *The Office,* changed it 100 percent. But the way they reacted to it was as if it didn't. Their goal was to try to re-create those story patterns as much as possible, to basically make Andy the new Michael, to give Robert California some of Michael's qualities. I completely get why they didn't want to change things too much, why NBC would be terrified if they said, "We're gonna completely reorganize the show." But there was no re-creating Michael Scott, and yet the show tried. And I think that attempt was doomed to failure. I don't think there was a way for them to just keep going as if that didn't happen, and I think they went on for a while believing that was possible and I just don't think it was.

Owen Ellickson: I think that the character Michael Scott was load bearing, basically. I think that it was worth trying it without him from a business perspective, and selfishly those were two of my favorite years of my career. I learned a ton and it was a great experience for me. But I don't think we ever got it to the point where you didn't miss Michael. He was the soul of the show.

Ricky Gervais: I thought it was over when Steve left. But, listen, I couldn't believe they were able to do twenty-two episodes a year and they'd already done seven of them. To me, it's all too much. I honestly haven't watched all of them.

chapter 27

LIFE IN THE BACKGROUND

("I learned not to count lines in a script.")

The number of people in the main cast swelled to new highs in the eighth season, making life even more difficult for the background players, some of whom had been around since the first season and rarely got more than a couple of lines of dialogue every season. Most shows didn't keep around the same background players season after season, but making Dunder Mifflin feel like an actual office that operated above a real warehouse made it necessary. For these actors, the job was an opportunity to get screen time on a major network show even if they had little to no dialogue and often just had to pretend to work for hours on end while the main cast shot a scene in the foreground. The single-camera format and giant cast also meant that even series regulars like Kate Flannery, Leslie Baker, and Oscar Nunez had to often spend day after day silently pretending to work as well.

Creed Bratton: Many times it would be late at night and they're shooting scenes with you in the back and you just have to just sit there even though you're tired and you just want to go home and go to bed. That was all part of the deal.

Kate Flannery: I learned not to count lines in a script. Sometimes they would write my story after the table read. I didn't always have it before that. And sometimes there were episodes where I didn't speak at all. I wasn't even given a line. I just learned to trust it. I remember one time someone else in the cast said to me, "You should be pissed. I don't speak and you don't speak in this scene." I was like, "No, no, no, no, no. That is not my fight. That might be your fight, but that is not my fight." This is the gift of getting a job when you're over forty. I was also in a situation where I really could trust Greg and I really could trust the show.

Creed Bratton: I didn't care when I didn't get lines. I was just happy to be there and happy to get in the show because I always felt getting onto it was a destiny thing. How lucky was I to be on it in the first place? I wasn't going to complain. I never complained. I mean, there was part of me that said, "Well, I'm capable of doing more." At that time, I thought, "Well, I know I can do this. I could do more of a serious side thing. Do I want to mention it?" Then my little voice said, "No." I always trust my little voice. "There's no reason to rock the boat." People come and go. Why would I even want to change anything about this? It all worked out.

Matt Sohn: We would always try to find moments to kind of build those minor characters up by giving them great reaction shots in group settings, whether they were reacting to Michael or to Dwight. We'd talk to them and say, "Hey, give me something in this area so I can find a reaction." And they were always excited to come through and to find something.

Claire Scanlon: If you watch *The Office*, keep your eye on Brian Baumgartner. He's always looking out for a way to infuse comedy in the background of a scene, like ending up at the receptionist's desk trying to get some jelly beans or trying to go in through a door that Ed just closed. He's just always looking for that extra button on a scene. No one was ever relaxed or lazy on that show. No one mailed it in. Everyone was always trying.

Matt Sohn: They'd sit there for hours and hours at a time. The funny thing is that they would always ask us what our [camera] angles were if they were at their desks, so they would know if their computer was being seen or not, because if their computer wasn't seen, they could put whatever they want on it, whether it was the fantasy football draft or whatever game they were doing or their personal e-mails and bills they were paying or whatever. And when we filmed the talking heads in the conference room, you could see into the bullpen through the window and right at Stanley's desk. That meant Leslie had to stay later than everyone else just to be in the background of those shots. He hated that.

Creed Bratton: Leslie slept most of the time. He'd sleep in his cubicle. It was a gift.

Randall Einhorn: Leslie played a lot of solitaire, in character and out of character.

Creed Bratton: I was writing songs at my desk a lot. I wrote two albums when I was on that show, in the greenroom and in my trailer. At the cubicle, when the camera was around and there was a possibility it was going to see me, I had to be playing spider solitaire because we were legally allowed to show it. I played a lot of spider solitaire.

Oscar Nunez: I was often looking at stupid things on YouTube. We would play games like Bejeweled or mahjong. . . . Phyllis played a lot of cards and then a lot of people just went on social media.

Devon Abner: There were many twelve-hour days where I had nothing to do. All I would do was either walk around or file papers or sit back and play spider solitaire, which I became addicted to, or I'd read a book. It was fun though. I learned a lot from watching the other guys. The big four were John and Jenna and Steve and Rainn. Rainn would always go out of his way to be really nice. They'd have parties and John invited me to one once. I thought, "Wow, he's a fucking kid and he went out of his way to include the fringe people." I thought it was really classy.

Robert Shafer: There was a dreaded thing called deep background. If you got stuck in deep background, you had to stay there and it didn't matter that you were doing nothing. I was always there at the parties and the weddings with Phyllis, but often I didn't really speak. That's very humbling. You had to learn to accept certain things. When I was a basketball player I started out at the very bottom and they'd only put me in at the end of the games. I worked as hard as I could to get in and then I worked to become the best I could be. It's the same thing there. You want the ball, you want to be driving the boat or at least contributing as much as you feel like you're capable of.

The warehouse workers had even less opportunity for dialogue and oftentimes were only seen far off in the background pretending to do manual labor.

Karly Rothenberg: On my first day of filming, I climbed up a ladder to put boxes on the top shelf when Michael came down to give checks to everybody. And then every time he walked down the steps for another take, I had to climb the stepladder again. We did that like fifty times. My butt hurt so bad by the end. After that, a friend of mine told me, "Always pick the easy thing to do."

Calvin Tenner: I used to be a supervisor at a corrugation plant, so I was certified to use the forklift, the scissor lift, and all the other equipment. Working in the warehouse on the show, you could pick the character you wanted to be, just like any other actor, and live the character through the whole scene. The only difference was you didn't have any dialogue. My character was pretty much always like, "Leave me alone. I'm here to do my job. I don't want to take no crap from you."

Karly Rothenberg: I tried to give Madge a backstory so that it would be there in case I needed to elaborate on it. I decided she definitely had a crush on Dwight, and that didn't pan out 'cause they wanted Dwight and Angela to have their thing. Then I decided she rides a Harley and that's how she gets to work every day and that maybe, maybe, maybe she likes girls. . . . My agent used to call me "Queen of the One Line" because I rarely got more than one line. But that was fine with me. I was grateful to be included.

Calvin Tenner: I had a trailer in the back of our warehouse with a futon bed, but I almost never used it. I would hang out on the stage and watch the other actors do their magic. My mind was constantly turning, like, "How can I be better?" Just watching everyone in that office work, especially Steve Carell, was mesmerizing. I was trying to figure out how I can be like that.

Karly Rothenberg: You're a day player and after a while you learn your place, I guess you could say. So I never imposed myself on anyone because I was just very grateful for the opportunity. When we shot the basketball episode in season one, I took a fall and I bashed my knee into the ground real hard. I didn't wanna go home and I was trying to hide it and I had an ice pack on and I was sitting there very discreetly. Jenna Fischer was sitting next to me on the sidelines and she looks down and she goes, "Oh my God!" And I'm like, "Shh." But they had to stop filming and they took me to the hospital. I just wanted to die because I was like, "No, I don't wanna be injured. I wanna stay here and play." I was so, so sad.

Hidetoshi "Hide" Imura moved to America from Japan when he was thirty-five and spoke very limited English when he got cast as a warehouse worker in season three. He stuck around until the very end of the series.

Hidetoshi Imura (Hidetoshi Hasagawa, Seasons 3–9): When I got to the audition, there were no other Japanese people and they were all native English speakers. I was very shocked. I can't speak English very well and I felt very negative about it, but two days later they called me and said I had the part. I was like, "Oh my God! They trust me!"

Karly Rothenberg: Hide was hysterical. He was just a really low-key guy, happy to be there, happy to be working, grateful for the paycheck. He never spoke much though.

Hidetoshi Imura: I was always very excited when we got to stay late and I got overtime pay.

As the years went by, the cast and crew started to reward the day players.

Calvin Tenner: I was getting married in South Beach on August eighth, 2008. But I learned soon beforehand they needed me the day before that, so I canceled my ticket and bought a red-eye to Florida the morning of my wedding so I could do it. I let everyone know what happened when I got there and Rainn put together a little package for me where everyone chipped in some money. When I got back from our honeymoon, I took my wife to the set to meet everyone and we brought them a box of chocolate strawberries from Edible Arrangements. The next day I got a call from my agent saying they'd written me into the show and I'd have lines. It was a shocker to me. I became a recurring.

Prior to this, there was such little care given to Calvin's character that his name tag changed from Lester to Calvin to Glenn without explanation. Once he became a recurring character, they stuck with Glenn and started throwing him lines and tiny scenes here and there.

Calvin Tenner: I was ecstatic. I was like, "Are you serious?" All my friends were jealous. They were like, "You are part of one of the shows that's going to be around forever."

Hide's limited English made it more difficult to expand on his role, but near the end of season six B. J. Novak decided it was finally time for viewers to hear his story. He wrote a hysterical tag to an episode where, at Darryl's urging, Hide explains to the camera that he was a heart surgeon in Japan who had to flee the country after killing a yakuza boss during an operation.

B. J. Novak: It was a particular mission of mine to get that into the episode. I liked the idea that Hide had a life story infinitely more dramatic than anyone else the documentary crew had been following, but that they never thought to ask.

Hidetoshi Imura: They gave me the script at ten P.M. the night before we shot and I was like, "Oh my God!" I thought it would be one or two lines, but I had so many lines. I couldn't sleep the night before and the next day I was so tired I couldn't remember my lines. B. J. and the director were like, "Okay, Hide, that's all right. Just relax." Then they called action again and I did it. They went, "Oh my God! Hide! Thank you very much!" And I was like, "Oh my God! I did it! I did it!" I was very happy.

B. J. Novak: Hide improvised one piece of monologue: the inclusion of "American car" among his good fortunes. I did not quite understand why someone from Japan would take such pride in owning an American car, but I enjoyed it and went with it.

Hidetoshi Imura: Many times on the streets since I'm asked, "Are you Hide? Are you the heart surgeon?" Many times.

In season one, stand-up comic Patrice O'Neal began appearing as temperamental warehouse worker Lonny Collins. Unlike the others, he was given dialogue.

Karly Rothenberg: He always got guest-star credit, which I never got. But I think he had the same kind of feeling that I had, wishing he could contribute more or be a more established character. But he was so funny when he would come in and do his one line or two lines that it almost didn't need any more than that.

Calvin Tenner: I remember this one time he was talking about how big guys like himself got chicks. He said something like, "I always look for the ones with low self-esteem." Man, he was so funny. He was a special person to have on set.

Craig Robinson: They wanted to put Patrice in more episodes, but he didn't want to be out in LA. They even, at one point, hit me up and were like, "Craig, do you know where Patrice is? We have a check for him." He was a different kind of cat, man, and there was no one funnier.

Once his stand-up career took off and Comedy Central gave him his own special, he was no longer willing to fly from his home in New York to appear on the show in such a minimal role. He died of a stroke in 2011.

Karly Rothenberg: Nobody knew he was sick. Nobody knew anything.

Calvin Tenner: He was just starting out. Had he lived, I think his role on the show would have gotten much bigger than what it was. He was a powerhouse.

Craig Robinson played the foreman of the warehouse on the show, and behind the scenes he was a fatherly figure to all of his fictional underlings.

Calvin Tenner: Craig Robinson was the man. He's one of my best friends to this day. Even right now, I'm his stunt double, right, for whatever he does. He's my brother in the entertainment business.

Karly Rothenberg: Bless his heart. Craig was the one character in the warehouse that got all of the story lines and he got the character development, which we were really incredibly happy for him because as long as he kept coming back, that meant somebody would be shooting in the warehouse. And every time they shot in the warehouse, I was like, "Oh, cool! Maybe I'll get to come back! Yay!" And then when he moved upstairs [in season six] I was like, "Oh, no."

Calvin Tenner: When Craig moved upstairs, Darryl moved upstairs. There wasn't that much time in the warehouse after that.

Karly Rothenberg: The more time went on, the less approachable people became. I don't mean that in a bad way. It's just that people can't help but change when they have that kind of success. People were always kind to me, but I was just window dressing. I wasn't an important character. At times I got frustrated because I contacted publicity at NBC and said, "Hey!

I'm available to go to Scranton for the convention or whatever you need," and no one ever reached out to me. They were only interested in the primary characters, which was cool, but I just wanted people to know I was available too.

Devon Abner: Now that the show is done, I keep hoping at some point I'll be offered to go to one of those autograph-signing conventions. [Creed, Oscar Nunez, and Kate Flannery have become regulars on that circuit.] But then I could also picture being there and nobody would want my autograph. I was just the obscure guy in the corner.

chapter 28

SEASON NINE

("A lot of us were low on gas.")

There wasn't even a hint that The Office *would end after its ninth season when the show was officially renewed in May 2012. Despite the sinking ratings in season eight and negative reviews, it was still NBC's highest-rated comedy. Once they secured the return of Ed Helms by giving him several weeks off to film* The Hangover Part III *and worked out raises for the other leads, a full-season order happened very quickly. "Remaining open is the question who will run The Office next season," Deadline reported. "I hear NBC is not close to naming a replacement for Paul Lieberstein, who will be leaving to focus on the spinoff [*The Farm*], which he co-created with Wilson." That replacement turned out to be Greg Daniels, who felt secure enough with Michael Schur running* Parks and Recreation *that he was able to return full-time for the first time since the first half of season five.*

Alysia Raycraft: Everything felt more cohesive after Greg returned. Mindy likened him to a dad at one point and it really felt like Dad was back.

Briton W. Erwin: Having Greg back made things feel more unified.

Greg Daniels: I hadn't been full-time on the show for a few years, and I just have a very strong connection to everybody. I feel responsible for everybody, and I couldn't imagine a scenario where I wouldn't be directing what was happening at the end.

Mark Proksch: Greg had such a clear insight into the show and how the show should work and how the relationships should work, better than anyone else, I think, other than possibly Paul Lieberstein. Him coming back really gave that last season direction. Season eight felt like Clown Town Frolics, which is a weird term I use sometimes. But Greg's whole idea was that it's a love story between Jim and Pam and he returned the focus back to that. I also think that he realized that Andy wasn't quite working out as boss and so he tried to spread that a little bit instead of focusing on Andy so much as they did in season eight. The writing felt more focused. I just felt season eight was a little . . . and who am I to say as just a recurring actor on the show, but I felt that the stories were a little wishy-washy at times and unfocused.

Greg Daniels: I wanted to have a tone of alternating comedy with seriousness, I guess. Then one of the things that we all as writers felt was that Andy Bernard was funnier as a bit of a dick. We took his character down a few notches. We went back to perhaps an earlier version of his character. Part of it was that he was going to be gone for like ten episodes in the middle of the season. So, it was clear that he couldn't headline the show as he had in season eight because he was missing for the middle. Part of it was, "What do we do if he's not going to be here for the middle of the season? We have to figure out something for Erin to do." But we also liked the Andy that was capable of more foolishness.

And even though the cast was huge by this point, he decided to bring on Jake Lacy and Clark Duke as young office workers.

Clark Duke: When Jake and I joined the show, the idea was that it was gonna be like *ER*. The three leads—Rainn, John, and Jenna—were all going to leave after the season and they were going to reboot the show the following year with new cast members basically. That was my understanding of what was going to happen when I was hired.

Owen Ellickson: I heard that bandied about, but I never thought it was going to happen. There was the road where—which is the road that ended up being taken—where you start a show and you start with a bunch of actors and you basically end with those same actors and that's the life of the show. The other version is you could theoretically imagine a sort of perpetual-motion machine, like a *Law & Order* or something, where, like in an actual office, people leave and new people come in.

Brent Forrester: Greg was initially thinking about a reboot of the show at the start of season nine. It was like, "Hey, you know what? Let's keep this show going on way beyond season nine." That's where you see him casting Clark Duke and Jake Lacy. That was going to be the future of *The Office*. On-screen they're quite deliberately referred to as, "Hey, look at new Jim and new Dwight." Greg anticipated if there had been a season ten that Krasinski and Jenna Fischer would move on, and then he would just replace them and build a new cast. There was an effective process of that from beginning to end. They had the core cast and then new characters were added effectively from time to time, like Andy Bernard and Erin. That would have just continued and old characters would have left and it just would have kept evolving.

Greg Daniels: From the storytelling standpoint the theme of this year was set in the premiere and it was the kind of realization on the part of Dwight and Jim that they'd been there a long time. That's sort of a prod for them to get their lives on to the next stage. By having these guys who everybody was seeing as the new Jim and the new Dwight—the point of that was just to kind of get them to think about how long they've been in the same job.

Clark Duke: There was supposed to be a Jim/Dwight thing with me and Jake. They kept playing with the meta-ness of it by saying that I looked like

Dwight. I think it would've been a fun thing if they'd kept it going longer and figured out the nuances of the characters.

Owen Ellickson: Greg sort of gathered everybody toward the end of season eight and asked how we thought we could rejuvenate the show. I said, largely to silence, that I think we have to fire a bunch of actors. Not that I think they deserve to be fired, but if you actually wanted to make it feel like you were starting a new chapter, you can't keep eighteen pieces in place. You're never going to start a new chapter if it's like, "Here's pieces nineteen through twenty-three." You have to give those people real slots. I think, totally understandably, partly for personal reasons, because everybody was friends with the actors, we were never going to quite pull that trigger. There may have been business concerns as well, but I think when Clark and Jake were told there was going to be a tenth season with them, I'm sure that Greg believed that in the moment. I think that was something he genuinely considered doing. But I'm not shocked it never went that way. I think you leave the dance with the date that brought you.

Just four episodes into the season, Daniels came onto the set and made a big announcement.

Kate Flannery: Bryan Cranston was on set that day directing the "Work Bus" episode [where everyone in the office is forced to work in a cramped, moving bus]. During lunch they told us this was going to be the last season and it was going to the press in an hour. They wanted to prep us for it going out. I just remember we were on this bus and inches from each other all day. I was like, "This is crazy." It just felt so emotional, but it also felt sort of perfect that we were in such close proximity feeling this all together and processing this together.

The exact reasoning has never been fully articulated, but it seems to be a mixture of creative exhaustion, the knowledge that the leads were unlikely to agree to another season, and Bob Greenblatt's desire to move NBC away from quirky, relatively low-rated shows like 30 Rock, Parks and Rec, Community, *and* The Office *and once again produce massive hits like the network did in the 1990s.*

Briton W. Erwin: When the ninth season rolled around, Greg went around and polled the cast and crew and said, "We can do a season ten if you want, but should we?" And I think pretty much everybody said, "Let's find a way to go out in style, not just try and drag it out for another season just because." I think everybody kinda liked the idea of a solid ten seasons and it's not like any of us wanted to stop working together, but I think the majority of the people kinda felt like it was time and it wasn't the same show anymore and it hadn't really found the traction that it needed to.

Brian Wittle: I remember there being some discussion of a reboot with Jake and Clark, but the general consensus was that we should just end it, that it's been nine years and if we try to start up with new guys, or even these new guys, it's not gonna be the same if everybody leaves except them. They were funny, but I think we would've lost most of the audience.

Warren Lieberstein: Greg wanted to get out before the show ever took a slide. By then we were always battling to try and find small office stories. That was the bread and butter of the show, but after a while [with] those small stories you begin to kind of circle around kind of the same stuff. And you're like, "Oh, we already did an episode that was kind of similar to that." Then when you start to remove yourself from the office and more and more stories start to be set in other locations, you can start to get the sense that the timing is right to leave.

Teri Weinberg: In thinking about a possible season ten, it was, "Does Greg have it in him? Does this writing staff have it in them? Does the cast want to come back and do this?" And I think we all decided that we felt like it was a great opportunity to have an incredible season nine and have that be our last season. We went out on our own terms.

John Krasinski: We all had a big say in whether or not we ended it. And it was a big discussion with the actors and producers and the crew and we all had a feeling about it. To us, it was just about maintaining the very special experience we've had all along, which is "I think we're a very special show, I think we're a very unique show, and because of it, I feel we deserve to leave rather than be asked to leave." Growing up I remember vividly the end of *Cheers* and the end of *Friends*, and I think it's such a special moment, and weirdly TV is an incredibly sentimental medium that you have a lot of people not only watching, but weirdly experiencing this with you, so everyone deserves to have that goodbye moment rather than, "Is that show still on?" We just didn't want that.

Oscar Nunez: Greg Daniels was like, "This is going to be the end." We're like, "No." And then he's like, "Should we keep going?" Everyone was like, "We don't know, we're just saying no, but we don't know." He's like, "I think we're done. I know I'm done." We were like, "He's right." For Greg it was so much work for so many years. He was ready for a break.

Steve Burgess: It was Greg being Greg and Greg wanting to end things the right way and on our terms and not on the network's terms.

Clark Duke: I thought NBC canceled it.

Bob Greenblatt: I made the decision with Greg Daniels to end it while it was still pretty strong because we didn't [want to] watch it erode on the air.

Randy Cordray: We believed that Bob Greenblatt wanted to move away from *The Office* and develop his own slate of comedies and dramas. And *The Office* was getting a little long in the tooth as far as he was concerned. And I don't think he planned on *The Office* going twelve seasons.

Owen Ellickson: I think that Bob Greenblatt was never particularly sold on *The Office*. I don't know him personally, but it certainly never felt like there was a consistent plug from the network, like, "We love you guys. We would like to find the next version of this show." It might have gone by the board anyway, but that element was certainly not in its favor.

Teri Weinberg: Bob couldn't have been more supportive when he first came to the network, and he's one of my closest friends. I love him dearly. He said, "I'm not going to come in and tell you guys how to make this show. I respect it. I'm a huge fan of it, and I'll support you, and I want you on the air as long as you want to be on the air."

Ben Silverman: Now that I look back, I think that Greg wanted to end it. I think there was just a little bit of fatigue around it that I'm sure that everyone regrets having because it could have kept going.

Halsted Sullivan: If the ratings were better at that time, maybe there would have been another season or two. But you also have to remember that, for both the cast and crew, we were doing twenty-six episodes a season at that point. A lot of us were low on gas—not low on love for the show, but it was challenging to find new and interesting ways to tell stories that hadn't been told before.

Kim Ferry: Most of the cast were still really interested in doing movies and maybe doing something completely different than the characters they'd been playing for nine years. I think they kind of got antsy.

Matt Sohn: It felt like the end. There was conversation of getting another season out of it, but everything leading up into it, it definitely felt like this was the last one. It seemed like that was the general chatter with the cast. There were cast members that were definitely ready to move on. There [were] other cast members that were happy to keep this going until they could just be done with the business.

Brian Wittle: I remember Greg saying, "At least we know it early on so that we can really savor this last season."

They had twenty episodes to wrap up the entire series.

Halsted Sullivan: When we knew we were marching toward the end, we were therefore able to take some bigger swings.

Owen Ellickson: It was a much more satisfying season to work on because we knew we were building to a head. Season eight was sort of like, "Here's some more stuff, but we don't really know what the upshot of any of it is." Season nine was totally different.

Brent Forrester: In some ways that was very energizing because it was like, "Hey, every single idea that you ever wanted to do on the show that you couldn't, now's your last chance." There was an abundance of leftover ideas. From the very beginning, Greg knew that a couple of things [were] going to happen before the show ended. One was that we were going to break the fourth wall and show the camera crew. You'd think we were talking about the end of the earth the way we debated this. People were going to lay down their lives for or against this issue back when Mike Schur was on the show. I remember speaking to Mike and saying, "Why are you so against showing the camera crew?" Mike said, "Why am I against this? Because it's like opening up the skin of the actor and pulling out its guts and showing that to the audience as entertainment." That's how passionate he was against this. Now that Mike Schur was gone Greg could finally show the boom operator.

Ken Kwapis: Greg decided we should start to get to know those people. But I do think that there's always been important moments where you get a sense that if a character says something to the camera, they're sort of having a conversation with the camera operator.

Justin Spitzer: In the back of our minds, that was always something that we would talk about. At some point, do we meet that person? I think Greg always had in the back of his mind that whenever the final season was, we would meet them, or we would jump forward in time to when they're screening the documentary and all that.

Owen Ellickson: I was a real camera-crew-reveal skeptic. I never really even thought of it so much from a creative perspective, but from a fan perspective. I just felt like even though I've often enjoyed meta stuff in other forms of comedy, that wasn't what I found interesting about the show. The presentation was part of what made the show fun, but I wasn't actually curious about who these people were living in Scranton. That just was a question that I felt viscerally I did not want to ask, personally. So, I was against it, but it was just season nine and we knew that was something we had to do, so we moved forward on it.

Briton W. Erwin: Our dream was that at the end of it, since it was a British documentary crew, that it would turn out to be Ricky Gervais and Stephen Merchant and some of the other people from the BBC show being the documentary crew. A bunch of us were rooting for that to be the end. But I think in a lot of ways, Greg was right to go out on a more emotional note because I think at that point, people were so invested in these characters.

Despite that investment, Greg wanted to throw a major wedge between Jim and Pam. It begins early in the season when Jim starts up a sports agency with college friends that forces him to divide his time between Philadelphia and Scranton.

Justin Spitzer: Early on, once we got Jim and Pam together we said that we're not gonna do the *Friends* thing of you split Ross and Rachel apart just to bring them back together. That season we thought, "Well, we've gone this long; maybe we do add a little bit of tension." It's so much fun to see characters get together and that would give us a cool place to end the season.

Steve Burgess: I remember Greg having a meeting with pretty much everybody in the cast about where they felt their character would be going and how their character would be ending the series. Greg actually took a lot of that into consideration as he planned out the final season.

John Krasinski: My whole pitch to Greg was that we've done so much with Jim and Pam, and now, after marriage and kids, there was a bit of a lull there, I think, for them about what they wanted to do. . . . For me it was, "Can you have this perfect relationship go through a split and keep it the same?" which of course you can't. And I said to Greg, "It would be really interesting to see how that split will affect two people that you know so well."

Greg Daniels: I was just very attracted to the idea of doing something that would matter, and where people would feel very involved, and I think there were a number of moments [that] year where you become really involved in what's happening. And in order to get that feeling of involvement there, you need some ups and some downs.

Brent Forrester: Greg really wanted to do something extremely risky and high-stakes, which was the documentary airs and we see what effect it has had on these characters. And there was going to be a reunion episode where you see that Jim and Pam have split up by this time, and they will have their reunion in the reunion episode.

Warren Lieberstein: I recall this slightly differently, though if Brent says it's true then I would believe it because he had a large part to do with that final season and Halsted and I were just working three days a week at that point. What I recall is that there might have been a faction of people who liked the idea of splitting up Jim and Pam, but it wasn't universally loved and Greg had the final say.

They built toward a possible Jim/Pam split through the early part of the season where they are increasingly at odds with each other over his new company, especially when she learns he lied to her about it at first and then put $10,000 of *their emergency savings in it. In the twelfth episode, "Customer Loyalty," they get into a nasty argument over the phone when Pam admits that she failed to record their daughter's dance recital. When it ends, Pam breaks down in tears and a voice off camera says, "Are you okay?" She shakes her head and says, "What am I doing wrong, Brian?" We then pan to a boom mic operator standing a few feet away from her desk. A camera operator is next to him. After nine years, we finally see the faces of the people making the documentary. The boom mic operator moves toward Pam to comfort her and orders the cameras off. It's clear they have affection for each other. The boom mic guy is named Brian Wittle.*

Brian Wittle: Brian is me, that's who it's supposed to be. Greg came to me and he said, "So we've been talking about you in the writing room. We're gonna introduce a character and we think it should be you. You're gonna audition and maybe you could play yourself." I was like, "Well, I haven't really done a lot of acting, but I'll try." I did an audition with Jenna and then they auditioned a bunch of other people, too. Greg sent me a very nice e-mail saying they had given it to someone else, which I expected to happen. [The part went to Chris Diamantopoulos.] We did a talking head where he introduces himself as Brian Wittle and I boomed it. It was really weird.

Owen Ellickson: It sucks to have a character named after you, then read for it and not get it. It always felt like it must have been a very existentially confusing moment for the real Brian Wittle.

Warren Lieberstein: There was always this notion that the person behind the camera might develop this certain affection toward the person they're shooting because it was so intimate. If you've ever been wired up for sound you know it's very intimate, the whole thing. So it made sense to us that a relationship would be drawn between filmer and subject.

Greg Daniels: [This] was something that came up in season five, I think. It was a pitch. I think Mindy was the first or one of the first champions of it. The idea was to introduce some romantic triangle with Jim when they were such soul mates that you had to say, "How could she possibly be interested in somebody else?" You think to yourself, "Well, I wouldn't believe it if I just was introduced to the character." You had to see it happening from scratch. What if that character had been secretly there the entire time and predated the relationship with Jim and had been a shoulder that she cried on for years? It just seemed very intriguing. But we also were like, "If we break the fourth wall in season five, it feels like that might be the last season for the show." So we kept putting that off. Ultimately, I didn't think it was about actually going there. They never did anything. It was just to introduce worry in the audience, which I think happened. I mean there are people who in season eight were like, "They're so boring. They just hang out together and there's no angst. We used to love the angst with their relationship."

Kelly Cantley: The rules we made up for our documentary, we always stuck to them. Then we were like, "Okay, so now some random guy walks in and starts talking to her. How is the doc going to shoot that?" My idea was that if you change the frame, like they weren't really paying attention, you could maybe believe it was found footage that we got by accident.

Halsted Sullivan: We knew at some point we were going to see the crew. And then, in trying to show Jim and Pam as real people, and a real couple with real stresses, we were like, "What happens when the cameras are put down and Jim and Pam are fighting a little bit? And this crew, who know these people really well, especially when you're cutting together their lives, what happens when they overstep?" This all came from a discussion about the story and process. It was like, "If we're gonna pull back the curtain, why not pull it back and create a new dynamic to explore?"

Over the next few episodes, the rift between Jim and Pam widens as it becomes quite clear that Brian has become infatuated with her after spending nearly a decade chronicling her every move.

Halsted Sullivan: We wanted to treat them as a real couple with real stresses. Are they gonna have a picture-perfect romance that maybe no other couple in America has or are they going to be a real, relatable couple that go through the same things that lots of people go through? We didn't want them to be sidelined into this perfect idyllic thing with Jim just pranking Dwight and Pam just being office managing. It was like, "No, this is our last season. Let's go back to the heart of the show and see what happens when that heart is put under stress."

Owen Ellickson: There was talk of Pam and Brian maybe hooking up a little bit. I have to say, as a writer, I never believed we were going to do that.

Briton W. Erwin: The whole Pam-and-the-sound-guy thing, that whole distraction . . . I don't think it was really necessary or really helped the show.

Claire Scanlon: Everything got better in season nine because Greg came back and James Spader wasn't there and they were really working toward an endgame so everyone's acting was on point. It just got better. The only thing I think that was off was the guy who was the sound guy. And that's such a bummer. I was so excited for the documentary crew to be incorporated into the storytelling and I just think that was bad casting. He was aggressive and mean and weird. I was like, "Why is this guy here?" He just didn't fit in. It didn't pay off the way I had hoped it would and I was a big proponent for that. Coming from documentary, I was like, "This is gonna be great. We're gonna get an idea of his point of view." And that was a mistake. We got out of it very quickly.

Owen Ellickson: The fans just didn't like that Brian guy. I think it's just this creepy lecherous guy who's been staring at her for nine years and was making his move now that she was vulnerable. I think it just didn't sit well with people. I felt like if [they] had cast kind of a schlubby guy, maybe it could have been okay. It would have been like, this guy likes Pam, but it's not really about Pam liking the guy back. It being this kind of fit handsome guy in a tight black T-shirt felt like we were trying to say there had been this kind of mutual sexy undercurrent between them all these years. The fans just did not want to be asked to think about [that].

Brian vanished after appearing just four more times.

Brent Forrester: We had to pull the ripcord on it because it was so painful to the fans of the show. John Krasinski said to me, "Brent, this final season is for the ultra fans of the show. They're the only ones really still left watching, right? This is for them. Jim and Pam splitting up is too painful for them to sustain all the way to the reunion. We have to get them back together immediately." I was like, "Wow, we can't allow this beautiful couple to be really like on the verge of divorce. It's too awful for them." It was obviously the direction that the show was going. Then they're just like, "No. Pull the plug on that. No. Nobody actually wants that."

Owen Ellickson: The episode that really spun people on a dime is one that I wrote ["Vandalism"] where Brian the boom guy heroically saves Pam from an attack from a warehouse guy. People just absolutely did not like that. They were bothered that there might be some triangle that Pam and Jim would be involved in and even more insulted that we thought they might believe that. That's how it felt to me. Greg absolutely turned on a dime after that and we pivoted away, I think pretty skillfully given how quickly we had to do that. It involved decently sized edits to the next two episodes, if I recall.

Another difficulty that season was the addition of Catherine Tate into the cast. The British comedian had a quick cameo at the end of season seven as one of the many candidates for Michael Scott's position and then joined the cast midway through season eight as vice president of Sabre's special projects. In her native England, Tate is a superstar best known for her work on Doctor Who *and the sketch program* The Catherine Tate Show, *but in America she was a complete unknown to most viewers. Her character of Nellie Bertram was introduced as a conniving schemer with basically no redeeming qualities. It didn't give her a lot of places to go comedically.*

Brent Forrester: Poor Catherine Tate, she really got swallowed up by the size of the cast. I remember certainly feeling like, "Oh my God. We have Catherine Tate in this ensemble!" and we're coming up with stories that we wanted to do for her, but ultimately in the last couple of seasons there are so many characters. There's a period where it's like, "Come on, we've got to give Oscar a story. We've got to give Kevin a story." Even if you are Catherine Tate, you've got to wait your turn. My feeling was always like, "Boy, we never really got to use this incredible English superstar in our cast."

Jeff Blitz: The writers loved her, but they never quite figured out exactly what her role should be.

Roxxi Dott: I loved her to pieces, but she was fucking miserable.

Owen Ellickson: She's brilliant. We were excited to get her, but I remember at one point in season nine, Greg saying, "I want the two of you to go off and start working on a G story for this episode." It just got fractured beyond a point I'd ever even heard of on any other sitcom . . . There wasn't enough oxygen to get a new character over. There had been a time when you really could sort of time and introduce a character, and really make them feel like they were woven into the core of the show, and they had their own unique comedy, but I think Ellie was the last one through the door. I think that it just got so crowded, which is a credit to the show that all these characters were fun, but I think Catherine was never quite given a clear path to becoming a real part of the fabric.

Rusty Mahmood: First of all, I didn't know who Catherine was. She's a huge, huge British comedy icon. She's the Steve Carell of Britain. I don't think the writers gave her what she's capable of. And she struggled with what was written for her. When I looked her up, I learned what she did in England and I looked at her with new eyes. I thought to myself, "Wow, she's coming in here and being treated like a recurring day player, like she's Pam's old boyfriend Roy or something." It would be like if Steve Carell went to England and nobody knew who he was. She was just so underutilized.

Mark Proksch: I was really psyched to work with her because she's the female Steve Coogan. She's so versatile and can do so much stuff. And she's just so funny to talk to in real life. She's just really funny, but I feel like they didn't quite know how to use her. They didn't know where and how to make that character a standout like they did with the other characters that they created. I felt like she was just an add-on in a show where so many of the characters are so well defined, and that's not her fault at all.

Kate Flannery: I really liked Catherine, but I felt like she didn't get to be that funny on the show, which was kind of a bummer because she's really funny. But I mean—and I understood what they were doing with her—but I felt like, I wonder if it would have been a missed opportunity for her to be the boss.

Steve Burgess: It was challenging for her, and for the writers, and I'm not sure they ever got the Nellie character the way they wanted it and the way Catherine wanted it.

Claire Scanlon: She thought they burned her character, like took her to crazy town too soon. And not everyone can work off-the-cuff like they want. It was just kind of like they threw her to the wolves and were like, "Okay, go play now." She was like, "Well, let's give me some more help here. Who's my character? What am I doing?"

Myles McNutt: I love Catherine Tate. I thought her character was super interesting during the interview phase in season seven. But the Nellie character was so aggressive and offensive that there was no balance to it. You met her during the Florida arc in season eight where she's just this absurd character they have to react to and engage with, and then they bring her to Scranton. They set her up as being this offensive woman who hates everybody, who nobody likes. How do you expect us to accept her as being part of this office? I remember watching that episode where they try to soften her and suggest all these sympathetic things about her. And I'm like, the deal was done. You can't do that retroactively if you've introduced somebody that aggressively.

Owen Ellickson: I'm all for villains, but you have to know that if you've presented somebody as a villain, especially on a show that has a lot of people that people like, they're not going to get that excited about turning themselves around on a villain.

Other plotlines of the season included Angela, now married with a new baby, discovering that her husband was having an affair with Oscar; Erin and Jake Lacy's character forming a relationship; Andy taking a long sailing trip (giving Ed Helms time to film The Hangover Part III*); Nellie taking over as manager; and the staff reacting to the upcoming debut of the documentary. The second-to-last episode, "A.A.R.M.," feels almost like a series finale. It features Angela revealing to Dwight that he's the father of her baby and the two of them deciding to wed, Jim asking the documentary crew to create a montage of his best moments with Pam and showing it to her, and new regional manager Dwight (he was promoted in the previous episode when Andy quit) getting pranked by Jim into competing in a contest to become the assistant to his own assistant. Pam begins to have second thoughts about forcing Jim to remain in Scranton instead of pursuing his dreams at the sports agency when she realizes that he truly loves her and Dunder Mifflin isn't allowing him to grow beyond silly pranks. At the end, everyone goes to Poor Richard's to watch the premiere of the documentary.*

Brent Forrester: I wrote that one. It's really plot heavy. Greg hired me to be the number two in season nine and what you see there is my work ethic and energy and drive in the penultimate episode. Then Greg takes over for the finale, and it becomes this meditative, almost melancholy meditation on people that he loved in the show. Much more than a plot episode, it's a mood episode. It was brilliant.

KEY EPISODE 12

"Finale"

The finale begins with a time jump of an entire year. The documentary has already aired; Dwight is firmly established as regional manager and he's dramatically increased business, even though he had to fire Kevin for gross incompetence, Stanley has retired to Florida, and Creed has vanished because the police were after him for crimes he committed in the 1960s. But the cameras are back for a reunion panel at a local theater just before Dwight marries Angela at Schrute Farms.

Halsted Sullivan: We talked a lot about great endings of great shows like *Six Feet Under* and *Bob Newhart*. What are the resonant endings? We wanted to say goodbye to these people who had become friends and know that everyone was in a good place.

Ken Kwapis, the director of the pilot and many of the best episodes, was brought back.

Ken Kwapis: I was thrilled to get the invite. In a way, I think for the cast my being there reminded people of the beginnings of the show. I think Greg just wanted me there to make everyone feel like we were bringing the whole process full circle. At the table read Greg said, "Ken was the country doctor who birthed this puppy and now he's come back to put the old dog down."

Brent Forrester: All the actors were invited to come in and pitch whatever they wanted for the end. That had not been encouraged early on. In fact, I remember season five, six, seven when Paul Lieberstein was running the show, he felt it was important not to invite too much pitching from the actors because they could overpower the writers with their tremendous personalities. That's a truism of television, by the way. Generally the writers and actors are balkanized. The reason is that the writers, we're just too meek relative to the actors. Their personalities are too strong. We get overwhelmed by them. But we invited them in and said, "Pitch us everything that you want to do. What's your dream?"

Owen Ellickson: It was a sort of a creative challenge on a scale I have not come close to encountering at any other point in my career. It was a weird thing in that if you watch seasons two, and three, and four, you would not say each of these eighteen people should get a least 4 percent of the finale. It ended in a way that was sort of more egalitarian than the show itself had been for most of its life.

Kate Flannery: My idea was that maybe Meredith falls in love with a cop and that way like she'll never have a problem with DUIs.

Brent Forrester: Creed had this beautiful song called "All the Faces" that he wrote years ago that deserved to be a hit and he had never recorded it. Early on, I remember him coming into the office and asking about it.

Creed Bratton: I played Greg "All the Faces" and said, "I think everybody should be in Poor Richard's and we get a close-up of their faces while I'm singing this song." I didn't hear a thing about it. Then we were at the table read and at the end of the script I look and there it says, "Creed sings his original song 'All the Faces.'" That was the second or third time that I cried. I had to pull it really together. People were seeing me over there with my head down when everyone's laughing and stuff like that. I was so emotional. It was a huge, huge gift to me. I also said to them, "I think it would be great if we could bring Devon Abner back again," because Devon and I stayed friends and we'd see each other on occasion too. I wanted to help him out.

In the episode, Dwight gives Devon his old job back after firing Kevin. He doesn't have any speaking lines, but he's back in the bullpen in several scenes after being gone since early in season two.

Devon Abner: I was in New York doing another play when I got a call. They said, "If you can make it out here tomorrow, we'll give you a couple of weeks on the show, but you have to pay your own airfare." The residuals I made from that one where I got fired were a lot of money since I wasn't an extra in it. I thought, "What the hell. I'll gladly do that if I have another shot at one of those." I used frequent flyers, got out there the next morning, and stayed at a friend's house. I remember Creed said to me, "Hey, do you have some lines?" I said no and he said, "I'm going to get you lines." I said, "No, that's okay," because as long as they [paid] me as a principal, I would get the residuals. It was a lot of fun and I'm very grateful they thought of me.

Devon wasn't the only old face back on the set for the finale shoot. Despite telling almost nobody, Steve Carell agreed to film a couple of quick scenes at Dwight's wedding.

Halsted Sullivan: There was a lot of talk about how to bring Michael back, and I think it was just as much Steve's idea. He wanted to come back but was like, "I don't want it to be all about me. The show has gone on for two years without me." But of course Michael would come back for Dwight and Angela's wedding. He had moved on with his life, so it wasn't gonna be Michael coming back and doing shenanigans.

Rusty Mahmood: It was a huge, huge secret. We had fake script pages and even the cast didn't know. We didn't know for sure if it was going to happen because we were negotiating it to the last minute. When he came, he had a little more gray in his hair and a little different look. It was so emotional that I think I remember Rainn crying.

The big reveal comes halfway through when Dwight is about to walk down the aisle and Jim tells him he can't serve as his best man. Dwight is confused and hurt until he turns around and sees Michael standing in the doorway. "Michael," he says. "I can't believe you came!" He briefly holds back a grin before delivering an inevitable, "That's what she said." Michael—now happily married to Holly and the father of young kids—has just one other quick scene at the wedding. "I feel like all my kids grew up," he said, "and then they married each other. It's every parent's dream."

Ken Kwapis: It's so wonderful that even though the character feels more mature . . . it's a relief to know that he's still capable of such a dunderheaded comment.

Jen Celotta: They didn't even tell the network Steve was coming back. I've never ever heard of anything like that happening.

Steve Burgess: Greg talked to Steve and Steve said he would come back, but he really didn't want to promote it and didn't want the show to be Michael Scott comes back to *The Office*. He wanted *The Office* to end without this big promotion of him coming back, and Greg agreed. His pages were numbered and collected, and anything that had Steve Carell's dialogue on it was only given to the people who needed to see it, and then it was collected again afterward so that no extra pages could get out.

Ken Kwapis: Some of the cast members didn't know until the morning. They were in the makeup trailer and suddenly Steve walked in to get his makeup done. It was like, "What the . . . ?" Everyone was flabbergasted.

Kate Flannery: Most of us found out maybe ten minutes before he got there. I'm so relieved because if I had known before and I somehow let it slip, I would never have been able to live with myself.

Robert Shafer: I was standing there talking to Phyllis and Creed and all of a sudden I hear Steve in the background. I said, "That sounds like Steve." They both nod their head and they smile a little bit and go, "He's here!" I wish our State Department was as tight with secrecy as the writers and producers of *The Office*.

Matt Sohn: It was such a pleasure to have him back after his two years of being gone, and to kind of feel that old energy again.

Alysia Raycraft: Steve was camera ready when he arrived. He just wore what he already had, but as how Michael looked at the end, which was a little more tailored and a nicer suit. And it was everybody's favorite camp counselor was back. Everybody wanted to have a minute with him. I would see him throughout the day laughing and hugging different people.

Ken Kwapis: Greg made the perfect choice for him to just show up at the wedding. It just made the wedding scene that much more festive and celebratory and emotional.

Steve Burgess: We had a bunch of extras at the wedding and I talked to them and said, "This is our giant secret. You guys are now part of our family. You have to keep the secret. You have to not tell anybody that Steve's gonna be on the show." And then I think the dailies were kept in a vault that was somewhere different than at Universal, so that there was no chance that there was any leak there. It was a major amount of secrecy and I kept telling Greg, "They're gonna fire me. They're gonna fire me." Greg kept saying, "What are you worried about? We're done after this week anyway."

Jen Celotta: It was edited down to time with a different scene so that nobody would know.

Steve Burgess: We basically didn't tell NBC that Steve was back on the finale until the day before it aired. We were worried that there were leaks at SAG and leaks at NBCUniversal and all that, so Steve signed his contract for the week and I kept it in my desk drawer until the day before we aired and then I turned it in and sent it through the system. But the NBC executives kept asking when could they see a cut of the finale, and Greg kept putting them off, and putting them off, and finally the day before it aired they said, "We have to see it before we air it." So we brought them into the edit bay and I sat there with them and as soon as Steve came on and they saw Steve on it I got really dirty looks from the NBC execs because they didn't know he was gonna be there. Somehow we pulled it off and we're very proud of that fact. I got a text from Steve Sauer, Steve Carell's manager, during the airing of the finale. He said something to the effect of, "What the fuck? We pulled it off! Amazing."

In the weeks building up to the finale, Daniels and the entire cast repeatedly lied and said that Carell wouldn't be returning.

Claire Scanlon: Ken Kwapis and Greg Daniels would do interviews and Ken would just lie with aplomb and after the interview Greg's like, "Don't you feel guilty about lying?" And he's like, "No, not even a little bit. It's for a good cause."

John Krasinski: I lied to Letterman! I have to apologize to him for that at some point. It was just one of those things that we all vowed and had to protect.

Steve Carell: I lied for months to the press, to almost everyone, really. And I felt terribly for the cast and for Greg Daniels, because they all lied, too. [But] I didn't want it to be a big thing. I did it out of respect for the show and for the actors. My only hope with it was I didn't want it to be about Michael coming back. I didn't want the story to be about him in any way. I wanted it to be more of a tip of the hat to the show.

A tougher job was wrapping up everyone's story line in just fifty minutes, but they did manage to give Ryan and Kelly a happy ending by having them run off together and by giving Ryan's baby to Nellie, fulfilling her dream of becoming a mother. Darryl finally gets together with his warehouse-worker crush, Val; Andy gets a job in the Cornell admissions department; Erin meets her birth parents; Oscar runs for state senate; and Pam surprises Jim by selling their house so they can move to Austin and he can work at the sports agency.

Ken Kwapis: It was such a massive production. I think the screenplay for the finale runs about seventy-five pages, maybe more. Then on top of that, there were like forty pages' worth of alternates and other ideas. There were so many stories to wrap up.

Halsted Sullivan: We were writing up until the last minute. We were even in a trailer just down the hill from that wedding banging out scenes because Greg would come up with ideas and be like, "Let's do this." In the end, fifty minutes of the show aired, but I think we had ninety minutes of show.

Near the end, everyone gathers in the warehouse for the unveiling of a massive mural created by Pam. They take a group photo, and in the final breaking of the fourth wall, Greg Daniels poses with them, along with many writers, producers, and members of the crew.

Brent Forrester: One thing that really stuck out to me about the finale was the way Greg was using the finale itself as this way of making a yearbook for himself. The final episode, Greg ends up shooting, of course, all of the actors in the show that he's loved, including Carell, who comes back for Dwight's wedding, but also the way he put in all the crew. Even his own manager appears. His wife appears. Writers appear. I appear asking a question in the audience during the reunion panel. All the people asking questions in the audience are writers. Greg was trying to capture on film the faces and voices of all the people that he loved in the making of *The Office*. It was so touching to me the way that, even more than plot, it was driving the episode.

Mary Wall: Everyone who ever worked on the show was in that scene pretty much. And then someone would be crying because it was their last talking head. So Greg would go and light another talking head. It's like, "No, it's not your last one now. Now you have a new last one!"

The main cast then goes up to the office to share some memories and final thoughts. "It took me so long to do so many important things," says Pam. "It's hard to accept I spent so many years being less happy than I could have been. Jim was five feet from my desk and it took me four years to get to him." Andy was equally reflective. "I spent so many years at Dunder Mifflin thinking about my old pals, my college a cappella group," he said. "The weird thing is now I'm exactly where I want to be. I got my dream job at Cornell and I'm still thinking about my old pals, only now they're the ones I made here. I wish there was a way to know you're in the good old days before you've actually left them."

Halsted Sullivan: That Andy Bernard quote has probably been said back to me more than any other thing. It's those tiny moments that resonate that people remember. In rewatching it, I always got choked up.

Matt Sohn: That last day there were a whole lot of tears. There was a whole lot of having to cut and bring makeup in and a whole lot of hugging and scenes dragging on and on. I remember Ken Kwapis being at a point where he was like, "Okay, guys, we've got to hold it together because we just need to get through this day. This is a long enough day as it is, let's just wrap this up and finish things up so that we can be done."

The last line goes to Pam. "I thought it was weird when you picked us to make a documentary," she said. "But all in all, I think an ordinary paper company like Dunder Mifflin is a great subject for a documentary. There's a lot of beauty in ordinary things. Isn't that kind of the point?" The final image is Pam's drawing of the Dunder Mifflin building, which transitions into the exterior of the place.

Ken Kwapis: A lot of people were in tears throughout the whole episode, but those scenes in particular were very emotional because they didn't even feel like scripted scenes so much as it just felt like the gang sitting around reminiscing. There was a scene that we ended up cutting, where they realize that poor old plant that's sitting in the middle of the bullpen has been there as long as any of the employees. They decide to take the plant out and plant it in front of the building. That was a possible ending for the finale, where they go take the plant out and I think they're chanting, "Planty, planty." Then Greg originally thought it would be nice to then just cut to a shot of the building the following morning where you just see that plant as the sun's coming up. I love the idea of the plant because it's a little unexpected thing to end on, but Pam's painting is perfect.

Halsted Sullivan: Pam's line about finding beauty in small places came from Greg, because that's basically what the whole show was about. It's finding beauty in the small things in this office in Scranton, Pennsylvania, with very few windows.

Steve Burgess: I think the last scene that we shot was Pam taking the picture off the wall. [*That's true, at least according to the call sheet for the day.*]

Mary Wall: Pam taking the photo off the wall was definitely the last shot. It felt so final to everyone there. Greg was standing off by the camera and Ken Kwapis was shooting it. And he shot it a few times, and I think everyone was exhausted, that whole crew. They had worked so hard that week. I mean, I don't even know how much they could emotionally process, because of how hard they worked that week. And even with all of that, there was sort of the feeling like no one wanted to yell cut on the scene. At one point, Ken just looked over at Greg and gave a look like, "I've got the scene.

You can keep shooting it, but we have it. We have good cuts of this. We're good to go." And usually, the director will yell *cut* or *wrap*. But Ken was like, "Well, Greg, you want to say it?" Then Greg said, "That's a wrap. That's a series wrap on *The Office*."

Ken Kwapis: As I remember it, the last shots that we did were just everyone walking past Pam's painting heading out toward the elevators. We did it a few times. Each time, the whole cast would walk past and exit and they'd end up huddled off-screen near the elevator. Then we'd go again and we did it a few times. Finally, I said to Greg, who was standing next to me, "I think we got it." Greg suddenly looked very emotional and a little flustered, and he said to me, "What do we do now?" I remember saying, "Well, go out and tell the cast we're done." That how we ended. I'm sure there was just a lot of complicated emotions, but I will tell you personally that at the end of that shoot, I was so tired. That was a mammoth episode of television to shoot. It basically was a feature film. Nine days. We started on Wednesday, March sixth, and we finished on Friday, March fifteenth, 2013.

Mark Proksch: It was definitely bittersweet. A lot of the actors were already going on to new projects that they were really interested in, but gosh, they cut their teeth on this show. It made them all famous and it gave them their careers, really. And so there were a lot of tears. I remember a lot of crying taking place. They even cried during my last scene and I was only in nineteen episodes for the last three seasons. Having them crying in my last scene was very, very sweet and definitely a testament to how much of a family the show was.

Brent Forrester: I remember people taking bets about when they would cry during the last episode, when other actors would cry. All kinds of bets were being taken.

Teri Weinberg: I could cry just talking to you about it. We had to say goodbye to our baby. But it was also a joyful thing, because we had the gift of being together for those ten years since we started to develop the show. We watched babies be born, we watched people fall in love. People got divorced, people lost partners, people had deaths in their families, all of those milestones in people's lives. Man, it was a hard last episode to shoot.

Kelly Cantley: It was really bad! It was like saying goodbye to eight years' worth of summer camp with some of your favorite people.

Kate Flannery: I just remember afterward the actors went into John's trailer and we all had a quick toast and a drink. But I felt like Greg didn't want it to end. I felt like it could have ended two hours before, but he just wanted to shoot it in a different way and then a different way and/or just a little more. I felt nobody wanted it to be over, to the point that we were late to our own wrap party, which was all the way across town. We all had to book it over there. It was just so crazy.

Brian Wittle: At the time we were shooting six-day weeks and the final week turned into a seven-day week. The way it was supposed to be is that the wrap party was on a Saturday and we were not supposed to work that day. Friday was supposed to be the last day of shooting, but for some reason we had to add Saturday. They originally thought, "Well, it'll just be half a day. We'll be done at noon and everyone can go home and get ready for the wrap party. We'll see everybody at the wrap party." But it ended up being a twelve-hour day and we were still at work while the wrap party was starting. The wrap party was way on the west side somewhere, and we were in Van Nuys. I was working in a suit so I'd be ready to go.

Mary Wall: There [were] a lot of people pretty dressed up for the final scene because they were going straight to the party.

Kim Ferry: The wrap party was amazing, oh my God. They had contortionists and these crazy carnival people doing all these crazy acrobatics and stuff. Everywhere you went there was the best of everything. There was a whole lobster bar, there was a whole sushi bar, there was food everywhere, including a World's Best Boss cake. There were drinks everywhere and they had this woman who was wearing this dress with a hoop skirt that had glasses filled with champagne that you would pull out of her hoop skirt and sip champagne. It was insane. Outside there was a red carpet for everybody and all the actors were coming in and doing paparazzi shoots. But what I loved is that it was just a party for the cast and the crew. It wasn't a thousand different executives, it wasn't all of the wannabes who would have wanted to come. It was us.

Alysia Raycraft: That was a huge, huge, huge event, and everybody was there. I think Craig [Robinson] led a *Soul Train* dance-off. That was fun. People were smashed. It was definitely a party and a genuine love fest. A lot of elegance. I remember seeing Emily [Blunt] with John, and God, the regal quality of those two is mind-blowing.

Creed Bratton: I hadn't had a drink or marijuana puff for ten years prior to that, but I might have smoked with somebody outside that thing before I walked into that party. I *might* have.

Kim Ferry: Greg got up and was very emotional and spoke about the show and said some incredibly elegant, wonderful, kind, moving words to everybody and we were all losing it.

Brian Wittle: I remember one disappointing thing about it is that they put Greg up on this staircase to give this farewell speech. It was loud through the whole thing and you couldn't really hear him. I don't even think his voice was amplified, and you could tell he had written this big couple pages of stuff. He went through the whole time and the whole story and mentioned everybody by name. I remember just feeling really bad that he didn't have a proper space to give that speech. It would've been as simple as if someone just gave him a speaker, which I'm sure they had at the club. They didn't turn the music off, though they might've lowered it. I just remember feeling it was noisy and I could barely hear him and feeling bad, like, "This moment should be bigger than this."

Matt Sohn: After the wrap party, there was also kind of a smaller, more intimate kind of drinks-and-dinner thing at the Chateau Marmont. It was just a happy and sad, very late night that I feel like went on until three or four in the morning of just hanging out with the rest of the cast and creators and a couple of the writers, and just talking about the last nine years and the amazing journey that we were all fortunate enough to be on together.

Kate Flannery: We were up until like four o'clock in the morning together at the Chateau and we had a little toast to Greg. There was like maybe fifteen of us along with some of the writers. I felt like Greg was so uncomfortable because it was almost like a funeral with the body there, but we got to thank him personally.

Clark Duke: This was way more private emotional stuff than anything from the wrap party, because that was gigantic. The more intimate stuff took place at the Chateau when it was just the cast and John rented a suite. The thing that really stands out in my head was that Krasinski's iPod was hooked up and I put on that LCD Soundsystem song "All My Friends," which is a really emotional song. And he *reacted*. He was like, "Oh, my God, you pulled that fucking song out. . . ." It was a real moment. Everyone was drinking and emotional. It was like three A.M. And it just felt like you were in a montage. I never hear that song and don't think of that moment.

chapter 29

THE AFTERMATH

("My fifteen-year-old niece is a fanatic.")

Even at the peak of its popularity around seasons four and five, The Office *never generated ratings even comparable to sitcoms like* Two and a Half Men *and* The Big Bang Theory, *procedural dramas like* CSI: Crime Scene Investigation *and* NCIS, *or, especially, reality competition shows like* American Idol *and* Dancing with the Stars. *But bars all over America in 2019 don't host* Dancing with the Stars *or* NCIS *trivia nights.* The Big Bang Theory *isn't breaking streaming records on Netflix and teens aren't bingeing* Two and a Half Men *on their phones. It's* The Office *that has emerged as the most beloved sitcom of the 2000s and just gets bigger with each passing year.*

John Krasinski: I was home visiting my parents recently and they said there was a girl up the street who was about fifteen, and that week she had had an *Office* sleepover party with her friends. Not only was it insane for me to hear someone that age loves the show, but this was just one week in the rotation, because they did it every weekend.

Jenna Fischer: I hear a lot from parents who watched the show when it was on originally. They now have kids that are like twelve years old to, like, twenty-two years old, and they're all discovering it. People who were kind of too young to get it when it came on are now getting it, and there's this second wave happening. What's really cool to me is that a lot of those parents are so excited, because they knew it was cool, and now their kids think it's cool, so they're cool. They're like, "See? My kids think I'm cool because I knew about this cool show," and so they love that they can watch it with their kids.

Kelly Cantley: When I go home, the only show that the cousins and the nieces and nephews, everyone, asks me about is *The Office*.

Amy Ryan: There's a lot more recognition now than when it was on the air, but I'm noticing it's a much younger generation. A lot of my friends who have teenagers, they've shared with me that they watch it as almost an emotional soother. If they're in a bad mood, they'll just pop on *The Office* and they'll binge-watch it. My daughter's in third grade and some of her friends are watching it now. I've gone from "Georgia's mom" to them looking at me a little differently. It's like, "You've been in my house since kindergarten, you know me. . . ."

Briton W. Erwin: My fifteen-year-old niece is a fanatic and has it playing round the clock all the time.

B. J. Novak: Kids respond more than you'd expect because Michael is such a child emotionally in some ways.

Aaron Shure: Thirteen-year-old boys in particular are about that age where it's like, "What will it be like to have a job? Will there be love there? Will I be the cool one or the nerdy one?"

Andy Buckley: My twelve-year-old is reluctantly now watching it. All his buddies were watching it and he was purposely avoiding it because I was on it. At the first he was like, "Dad, I don't want to watch this." But now he watches all the episodes that I'm not in, which is most of them. The thing is, if you're in high school or college now you would have probably been too young then. And even people in their twenties, they might have been in high school and they didn't necessarily watch it. You know, I sit down and watch a few of them from time to time with my son and boy oh boy, it's so darn funny.

Melora Hardin: I enjoy the success of *The Office* more now than I did when it was on. People come up to me every day and they're like, "Oh my God, I just binge-watched the first five seasons." I actually just ran into a woman on the metro that said, "Oh my God, I just was watching you last night!"

Tucker Gates: I just finished working with Steve Carell on something else and he was telling me that there's this whole resurgence of it, especially on college campuses, and that he had taken his daughter on a college tour and he got mobbed so much that he couldn't take her on any of the other college visits and he was really upset about that.

Mari Potis: It definitely shines a different light on Scranton and it's made us a cool city. We get tons of millennials that come to visit. They wanna go to Steamtown mall and Poor Richard's and they wanna go get their picture taken at the welcome sign and I'm like, "Well that's just nuts." Somebody just had their bridal shower in Scranton this weekend and it was *Office* themed. Each year the show seems to become more popular.

Robert Durkin (Greater Scranton Chamber of Commerce President and CEO): People still come here on a constant basis to visit places like Poor Richard's, Cooper's Seafood House, and Steamtown mall. They might even try to find Lake Scranton, even though you can't actually drive around it. If any of them contact us I say, "Stop by and we'll give you a Dunder Mifflin stock certificate." People seem to get a kick out of that.

Kevin Reilly: I'm involved with Cornell and often I speak at classes, and literally every year someone's asked me if Andy Bernard is based on me. Literally every year. And it's a new generation of freshmen every year.

Mark Proksch: I think this is a testament to how actually smart younger people are these days, but also they're not used to seeing actually funny TV. And if a show is funny to them on TV these days, it's usually canceled after the first or second season. And so, to know that you have nine seasons of the show, back when they were giving shows twenty-two-, twenty-three-episode orders, that's something unique to them and it's a novel idea. That they can keep watching these shows without getting a rerun every few episodes is very rare.

Anthony Farrell: Michael Scott and Dwight are just big kids. Young people are watching these characters because they really are enjoying the silly things that they get up to inside of an office. It's almost kind of like wishful thinking about what they would be able to do once they go out of school. And *The Office* is like school, and these kids are getting into all kinds of mischief at school, so I can kind of see why they love it so much. But I've been approached by a bunch of people who are like, "My son is so into the show now and he's thirteen." Any time I meet people, if I'm working on a kids' show or whatever and someone's like, "Oh, can my son come to the set? He wants to talk to you. He knows you wrote on *The Office* and he's sixteen and he really wants to ask you questions. He's seen every episode like four times," I'm like, "Well, he might know the show better than I know the show at this point. Maybe I can talk to him about some stuff."

Briton W. Erwin: I think the simple explanation is that the characters may be exaggerated, but they're all people you know. And people don't really change that much in the macro sense over time. You always have the guy who thinks he knows everything, and you have, whether you're in high school or at a job, you have the two people that have a crush on each other but you don't know if they're going to get together or not. You have the boss who barely knows what he's doing but somehow manages to endear himself to people.

Caroline Williams: I think it's because it's so timeless in its depiction of life. Also, the characters are weirdly ageless. If you didn't see Michael and you just read about what he did, it would be unclear how old he is. And Dwight, the same thing. All of them, they kind of inhabit this magical world where it's always 2003. And everyone is eight. I think there's so much TV now that there is a show for every niche, and that you can find a show that fits you. The idea that there's this show that appeals to everybody is just, I think, a unique idea.

J. J. Abrams: All I can say is that when something works as well as it does and is as smartly written as that show was and has the kind of cast that is just undeniable, as that show did, there is a kind of timelessness to it. Certain things can become sort of phenomenons in different moments, different times, different ways. But the way that some series live on, where people will still be laughing at *I Love Lucy* now so many years later . . . I feel like [when] it's fifty years, a hundred years from now, I don't think the discomfort and awkwardness of working with odd people is ever gonna go away and that show captured that beautifully.

Teri Weinberg: It doesn't matter where you work, what you do, if it was twenty years ago or twenty years from now, people are still going to go into a workplace and they're going to be surrounded by people that they see day in and day out. And we're going to feel the growing pains of the economy and what's happening, and how we have to coexist with people and find the joy in difficult situations, and that you can actually wake up in the morning and laugh with a family of people who you can feel a part of. And *The Office* is part of that culture. We're so divided as a nation, we're so divided as a world, but the one thing that brings us together always is love and smiles and comedy and an outside family that makes you feel a part of it.

The availability of the show on Netflix plays no small role in this since every single episode is on demand and thus it's effortless to binge.

Brent Forrester: I have some inside information and I don't know if I'm allowed to know it, but I could say to you that it is fairly well understood by people in the know that *The Office* is the biggest performer on Netflix, at least in terms of comedies. The way Netflix rates shows is by seasons of TV, so like season five of *Friends* is like the thirtieth most watched show on Netflix. They do it by season of TV. My understanding is that eight of the top twelve shows on Netflix by viewership are seasons of *The Office*.

John Krasinski: Netflix is really giving a lot of shows new life, but certainly ours. Maybe you had to be a certain age to be up at nine P.M. and watch it, but you know, you no longer have to do that. You can watch it any time you want. I think that really helps.

Claire Scanlon: Greg was recently showing me how *The Office* is the number one show on Netflix and I was like, "Holy mackerel." He was like, "Yeah, I guess we negotiated that deal a little too soon, a little too fast, not realizing all that we were giving them."

Ben Silverman: Netflix has expanded the reach of *The Office* and it's also a giant hit for Comedy Central. Ricky [Gervais], Stephen [Merchant], me, and Greg all own it. Carell has a little bit, as does Universal and NBC. None of us are making as much as we should from it. They didn't do a good enough deal and NBC is weird about how it accounts for things. But it's cool because people like it and Angela and Brian and Creed get to go to, like, conventions and Comic-Con.

Bob Greenblatt: I believe it's the number one or two show on Netflix that they acquired, and there are millions of streams of those episodes. A stream is not the same as a linear rating, so the apples-to-oranges thing comes in, but I believe that Netflix has helped make *The Office* extraordinarily popular, and more popular than it was when it was on the network. And they pay us a lot of money for it. If we knew how popular it was going to be before they made the deal, we would have asked for more money from them!

Ricky Gervais: It's still not *Seinfeld* syndication, nowhere near. And everyone gets a piece of it.

Creed Bratton: I still get paid from it. It's just the gift that keeps giving in so many ways, so many ways. It frees us all up to do whatever projects we want to do, not for the money but for just the love of a good project. For me, the checks I get are astronomical, certainly more money than I ever would make in my Grass Roots days. No comparison. It's a whole other ball game. Rarefied earth.

*But even though it inspired a handful of mockumentary-style shows (*Parks and Recreation, Modern Family, American Vandal*) and made the laugh track and most other traditional sitcom elements feel hopelessly dated (not a single NBC show right now utilizes one), most people involved feel it hasn't changed TV nearly as much as they'd hoped.*

Brent Forrester: I spoke to Greg recently and he was a bit concerned that it hadn't changed television, that it showed that taste makers and lovers of great comedy will give ovations to naturalistic comedy, but it has not changed the tone of comedy overall on network television. It seems like they may have been an outlier. The more realistic a show is, the more you have a chance of emoting and feeling something deep and real. That is why all of these taste-making writers and performers and fans love the show. But I don't think it changed TV the way everybody involved in the show hoped it would.

Danny Chun: I've heard it said that whenever there is something really special and successful in the entertainment industry, the industry will learn all the wrong lessons from it. And I think that's true in this case. It felt like people thought the lesson was, "Okay, let's do stuff in a mockumentary style." And one of them was really successful, *Modern Family.* Okay, there's also *Parks and Rec,* but that didn't feel very mockumentary to me. So there was this feeling of, "Let's do shows that look like *The Office* or that have the same conceit as *The Office.*" They thought that rather than what I think the real lesson is, that you nurture something comedically, you take a really well-observed, intelligent premise and you let a really excellent writer assemble a team that he or she wants and you have faith in it and you trust it. Obviously, that doesn't happen very often. But it did with *The Office*.

Owen Ellickson: There are people who will tell you that it's a super-grounded show. I think that's crazy. I think it was grounded in spots, and then unbelievably broad in spots, and I don't think that's a bad thing. I think there is a tendency in TV to call anything you liked "grounded" and anything you don't like "broad." I think it was both, and it was a good mix of both more often than not. But there weren't that many talking-head shows that followed. I feel like in some ways there's *The Office*, and *Parks*, and *Modern Family*, and somehow those three established such a beach-head that people are actually kind of leery of copying. There were some rip-off attempts afterward in the first couple years, but it's surprising that people don't do more of that. I feel like in a sort of crass network sense it actually never was profitable enough to change what networks looked for. That's why I can't tell how much of a footprint it actually has. I almost feel like if it had more of a footprint maybe it would have less of a following now.

Mark Proksch: I think it's a seminal show and I think it's a classic TV show already and that's proven by those Netflix numbers, but it certainly didn't change network TV. Network TV still tries to just put models, both male and female, into comedies, thinking that, "Oh, it will work." And they shoehorn in the goofy actor for the crazy role. They don't understand that you have to have really good scripts, first of all, bring in actual funny people even if they're not famous yet. I mean, I really do not think that they could make *Seinfeld* nowadays. Those actors weren't models. They weren't beautiful looking and most of them were relatively unknown. Same with *The Office*. People love this show because it was clever and it had a point of view. You cannot tell me *Abby's* [a recent show about beautiful people at a San Diego bar that NBC canceled after ten episodes] had a point of view.

For the two original creators who merely wanted to make a handful of episodes on BBC Two about a goofy office, the incredible afterlife is still a little hard to understand, especially when it started getting remade in countries like India, Sweden, Germany, Chile, and the Czech Republic.

Ricky Gervais: I've never known [of] a sitcom, particularly a British one, getting remade in so many countries.

Stephen Merchant: We worked quite hard early on to identify what seemed like truthful observations about office life. We felt like there were lots of shows that had taken place in offices, but they were normally just a background to kind of high jinks in the foreground. And there was something about the actual mechanics of the office itself, the literal day-to-day goings-on, that hadn't been mined sufficiently, whether it was health and safety training or people were coming in from outside to sort of teach you how to do your job better. I think the urge we had to be observational and authentic and sort of precise is I think one of the reasons it has both translated to America and elsewhere, because I think the observations are truthful. I don't know what it says about mankind that clearly office life in many, many countries is very similar. Which I guess is a good thing? I guess it brings us together? But it also suggests that we're all living these quiet lives of despair in one way or another.

chapter 30

REBOOT?

("I hope we can do it before any of us kick the bucket.")

TVLine caused an Internet firestorm in December 2017 when they posted a story with the headline "The Office *Revival Eyed at NBC for 2018–2019 Season." "Sources confirm to TVLine exclusively that the Peacock network is eyeing a continuation of the beloved workplace comedy for the 2018–2019 season," read the article. "The revival would once again be set at Dunder Mifflin's Scranton, PA., branch, and feature a mix of new and old cast members. Steve Carell, who starred as the branch's regional manager, Michael Scott, for seven of the comedy's nine seasons, will* not *be involved in the new series. The search for a new RM/boss is said to be already underway." Well, the 2018–19 season came and went without a new edition of* The Office, *but that hasn't stopped new rumors from popping up online every few months. Cast and crew reactions to this possibility are all over the place.*

Kate Flannery: I've heard many of those rumors and I'm pro-reboot; that is my politics. I would love it and would totally be on board. I'm not banking on it though. I'm not overspending and expecting it to happen, but it would be wonderful even if we just did something for the fans, like a special or something. I hope we can do it before any of us kick the bucket.

Creed Bratton: I don't think you're going to be able to get everybody together. A Christmas special would be the thing, wouldn't it? That would be so much fun. It would be really monumental. We would have so much fun to get to do that. You know I'm on board to do something like that.

Oscar Nunez: Maybe we can do it once a year for a Christmas special. I don't know though. There'd be so much pressure on us if we did that once a year. And they can't afford that. There's nine seasons of the show. People watch it over and over again. They finish watching a season, then they go right back again and they watch it like five, six, seven times. Over and over. There it is. We don't need to do new ones. People keep asking, but it's not going to happen, I think.

Robert Shafer: What I read was that they would get some of the old cast and some new people, so half new and half old. I would desperately want to be part of it. I know that John Krasinski said that he would be part of it, which is a stunner 'cause he's playing Jack Ryan now and also he had that huge movie [*A Quiet Place*].

John Krasinski: It's hard to say I would never do that again because there will always be a part of me that feels the people on that show are my family, so I'd always want to hang out with my family again. I always admired that the British show and other British TV shows do like a Christmas special, so maybe there's always something like that where we can all get together. I'm sure everybody's really busy and it would be hard to put us all together for an actual reboot of the show, but certainly like a Christmas special or something would be amazing. Truth is I've never gotten a call about it so I can't tell if it's just rumor or they don't want me on the show. [*Laughs*] I don't know. I haven't heard one thing.

Jenna Fischer: I'm not gonna comment on it. I have nothing to offer. Sorry.

Andy Buckley: Would I go back? Is that a trick question? Of course!

Ed Helms: I would just say I'm open-minded about anything, but it's hard to say without knowing what it might be. Who knows?

Angela Kinsey: I'm a fan of the show. I actually find it really funny and just as a fan of the show, not even as someone who acted in it, I would love to see where these characters are right now. I would love some kind of reunion and to see where they're at. I think that would be so much fun. But it would have to be done the right way because what you don't want to do is mess with this great legacy. I feel like when we left we wrapped everything up so beautifully and it would have to be done right, and I think Greg Daniels would know how to do that. I would trust him to know how to do that. But, of course, I would love to see where everyone is. So I say, why not? But do it smart. Do it justice. And sign me up. No one has called any one of us, but hit me up. [*Laughs*]

Kim Ferry: I know John had said something about doing a two-hour special, that he would be up to it. Rumors started circulating and when I heard about it the first thing I did was e-mail Greg Daniels. And I said, "If this goes I'm on it. You don't have a choice. But is this even a possibility? What are your thoughts?" He wrote back, actually pretty quickly, and was like, "I don't know if I could do that. NBC wants it." He made that clear, but he said, "I don't know if it should be revisited. But, you know what, I'm willing to think about it. I'm thinking about it. I just don't know." He seems very torn on it. Does he want to do it again or not? I don't know. I said, "Well, if that ever happens you know where I am." And he's like, "Absolutely you'd be on it." I would love to do a two-hour special. I think everybody [would].

Amy Ryan: I would join the party, for sure, but I would be surprised if it came back just because it's such a large group and everybody is so busy. I don't know how you coordinate that schedule. And it's different for me stepping back in, but I wonder how many other people might have been like, "You know what, ten years is enough of playing that character," and you really want to start exercising other muscles as an actor, even though it was fun and joyous and a positive thing. I don't know. I just feel like there's so much else to try to do and approach in this world. A special could be interesting though. Maybe we all go on the Love Boat or something. *Fantasy Island*! That would be amazing.

Warren Lieberstein: I don't necessarily think it's a bad idea. I think the way to do it would be to see if you can get one or two of the old cast and have them transfer to a new branch and do the new branch. Or do an *Office* that's not paper, that's something else in a different part of the country altogether and just call it *The Office* but it's following something completely different. Maybe one of the companies that Dunder Mifflin supplies paper to, just something that's different altogether. But I don't think the way to do it would be to jump back into Scranton. That would be just too weird for people I think. I wouldn't want to see that old office building again. It's like your parents have sold the house and a construction company came in and tore it down. And they rebuilt something new. You just can't go back.

Owen Ellickson: I am as rebooted out as most people, but that doesn't mean that it couldn't work. I think that if I were sort of king of TV I would say, "Let's let this one lie. I like it the way it is." But to say "*The Office* shouldn't be rebooted" is just to build a sandcastle an inch from the water. It's coming.

Jen Celotta: I think it would have to be exactly the right idea, but I think it could work. *The Office* was the best show I've ever worked on. Going to the show similar to how it existed, I wouldn't want to touch it. I don't have any interest, slash think it should be done, but if there's a take on it that's just inventive and interesting, where it opens up a world of new stories in a different way, I could see that. Because I don't know, man, I miss working with those writers and I miss working with those actors. That was just incredible.

Ben Silverman: I think there will be a moment to continue what *The Office* did. It's got so many characters and so many worlds, the style is so unique, and there are all these clones; why not clone ourselves? You could seed a couple characters from the old show into the new one. Many of them would come back.

J. J. Abrams: I can't imagine that this is not a discussion that someone is having somewhere right this second.

Allison Jones: It's a bad idea, in my opinion. I mean, my theory is everything is all in the execution, but I think if it were a 100 percent new version of *The Office*, who knows? Maybe that could work. But doing a reboot seems to me like it could do more harm than good. It's like getting married to the same guy twice. You don't want to do that.

Halsted Sullivan: I would love for it to come back. Would it come back in its current iteration? I don't think so. And look at *Will and Grace*. The ratings aren't that great right now even though it was the talk of Hollywood. So, if it came back, I would want it to come back in the right way. Do I know what that way is? Absolutely not. Do I think that if anyone could do it, it would be Greg? Yes. Absolutely.

Brent Forrester: This isn't just a rumor on the outside from fans. It's absolutely being talked about by NBC. I think if Greg wanted to do a reboot, of course, they would do it in a second. But the only reason Greg hasn't is it's just because creators have only so much bandwidth, and he's doing other stuff.

Justin Spitzer: I think it could come back from a creative standpoint and from an is-America-ready-and-receptive standpoint. I don't know from a behind-the-scenes standpoint. I don't know what those discussions have been, how much of it is true, how much of it is rumors. I ran into Rainn a little while ago. I was like, "What is going on?" He's like, "You tell me. No one's talked to me about it." But I think it could come back.

Kelly Cantley: I was working with Greg on a pilot when the reboot rumors started. I think the reboot rumors started online at about four P.M.

and by the time I got to my car, I think I had eighty-five messages from crew going, "Hey, have you heard anything about this?" So, the next day I walked in and said, "Hey, Greg, guess what's all over the Internet!" He goes, "What?" I go, "*Office* reboot." He goes, "No, no. I don't know where that came from!"

Clark Duke: I would not advise doing it without Greg. I mean, to me, the show's sensibility is Greg's sensibility.

Mark Proksch: If Greg's involved, I think they could do it. I don't know what that scenario would be or if any of the cast would be involved in any way. I know someone had brought up that they might do it completely new, and that could certainly work. In fact, that almost interests me more, if it's a completely new cast somewhere, as opposed to bringing some people back. But I don't know if that's what the audience would want. I think the audience would want to see certain people back. If anyone can do it, I think Greg could do it. Whether you'd be able to get some of the cast would be another story.

Danny Chun: I guess it depends on what you mean by "reboot." On first blush, it does smack of learning the wrong lesson from the success of the show. What does it mean to reboot it if it's not the same caliber of comedic actors, if it's not necessarily the same person running the writers' room? I don't really know what that means, if you're just taking the title and the concept; I don't think that's really the essence of what made *The Office* so good.

Teri Weinberg: In truth, I hope it doesn't come back. I mean, I hope it is what it was and we get to just live with the beautiful memory of it. I'm sure you got a lot of other opinions, but my heart says it's one of the most incredible experiences of my producorial life and I'll never forget it. And it made me the producer I am, and I still am today. It makes me want to continue to be a producer and tell stories about people. But I don't know, to me, it was such a special thing and when you get hit by lightning, you just want to get hit once by that thing.

Rob Sheffield: Clearly, it would be a mistake to reboot it. But on the other hand, it was a mistake to do it in the first place. The whole premise of this show was a really stupid idea and I remember there was a point around the third or fourth season where you started to hear people say, "It's so weird that this is better than the UK one." And when people first started to say that it seemed so shocking and counterintuitive, and it stayed that way for a long time. By 2009, when people were making their best-of-the-2000s TV lists, it was really weird that people had to specify the US one. It's historically unprecedented and unique in a way that the UK one wasn't. So I would say a reboot is clearly the wrong idea, but doing the show in the first place was clearly the wrong idea and I was delighted to be proved wrong then.

Alan Sepinwall: They could do it, but I don't think it's a good idea unless you have a great creative team involved. Just saying, "Let's do another *Office*," in and of itself does not excite me. If a really good creator with a good cast comes in and says, "I want to do another mockumentary set in an office," you could easily do that. Because it doesn't need a Michael. It doesn't need a Jim. It doesn't need a Pam. It just needs the setting and whatever idea you have that you want to do with it.

Ricky Gervais: They've talked to me about bringing it back. I went, "Yeah, whatever, whatever." It doesn't affect me. It doesn't touch me. I used a really poor metaphor at the time. I said, "It's like I've donated my DNA, but I don't want to bring up the kid."

Stephen Merchant: At some point it goes beyond you. We used to talk about it like it's Frankenstein's monster. You've created it, but then it just has to go off and rampage across the countryside on its own because you can't kind of control it anymore.

Ricky Gervais: I still think that everything about it is arbitrary except Brent wanting to be famous; that's essential. You can change everything else, but you can't not make this buffoon want to be famous and loved, with love being more important and fame his weird way of getting there. Without that, the show is nothing.

acknowledgments

The creation of any book is a team effort, but that's especially true when it comes to an oral history. Were it not for the eighty-six individuals who graciously agreed to talk to me for this book, it simply wouldn't exist. Many of them spoke to me on the phone, but others sat with me in restaurants, hotel rooms, all around the *Rolling Stone* offices, and even their own homes. They shared scripts, call sheets, behind-the-scenes photographs, and, in one case, the actual pig nose that Dwight wore in the season nine episode "Here Comes Trouble." (It proudly sits on my desk to this day.)

I want to start by thanking them all by name: Devon Abner, J. J. Abrams, Shelley Adajian, Ash Atalla, Carey Bennett, Jeff Blitz, Creed Bratton, Andy Buckley, Steve Burgess, Kelly Cantley, Jen Celotta, Danny Chun, Randy Cordray, Roxxi Dott, Clark Duke, Robert Durkin, Randall Einhorn, Lee Eisenberg, Idris Elba, Owen Ellickson, Briton W. Erwin, Anthony Farrell, Paul Feig, Kim Ferry, Kate Flannery, Brent Forrester, Michael Gallenberg, Tucker Gates, Ricky Gervais, Sergio Giacoman, Amelie Gillette, Richard Gonzales, Bryan Gordon, Bob Greenblatt, Anil Gupta, Melora Hardin, Donald Lee Harris, Dean Holland, Andy Hollis, Jeff Immelt, Hidetoshi Imura, Allison Jones, Jason Kessler, Ken Kwapis, Warren Lieberstein, Ewen MacIntosh, Rusty Mahmood, Myles McNutt, Stephen Merchant, Oscar Nunez, Peter Ocko, Ben Patrick, Jon Plowman, Mari Potis, Mark Proksch, Nathan Rabin, Alysia Raycraft, Kevin Reilly, Karly Rothenberg, Amy Ryan, Henry Saine, Claire Scanlon, Alan Sepinwall, Robert Shafer, Rob Sheffield, Aaron Shure, Ben Silverman, Peter Smokler, Stacey Snider, Matt Sohn, James Spader, Justin Spitzer, Gene Stupnitsky, Halsted Sullivan, Jennie Tan, Calvin Tenner, Kasia Trojak, Mary Wall, Teri

Weinberg, Ken Whittingham, Caroline Williams, Larry Wilmore, Brian Wittle, Lisa Hans-Wolf, Christopher Wood, and Jeff Zucker.

Along the way, many agreed to multiple interviews, passed on invaluable contacts, vouched for me to others, and never expressed even the slightest bit of irritation when I asked them to divulge bits of trivia about episodes they worked on, in many cases, well over a decade ago. I want to especially call out Randy Cordray for the countless hours he spent on the phone with me across several months, and Allison Jones for sending me all her original casting documents. Warren Lieberstein, Matt Sohn, Ben Silverman, Carey Bennett, Jennie Tan, Kim Ferry, Roxxi Dott, Jen Celotta, and Brian Wittle all went the extra mile as well.

Before I even had the slightest inkling I'd ever write a book about *The Office*, I interviewed Greg Daniels, Jenna Fischer, John Krasinski, Ed Helms, Ellie Kemper, Angela Kinsey, and Paul Lieberstein about their work on the show as part of my duties at *Rolling Stone*. Many of their quotes have never been printed anywhere, and they gave me a huge cache of material to draw from before I started to conduct new interviews. I'm enormously grateful to all of them.

This whole journey would have never started if I hadn't received an e-mail from literary agent extraordinaire Rick Richter to see if I had any ideas for a book. It just so happened I was nearly done reporting an oral history of "The Dinner Party" episode of *The Office* that I felt could be the beginning of a book. Before I knew it, we were signing a deal with Dutton. He not only made everything happen, but he made it happen astonishingly fast.

My editor, Jill Schwartzman, and her colleague Marya Pasciuto guided me through every step of the writing and reporting process. Their optimism, resolve, and editorial brilliance gave me strength even during the difficult moments when I feared I'd never even finish the first draft. They always believed in this book and allowed me to believe in myself. I can't imagine how I could have done this without them.

I wrote this book during the course of a single year while keeping my full-time job as a senior writer at *Rolling Stone*. I never would have attempted such a crazy thing had Jason Fine and Christian Hoard not given me the go-ahead the moment they heard about this. It was a year when *The Office* seemed to fill my every waking thought, but somehow they never uttered a word of complaint and trusted me to juggle all my tasks. They were my biggest supporters and remain dear friends. The same goes for other *Rolling Stone* staff members past and present, including Sean Woods, Brian Hiatt, Patrick Doyle, Alison Weinflash, Jason Newman, Gus Wenner, Jerry Portwood, Hank Shteamer, Kory Grow, David Fear, Maria Fontoura, David Browne, Elisabeth Garber-Paul, Tessa Stuart, Joe Levy, Nathan Brackett, Will Dana, Caryn Ganz, Jonathan Ringen, Cady Drell, Marielle Anas, and Daniela Tijerina. I have learned so much from working with each and every one of you over these many years.

I got my first job at the Rock and Roll Hall of Fame when I was eighteen. Sharon Uhl, Carole Bell, Brian Kenyon, Howard Kramer, and the late Jim Henke took me under their wings and showed me a kindness I'll never be able to repay as long as I live. Were it not for the pivotal time I spent there in the early 2000s, I have no idea where my career would have gone.

Jann Wenner hired me to write for *Rolling Stone* when I was less than a year out of college. I barely knew how to put two words together, but he somehow saw potential, and I work every day to make him proud. He is one of my all-time heroes. Jay Penske was kind enough to keep me on staff, along with the entire edit team, when he bought the magazine in 2017. To say that I'm eternally grateful for that would be a gross understatement.

Rob Sheffield was my favorite pop culture writer before I even met him. He's been a close friend for years, but I'm still in absolute awe of his genius and his generosity. Likewise, Alan Sepinwall is an amazing addition to the *Rolling Stone* team (not to mention a walking TV encyclopedia), and he was an invaluable resource during this process.

My dear friends Daniel Jacobson, Jessie Katz, Sarah Silberman, Mary Coffman, Sarah Abrams Beraha, and Andrew Kilpatrick were there for the ups and downs of this whole saga. I'm very luck to have them in my life. In that same vein, Creed Bratton became an unlikely friend when I met him nearly a decade ago, when I wrote an article about him in *Rolling Stone*. He was the first person in *Office* world I told about this book, and he was incredibly helpful and supportive as I worked on it, even feeding me sushi in his home while we spent hours going over his incredible story. He's a living example of the fact that it's never too late in life to find success if you work hard enough.

My most sincere gratitude goes toward my family. My sister, Jennifer Wolinetz; brother-in-law, Adam Wolinetz; and nephews, Chase and Spencer, cheered for me throughout this whole time, and I don't even mind that they've never really watched *The Office*. I do hope that one day they give it a fair chance, though. I really think they'd like it.

My girlfriend, Angie Martoccio, kept me sane and grounded throughout all of this and was always understanding of the late nights, mood shifts, endless conversations about the greatness of season two, and the weekends when I was chained to my computer working on this thing. She also maintained my interview schedule, traveled with me to London to interview the *Office* UK gang, and helped me find some of the more obscure interview subjects. If anyone was my coauthor on this, it was her. She is the love of my life.

Finally, thanks to my mother and father, Bill and Sally Greene, for never pushing me to go to law school or insisting I find a more practical career path. You also filled our house with television sets and let me watch whatever I wanted at all hours of the day. It finally paid off. I love you both more than I can ever say.

sources

Introduction: An American Workplace

Author interviews with J. J. Abrams, Creed Bratton, Jen Celotta, Clark Duke, Lee Eisenberg, Paul Feig, Kate Flannery, Amelie Gillette, Melora Hardin, Jason Kessler, Ken Kwapis, Oscar Nunez, Nathan Rabin, Alan Sepinwall, Rob Sheffield, Aaron Shure, Gene Stupnitsky, and Larry Wilmore.

Archival author interview with Jenna Fischer (2018).

Chapter 1: The Original *Office*

Author interviews with Ash Atalla, Ricky Gervais, Anil Gupta, Andy Hollis, Ewen MacIntosh, Stephen Merchant, and Jon Plowman.

Chapter 2: Coming to America

Author interviews with Ash Atalla, Ricky Gervais, Jeffrey Immelt, Stephen Merchant, Nathan Rabin, Kevin Reilly, Alan Sepinwall, Rob Sheffield, Ben Silverman, Teri Weinberg, Larry Wilmore, and Jeff Zucker.

Quotes from Greg Daniels: DVD commentary. *The Office*. "Pilot." Universal Studios, 2005.

Chapter 3: Casting

Author interviews with Kate Flannery, Allison Jones, Ken Kwapis, Oscar Nunez, Kevin Reilly, Ben Silverman, Stacey Snider, and Jeff Zucker.

Archival author interview with Angela Kinsey (2018).

Quotes from B. J. Novak: Chun, Wing. "It Was Just so Intellectually Stimulating and Inspiring; It Was All I Wanted to Do." Television Without Pity, March 1, 2006, www.brilliantbutcancelled.com/show/the-office/the-bj-novak-interview.

Quotes from Jenna Fischer: Fischer, Jenna. *The Actor's Life: A Survival Guide*. Dallas: BenBella Books, 2017.

Quotes from John Krasinski: Jones, Sam. "John Krasinski on the Story Behind His Audition for 'The Office.'" *Off Camera with Sam Jones*, August 24, 2016, www.youtube.com/watch?v=SAdJ7VxzquU.

Quotes from B. J. Novak: Muther, Christopher. "Class Reunion: Schoolmates from Newton Meet Again in 'The Office.'" *Boston Globe*, December 6, 2005.

Quotes from Rainn Wilson: Wilson, Rainn. *The Bassoon King: Life in Art, Faith, and Idiocy.* New York: Dutton, 2015.

Quotes from Brian Baumgartner, Steve Carell, and Greg Daniels: Academy of Television Arts & Sciences. *Inside "The Office."* Panel discussion at the Leonard H. Goldenson Theatre, March 18, 2009.

Quotes from Greg Daniels and John Krasinski: DVD commentary. *The Office.* "Pilot." Universal Studios, 2005.

Quotes from Greg Daniels and John Krasinski: "Greg Daniels/John Krasinski Press Call." OfficeTally, May 1, 2013, www.officetally.com/greg-danielsjohn-krasinski-press-call.

Quotes from Leslie David Baker: "Stanley from NBC's The Office—Interview." Hollywood Press, May 15, 2007, www.youtube.com/watch?v=2jts9yF9qvU&t=499s.

Quote from Phyllis Smith: Sepinwall, Alan. "How Phyllis Smith's Sadness Became the Unlikely Heart of 'Inside Out.'" Uproxx, June 22, 2015, uproxx.com/sepinwall/how-phyllis-smiths-sadness-became-the-unlikely-heart-of-inside-out.

Quote from Craig Robinson: "Craig Robinson Talks About New Book Jake the Fake." TheCelebrityCafé.com, April 27, 2017, https://www.youtube.com/watch?v=wazRXAiEekE.

Chapter 4: Setting the Stage

Author interviews with J. J. Abrams, Carey Bennett, Randall Einhorn, Donald Lee Harris, Jason Kessler, Ken Kwapis, Mari Potis, Henry Saine, Matt Sohn, and Larry Wilmore.

Quotes from Greg Daniels: "Writer's Block 2007." Panel discussion at the Office Convention, Scranton, Pennsylvania, October 2007.

Chapter 5: The Pilot

Author interviews with Carey Bennett, Creed Bratton, Paul Feig, Ricky Gervais, Melora Hardin, Ken Kwapis, Alan Sepinwall, Ben Silverman, Peter Smokler, and Larry Wilmore.

Archival author interview with Greg Daniels (2018).

Barnhart, Aaron. "NBC's 'Office' Knockoff Needs Repairs." *Kansas City Star*, March 24, 2005.

Bianco, Robert. "NBC Copy Machine Misfeeds at 'The Office.'" *USA Today*, March 24, 2005.

Bianculli, David. "It Doesn't Work for Us: NBC Remake of Brit 'Office.'" *Daily News* (New York), March 23, 2005.

Brownfield, Paul. "'Office' Wit Wilts a Bit Crossing Atlantic." *Los Angeles Times*, March 23, 2005.

Flynn, Gillian. "The Office." *Entertainment Weekly*, March 15, 2005.

Maynard, John. "'Office' Humor and a Joyless 'Stick.'" *Washington Post*, March 20, 2005.

Quotes from Steve Carell, Jenna Fischer, John Krasinski, B. J. Novak, and Rainn Wilson: DVD commentary. *The Office.* "Pilot." Universal Studios, 2005.

Quotes from Greg Daniels and John Krasinski: "Greg Daniels/John Krasinski Press Call." OfficeTally, May 1, 2013, www.officetally.com/greg-danielsjohn-krasinski-press-call.

Key Episode 1: "Diversity Day"

Author interviews with Paul Feig, Kate Flannery, Ken Kwapis, Oscar Nunez, and Larry Wilmore.

Archival author interview with Greg Daniels (2018).

Quotes from Greg Daniels, Angela Kinsey, and Michael Schur: Burns, Ashley, and Chloe Schildhause. "The Behind-the-Scenes Story of 'Diversity Day,' the Episode That Defined NBC's 'The Office.'" Uproxx, March 23, 2015, uproxx.com/feature/feature-the-behind-the-scenes-story-of-diversity-day-the-episode-that-defined-nbcs-the-office.

Quotes from Greg Daniels: McGrath, Denis. "In Conversation: Greg Daniels, Executive Producer/Showrunner of The Office." Dead Things on Sticks, June 20, 2007, http://heywriterboy.blogspot.com/2007/06/in-conversation-greg-daniels-executive.html.

Quotes from Steve Carell, Greg Daniels, and B. J. Novak: DVD commentary. *The Office*. "Diversity Day." Universal Studios, 2005.

Chapter 6: Season One

Author interviews with Jen Celotta, Randall Einhorn, Paul Feig, Kate Flannery, Jason Kessler, Ken Kwapis, Oscar Nunez, Ben Silverman, Matt Sohn, Ken Whittingham, and Larry Wilmore.

Quotes from Steve Carell, Greg Daniels, and B. J. Novak: DVD commentary. *The Office*. "Basketball." Universal Studios, 2005.

Quotes from John Krasinski: "Greg Daniels/John Krasinski Press Call." OfficeTally, May 1, 2013, www.officetally.com/greg-danielsjohn-krasinski-press-call.

Chapter 7: The Fight for Survival

Author interviews with Kim Ferry, Kate Flannery, Ricky Gervais, Jeffrey Immelt, Jason Kessler, Kevin Reilly, Alan Sepinwall, Ben Silverman, Matt Sohn, Jennie Tan, Mary Wall, Teri Weinberg, Larry Wilmore, and Jeff Zucker.

Heffernan, Virginia. "Upfronts Journal." *New York Times*, May 20, 2005, archive.nytimes.com/www.nytimes.com/ref/arts/television/tv-upfronts-journal.html.

Chapter 8: Dwight

Author interviews with Jeff Blitz, Creed Bratton, Danny Chun, Randall Einhorn, Lee Eisenberg, Owen Ellickson, Jason Kessler, Mark Proksch, Nathan Rabin, Rob Sheffield, Justin Spitzer, Gene Stupnitsky, Halsted Sullivan, Caroline Williams, and Larry Wilmore.

Quotes from Rainn Wilson: Gross, Terry. "Rainn Wilson: 'The Office' Drone Outside of Work." *Fresh Air*, NPR, July 30, 2008.

Quotes from Rainn Wilson: Rooney, Brian. "The Man Behind *The Office*'s Favorite Suck-Up, Dwight Schrute." *Nightline*, ABC, September 7, 2007.

Quotes from B. J. Novak: DVD commentary. *The Office*. "Business School." Universal Studios, 2005.

Quotes from Rainn Wilson: Paley Center for Media. *The Office: Cast & Creators Live at the Paley Center*, 2007.

Chapter 9: Season Two

Author interviews with Creed Bratton, Andy Buckley, Jen Celotta, Randall Einhorn, Lee Eisenberg, Paul Feig, Kim Ferry, Kate Flannery, Melora Hardin, Jason Kessler, Oscar Nunez, Ben Patrick, Kevin Reilly, Alan Sepinwall, Ben Silverman, Matt Sohn, Gene Stupnitsky, Larry Wilmore, and Jeff Zucker.

Quotes from Craig Robinson: Rabin, Nathan. "Craig Robinson Interview." AV Club, January 6, 2009.

Quotes from John Krasinski: Academy of Television Arts & Sciences. *Inside "The Office."* Panel discussion at the Leonard H. Goldenson Theatre, March 18, 2009.

Quotes from Mindy Kaling: DVD commentary. *The Office*. "The Dundies." Universal Studios, 2006.

Key Episode 2: "The Dundies"

Author interviews with Randall Einhorn, Kate Flannery, Michael Gallenberg, Jason Kessler, Jennie Tan, and Christopher T. Wood.

Quotes from Jenna Fischer: Fischer, Jenna. "The Office Goes for the Gold Again." *TV Guide*, April 13, 2006.

Quotes from B. J. Novak: Novak, B. J. "Office Gossip's First Exclusive Blog." *TV Guide*, September 20, 2005.

Quotes from Greg Daniels, Jenna Fischer, Mindy Kaling, John Krasinski, and B. J. Novak: DVD commentary. *The Office*. "The Dundies." Universal Studios, 2006.

Key Episode 3: "The Injury"

Author interviews with Jen Celotta, Randall Einhorn, Bryan Gordon, and Dean Holland.

Quotes from Jenna Fischer: Fischer, Jenna. "The Office Blog Is Back, and It's Pam-tastic!" *TV Guide*, January 12, 2006.

Quotes from Mindy Kaling: Martin, Denise. "Mindy Kaling on the End of *The Office* and Her Favorite Episode." Vulture, August 22, 2012.

Quotes from Mindy Kaling: Sepinwall, Alan. "Mindy Kaling on 'The Mindy Project,' 'The Office' and More." Uproxx, September 4, 2012.

Quotes from Mindy Kaling: "Writer's Block 2007." Panel discussion at the Office Convention, Scranton, Pennsylvania, October 2007.

Key Episode 4: "Casino Night"

Author interviews with Carey Bennett, Michael Gallenberg, Jason Kessler, Ken Kwapis, and Jennie Tan.

Quote from Jenna Fischer: Fischer, Jenna. *The Actor's Life: A Survival Guide*. Dallas: BenBella Books, 2017.

Quotes from Steve Carell and Greg Daniels: Rosen, Lisa. "Office Manager Takes on New Task." *Los Angeles Times*, May 10, 2006.

Quotes from Greg Daniels, Jenna Fischer, and Rainn Wilson: DVD commentary. *The Office*. "Casino Night." Universal Studios, 2006.

Chapter 10: The Rise of Creed

Author interviews with Devon Abner, Creed Bratton, Kelly Cantley, Randall Einhorn, Lee Eisenberg, Paul Feig, Allison Jones, Jason Kessler, Ken Kwapis, Alysia Raycraft, Matt Sohn, and Larry Wilmore.

Archival author interviews with Greg Daniels (2010) and Ed Helms (2010).

Chapter 11: Mindy

Author interviews with Carey Bennett, Jen Celotta, Lee Eisenberg, Richard Gonzales, and Ken Kwapis.

Quotes from Mindy Kaling: Blyth, Antonia. "Mindy Kaling on How 'Late Night' Was Inspired by Her Own 'Diversity Hire' Experience and the Importance of Holding the Door Open for Others." Deadline Hollywood, May 18, 2019, deadline.com/2019/05/mindy-kaling-late-night-the-office-disruptors-interview-news-1202610283.

Quotes from Oscar Nunez: Burns, Ashley, and Chloe Schildhause. "The Behind-the-Scenes Story of 'Diversity Day,' the Episode That Defined NBC's 'The Office.'" Uproxx, March 23, 2015, uproxx.com/feature/feature-the-behind-the-scenes-story-of-diversity-day-the-episode-that-defined-nbcs-the-office/.

Quotes from Greg Daniels and Mindy Kaling: Gross, Terry. "Executive Producer Greg Daniels and Writer-Actor Mindy Kaling Discuss Their TV Comedy Series, 'The Office.'" *Fresh Air*, NPR, September 2, 2006.

Quotes from Mindy Kaling: Kaling, Mindy. *Is Everyone Hanging Out Without Me? (And Other Concerns)*. New York: Three Rivers Press, 2011.

Quotes from Mindy Kaling and B. J. Novak: "Mindy Kaling and B. J. Novak Talk *Why Not Me?* at BookCon 2015." Penguin Random House, June 2, 2015, www.youtube.com/watch?v=53i2008nt1M.

Quotes from Mindy Kaling: Phipps, Keith. "Mindy Kaling Interview." AV Club, April 4, 2007.

Quotes from Mindy Kaling: Yuan, Jada. "Thirty-Three Facts You Learn About Mindy Kaling by Hanging Around Her." *New York*, September 25, 2012.

Chapter 12: Season Three

Author interviews with Carey Bennett, Creed Bratton, Jen Celotta, Randall Einhorn, Lee Eisenberg, Kim Ferry, Kate Flannery, Brent Forrester, Melora Hardin, Allison Jones, Jason Kessler, Ken Kwapis, Oscar Nunez, Matt Sohn, Justin Spitzer, Gene Stupnitsky, Teri Weinberg, Ken Whittingham, Caroline Williams, Larry Wilmore, and Brian Wittle.

Archival author interview with John Krasinski (2018).

Quotes from Ed Helms: Academy of Television Arts & Sciences. *Inside "The Office."* Panel discussion at the Leonard H. Goldenson Theatre, March 18, 2009.

Quotes from Rainn Wilson: DVD commentary. *The Office.* "The Coup." Universal Studios, 2007.

Quotes from Leslie David Baker, B. J. Novak, and Rainn Wilson: DVD commentary. *The Office.* "Initiation." Universal Studios, 2007.

Quotes from Jenna Fischer and Dave Rogers: DVD commentary. *The Office.* "The Job." Universal Studios, 2007.

Quotes from Rainn Wilson: DVD commentary. *The Office.* "Business School." Universal Studios, 2007.

Fickett, Travis. "At the Office with Ed Helms." IGN, August 21, 2007.

Quotes from Greg Daniels and Rashida Jones: Fierman, Daniel. "Audiences Love to Love Rashida Jones." *Entertainment Weekly,* February 9, 2007.

Quotes from Rashida Jones: Paley Center for Media. *The Office: Cast & Creators Live at the Paley Center,* 2007.

Key Episode 5: "Beach Games"

Author interviews with Jen Celotta, Randall Einhorn, Kate Flannery, and Gene Stupnitsky.

Quotes from Brian Baumgartner and Ed Helms: DVD commentary. *The Office.* "Beach Games." Universal Studios, 2007.

Chapter 13: Who Is Michael Scott?

Author interviews with Jen Celotta, Lee Eisenberg, Anthony Farrell, Brent Forrester, Tucker Gates, Jason Kessler, Warren Lieberstein, Alan Sepinwall, Justin Spitzer, Gene Stupnitsky, Halsted Sullivan, and Caroline Williams.

Archival author interviews with Jenna Fischer (2018), John Krasinski (2018), and Paul Lieberstein (2011).

Quotes from Greg Daniels: Gross, Terry. "Executive Producer Greg Daniels and Writer-Actor Mindy Kaling Discuss Their TV Comedy Series, 'The Office.'" *Fresh Air,* NPR, September 2, 2006.

Quotes from Steve Carell: Kronke, David. "Office Politics." *Daily News* (Los Angeles), March 24, 2005.

Quotes from Steve Carell: Paley Center for Media. *The Office: Cast & Creators Live at the Paley Center,* 2007.

Quotes from Rainn Wilson: DVD commentary. *The Office.* "The Return." Universal Studios, 2007.

Chapter 14: Filming *The Office*

Author interviews with J. J. Abrams, Carey Bennett, Creed Bratton, Andy Buckley, Kelly Cantley, Randall Einhorn, Paul Feig, Kim Ferry, Kate Flannery, Tucker Gates, Richard Gonzales, Lisa Hans-Wolf, Melora Hardin, Dean Holland, Jason Kessler, Ken Kwapis, Oscar Nunez, Ben Patrick, Mark Proksch, Amy Ryan, Robert Shafer, Ben Silverman, Matt Sohn, and Brian Wittle.

Archival author interviews with Greg Daniels (2018), Ed Helms (2018), and John Krasinski (2018).

Quotes from Jenna Fischer and B. J. Novak: DVD commentary. *The Office*. "Pilot." Universal Studios, 2005.

Quotes from Greg Daniels and John Krasinski: "Greg Daniels/John Krasinski Press Call." OfficeTally, May 1, 2013, www.officetally.com/greg-danielsjohn-krasinski-press-call.

Quotes from Greg Daniels and Mindy Kaling: Paley Center for Media. *The Office: Cast & Creators Live at the Paley Center*, 2007.

Chapter 15: Season Four

Author interviews with Carey Bennett, Creed Bratton, Kelly Cantley, Jen Celotta, Lee Eisenberg, Anthony Farrell, Kim Ferry, Kate Flannery, Brent Forrester, Ricky Gervais, Jason Kessler, Ben Patrick, Ben Silverman, Matt Sohn, Justin Spitzer, Gene Stupnitsky, Larry Wilmore, and Brian Wittle.

Archival author interviews with Jenna Fischer (2018), Ed Helms (2018), Angela Kinsey (2018), and John Krasinski (2018).

Quotes from Michael Schur: DVD commentary. *The Office*. "Money." Universal Studios, 2008.

Quotes from Angela Kinsey and Rainn Wilson: Hochman, David. "Rainn Wilson and Angela Kinsey Deconstruct *The Office*'s 'Dwangela.'" *TV Guide*, November 29, 2006, www.tvguide.com/news/rainn-wilson-angela-37533/.

Key Episode 6: "Dinner Party"

Author interview with Mary Wall.

Archival author interviews with Greg Daniels (2018), Lee Eisenberg (2017), Todd Fancey (2018), Paul Feig (2018), Jenna Fischer (2018), Beth Grant (2018), Melora Hardin (2018), Ed Helms (2018), Angela Kinsey (2018), John Krasinski (2018), and Gene Stupnitsky (2017).

Chapter 16: The Writers' Room

Author interviews with Jen Celotta, Lee Eisenberg, Owen Ellickson, Anthony Farrell, Brent Forrester, Melora Hardin, Jason Kessler, Warren Lieberstein, Peter Ocko, Claire Scanlon, Aaron Shure, Justin Spitzer, Gene Stupnitsky, Halsted Sullivan, Mary Wall, Caroline Williams, amd Larry Wilmore.

Quotes from Mindy Kaling: Academy of Television Arts & Sciences. *Inside "The Office."* Panel discussion at the Leonard H. Goldenson Theatre, March 18, 2009.

Chapter 17: Greg

Author interviews with Shelley Adajian, Jeff Blitz, Creed Bratton, Andy Buckley, Kelly Cantley, Jen Celotta, Briton W. Erwin, Paul Feig, Kim Ferry, Kate Flannery, Brent Forrester, Melora Hardin, Dean Holland, Jason Kessler, Ken Kwapis, Rusty Mahmood,

Oscar Nunez, Alysia Raycraft, Claire Scanlon, Alan Sepinwall, Robert Shafer, Justin Spitzer, Caroline Williams, Larry Wilmore, and Brian Wittle.

Quotes from Mindy Kaling: Kaling, Mindy. *Is Everyone Hanging Out Without Me? (And Other Concerns)*. New York: Three Rivers Press, 2011.

Chapter 18: Season Five

Author interviews with Jeff Blitz, Andy Buckley, Kelly Cantley, Jen Celotta, Randy Cordray, Lee Eisenberg, Idris Elba, Anthony Farrell, Paul Feig, Kate Flannery, Brent Forrester, Ken Kwapis, Warren Lieberstein, Oscar Nunez, Amy Ryan, Aaron Shure, Justin Spitzer, Gene Stupnitsky, Halsted Sullivan, Jennie Tan, Mary Wall, Ken Whittingham, and Brian Wittle.

Quotes from B. J. Novak: DVD commentary. *The Office*. "Dream Team." Universal Studios, 2009.

Quotes from Jenna Fischer: DVD commentary. *The Office*. "Michael Scott Paper Company." Universal Studios, 2009.

Key Episode 7: "Weight Loss"

Author interviews with Jen Celotta, Randy Cordray, Randall Einhorn, Michael Gallenberg, Dean Holland, Matt Sohn, Halsted Sullivan, and Brian Wittle.

Key Episode 8: "Stress Relief"

Author interviews with Jeff Blitz, Jen Celotta, Randy Cordray, Randall Einhorn, Lee Eisenberg, Anthony Farrell, Paul Feig, Kate Flannery, Warren Lieberstein, Ben Silverman, Gene Stupnitsky, and Halsted Sullivan.

Chapter 19: 13927 Saticoy Street

Author interviews with Shelley Adajian, Carey Bennett, Creed Bratton, Steve Burgess, Kelly Cantley, Randy Cordray, Briton W. Erwin, Paul Feig, Kim Ferry, Kate Flannery, Michael Gallenberg, Sergio Giacoman, Richard Gonzales, Lisa Hans-Wolf, Jason Kessler, Ken Kwapis, Rusty Mahmood, Oscar Nunez, Claire Scanlon, Aaron Shure, Matt Sohn, Justin Spitzer, Halsted Sullivan, Kasia Trojak, and Brian Wittle.

Archival author interview with Ed Helms (2010).

Quotes from Jenna Fischer and Rainn Wilson: DVD commentary. *The Office*. "Money." Universal Studios, 2008.

Chapter 20: The Trouble with Movies

Author interviews with J. J. Abrams, Carey Bennett, Randy Cordray, Kim Ferry, Kate Flannery, Ken Kwapis, Rusty Mahmood, Oscar Nunez, and Ken Wittingham.

Chapter 21: Season Six

Author interviews with Jeff Blitz, Kelly Cantley, Jen Celotta, Danny Chun, Randy Cordray, Briton W. Erwin, Anthony Farrell, Kate Flannery, Brent Forrester, Allison Jones,

Warren Lieberstein, Rusty Mahmood, Myles McNutt, Ben Patrick, Claire Scanlon, Aaron Shure, Justin Spitzer, Gene Stupnitsky, Halsted Sullivan, Teri Weinberg, and Brian Wittle.

Archival author interview with Ellie Kemper (2011).

Quotes from Zach Woods: BUILD Series. "Zach Woods Compares His Character in 'The Office' to His Character Now in 'Silicon Valley.'" May 10, 2017, www.youtube.com/watch?v=gcmr-fUziwo.

Key Episode 9: "Niagara"

Author interviews with Steve Burgess, Danny Chun, Randy Cordray, Randall Einhorn, Paul Feig, Brent Forrester, Warren Lieberstein, Claire Scanlon, Justin Spitzer, Gene Stupnitsky, Halsted Sullivan, and Brian Wittle.

Quotes from Greg Daniels: DVD commentary. *The Office*. "Niagara." Universal Studios, 2010.

Chapter 22: Spin-off Blues

Author interviews with Steve Burgess, Briton W. Erwin, Kate Flannery, Brent Forrester, Claire Scanlon, Aaron Shure, Ben Silverman, Justin Spitzer, and Teri Weinberg.

Chapter 23: Steve

Author interviews with J. J. Abrams, Carey Bennett, Creed Bratton, Andy Buckley, Jen Celotta, Randy Cordray, Randall Einhorn, Lee Eisenberg, Briton W. Erwin, Paul Feig, Kim Ferry, Kate Flannery, Ricky Gervais, Richard Gonzales, Melora Hardin, Dean Holland, Ben Patrick, Mark Proksch, Alysia Raycraft, Amy Ryan, Claire Scanlon, Robert Shafer, Stacey Snider, and Teri Weinberg.

Archival author interview with Jenna Fischer (2018).

B. J. Novak quotes: DVD commentary. *The Office*. "Business School." Universal Studios, 2005.

Chapter 24: Season Seven

Author interviews with Danny Chun, Randy Cordray, Roxxi Dott, Kim Ferry, Brent Forrester, Amelie Gillette, Bob Greenblatt, Allison Jones, Warren Lieberstein, Rusty Mahmood, Peter Ocko, Amy Ryan, Alan Sepinwall, Aaron Shure, Ben Silverman, Halsted Sullivan, Teri Weinberg, Brian Wittle, and Jeff Zucker.

Archival author interview with Ellie Kemper (2011).

Quotes from Will Ferrell: Bergman, Ben. "Will Ferrell Ends His Short-Lived 'Office' Run and Promises He's Not the New Boss." NPR, May 5, 2011.

Quotes from Greg Daniels, Paul Lieberstein, and Dave Rogers: DVD commentary. *The Office*. "Goodbye, Michael." Universal Studios, 2011.

Quotes from Paul Lieberstein and B. J. Novak: DVD commentary. *The Office*. "Nepotism." Universal Studios, 2011.

Quotes from Will Ferrell: Itzkoff, Dave. "Meet the New Boss: Will Ferrell Clocks in at 'The Office.'" *New York Times*, April 6, 2011.

Key Episode 10: "Threat Level Midnight"

Author interviews with Steve Burgess, Randy Cordray, Kate Flannery, Tucker Gates, Amelie Gillette, Peter Ocko, Halsted Sullivan, and Calvin Tenner.

Quotes from B. J. Novak: DVD commentary. *The Office*. "Threat Level Midnight." Universal Studios, 2011.

Quotes from B. J. Novak: "'Threat Level Midnight' Q & A with B. J. Novak." OfficeTally, February 25, 2011.

Key Episode 11: "Goodbye, Michael"

Author interviews with Creed Bratton, Danny Chun, Randy Cordray, Randall Einhorn, Owen Ellickson, Paul Feig, Kim Ferry, Brent Forrester, Warren Lieberstein, Oscar Nunez, Peter Ocko, and Rob Sheffield.

Quotes from Brian Baumgartner, Greg Daniels, Ellie Kemper, and Dave Rogers: DVD commentary. *The Office*. "Goodbye, Michael." Universal Studios, 2011.

Quotes from Jenna Fischer: Gallucci, Nicole. "Jenna Fischer Finally Reveals What Pam Said to Michael During Their Airport Goodbye." Mashable, May 2, 2018.

Chapter 25: Meet the New Boss

Author interviews with Danny Chun, Owen Ellickson, Kate Flannery, Brent Forrester, Amelie Gillette, Warren Lieberstein, Peter Ocko, Ben Patrick, Mark Proksch, Alan Sepinwall, Aaron Shure, Ben Silverman, James Spader, Justin Spitzer, Halsted Sullivan, and Teri Weinberg.

Archival author interview with Paul Lieberstein (2011).

Chapter 26: Season Eight

Author interviews with Jeff Blitz, Creed Bratton, Andy Buckley, Kelly Cantley, Danny Chun, Randall Einhorn, Owen Ellickson, Briton W. Erwin, Paul Feig, Kim Ferry, Kate Flannery, Brent Forrester, Ricky Gervais, Amelie Gillette, Melora Hardin, Warren Lieberstein, Rusty Mahmood, Myles McNutt, Oscar Nunez, Ben Patrick, Mark Proksch, Alysia Raycraft, Karly Rothenberg, Claire Scanlon, Alan Sepinwall, Rob Sheffield, Aaron Shure, Ben Silverman, Matt Sohn, James Spader, Justin Spitzer, Halsted Sullivan, and Brian Wittle.

Chapter 27: Life in the Background

Author interviews with Devon Abner, Creed Bratton, Randall Einhorn, Kate Flannery, Hidetoshi Imura, Oscar Nunez, Karly Rothenberg, Claire Scanlon, Robert Shafer, Matt Sohn, and Calvin Tenner.

Quotes from Craig Robinson: Juul, Matt. "Craig Robinson on Morris From America and Patrice O'Neal's Boston Side." *Boston Magazine*, September 9, 2016, https://www

.bostonmagazine.com/arts-entertainment/2016/09/09/craig-robinson-morris-from-america-interview.

Quotes from B. J. Novak: "B. J. Novak Talks About the 'Happy Hour' Tag." OfficeTally, March 29, 2010.

Chapter 28: Season Nine

Author interviews with Jeff Blitz, Steve Burgess, Kelly Cantley, Randy Cordray, Roxxi Dott, Clark Duke, Owen Ellickson, Briton W. Erwin, Kim Ferry, Kate Flannery, Brent Forrester, Bob Greenblatt, Ken Kwapis, Warren Lieberstein, Myles McNutt, Oscar Nunez, Mark Proksch, Alysia Raycraft, Claire Scanlon, Ben Silverman, Matt Sohn, Justin Spitzer, Halsted Sullivan, Teri Weinberg, and Brian Wittle.

Quotes from Greg Daniels and John Krasinski: "Greg Daniels/John Krasinski Press Call." OfficeTally, May 1, 2013, www.officetally.com/greg-danielsjohn-krasinski-press-call.

Quotes from John Krasinski: "John Krasinski and the End of the Office." *Off Camera with Sam Jones*, April 23, 2013, www.youtube.com/watch?v=S9ROHotAAQk.

Quotes from Greg Daniels: Keller, Joe. "Greg Daniels on Writing the Final Season of 'The Office.'" Fast Company, May 8, 2013.

Quotes from Greg Daniels: Radish, Christine. "Executive Producer Greg Daniels Talks Returning Full Time for Season 9, Ending the Show, and the Goal of the Finale on *The Office* Set." Collider, January 21, 2013, collider.com/the-office-series-finale-greg-daniels-interview/.

Key Episode 12: "Finale"

Author interviews with Devon Abner, Creed Bratton, Steve Burgess, Kelly Cantley, Jen Celotta, Clark Duke, Owen Ellickson, Kate Flannery, Brent Forrester, Ken Kwapis, Rusty Mahmood, Mark Proksch, Alysia Raycraft, Claire Scanlon, Robert Shafer, Matt Sohn, Halsted Sullivan, Mary Wall, Teri Weinberg, and Brian Wittle.

Quotes from John Krasinski: Michaud, Sarah. "John Krasinski on *Office* Finale: 'We Flat-Out Lied.'" *People*, June 6, 2013, people.com/tv/john-krasinski-on-office-finale-we-flat-out-lied/.

Quotes from Steve Carell: Roots, Kimberly. "Steve Carell Admits His *Office* Finale Sin: 'I Lied.'" TVLine, June 18, 2012, tvline.com/2013/06/18/steve-carell-the-office-series-finale-lied/.

Chapter 29: The Aftermath

Author interviews with J. J. Abrams, Creed Bratton, Andy Buckley, Kelly Cantley, Danny Chun, Robert Durkin, Owen Ellickson, Briton W. Erwin, Anthony Farrell, Brent Forrester, Tucker Gates, Ricky Gervais, Melora Hardin, Stephen Merchant, Mari Potis, Mark Proksch, Kevin Reilly, Amy Ryan, Claire Scanlon, Aaron Shure, Ben Silverman, Teri Weinberg, and Caroline Williams.

Archival author interviews with Jenna Fischer (2018) and John Krasinski (2018).

Quotes from Bob Greenblatt: Adalian, Josef. "Bob Greenblatt Saved NBC. Now What?" Vulture, September 17, 2018.

Quotes from B. J. Novak: DVD commentary. *The Office*. "Safety Training." Universal Studios, 2007.

Chapter 30: Reboot?

Author interviews with J. J. Abrams, Creed Bratton, Kelly Cantley, Jen Celotta, Danny Chun, Clark Duke, Owen Ellickson, Kim Ferry, Kate Flannery, Brent Forrester, Ricky Gervais, Allison Jones, Warren Lieberstein, Stephen Merchant, Oscar Nunez, Mark Proksch, Amy Ryan, Robert Shafer, Rob Sheffield, Alan Sepinwall, Ben Silverman, Justin Spitzer, Halsted Sullivan, and Teri Weinberg.

Archival author interviews with Jenna Fischer (2018), Ed Helms (2018), Angela Kinsey (2018), and John Krasinski (2018).

index

Note: *Names in italics* refer to character names.

Index

Index

about the author

Andy Greene is from Cleveland, Ohio; attended Kenyon College; and is now a senior writer for *Rolling Stone*, where he's worked for the past fifteen years. He's written cover stories about Radiohead and Howard Stern and feature articles about Bill Withers, Nathan Fielder, Steve Perry, Pete Townshend, Stephen King, and many others. He lives in Brooklyn.